# Petrarchan Love and the English Renaissance

# Petrarchan Love and the English Renaissance

GORDON BRADEN

Great Clarendon Street, Oxford, OX2 6DP,
United Kingdom

Oxford University Press is a department of the University of Oxford.
It furthers the University's objective of excellence in research, scholarship,
and education by publishing worldwide. Oxford is a registered trade mark of
Oxford University Press in the UK and in certain other countries

© Gordon Braden 2022

The moral rights of the author have been asserted

Impression: 1

All rights reserved. No part of this publication may be reproduced, stored in
a retrieval system, or transmitted, in any form or by any means, without the
prior permission in writing of Oxford University Press, or as expressly permitted
by law, by licence, or under terms agreed with the appropriate reprographics
rights organization. Enquiries concerning reproduction outside the scope of the
above should be sent to the Rights Department, Oxford University Press, at the
address above

You must not circulate this work in any other form
and you must impose this same condition on any acquirer

Published in the United States of America by Oxford University Press
198 Madison Avenue, New York, NY 10016, United States of America

British Library Cataloguing in Publication Data

Data available

Library of Congress Control Number: 2022943694

ISBN 978–0–19–285836–8

DOI: 10.1093/oso/9780192858368.001.0001

Printed and bound by
CPI Group (UK) Ltd, Croydon, CR0 4YY

Links to third-party websites are provided by Oxford in good faith and
for information only. Oxford disclaims any responsibility for the materials
contained in any third-party website referenced in this work.

*Clare's book*

# Acknowledgements

Clare Kinney's contribution extends well beyond the specific places I have been able to acknowledge it. Decades of conversation with Elizabeth Hull have also shaped my interest in and understanding of this poetry (and many other things), in ways I could not begin to localize. Karen Ryan is in here too, whether she realizes it or not. Tony Spearing and Richard Strier offered specific suggestions, which I took; an acute query from David Quint redirected my thinking on the end of "Wodmanship." Mac Pigman's magnificent edition of Gascoigne, arriving in my mailbox at a crucial moment, is responsible for chapter two. The whole project descends from a throwaway question that Robert Kellogg asked on a dissertation defense shortly after I came to Virginia; it became a bone to gnaw upon. Three friends whom I always imagined would be reading this book—William Kerrigan, Eve Sedgwick, Bari Watkins—are no longer with us. Their reactions are likely to have been very different, but you never know. I miss them.

A version of chapter one was published as "Wyatt and Petrarch: Italian Fashion at the Court of Henry VIII" in *Annali d'Italianistica*, vol. 22 (2004); I am grateful to Dino Cervigni for his help and advice on it. An overview of English Petrarchism that Catherine Bates asked me to write for her *Companion to Renaissance Poetry* (Wiley-Blackwell, 2018) proved to be the portal into finally finishing things. Appendix C resulted from Stuart Gillespie's timely request to do a book review for *Translation and Literature*. I am grateful for permission to quote from "All we were going strong last night this time" from *Collected Poems: 1937-1971* by John Berryman. Copyright © 1989 by Kate Donahue Berryman, reprinted by permission of Farrar, Straus, and Giroux. All Rights Reserved.

# Contents

*Note on Texts* viii
*Introduction* ix

1. Thomas Wyatt  1
2. George Gascoigne  38
3. Philip Sidney  82
4. Sonneteers  122
5. Courtiers  178
6. William Shakespeare  206

Afterword  250

Appendix A: Astrophil and Stella: *Utrum Copularentur*  253
Appendix B: The Afterlife of Petrarch, *Canzoniere* 23  260
Appendix C: The *Trionfi*  269

*Bibliography (Works Cited)*  273
*Index*  291

# Note on Texts

For Petrarch's *Canzoniere* I quote the Italian text (adapted from the edition of Gianfranco Contini) and English translation in *Petrarch's Lyric Poems*, ed. and trans. Robert M. Durling. The Italian text of Petrarch's *Trionfi* is quoted from *Triumphi*, ed. Marco Ariani.

Quotations of Wyatt's poetry are taken, with caution, from the old-spelling text in *Collected Poems of Sir Thomas Wyatt*, ed. Kenneth Muir and Patricia Thomson; for references I give the poem numbers in this edition (MT) and also in the widely used modern-spelling edition (R) of R. A. Rebholz. Jason Powell's new Oxford edition of the poems is eagerly awaited.

Quotations of Gascoigne's *Flowres* and *Posies* are from *A Hundreth Sundrie Flowres*, ed. G. W. Pigman III, with references (P) to pages in this edition. Quotations from Gascoigne's other works are from the second volume of *The Complete Works of George Gascoigne*, ed. John W. Cunliffe, with references (C) to pages in this edition.

Quotations of Philip Sidney's poetry are from *The Poems of Sir Philip Sidney*, ed. William A. Ringler, Jr. References to *Astrophil and Stella* are to poem number, using Ringler's system of Arabic numerals for the sonnets and lower-case roman numerals for the songs. Other references are to pages in this edition.

Quotations of Shakespeare use the text in *The Complete Works: Original-Spelling Edition*, ed. Stanley Wells and Gary Taylor et al; for references to the plays, I give act-scene-line numbers from *The Riverside Shakespeare*, ed. G. Blakemore Evans et al.

I make minor, usually silent adjustments to quotations from all sources. Most abbreviations are expanded, quotation marks and some other later editorial intrusions removed, punctuation and capitalization occasionally regularized, uncontroversial emendations accepted. A few more significant departures from my source texts are identified where they happen. Translations not otherwise identified are my own.

# Introduction

This book is a long-intended complement to *Petrarchan Love and the Continental Renaissance* (Yale, 1999). I wrote a version of the first chapter 20 years ago, then other things came along. The project has benefited from the delay, especially from Jackson Boswell's invitation to help with *Petrarch's English Laurels, 1475–1700* (Ashgate, 2012), for which he had already assembled unprecedentedly detailed documentation of Petrarch's presence before the English reading public. The last two decades have also seen an impressive if belated harvest of scholarship and criticism on Mary Wroth, whose *Pamphilia to Amphilanthus* has finally taken its place as the work that rounds off the legendary if frequently maddening and baffling episode in English literary history that is my subject here. Like most people, I had not paid Wroth much mind, but my colleague Clare Kinney was persistent in insisting that I should, and she was right. Other developments in scholarship have added significantly to a literary historical narrative that had come to seem stale and obsolete and for many specialists not all that interesting. It is time for a fresh telling, open to much that had previously been unknown or (in some cases) fended off, of a traditional story.

In general, that story remains the same, of English Renaissance love poetry as an idiosyncratic, late-arriving chapter in the international phenomenon of Petrarchism, not restricted to sonneteering but dominated by it to a remarkable, even astonishing degree. The sonnet itself was at least a century old when Petrarch took it up, but he gave it a prominence it never had before, and displayed it within a structure he did invent, for which the Renaissance never came up with a name but which was adopted by vernacular poets across western Europe (and as far east as Croatia and Cyprus) from the fifteenth into the seventeenth centuries. We now call it the sonnet sequence, successive lyric moments with innuendos of continuity (sometimes leading somewhere, sometimes not) whose usual story of hopeless desire for a beautiful and unattainable beloved follows expectations set by Petrarch. Episodes of sonneteering in a Petrarchan manner occur at different times in different places as aspirational announcements that another national culture has reached a certain level of maturity and refinement, tracking with impressive consistency the self-conscious cultural event that comes to be called the Renaissance. The English version starts with a flurry in the court of Henry VIII in the early sixteenth century, lapses for several decades, gathers momentum again with the accession of Elizabeth I, crests in the 1590s with an almost deranged storm of popularity, and in its wane leaves an enigmatic but intense exemplar from, as it happens, the greatest poet in the language. I think all of the poetry involved—some of it first-rate by any standard, some of it rightly mocked in its own time as awesomely bad—benefits from being seen in this context.

On the widest view, the continuity of the tradition is so obvious as to be almost trivial, a lot of it decorative glitter sprinkled over very different poems by very different poets writing in very different contexts. The continuity also happens simultaneously on several levels, on some of them active, conscious imitation of Petrarch's own poems or the poems of his imitators, and on others mute absorption of things that were simply in the air that any poet had to breathe. It is important to discriminate such levels, when possible, but it is also important not to discount the more penumbral kinds of influence, which can be the more important. The result in my discussion is a certain vagueness or nonchalance, which I think is answerable to the phenomenon itself, about what I mean by "Petrarchan." That is a term I prefer to the even vaguer "courtly love," a bland label which has the further disadvantage of being a nineteenth-century formulation. I nevertheless do not attempt any rigorous or exclusionary definition of Petrarchism (I would not be especially interested in one), nor am I claiming for that category some specially authoritative paradigm for the poems in question. I am concerned throughout with the distinctiveness of particular poets and their work, and this involves many other things besides their Petrarchan filiations, including, where we have the evidence, a good deal of biographical and historical circumstance. Biographical context, for instance, is crucial in appreciating Wroth's poetry; we now know a surprising amount about that context, and the neo-Platonic abstraction in her poems gains significantly in power when you understand what it is striving to transcend. My main interest throughout, to which each of the following chapters comes by the end, is literary, the poetry we have before us.

The claim I do make is that the larger phenomenon of Petrarchism, by which no practicing poet of the time could be untouched, repeatedly offers an insightful way into that poetry, even if beyond a certain point Petrarchism as such all but disappears from the discussion. When that happens here, it is not through inattention on my part. Chapter one concludes with Thomas Wyatt's "They fle from me" because I agree with the common wisdom that it is Wyatt's greatest poem, though it is not a sonnet or otherwise a poem there is any particular reason to saddle with the label "Petrarchan." What is great about it, though, is something that can be brought out through its relation to the Petrarchan translations and imitations that elsewhere loom large in Wyatt's *oeuvre* and influence. My most eccentric decision may be to devote a chapter to George Gascoigne, whose dealings with Petrarchism, sometimes explicit, are also modest and do not in any obvious way impinge on his greatest poem, "Gascoignes wodmanship," which is not even a love poem. Once more, I think coming upon the poem as I do helps explain that greatness more effectively than previous critics have. A similar route leads me with Walter Ralegh to "The Ocēans love to Scinthia," a strange poetic ruin that defies any attempt to fit it into any known genre but is also in its eerie, haunted way one of the age's defining literary works.

Concluding with Shakespeare's sonnet sequence needs no explanation, though it does violate a generally chronological presentation that I have tried to make as continuous as possible. Among other things, I have hoped to restore some respectability to the idea of narrative literary history. The cast is large but the coverage by no means comprehensive; I am conscious of not doing justice to certain figures along the way (the Earl of Surrey, Edmund Spenser), but it seemed better not to take up space where I had nothing special to say. For the poets to whom I do give more than passing attention—Wyatt, Gascoigne, Philip Sidney, Samuel Daniel, Fulke Greville, Wroth, Ralegh, and Shakespeare—what I do have to say is for better or worse the justification for the general approach I take; it is of course for the reader to judge by the results.

# 1
# Thomas Wyatt

In the last years of the fifteenth century, a Venetian accompanying his city's ambassador to England puzzled over the people there: "although their dispositions are somewhat licentious [*inclinati alla libidine*], I never have noticed any one, either at court or among the lower orders, to be in love [*sia alcuno innamorato*]." Two possible explanations: "either that the English are the most discreet lovers in the world [*più segreti amatori del mundo*], or that they are incapable of love." He assures us he is speaking only of the men—"I understand it is quite the contrary with the women, who are very violent in their passions"—but in a way that implies he is not writing from direct observation; female passion may have been reported but was not on display ("the English keep a very jealous guard over their wives"). The writer links all this to the way these people treat their children, and clearly thinks of it as a flaw in the national character: *il poco amore delli Inglesi*.[1]

The diagnosis tells us as much about Italy as about England. The *innamorato* was an established figure in the Italian public landscape. You would expect to find him and know him when you saw him; he might want to be discreet about the details, but he would not be concealing his affective state behind any cover that a knowing observer would not be expected to penetrate. Being in such a state and recognizing it in others were important components of civilized existence, the subject of some of the best-known products of Italian culture:

> Se 'n solitaria piaggia rivo o fonte,
> se 'nfra duo poggi siede ombrosa valle,
> ivi s'acqueta l'alma sbigottita;
>     et come Amor l'envita
> or ride or piange or teme or s'assecura,
> e 'l volto, che lei segue ov' ella il mena,
> si turba e rasserena
> et in un esser picciol tempo dura:
> onde a la vista uom di tal vita esperto
> diria: Questo arde et di suo stato è incerto.
>                                    (Petrarch, *Canz.* 129.4–13)

---

[1] *A Relation ... of the Island of England*, ed. and trans. Charlotte Augusta Sneyd, p. 24. The report is dated 1500; the visit appears to have taken place 1496–97.

If there is on some solitary slope a river or spring, or between two peaks a shady valley, there my frightened soul is quieted; and, as Love leads it on, now laughs, now weeps, now fears, now is confident: and my face, which follows wherever my soul leads, is clouded and made clear again, and remains but a short time in any one state; and at the sight anyone who had experienced such a life would say: "This man is burning with love and his state is uncertain."

By the end of the fifteenth century Petrarch's vernacular poetry had become the focus of a larger complex of cultivated social life intimated in these lines: the very passion that isolates the lover becomes the object of acknowledgment and empathy in select others. Petrarch is drawing on Ovid, whose tone is cynical in comparison: "*ut voto potiare tuo, miserabilis esto, / ut qui te videat, dicere possit 'amas'*" (*Ars amatoria* 1.737–8 [to get what you're after, be pitiful, so that whoever sees you can say, You're in love]). Petrarch elaborates this advice into something melancholy and picturesque, which becomes the aesthetic for a community of those who are or would be thought expert in such a life. That aesthetic is at the center of Italian cultural prestige in the Renaissance, and a major export. The lack which the Venetian visitor felt may or may not have had something to do with the emotional lives of actual individuals; it certainly had to do with the low profile of Italianate culture in the England of Henry VII, and in particular with the absence of any trace of the international literary phenomenon that had elsewhere begun to manifest itself under Petrarchan inspiration. We may link the supposed low incidence of love among the English to another perplexity the Venetian visitor recorded a little earlier: "They are gifted with good understandings, and are very quick at every thing they apply their minds to; very few, however, excepting the clergy, are addicted to the study of letters."[2] The spread of Petrarchist love poetry is entwined with the growth of a secular reading public, and is indeed one way of tracking its growth; the Venetian's observation on this score is probably true.

Some thirty years later the picture is different. The most famous evidence is the poetry of Thomas Wyatt, including some two dozen English versions of poems from Petrarch's *Canzoniere*, and a comparable number of translations from more recent Italian and French poets who were themselves writing under Petrarch's influence. Among these poems are the first known free-standing sonnets in English.[3] The project seems to have been largely one man's doing; the records we have of other poetry composed in Wyatt's vicinity (other than that of the Earl of Surrey, who was following Wyatt's lead) show few traces of such overtly Italianate borrowing. The inspiration for Wyatt's effort is often attributed to his ambassadorial service on the continent, though developments at home could have been sufficient to explain his interest, indeed make it seem almost inevitable.

---

[2] *Relation*, p. 22.
[3] There is an embedded sonnet in an anonymous Middle English romance from the fifteenth century; see John Metham, *Amoryus and Cleopes*, ed. Stephen F. Page, pp. 43–4. For the form's more general pre-history in English, see Amanda Holton, "An Obscured Tradition."

The accession of Henry VIII in 1509 changed the tenor of the English court; the figure he presented in 1515 to a new delegation of ambassadors from Venice seemed bright with erotic promise: "the handsomest potentate I have ever set eyes on; above the usual height, with an extremely fine calf to his leg, his complexion very fine and bright [*bianchissimo vivacissimo*], with auburn hair combed straight and short, in the French fashion, and a round face so very beautiful, that it would become a pretty woman [*staria ben ad una bella donna*]."[4] Aspects of Italian fashion had already found their place; the Venetians discovered at court the noteworthy Brescian musician Zuan Piero, "to whom this King gives 300 ducats annually for playing the lute," and with whom the ambassador's secretary played an impromptu duet on the *clavicembalo*.[5] Piero was the first of several Italian musicians who can be placed at Henry's court. It would be surprising if lyrics by Petrarch were not on their playlist; numerous poems from his *Canzoniere* had been set to music and figured prominently in the usual Italian repertoire. At least seven of the poems Wyatt translated were so treated, including the especially popular *Canzoniere* 121, "Or vedi, Amor," for which no fewer than eighteen settings survive. Wyatt enters his English version first in the Egerton manuscript, his personal collection: "Behold, love, thy power how she dispiseth" (1R/1MT—the poem keeps its priority in modern editions as well). The last poem inserted into the *Canzoniere*, it marks the start of English Renaissance literature's direct encounter with Petrarch's sequence and its offspring.

\*

That start is conditioned both by the conventions of English love poetry as already being practiced and by the impress of Wyatt's own literary personality. That conditioning can deprive the imported material of some of what one might have thought would make it most attractive, especially within an aspiring Renaissance court:

> Or vedi, Amor, che giovenettta donna
> tuo regno sprezza et del mio mal non cura,
> et tra duo ta' nemici è sì secura.
>
> Tu se' armato, et ella in treccie e 'n gonna
> si siede et scalza in mezzo i fiori et l'erba,
> ver me spietata e 'ncontr' a te superba. (1–6)

Now see, Love, how a young woman scorns your rule and cares nothing for my harm, and between two such enemies is so confident. You are in armor, and she

---

[4] *Four Years at the Court of Henry VIII*, ed. and trans. Rawdon Brown, 1: 86; the text is a letter by one of the ambassadors, Piero Pasqualigo.

[5] *Four Years* 1: 80; from a letter by Nicolo Sagudino, secretary to Pasqualigo's colleague. On the musician's identity and the information that follows, see Ivy L. Mumford, "Petrarchism and Italian Music at the Court of Henry VIII."

in a mere robe with braided hair is sitting barefoot amid the flowers and the grass, pitiless toward me and proud toward you.[6]

> Behold, love, thy power how she dispiseth!
> My great payne how little she regardeth!
> The holy oth, wherof she taketh no cure
> Broken she hath: and yet she bideth sure,
> Right at her ease: and litle she dredeth.
> Wepened thou art: and she unarmed sitteth:
> To the disdaynfull, her liff she ledeth:
> To me spitefull, withoute cause, or mesure.
>     Behold, love! (1–9)

Even as it takes longer to say what it has to say, the English poem removes almost all visual and circumstantial information from the original. The picture of the woman in the landscape, amid flowers and grass, is gone, the casual dress and beguiling hair reduced to "unarmed." Nor is there an English word corresponding to *giovenetta* or even *donna*: we know she is a woman only from the pronoun, and can only presume she is young. This is not to remove her from the poem; quite the contrary, the emotions attributed to her—the pride and spite behind her indifference—now fill the poem all the more completely. What has been taken out is anything to explain the speaker's own longing, any direct presentation of the woman as an object of desire.

Part of what is involved here is a soberer taste in decoration, a comparative dislike for glitter. Where Petrarch has "*non di diamante ma d'un vetro*" (*Canz.* 124.12 [made not of diamond but even of glass]), Wyatt writes "not of steill but of brickell glasse" (22R/31MT.12). Diamonds are not out of the question for Wyatt; the motto on the collar of the deer in "Who so list to hounte" is "graven in Diamondes in letters plain" (11R/7MT.11), but this is still an economy over the original: "*di diamanti et di topazi*" (*Canz.* 190.10 [with diamonds and topazes]). The category of *décor* for which Petrarchism is famous, the precious objects used to praise parts of the woman's body, is barely in evidence.[7] There is a modest cluster of them in a loose adaptation of *Canzoniere* 199 into song form:

> With Lilis whight
> And Roses bright
> Doth stryve thy colour faire;

---

[6] Durling translates *treccie* as "loose hair"; I am indebted to Dino Cervigni for the correction.

[7] There is some of this already in English poetry, apparently without direct Italian sanction:

> hur lyppes ar lyke unto cherye
> with Tethe as whyte as whalles bone
> hur browes bente as any can be
> with eyes as clere as crystall stoune

(4.13–16 in *The Welles Anthology*, ed. Sharon L. Jansen and Kathleen H. Jordan.) Other *blasons* in this collection are less metaphorical; see n. 56.

> Nature did lend
> Eche fyngers ende
> A perle for to repayre. (140R/86MT.13–18)

In a translation of *Canzoniere* 37, Wyatt not only keeps one of the conventional metaphors but inserts one not in the original: "The cryspid gold that doth sormount Apollos pryd, / The lyvely strenes off pleasaunt sterres that under it doth glyd" (76R/98MT.69–70; translating 81–5 in the Italian); Petrarch provides the gold but not in this instance the stars. Elsewhere Wyatt writes of ideal female beauty, "The tresse also shuld be of cryspyd goold" (67R/118MT.6). This is sufficiently unlike him to suggest special circumstances; we may be learning the otherwise unattested hair color of Elizabeth Darrell, a maid of honor to Katherine of Aragon and later the mistress with whom Wyatt, when he was allowed to be with her, seems to have been happy in the last part of his life. But the bright color here emphasizes the prevailing monochrome. "Behold, love" is paradigmatic; most of the visual drama in Wyatt's Petrarchan texts is severely curtailed by the passage into English.

> Una candida cerva sopra l'erba
> verde m'apparve con duo corna d'oro,
> fra due riviere all'ombra d'un alloro,
> levando 'l sole a la stagione acerba.
>                (*Canz.* 190.1–4)

A white doe on the green grass appeared to me, with two golden horns, between two rivers, in the shade of a laurel, when the sun was rising in the unripe season.

In Wyatt's version, this entire quatrain corresponds to a single line: "Who so list to hounte I know where is an hynde" (11R/7MT.1). C. S. Lewis's observation on another site has general relevance: "Wyatt (perhaps not for purely aesthetic reasons) has, so to speak, turned down the lights of the Petrarch."[8]

Vanishing without apparent fuss from the Italian original here is the symbolic lynchpin of Petrarch's entire sequence: the laurel. In this case its disappearance need not imply deliberate thought on Petrarch's central trope, the coincidence of erotic and literary ambition, though another text of Wyatt's does. In a generally close translation of the penultimate *canzone* of the sequence, where Reason is called upon to decide whether Love has done the speaker more good than harm, Wyatt pointedly omits the passage in which Love describes his gift of poetic fame and the circulation of the lover's collected poems:

> Sì l'avea sotto l'ali mie condutto
> ch'a donne et cavalier piacea il suo dire;
> et sì alto salire

---

[8] C. S. Lewis, *English Literature in the Sixteenth Century*, pp. 326–7.

> il feci che tra' caldi ingegni ferve
> il suo nome, et de' suoi detti conserve
> si fanno con diletto in alcun loco;
> ch'or saria forse un roco
> mormorador di corti, un uom del vulgo!
> I' l'esalto et divulgo
> per quel ch'elli 'mparò ne la mia scola
> et da colei che fu nel mundo sola. (*Canz.* 360.110–20)

I had so carried him under my wings that his speech pleased ladies and knights; and I made him rise so high that among brilliant wits his name shines, and in some places collections are made of his poems; who now would perhaps be a hoarse murmurer of the courts, one of the mob! I exalt him and make him known by what he learned in my school and from her who was unique in the world.

This part of Love's case largely disappears into the gap between Wyatt's sixteenth and seventeenth stanzas (73R/8MT); a trace survives as a brief addition at a later point:

> da volar sopra 'l ciel li avea dat' ali
> per le cose mortali,
> che son scala al Fattor, chi ben l'estima. (137–9)

I gave him wings to fly above the heavens through mortal things, which are a ladder to the Creator, if one judges them rightly.

> I gave him wynges wherewith he myght flye
> To honour and fame, and if he would farther
> By mortall thinges above the starry skye (128–30)

Even here we are not actually told that the honor and fame would be due to the lover's achievement as a poet. Wyatt declines to voice the specifically laureate ambition that marks Petrarchan love off from its near relatives. The sole appearance of a laurel in Wyatt's poetry, in his translation of Psalm 37, looks like a considered judgment on that ambition:

> I have well seene the wicked sheene lyke goolde,
>     Lustie and greene as lawrell lasting aye;
>     But even anon and scantt his seate was colde (266R/94MT.97–9)

There is a history of uncertainty about the tree here. The Hebrew (Psalm 37:35) is problematic; it appears to liken the wicked to something green or flourishing

(רַעֲנָן, *ra'anan*), often interpreted or emended (insofar as one can emend Scripture) to be the cedars of Lebanon. The Septuagint and the Vulgate adopt this solution, but sixteenth-century scholarship proposes the bay tree, and the Coverdale, Geneva, and King James Bibles so translate. We are confident Wyatt used the Latin paraphrase by Jean de Campen (Ioannis Campensis), where the line in question reads: "*Vidi impium potentem, & virentem, & similem lauro quae viret perpetuò*" [I saw the evil man powerful and flourishing/green, and like the laurel which is perpetually green].[9] The golden sheen is Wyatt's addition; the result is a concentrated burst of Petrarchan color, but in a lurid and menacing light. *Décor* that Wyatt culls from his love poetry serves his turn as an object of moral outrage, the badge of a perverse and unsupportable aspiration to the wrong kind of immortality.

Wyatt's usage here is consistent with an absence that Anne Ferry notes in his borrowings from the continent: "Even in 'There was never ffile' [32R/16MT], Wyatt does not explicitly identify his speaker as a poet, or present him in the act of writing verses .... Nor elsewhere in Wyatt's sonnets, either translated or original, is the speaker identified as a poet-lover."[10] For a Petrarchist, this is a momentous absence. When a poem in the Devonshire manuscript considers what "some redres" (readers) might make of "this boke" (177R/214MT.9, 28)—in a manner that has prompted comparisons to the opening sonnet of the *Canzoniere*—those references are themselves evidence against Wyatt's authorship. His poems were of course circulated in written form and did indeed have readers, but the performative self-consciousness on view in the poetry that we can be sure is Wyatt's is almost never literary.[11] He never uses the word "poem"; his compositions, when he refers to them, are songs, and on occasion he presents himself in them as a singer and lutanist:

> My lute, awake! perfourme the last
> Labour that thou and I shall wast
> And end that I have now begon;
> For when this song is sung and past,
> My lute be still, for I have done. (109R/66MT.1–5)

---

[9] Johannes Campensis, *Enchiridion Psalmorum*, sig. i6ʳ–7ᵛ. See H. A. Mason, "Wyatt and the Psalms."

[10] Anne Ferry, *The "Inward" Language*, pp. 92–3.

[11] Only twice is a love poem referred to as a written text: when Wyatt complains to a woman who has torn "The weping paper that to you I sent, / Wherof eche letter was written with a teare" (125R/251MT.3–4); and when, writing from abroad, he imagines the woman receiving the poem as a letter: "When she hath red and seene the dred wherein I serve / Be twene her brestes she shall the put there shall she the reserve" (76R/98MT.98–9—translating *Canz*. 37, though this particular imagining is Wyatt's addition). The most serious exception to the rule here would be "My pen, take payn a lytyll space" (208R/179MT), but the attribution to Wyatt is uncertain; it is anonymous in the Devonshire and two other manuscripts.

We do not know that Wyatt actually performed in those roles.[12] If he did not, his assumption of them is in a way all the more interesting as the fictional appropriation of a still foreign Italian manner—a manner that very possibly mediated his own first encounter with Petrarch's texts. Such an encounter would have placed them in a significantly un-Petrarchan or at least pre-Petrarchan situation: one like that of the troubadours, their eyes not on a distant audience to be reached by writing but on a present audience waiting to be entertained here and now. I suspect the role of singer attracted Wyatt in great part because of the way it implied that context.

As with the troubadours, the available information does not allow us to be much more specific than that. Scholars are thrown back on their own imaginative powers, with results that do not always age well. As Lewis envisions it: "The whole scene comes before us .... We are having a little music after supper."[13] Stephen Greenblatt confronts that picture with an influential jibe that is just as obviously a kind of historical mythmaking: "conversation with the king himself must have been like small talk with Stalin."[14] The real failure of imagination on Lewis's part is not so much the benign glow he gives to the courtly scene as the generalization with which he short-circuits his own argument: "In that atmosphere all the confessional or autobiographical tone of the songs falls away .... The song is still passionate: but the passion is distanced or generalized by being sung." Repeated intimate performances among people who see each other all the time are more likely to acquire just the opposite weight, a complicated sense of relevance to the lives and affections of the people involved. H. A. Mason offers a more convincingly fraught version of Lewis's scene:

After dinner the company began to sing, to play on instruments or to dance. And while one lady led the dance, the master of ceremonies ordered a lady to recite to music a poem .... The lady complied and in her poem spoke of her fears that the other ladies of the party might steal from her the love of the man she admired, and thus cause her to fall into a fury of jealousy. When she had finished her song, one of the gentlemen went up to her and said with a smile: "Lady, you would oblige us if you would tell all the company here who was the man you were alluding to

---

[12] See the negative conclusions of John Stevens, *Music and Poetry in the Early Tudor Court*, pp. 132–8. The absence of positive testimony fits with what strikes Stevens as the unconvincing quality of the musical references in Wyatt's poetry: "He blames his lute, or not, as the fancy takes him, but never talks about it in the way of a man who really understands and cares for it" (p. 134). Stevens argues against the myth of "a tradition of courtier-poets singing extempore to their lutes, comparable to the Italian," which seems to him to involve projecting an Elizabethan image back on "a French-Burgundian court culture, still distinctly un-Italianate" (p. 138). Winifred Maynard, "The Lyrics of Wyatt: Poems or Songs?," attempts a counterargument, but admits that, in the absence of further evidence, "It is a matter of weighing probabilities" (p. 256).

[13] Lewis, p. 230.

[14] Stephen Greenblatt, *Renaissance Self-Fashioning*, pp. 136–7.

in your poem, in case any one of the ladies through ignorance of the name might gain possession of his love and thus throw you into a rage."[15]

We may safely assume that if she did answer, it would be not to the company at large but privately to the gentleman himself, swearing him to a confidentiality she understood would be selectively observed. He probably already knew the answer anyway.

In Wyatt's case we can sense such a context in the vehemence with which he insists that what he is doing with his lute is conducting a conversation, responding to particular actions on someone else's part:

> Spyght askyth spight and changing change,
> And falsyd faith must nedes be knowne,
> The faute so grett, the case so strange,
> Of Right it must abrod be blown:
> Then sins that by thyn own desartte
> My soinges do tell how trew thou art,
>     Blame not my lute. (94R/205MT.22–8)

The lute—the word an Italian import, possibly Wyatt's contribution to English love poetry—is the closest thing in Wyatt's work to the Petrarchan laurel, a symbol for the artistic ambition accompanying his erotic desire. Here he goes out of his way to insist in an un-Petrarchan spirit that the lute has no independent power of its own but is strictly subservient to his own intent in holding up his end of this conversation:

> My lutte, alas, doth not ofend
> Tho that perfors he must agre
> To sownd such teunes as I entend
> To sing to them that hereth me;
> Then tho my songes be some what plain,
> And tocheth some that use to fayn,
>     Blame not my lutte. (8–14)

In the longest poem in his *Canzoniere* Petrarch links the displacement of speech by song—"*volendo parlar, cantava sempre*" (23.62 [wishing to speak, I sang always])—to his fatal inability to move Laura with his poetic voice:

> né mai in sì dolci o in sì soavi tempre
> risonar seppi gli amorosi guai

---

[15] H. A. Mason, *Humanism and Poetry in the Early Tudor Period*, p. 173.

> che 'l cor s'umiliasse aspro et feroce. (64–6)
>
> nor was I ever able to make my amorous woes resound in so sweet
> or soft a temper that her harsh and ferocious heart was humbled.

He writes as if making his song sweeter or softer might finally reach her, but he also knows that will not be the case; the price his poetry pays for beauty is effectiveness as speech. Wyatt imagines no such negotiation. His lute is simply one of his tools for speaking to those that hear him.

Such a conviction may be felt in many of Wyatt's lyrics.[16] It helps explain the disappearance of the woman's image from "Behold, love." Though he keeps the fiction of addressing Love rather than the woman, Wyatt's poem has, notably more than Petrarch's, the force of a complaint that she is meant to hear. Painting a picture of her beauty would be primarily for the benefit of others, and largely beside the point as far as persuading her is concerned. Translating *Canzoniere* 206, Wyatt explicitly changes the woman from third-person object (to whom Love is supposed to speak on the poet's behalf) to second-person addressee, and builds the poem to a righteous appeal much in the spirit of "Blame not my lute" but corresponding to nothing at all in the Italian:

> Then that that ye have wrowght
> Ye must hyt now redresse;
> Off ryght therfore ye ought
> Such rygor to represse.
>
> And as I have deservyd,
> So grant me now my hyer;
> Ye know I never swarvyd,
> Ye never fownd me lyer. (77R/158MT.37–44)

In its very rudeness (which begins with the poem's abrupt opening: "Perdy I sayd hytt nott"), this disposition is part of what makes Wyatt's lyrics seriously courtly in the literal sense: showing the abrasions of life at court, of frequent close encounters within a small circuit. Petrarch's life and work were strongly shaped by the deliberate withdrawal from such encounters, and he has Love list among the benefits of poetic fame that it allowed him to avoid becoming "*un roco / mormorador di corti*" (*Canz*. 360.116–17 [a hoarse murmurer of the courts]). Petrarchism as a literary movement seeks out the courts of western Europe as if they were its natural home, and that tensely crowded environment exerts a felt pressure on the dynamics of erotic reverie. The lyric soliloquy becomes more like direct speech in a dramatic occasion.

---

[16] I am indebted on some of the following to Reed Ray Dasenbrock, *Imitating the Italians*, pp. 24–6.

The metamorphosis of one of Petrarch's most imitated set of poems displays the process with particular clarity. Laura has removed a glove, and the poet now holds it; both the sight of the exposed hand and the possession of an article of Laura's clothing are sources of unaccustomed pleasure:

> O bella man che mi destringi 'l core
> e 'n poco spazio la mia vita chiudi,
> man ov'ogni arte et tutti loro studi
> poser Natura e 'l Ciel per farsi onore,
>
> di cinque perle oriental colore,
> et sol ne le mie piaghe acerbi et crudi,
> diti schietti soavi: a tempo ignudi
> consente or voi per arrichirme Amore.
>
> Candido leggiadretto et caro guanto
> che copria netto avorio et fresche rose:
> chi vide al mondo mai sì dolci spoglie?
>
> Così avess'io del bel velo altrettanto!
> O inconstanzia de l'umane cose,
> pur questo è furto, et vien chi me ne spoglie.
> *(Canz.* 199)

O beautiful hand that grasps my heart and encloses in a little space all my life, hand where Nature and Heaven have put all their art and all their care to do themselves honor, neat soft fingers, the color of five oriental pearls, and only bitter and cruel to wound me: to make me rich, Love now opportunely consents that you be naked. White, light, and dear glove, that covered clear ivory and fresh roses: who ever saw in the world such sweet spoils? Would I had again as much of that lovely veil! Oh the inconstancy of human life! Even this is a theft, and one is coming who will deprive me of it.

This is unusually specific narrative action for Petrarch's sequence, though characteristically many of the details are obscured by the very intensity of the lover's response. A decent guess is that Laura dropped the glove inadvertently and the lover picked it up and held it for a few minutes before giving it back. Subsequent details imply that the one who came to ask for it was Laura herself, though no specific dialogue is reported. The last poem in the episode expresses regret at having readily granted her request, and goes as far as a fantasy of *vendetta*:

> Né mi riede a la mente mai quel giorno
> che mi fe' ricco et povero in un punto

> ch' i' non sia d'ira et di dolor compunto,
> pien di vergogna et d'amoroso scorno
>
> che la mia nobil preda non più stretta
> tenni al bisogno et non fui più costante
> contra lo sforzo sol d'un'angioletta,
>
> o, fuggendo, ale non giunsi a le piante
> per far almen di quella man vendetta
> che de li occhi mi trae lagrime tante.
> (*Canz.* 201.5–14)

Nor does that day, which made me rich and poor at the same time, ever come to mind without my being moved with anger and sorrow, full of shame and amorous scorn that I did not hold my noble spoils more tightly when it was needful, and was not more constant against the force of a mere angel, or, fleeing, did not add wings to my feet and take vengeance at least on that hand which draws from my eyes so many tears.

But the revenge in question—fleeing the scene—is precisely what did not happen, and none of the angry words now stirring were spoken at the time. An observer would probably have witnessed an exchange polite to the point of meaninglessness.

Things in this vignette clearly interest Wyatt. He makes the octave of the first poem the starting point for one of his songs:

> O goodely hand,
> Wherin doeth stand
> My hert distrast in payne,
> Faire hand, Alas,
> In litle spas
> My liff that doeth restrayne. (140R/86MT.1–6)

For three stanzas he stays close to the original, going against his own grain in reproducing the Petrarchan preciousness of the *blason* of the hand. Having done so, though, he again turns the poem into a song of Wyatt's with what Petrarch avoids, an appeal to the woman in the here and now:

> Consent at last,
> Syns that thou hast
> My hert in thy demayne,
> For service trew
> On me to rew,
> And reche me love againe. (19–24)

This is a feudal contract negotiation.[17] If she will not grant his first request he has a second:

> And if not so,
> Then with more woo
> Enforce thiself to strayne
> This simple hert,
> That suffreth smart,
> And rid it owte of payne. (25–30)

Make it right or end it. The status quo is no longer bearable, and the man wants the woman to know that he needs a decision.

In that spirit Wyatt has no use for the glove, a Petrarchan MacGuffin, a trivial object that acquires extravagant importance because the larger situation cannot change. Unable to possess Laura or to cease desiring her, the poet could imagine contenting himself with something he might conceivably possess, a fetishized surrogate—though the point of the episode is that even this he cannot hold on to. The woman's glove does interest Wyatt, however, when it figures in a more confrontational scenario. He is shown the way by his favorite Petrarchist:

> A che minacci, a che tanta ira e orgoglio?
> Per questo non farai che'l furto renda.
> Non senza causa la tua man dispoglio,
> Rapir quel d'altri non fu mai mia menda.
> Famme citar davanti Amor, ch'io voglio
> Che la ragion de l'uno & l'altro intenda:
> Lei il cor mi tolse & io gli ho tolto un guanto,
> Vorró saper da te se un cor val tanto.
>             (Serafino, *Strambotto* 415)[18]

What's the point of threatening? what's the point of such anger and haughtiness? You will not this way make me give back the theft. Not without cause did I despoil your hand; that I stole this from someone was not my crime. Have me summon here Love, whom I want to judge the case of the one and the other. She took my heart, and I took a glove; I will want to know from you if a heart is worth that much.

Petrarch leaves it unsaid how he came into possession of the glove; Serafino's speaker just took it, and boasts of his rightness in doing so. The addressee in

---

[17] There is a good note on this in Rebholz, *Sir Thomas Wyatt*, pp. 433–4. On such language elsewhere in Wyatt's love poetry, see Danila Sokolov, "Love under Law."
[18] I quote Serafino from *Die strambotti*, ed. Barbara Bauer-Formiconi.

the poem shifts from the woman to Love, but we sense no withdrawal from the site of conflict; rather, Love is the judge who will settle this now. The heightened aggression of situation and tone is a distinguishing mark of Serafino's generation of Petrarchists. Wyatt shows some interest in other members of this generation, but he turns to Serafino almost as often as he turns to Petrarch himself.[19] Even when Wyatt's eyes are on Petrarch, Serafino can be a presence; the change of addressee from Love to the woman in "Perdy I sayd hytt nott" is anticipated by a *strambotto* of Serafino's based on the same original (412). With the *strambotto* on the glove, Wyatt reproduces the verse form[20] and translates fairly closely:

> What nedeth these thretning wordes and wasted wynde?
> All this cannot make me restore my pray.
> To robbe your good, I wis, is not my mynde,
> Nor causeles your faire hand did I display.
> Let love be judge, or els whome next we meit,
> That may boeth here what you and I can say.
> She toke from me an hert and I a glove from her:
> Let us se nowe, if th'one be wourth th'othre. (40R/48MT)

The most significant change is the insertion of "or els whome next we meit," which if anything improves the original on its own terms: "Wyatt, in adding this, gets the appropriate spirit, almost the social environment, perfectly."[21] Not only does the lover not flee the confrontation, but it takes place in a populated world in which others might show up and become part of the scene.

*

---

[19] The best discussion is still Patricia Thomson, *Sir Thomas Wyatt and His Background*, pp. 209–37; see also Vincenzo Bonanno, *Serafino l'Aquilano e Sir Thomas Wyatt*. A spiteful glee in Serafino matches a streak in Wyatt's own temperament:

> Fui serrato nel dolore
> Con la morte a canto a canto.
> Ha ha ha! men rido tanto
> Ch'io son vivo e son di fuore! (*Barzelletta* 9)

> I was shut up by pain with death in every corner. But ha! ha! ha! I am laughing so much because I am alive and on the outside.

An unattributed poem in the Devonshire manuscript is built around a version of this refrain: "But ha, ha, ha, full well is me, / For I am now at libertye" (203R/224MT.5–6). The connection with Serafino argues in favor of Wyatt's authorship.

[20] With one lapse, the unrhymed l. 5, repaired by changing "meit" to "finde" when the poem is first printed by Richard Tottel in 1557; see *Tottel's Miscellany*, ed. Hyder Edward Rollins, 2nd ed., vol. 1, poem 56. This is an edition of the first edition of the anthology, with a supplement of poems added in the numerous subsequent editions. The more influential second edition has now been edited by Paul A. Marquis as *Richard Tottel's Songes and Sonettes: The Elizabethan Version*, where the poem in question is number 61. Subsequent citations of the anthology use Rollins's text and give the number of the poem in Rollins (R), together with the number in Marquis (M) for poems included in the second and later editions.

[21] Thomson, p. 232.

Contemporary Italian poetry had models for even more summary judgement in the matter of male-female courtship. A madgrigal by one Dragonetto Bonifacio caught Wyatt's attention:

> Madonna, i' non so far tante parole!
> o voi volete o no. Si voi volete,
> oprate al gran bisogno il vostro senno,
> che voi sarrete intesa per un cenno.
> E si d'un, che sempre arde, pur ve dole,
> un presto *si* o *no* li rispondete.
> Si serrà un *si*, io scriverovvi in rima:
> quando che *no*, amici come prima!
> voi cercherete un altro amante, et io,
> si non posso esser vostro, sarrò mio.[22]

My lady, I do not know how to make long talk. Either you are willing or not. If you are willing, apply your good sense to this important business, for you will be understood with a gesture, and if you feel any pain for one who burns forever, answer him with a prompt Yes or No. If it will be a Yes, I will write a poem about you. If it's No, friends as before; you will find another lover and I, if I cannot be yours, will be my own.

Wyatt passes up an opportunity to refer to himself as a writer of poetry, but otherwise embraces the poem and translates with evident relish:

> Madame, withouten many wordes,
> Ons I am sure ye will or no:
> And if ye will, then leve your bordes,
> And use your wit and shew it so.
>
> And with a beck ye shall me call,
> And if of oon that burneth alwaye
> Ye have any pitie at all,
> Aunswer him faire with yea or nay.
>
> Yf it be yea, I shalbe fayne;
> If it be nay, frendes as before;
> Ye shall an othre man obtain,
> And I myn owne and yours no more. (96R/34MT)

---

[22] Text from Erasmo Pèrcopo, "Dragonetto Bonifacio," p. 220. The source was first identified by Joel Newman, "An Italian Source for Wyatt's *Madame, withouten many wordes*."

The clarity of the reasoning at the end makes the speaker's goal comparably clear. This is a seduction poem, and what is being sought is the woman's sexual consent. The centerpiece of the argument is an honorable respect for her freedom of choice, but it is also the unproblematically sexual character of the request that makes possible the brisk confidence of the conclusion: if your answer is No, I will have no trouble moving on. That confidence is the most anti-Petrarchan feature of the poem. The only thing that links the Italian poem in any meaningful way to Petrarchism is the perpetual ardor in l. 5—a reference that if not exactly contradicted is certainly given a new meaning by the last lines: I may burn always, but not necessarily for the same object. Petrarchan passion survives as part of the seducer's advertising, which even he probably does not expect to be taken at face value.

Most of the evidence we have about Wyatt's erotic adventures at court is too contradictory and uncertain for us to be sure about any of the details—especially those concerning Anne Boleyn—though in the course of defending himself in 1541 against the accusations of Edmund Bonner and others he does make one forthright statement: "I graunte I do not professe chastite."[23] At the time (Wyatt being bound by a failed marriage from which there was no prospect of his legally extricating himself) the specific reference is presumably to Bess Darrell, pregnant with his son Francis, but the statement has a longterm sound to it. An edgy but smug knowingness about sexual love and its brevity hangs over many of Wyatt's lyrics:

> Alas it is a pevishe spight
> To yelde thi self and then to parte;
> But sins thou settst thie faithe so light,
> Yt doth suffise that myne thou warte. (184R/219MT.13–16)

It is easy to suppose the place of such poems in a life of courtly promiscuity. Bonifacio's madrigal would appeal as a *jeu d'esprit* that clarified the reality of that life while disabling some of its hypocrisies. Petrarchan devotion would be one such hypocrisy. Yet the Petrarchan moment in "Madame, withouten many wordes" is not necessarily just part of the joke. In two manuscripts the poem is accompanied by the woman's reply, apparently by Wyatt's friend George Blage (the owner of one of the manuscripts), in which she takes offense at such light wooing and seizes on the profession of Petrarchan ardor as one that *ought* to be true:

> For he that wyl be cawlyd wythe a bek
> Makes haste sute on Lyght desier
> Is ever redi to the chek
> And burnythe in no wastynge fyer.

---

[23] Wyatt, *Prose*, ed. Jason Powell, p. 317. This comes in the context of claims that Wyatt "leved viciously amongest the nunnes of Barsalona"; doing so would be crossing a line even for the unchaste: "I graunte I do not professe chastite, but yet I use not abhomination."

That being the case, "Content you wythe nay for you get no moer."[24] She expects to be made a fuss over, and is holding out for a wasting fire of somewhat more credibility. There are reasons to think the middle two lines of the proposition to which the woman is responding are meant to supply a lilt rather than just set up the punchline. Another translator of the madrigal, the French poet Mellin de Saint-Gelais, eliminated the Petrarchan touches altogether; Wyatt actually heightens them, expanding them from one line to two and introducing the more or less technical term "pity" to designate the woman's desired response. And we are dealing here with one of the areas of Petrarchan convention which appears to have actively attracted Wyatt—an attraction which takes on particular meaning in view of the rather lengthy list of conventions which he seemed comparatively uninterested in bringing into English.

The attraction may have had to do with the way in which the conventions in question would not seem especially foreign. The tumultuous, hyperbolic symptomology of Petrarchan love already had its presence in English love poetry; we can find its components spread about the Welles anthology, which gives us a look at Wyatt's immediate background in this regard. Being in love entails specific somatic disturbances—

> my ees dyd loke redde
> my colour be gane to wax wanne and pale
> upon my chekes Soo þe dropes were sprede
> whych fro my eyes be gan to advale
> from my hart Sore I dyd the sykes hale
>
> . . .
>
> I wypyd my chekes the Sorow to cloke
> outwardly faynyng my selfe glade and mery
> þat the people shuld nott perceyve the smoke
> of owr whot fyre to lyght the emysperye (13.85–9, 92–5)

—and a sense of obsessed distraction that feels inclusive and endless:

> Thys have I lyed allwey languyshyng
> In vareance be twene love hope and drede
> With pensyfe thou3tes allwey Imagenyng

---

[24] Muir-Thomson, p. 298. On the likely circumstances of this exchange of poems during a rough patch in Wyatt's embassy to Spain, see Susan Brigden, *Thomas Wyatt*, pp. 358–60; on the manuscript page, see Chris Stamatakis, *Sir Thomas Wyatt and the Rhetoric of Rewriting*, pp. 186–90. An Italian reply finds another way to disable the man's fantasy of cheerful cooperation: "*Moneta, signor mio, non più parole, / se 'l dolce frutto del mio amor volete*" [money, my lord, no more words, if you want the sweet fruit of my love]; that being the case, "*basta con la borsa far un cenno*" [it is enough to make a gesture with your purse]. See Alfred Einstein, *The Italian Madrigal*, p. 178.

> of my purpose how þat I myght spede
> and yf I shuld be now on rewardyde
> for the love þat I unto hur doo beyre
> thys am I all wey putt yn thou3t and feyre
>
> . . .
>
> ... at noo tyme I am In any reste
> but by desyre and fere allwey oppreste (16.148–54, 160–1)

Such writing is done under the strong influence of Chaucer and especially of *Troilus and Criseyde*, and may in that sense rely on an indirect kind of Petrarchan sanction. A heightened version of this strain of love sickness becomes a pervasive feature of Wyatt's poetry:

> What rage is this? What furour of what kynd?
> What powre, what plage, doth wery thus my mynd?
> Within my bons to rancle is assind
>     What poyson, plesant swete?
>
> Lo, se myn iyes swell with contynuall terys;
> The body still away sleples it weris;
> My fode nothing my faintyng strenght reperis,
>     Nor doth my lyms sustayne. (117R/101MT.1–8)

We sense the direct influence of Petrarchan example in the frequent turn to paradox—

> Of hete and cold when I complain
> And say that hete doeth cause my pain,
> When cold doeth shake me every vain,
> And boeth at ons, I say again
> It is impossible. (113R/77MT.6–10)

—but even this has Chaucerian precedent: "For hete of cold, for cold of hete, I deye" (*Troilus* 1.420).

    Two of the Petrarchan sonnets which Wyatt translates list things to look for in spotting an *innamorato*:

> Yf in my visage eche thought depaynted,
>   Or else in my sperklyng voyse lower or higher,
>     Which nowe fere, nowe shame, wofully doth tyer,
>     Yf a pale colour which love hath stayned ... (13R/12MT.5–8)[25]

---

[25] Translating *Canz.* 224; see also 17R/26MT, translating *Canz.* 134.

Such display presents a ready target when Petrarchism becomes an object of fun, but I sense no mockery in Wyatt. The exaggeration seems rather to affirm the speaker's seriousness, as can be seen with special clarity when the un-Petrarchan nature of the situation is most evident. A sonnet late in the Egerton manuscript opens as if it were another adaptation of the same Petrarchan original as that behind the one just cited:

> If waker care if sodayne pale Coulour
> If many sighes with litle speche to playne
> Now joy, now woo, if they my chere distayne,
> For hope of smalle, if muche to fere therfore,
> To hast, to slak my pase lesse or more,
> Be signe of love

In the middle of the second quatrain, though, with a twist George Puttenham would single out for praise in his Elizabethan *Arte of English Poesie* (1589),[26] the poem begins to break some important rules:

> then do I love agayne.
> If thow aske whome, sure sins I did refrayne
> Brunet that set my welth in such a rore,
> Th'unfayned chere of Phillis hath the place
> That Brunet had: she hath and ever shal.
> She from my self now hath me in her grace:
> She hath in hand my witt, my will, and all
> My hert alone wel worthie she doth staye,
> Without whose helpe skant do I live a daye. (28R/97MT)

The speaker's insomnia and pallor come in the wake of successfully ending his love for one woman and falling in love with another. "I did refrayne / Brunet" suggests direct and decisive action—the kind of willful change of affections whose impossibility is one of the most popular protestations of Petrarch's imitators. Those imitators do nevertheless come at times to the same pass Wyatt has reached here, and can have interesting things to say when they do; Ronsard and Gaspara Stampa are notable examples.[27] In Wyatt's case the rationality of the change is quite obvious. Brunet's effect on his life was clearly destructive, while everything about Phillis suggests a happy ending. Not only is she a more worthy object of admiration ("unfayned chere" seems to look back to a capacity for deceit on the

---

[26] See Puttenham, *The Arte of English Poesie*, ed. Gladys Doidge Willcock and Alice Walker, p. 176 (3.16).
[27] See Braden, *Petrarchan Love and the Continental Renaissance*, pp. 111–14, 127–8. Nicola Shulman, with forgivable exaggeration, calls Wyatt's poem "a momentous occasion in the history of relations between men and women"; *Graven with Diamonds*, p. 159.

other woman's part), but his love for her is already reciprocated with badly needed care and affection that he is confidently affirming to be permanent. This happy ending moves us so far from Petrarchan precedent that the opening looks in retrospect strangely incongruous: the established rhetoric of erotic despair is offered as evidence of the speaker's commitment to a woman who is nothing but good news. By the end of the poem one would guess he now breathes easily, sleeps quite well, and has plenty of blood in his cheeks.

I take that incongruity to be largely a by-product of biographical reality. The previous love has the same hair color as Anne Boleyn, an identification made even harder to avoid by the original reading of l. 8 in the Egerton manuscript, which Wyatt changed with his own hand: "her that did set our country in a rore." Phillis is almost certainly Bess Darrell; this poem is another reason for thinking that her hair was not dark.[28] Wyatt's passion for Boleyn, very likely the latent subject of other poems of his, would have been a much more appropriate occasion for Petrarchan suffering, especially if that passion was indeed unconsummated.[29] It would also make sense for his love for Darrell to inspire such suffering in times of forced absence—and indeed Wyatt's translation of one of Petrarch's *canzoni* of distant longing becomes, with the help of a few signals, a lament for his separation from Darrell during his ambassadorial service in Spain (76R/98MT, from *Canz.* 37).[30] But in "If waker care" there is no separation—the woman's intimate emotional support for the man is happening in the present, and on a daily basis—and the sonnet's first five lines constitute a hasty version of one of the rarest metamorphoses that Petrarchism is called upon to perform: its evolution into the poetry of successfully mutual love. Later in the century, Spenser will require an entire sequence to enact that evolution. Wyatt, at the beginning of the century, effects an often-incautious generalization of the Petrarchan symptoms to a wider range of erotic experience,

---

[28] The name Phyllis descends from Greek pastoral, and Shulman (p. 102) argues that Wyatt intended knowing readers to see a country / city contrast in the two women. Boleyn came to the English court after a cosmopolitan finishing in France; Darrell came from Littlecote, Wiltshire.

[29] There is a canvass of the available evidence, poetic and otherwise, in Eric Ives, *Anne Boleyn*, pp. 83–99, who finds nothing to disturb the likely conclusion "that she and Thomas flirted together with increasing seriousness on his part but with little more than courtly convention on hers" (p. 97). Brigden leaves some windows open on the possibility, but also suggests that before Darrell Wyatt may have been romantically interested in Anne Zouche or even Mary Shelton (pp. 145–51, 190–5). A letter from the imperial ambassador to the Queen of Hungary reports that in 1541 there were said to be two former loves whom Wyatt might prefer to the repudiated wife he still shunned (Brigden, pp. 190, 547–8; Shulman, pp. 348–9).

[30] The poem is subscribed "In Spayne" in the Egerton manuscript; in the final version of a much-revised line, Wyatt inserts what is almost certainly a reference to Henry's responsibility for keeping him where he is: "At other will my long abode my diepe dispaire fulfilles" (88). Wyatt also alters the conclusion to strengthen the speaker's expectation that the lady will read and treasure what he is writing. Wyatt also appears to have been separated from Darrell in the last year of his life, again by Henry's doing; with his usual solicitude for the sanctity of other people's marriages, the king is said to have insisted that Wyatt leave Darrell and reconcile with his wife as a condition for being freed on the charges that sent him to prison in 1541. Wyatt was freed but there is no evidence the reconciliation ever happened. At his death he left a will providing for Darrell.

as if Petrarchan rhetoric were the language of love pure and simple. That often unsatisfying generalization is itself part of Wyatt's legacy to English Renaissance poetry, and possibly played a role in making England so slow to produce a real Petrarchan sequence on the continental model.

\*

The incongruities of "If waker care" are consistent with the seriousness behind "Madame, withouten many wordes." Petrarchan ardor is a possibility of extravagant emotional commitment that is also governable by choice, a choice which is itself a response to what the object of desire is minded to do. Wyatt's love poetry is marked both by the capacity, indeed longing for such extravagance, and by what can seem like a cold respect for the logic of choice in this matter. In that logic we sense the populated world around his lyrics, where questions of love merge with all the other questions that need answering. Wyatt can make us unsure whether he is talking about love or about human relations generally:

> Eche man me telleth I chaunge moost my devise.
> And on my faith me thinck it goode reason
> To chaunge propose like after the season,
> Ffor in every cas to kepe still oon gyse
> Ys mytt for theim that would be taken wyse,
> And I ame not of suche maner condition,
> But treted after a dyvers fasshion,
> And thereupon my dyvernes doeth rise.
> But you that blame this dyvernes moost,
> Chaunge you no more, but still after oon rate
> Trete ye me well, and kepe ye in the same state;
> And while with me doeth dwell this weried goost,
> My word nor I shall not be variable,
> But alwaies oon, your owne boeth ferme and stable.
> (30R/10MT)

If this is a poem of courtship addressed to a woman, it is one in which the question of desire is wholly assimilated to the question of fidelity.[31] Initially the diversity of which the speaker stands accused might be just antic behavior of some unspecified sort; but when the general wisdom of the opening becomes the particular

---

[31] The argument has some affinity with Wyatt's advice to his son about marriage: "Frame wel your self to love, and rule wel and honestly your wife as your felow, and she shal love and reverens you as her hed. Such as you are unto her such shal she be unto you" (*Prose*, pp. 64–5). A few lines later he makes his only known comment on his own marriage: "the blissing of God for good agrement betwen the wife and husband is fruyt of many children, which I for the like thinge doe lack, and the faulte is bothe in your mother and me, but chieflye in her." The theory of mutual responsibility follows him almost to the end, but he cannot at last be quite that generous.

reproach to the addressee in the third quatrain, we understand that what is at stake is individual loyalty in a world of continually changing circumstance. The changing season brings changes of allegiance—but the poem also affirms that, at least with this addressee, an exemption from that necessity can be earned. What earns it is a more soberly formulated version of the arrangement proposed in "Madame, withouten many wordes": I will treat you as you treat me, and if you are minded to be faithful we can create a site of stability in an otherwise shifting and treacherous world.

That world is of course Henry's court. At moments like these Wyatt's love poetry seems to manifest a political content broader than what may or may not have happened with Anne Boleyn. What Raymond Southall calls "the proximity between the conventions of courtly love and the conditions of courtly life"[32] is itself a legacy of *fin' amors* and the political situation in which it was crafted. As assimilated by Petrarch, the political dimension is largely displaced by the literary, and what is left of it is relatively disengaged from the love story. But the nexus remains, and Henry's court gives it new embodiment and life; no less a figure than Wolsey will reassure his king in overtly erotic terms: "ther was never lover more desirous of the sight of his lady, than I am of your most noble and roiall personne."[33] Wyatt's sole authorized appearance in print during his lifetime involves a gesture quite specifically in the troubadour tradition, when he subscribes himself "most humble subject and slave" to Katherine of Aragon, his king's wife.[34] Love poetry such as Wyatt's can be read against this context in several ways. On a practical level, "the poetry of amorous complaint was admirably suited to the purpose of seeking the patronage of well-placed ladies of the Court. [It] offered them present and future service, reminded them of past service, extolled the supplicant's faithfulness and trustworthiness or, alternatively, chided them with lack of gratitude in a tone of servility properly becoming to a dependent."[35] More darkly, the turmoil in these poems displaces more general anxieties attendant on being a courtier in Wyatt's situation:

> the convention of the love-lament offered indirect expression to a range of feelings—depression, protest at bad faith, weariness from unrewarded service—that may have arisen from quite other sources, such as the difficulties and disappointments of his diplomatic work, fluctuations in the King's regard for him, and the hazards of his position as a courtier among intriguing rivals.[36]

---

[32] Raymond Southall, *The Courtly Maker*, p. 48.
[33] From a letter dated September 13, 1527; *State Papers of the Reign of King Henry VIII* 1: 278–9.
[34] In the dedication of *The Quyete of Mynde*, a translation from Plutarch that he offers Katherine in place of the translation of Petrarch's *De remediis* that she had requested; *Prose*, p. 17.
[35] Southall, p. 49.
[36] D. W. Harding, "The Poetry of Wyatt," p. 204. The most influential discussion along these lines has been that of Greenblatt, *Renaissance Self-Fashioning*, pp. 115–56. Alistair Fox makes an attempt to

Even poems making no particular reference to courtly matters and asking to be read primarily as love poems can be felt drawing urgency from this environment.

In Wyatt's case, that urgency is often registered in a complex of terms having to do with stability and permanence. They nuance his appropriation of Petrarch in one of his best-known translations. "*Amor, che nel penser mio vive et regna*" [Love, who lives and reigns in my thought] acquires an opening reminder, metrically emphasized, of the extraordinary length of this habitation: "The longe love, that in my thought doeth harbar."[37] It closes with the assimilation of love to fidelity, as "*bel fin fa chi ben amando more*" [he makes a good end who dies loving well] becomes "goode is the liff, ending faithfully" (*Canz.* 140, 10R/4MT). Read in this context, the speaker's profession of ardor in "Madame, withouten many wordes" emphasizes "alwaye" as much as "burneth." "Eche man me telleth" stands out as one of the few places where the speaker admits that his own devotion has been erratic. More commonly, the speaker has kept faith only to be let down by undependable others. The second poem in the Egerton manuscript sets the tone:

> What vaileth trouth? or, by it to take payn?
> To stryve, by stedfastnes, for to attayne,
> To be juste, and true: and fle from dowblenes:
> Sythens all alike, where rueleth craftines
> Rewarded is boeth fals, and plain.
> Sonest he spedeth, that moost can fain;
> True meanyng hert is had in disdayn.
> Against deceipte and dowblenes
>     What vaileth trouth? (4R/2MT.1–9)

We are not told for sure until the next stanza that this is a love poem, and no first-person pronoun is used. The Petrarchan conclusion, however, is previewed in l. 7, and we may confidently identify the speaker with the lover there being disdained. What is set against this lady's disdain is not her lover's pitifulness or even the strength of his desire but the truth of his heart. He maintains this truth in a world of endless duplicity; modernized spelling obscures a linkage operative throughout Wyatt's work between truth and troth, keeping one's word. His declaration of his feelings is also a pledge, and one he has stood by; his courtship, as the poet characterizes it, has been one of striving by steadfastness. That the woman has not responded in kind makes her of a piece with the corrupt world surrounding them both.

---

relate Wyatt's poetry to a specific timeline of political events; *Politics and Literature in the Reigns of Henry VII and Henry VIII*, pp. 257–85.

[37] The phrase "lungo amor" occurs nowhere in Petrarch's sequence, but it may have caught in Wyatt's ear from chapter 8 of Jacopo Sannazaro's *Arcadia*, a popular work first published in 1502: "Ay me, and how can it be that the long love that I am certain you bore me at one time should be now altogether fled from you?" *Arcadia and Piscatorial Eclogues*, trans. Ralph Nash, p. 83.

One encounters versions of this posture on almost every page of Wyatt's collected lyrics:

> Dryven by Desire I Dyd this Dede,
>     To daunger my self without cause why:
>     To trust the untrue, not Lyke to sped,
>     To speke and promas faithfully;
>     But now the prouf Doth verefy
>     That whoo soo trustith ere he knoo
>     Doth hurt hym self and please his foo. (64R/128MT.1–7)

The repeated declarations of aggrieved righteousness have not helped Wyatt with modern readers: "some of us find in him an atmosphere which is from the first oppressive and finally suffocating. Poor Wyatt seems to be always in love with women he dislikes .... I feel how very disagreeable it must be for a woman to have a lover like Wyatt."[38] Greenblatt is aggressively diagnostic:

The single self, the affirmation of wholeness or stoic apathy or quiet of mind, is a rhetorical construct designed to enhance the speaker's power, allay his fear, disguise his need. The man's singleness is played off against the woman's doubleness—the fear that she embodies a destructive mutability, that she wears a mask, that she must not under any circumstances be trusted, that she inevitably repays love with betrayal. The woman is that which is essentially foreign to the man, yet the man is irresistably drawn in to relations with her.[39]

The gender contrast implies an unfriendly sense of Wyatt's "manliness": "The qualities that seem to evoke this term are sarcasm, the will to dominate, aggression toward women, concern for liberty and invulnerability, and hence resistance to the romantic worship of the lady, a deliberate harshness of accent and phrasing, and ... a constant and unappeasable restlessness."[40] We can readily divine in Wyatt's love poetry personality traits that could play a largely unreckoned role in its habitual unsatisfaction.

---

[38] Lewis, p. 229.
[39] Greenblatt, *Renaissance Self-Fashioning*, pp. 141–2.
[40] Greenblatt, *Renaissance Self-Fashioning*, p. 154. A decade later Jonathan Crewe can write of "an openly sadomasochistic brutality not uncommonly regarded as Wyatt's special contribution to Petrarchanism"; *Trials of Authorship*, p. 33. In a similar spirit, see Barbara L. Estrin, *Laura*, though she sees the feared female presence as finally dominant: "she prompts the poet to distrust the nets of form that Petrarch uses to idealize Laura as his influence .... In admitting his inability to materialize anything, Wyatt dissociates himself from the male power complex" (p. 146).

In at least one instance Wyatt sounds as if he may be attempting such a reckoning, though a key line is clouded by textual uncertainty:

> If fansy would favour
> As my deserving shall,
> My love, my paramour,
> Should love me best of all.
>
> But if I cannot attain
> The grace that I desire,
> Then may I well complain
> My service and my hiere. (127R/43MT.1–8)[41]

The righteous sense of deserving to be loved is as straightforward as ever, but the relation between deserving and love is given a twist by personifying the latter as Fancy. "Fancy," a more casual term for desire than "love," is virtually interchangeable with "fantasy"—desire with the freedom of the imagination. Happiness for the speaker would be for Fancy to make an alliance with his own values—

> Fansy doethe knowe how
> To fourther my trew hert
> If fansy myght avowe
> With faith to take part. (9–12)

—yet he also knows that Fancy is by its very nature incompatible with those values:

> But fansy is so fraill
> And flitting still so fast,
> That faith may not prevaill
> To helpe me furst nor last.
>
> For fansy at his lust
> Doeth rule all but by gesse;
> Whereto should I then trust
> In trouth or stedfastnes? (13–20)

The direction of that last question is not what it might have been in a different poem, a reaffirmation of the speaker's own pride in possessing those stable virtues that Fancy does not—because he really does want this woman, understands that striving by steadfastness will not win her, and wants to know what will:

---

[41] For an extended discussion of this poem, with particular attention to the relation between fancy and fantasy, see Donald M. Friedman, "Wyatt and the Ambiguities of Fancy," though his understanding of the direction of the poem in its sixth and seventh stanzas is different from mine.

> Yet gladdely would I please
> The fansy of her hert,
> That may me onely ease
> And cure my carefull smart. (21–4)

He speculates, maybe, that the thing to do is to suspend his own rectitude and adopt her own style of fanciful unpredictability—a sufficiently uncharacteristic move on his part that he will need her help:

> Therefore, my lady dere,
> Set ons your fantasy
> To make som hope appere
> Of stedfastnes remedy. (25–8)

Maybe, if l. 28 does indeed read "stedfastnes remedy" and the phrase means something like "cure for steadfastness." Both the Egerton and Arundel manuscripts read "stedfastnes"; the Devonshire manuscript has "stedfast," which is metrically tidier, and most editors accept it.[42] Doing so, however, or parsing "stedfastnes remedy" as appositive nouns, scants the argument of the preceding lines where Fancy is recognized as incapable of steadfastness, and also deprives the poem of its interesting flirtation with the idea of joining Fancy's company rather than simply pining that the woman will not change her ways. That this would be a significant break with pattern on Wyatt's part is not in itself sufficient grounds for denying the possibility.

Still, in the long run the speaker cannot dismiss his longing for permanence or his sense that justice has its claim in these matters:

> For if he be my frend
> And undertake my woo,
> My greife is at an ende
> If he continue so.
>
> Elles fancy doeth not right,
> As I deserve and shall,
> To have you daye and nyght
> To love me best of all. (29–36)

The relative mildness of tone here has to be measured against a capacity elsewhere for being almost uniquely demanding:

---

[42] Most editors have accepted "stedfast." Ruth Hughey retains "stedfastnes" but claims that no difference in meaning is at stake; *The Arundel Harington Manuscript* 2: 165–6. Richard S. Sylvester prints "stedfastnes" and is as far as I know the only scholar to gloss the line as I do here: "a remedy for my steadfastness"; *The Anchor Anthology of Sixteenth-Century Verse*, p. 142.

> It was my choyse, yt was no chaunce,
> That browght my hart in others holde,
> Wherby ytt hath had sufferaunce
> Lenger perde then Reason wold;
> Syns I ytt bownd where ytt was ffree,
> Me thynkes, ywys, of Ryght yt shold
>       Acceptyd be. (93R/192MT.1-7)

Even Yvor Winters, the least compromising twentieth-century advocate of Wyatt's righteous plain speaking, finds the argument here "curious and unreasonable"; from the woman's point of view, it "might well seem arrogant."[43] We have evidence that this might indeed be the reaction of a woman in Wyatt's circle. In the Devonshire manuscript—"the facebook of the Tudor court"[44]—Mary Shelton annotates a less extreme complaint about her own unjust treatment of a prospective lover ("Who wold not Rew to se how wrongfullye / Thus for to serve and suffer styll I must"; 210R/165MT.24-5) with a deft and calm rebuff that is unimpeachably logical and a small poem in its own right: "ondesyard sarwes / reqwer no hyar," undesired service requires no hire.[45] You cannot obligate me with service I have not asked for.

We may be tempted to categorize the pose as specially masculine, but it is not exclusively coded that way in the context in which Wyatt wrote. Female speakers, possibly ventriloquized by male writers but possibly not, are capable of making comparable assertions:

> Yet Reasone wold that trewe love wer regardyd
>   Without ffayninge, wher ment ffaythfully,
> And not with unkyndnes ys to be rewardyd. (200R/164MT.
>   17-19)[46]

---

[43] Yvor Winters, *Forms of Discovery*, p. 11.
[44] Shulman, p. 142.
[45] *A Social Edition of the Devonshire Manuscript*, p. 97; also poem 8 in the modernized text of Elizabeth Heale, *The Devonshire Manuscript*. It is possible that "sarwes" means "sorrows," but "service" fits the sense better and clearly means "service" elsewhere in the manuscript (*Social Edition*, p. 215; 64.17 in Heale's edition). The hand of the annotation is identifiable as Shelton's; handwriting also allows us to identify an exchange in the margin on the poem's merits between Margaret Douglas ("forgett thys") and Shelton ("yt ys worthy"). The two women played an important role in curating the manuscript, and their annotations here give us a brief but unusually intimate look at the functioning of such manuscripts in the upper levels of court society. See Heale, "Women and the Courtly Love Lyric"; Bradley J. Irish, "Gender and Politics in the Henrician Court." The seven-stanza poem spells out SHELTUN with the first letters of each stanza. The poem itself is unattributed; no confident claims for Wyatt's authorship have been made.
[46] An unattributed poem in the Blage manuscript; the gender of the speaker is implied in the first stanza by her reproach against "want of truthe and ffaythfull stedfastnes / Of hym that hathe my hart onlye" (6-7).

And the extreme character of "It was my choyse" clarifies something often implied but not quite said; it makes explicit a rationale to *fin' amors* and the traditions descending from it, of which Petrarchism is not on this point the most relevant. Making that rationale overt is a sensitive business, and tends to require the help of a commentator. Elizabeth Hull is especially incisive:

> poets insist upon bonds of knots, servitude or pain. These bonds knit lovers to women who do not actively cooperate, who may indeed be absent, unaware, or even dead .... But the association must be manufactured: fortunately it can be created abstractly and without the active participation of the woman. If he does not have her, but she possesses him ... he can invert that possession and have her *because* she has him. He is overwhelmed; therefore she is his conquerer. ... He is wounded by her, therefore she is his torturer.[47]

For courtship so conducted, poetry plays a role different from that of Petrarchan memorialization in the indefinite future:

> Out of his private pain the poet creates a relationship, and validates it by making it public. ... Not only does he publish the behavior he projects upon [the beloved], but the publication itself may make his projection real, whether or not she succumbs to guilt. If she denies him a relationship she is by that fact engaged in a relationship with him—it's called cruelty—and everyone knows it.[48]

The most exhilarating claim that poets traditionally make for themselves is of the godlike power of creation *ex nihilo*, bringing something into existence where there had been nothing. Love poetry such as Wyatt's looks to such creation in a less abstract mode than theory usually has in mind, the contribution of new reality to the erotic and social network in its vicinity.

*

If the woman herself is not convinced but third parties are, and if she persists in her indifference despite the resulting pressure, we are moving toward the Petrarchan laurel, whereby the poet hopes for vindication, or at least empathy, from a more distant readership. But that movement is one Wyatt resists, and in comparison with other possibilities his love poetry distinguishes itself by keeping the woman's response central: what she does at the end of the poem will make all the difference, will determine whether an ostensibly seductive argument will indeed seduce. We of course (who are not the ones being seduced) are not usually in a

---

[47] Elizabeth M. Hull, "The Remedy of Love," p. 118. Shakespeare's Theseus understands the logic here: "Such trickes hath strong imagination, / That if it would but apprehend some joy, / It comprehends some bringer of that joy" (*Midsummer Night's Dream* 5.1.18–20).

[48] Hull, "Remedy," p. 119.

position to make that call. The state of Wyatt's poems as we have them returns us to a problem presented by the poems of the troubadours; without more in the way of narrative context or at least definitive ordering, readers outside the original circle in which the poems functioned can in most cases only guess where things are headed. Shelton's seemingly decisive reply is not always decisive in lived experience; we are not dealing just with literary convention but with the enduring lore of European eroticism, which knows that things can in fact work this way: "There are few women who can remain indifferent to my way of being obsessed and dominated by them."[49]

When it does work this way, the sensation is extraordinary—like a dream coming true. Boccaccio in his *Ameto* and his *Fiammetta* gives that simile narrative form as a way of moving a Petrarchan love story to an un-Petrarchan consummation: a character in the grip of a powerful erotic dream wakes to the amazing truth of physical love with a very real beloved.[50] Boccaccio is remembering Laura's dream visitations in the *Canzoniere*; Petrarch reports nothing overtly sexual in these encounters, but Laura's simple presence and willingness to speak make these moments of privileged intensity. Imitators from the late fifteenth century on will develop the dream poem as one of the premier sites where such success can be experienced and described:

> Hor ne le braccia io tengo il corpo adorno
> D'ogni valore, hor son con la mia dea,
> Hor mi concede Amor lieta vittoria ...—
> Così parlar dormendo mi parea;
> Ma poi che gli occhi apersi & vidi il giorno,
> In ombra si converse ogni mia gloria.
> (Il Cariteo, *Endimione* sonnet 15.9–14)[51]

"Now I hold in my arms the body adorned with everything of value, now I am with my goddess, now Love grants me happy victory..." So I seemed to be saying in my sleep; but when my eyes opened and I saw the day, all my glory turned into shadow.

Without any obvious sign of Petrarchan influence, a parallel genre appears in late medieval English lyric:

> Soo glade I was of my dreme verely
> that In my slepe loude I be gane to synge

---

[49] Benjamin Constant, in his diary for September 7, 1814, quoted and translated by Dennis Wood, *Benjamin Constant*, p. 211. The woman of the moment, Juliette Récamier, turned out to be one of the few, but Constant's record as a seducer was sufficient to give the remark authority.
[50] See Braden, *Petrarchan Love and the Continental Renaissance*, pp. 69–70.
[51] I quote from *Le rime*, ed. Erasmo Pèrcopo.

> and when I awoke by hevyn kynge
> I wente aftur hur and she was gone
> I had no thyng but my pylowe yn my armys lyyng
> for when I awoke ther was but I alone
> (Welles 36.43–8)[52]

So vivid is the experience that some poets will affirm its value even in waking reality:

> Se 'l viver men che pria m'è duro e vile,
> né più d'Amor mi pento esser suggetto,
> né son di duol, come io solea, ricetto,
> tutto questo è tuo don, sogno gentile.
> (Pietro Bembo, *Rime* 89.1–4)[53]

If life is less hard and vile to me than before, and I repent less at being Love's subject, and I am not the refuge of pain that I used to be, all this is your gift, gentle dream.

Indeed, it can be the occasion to celebrate the powers of illusion: "*Le bon sommeil ainsi / Abuse par le faux mon amoureux souci. / S'abuser en amour n'est pas mauvaise chose*" (Ronsard, *Sonets pour Helene* 2.23.12–14 [Kind sleep thus deceives my amorous care with falsehood. To deceive oneself in love is not a bad thing]).

Wyatt comes to no such conclusion. He regularly edits dreaminess out of his Petrarchan borrowings; among the things that disappears from "*Una candida cerva*" is the entire final tercet, in which the rest of the poem is framed as a kind of visionary trance:

> Et era 'l sol già vòlto al mezzo giorno,
> gli occhi miei stanchi di mirar, non sazi,
> quand'io caddi ne l'acqua et ella sparve.
> (*Canz.* 190.12–14)

And the sun had already turned at midday; my eyes were tired by looking but not sated, when I fell into the water, and she disappeared.

Wyatt's deer is not a noontime hallucination but lightly allegorized reality, the inspiration not for poetic revery but urgent advice: "Who list her hount I put him

---

[52] See P. J. Frankis, "The Erotic Dream in Medieval English Lyrics." There are two other examples in the Welles anthology (37, 46). A non-Petrarchan lineage is possible through Charles d'Orléans; see ll. 561-8 (the second stanza of "Syn that y absent am thus from yow fare") in *Fortunes Stablines*, ed. Mary-Jo Arn.
[53] I quote from Bembo, *Opere in volgare*, ed. Mario Marti.

owte of dowbte" (11R/7MT.9). Where Wyatt does entertain erotic dreaming as a beguiling alternative to his own unhappiness, it appears to involve no revising of his failure:

> Let me in bed lye dreming in mischaunce;
>   Let me remember the happs most unhappy
>   That me betide in May most commonly,
> As oon whome love list litil to avaunce. (33R/92MT.5–8)

The happy dreaming is of the success of others:

> You that in love finde lucke and habundance
>   And live in lust and joyful jolitie,
>   Arrise for shame! do away your sluggardie!
> Arise, I say, do May some observance!
>       .   .   .
>   Rejoyse! let me dreme of your felicitie. (1–4, 14)

The very way the audience is defined means that these dreams will be true ones. When a more conventional version of the Petrarchist erotic dream does occur in Wyatt, it is recounted with an arresting vehemence:

> Unstable dreme according to the place
>   Be stedfast ons: or els at leist be true:
>   By tasted swetenes make me not to rew
>   The sudden losse of thy fals fayned grace.
> By goode respect in such a daungerous case
>   Thou broughtes not her into this tossing mew
>   But madest my sprite lyve my care to renew,
>   My body in tempest her succour to embrace.
> The body dede, the spryt had his desire;
>   Paynles was th'one: th'othre in delight.
>   Why then, Alas, did it not kepe it right,
> Retorning to lepe into the fire,
>   And where it was at wysshe it could not remain?
>   Such mockes of dremes they torne to dedly pain. (27R/79MT)

The tumult here includes some serious problems following the simple sense. Ronald Rebholz, the only critic to engage seriously with the difficulties, argues that ll. 7–8 deal with the experience of waking (usually in such poems relegated to the end), while ll. 9–10 return to the dream experience itself. In this case, the speaker apparently awakes to full sexual arousal ("My body in tempest"—which would also be the fire in l. 12); if "madest my sprite lyve" means "woke me up" (at that moment renewing his cares), then he is attributing to the dream itself the sadistic power not only to craft deceitful illusions but also to say when they end, presumably through the very mechanism of that arousal. The opening of the third quatrain, however, strongly implies that in the dream state the spirit was the opposite of dead—the body's death in sleep is the spirit's life in fantasy—and consistency would need the life of the spirit two lines earlier to have the same sense (the renewing of cares being not simultaneous with the spirit's life, but rather being set up by it as a cruel punchline later on). Consistency of course may not be the right criterion here.

None of this seriously confuses the powerful feeling of anger at the experience, the absence of anything like Bembo's gratitude to his *sogno gentile*. Continental precedents for that anger are regularly cited, but they are not at Wyatt's pitch:

> Ma il gran piacer mutosse in gran tormento
> quando che solo me trovai nel lecto.
> Né duolmi già che 'l sonno m'ha ingannato,
> ma duolmi sol che sonno sogno è stato.[54]

But the great pleasure turned into great torment when I found myself alone in bed. Indeed, it does not grieve me that sleep deceived me, but it grieves me only that sleep remains a dream.

Wyatt's anger is inclusive and layered. At one extreme it includes the implication in ll. 4–5 that the dream had the power to bring the woman to the speaker's bed, to make the dream come true as it does in Boccaccio, and decided not to; the commendation of the dream's good judgment is sarcastic. The soberest complaint is that the dream is a "fals fayned grace"—the illusion of a pleasure that is not in fact taking place—but that reproach is knit with anger at the "sudden losse" of this unreal joy. These two sources of bitterness are refracted in the appeals with which the poem opens. Either let the dream be true—presumably, a dream in which the woman is, as she is in reality, absent, and hence a dream with no deceitful sweetness to offer—or let it last. These are the two ways in which dreaming could be assimilated to Wyatt's central complex of virtues, to truth or steadfastness. Usually treated by Wyatt as virtual synonyms, those two virtues here mark contrasting possibilities, intriguingly ranked: truth is the second choice ("at leist"); an untrue dream that would endure is first. That is about as close to a Petrarchan embrace of the unreal as Wyatt ever comes, and the poem offers no encouragement in thinking that the appeal could be answered, that such a dream could be stable. We may associate Wyatt's reticence on this point with a general lack of color and risk in his work, and feel a love poet should show more of both. Yet Wyatt's greatest and

---

[54] Marcello Filosseno, *Sylve*, sig. i2r; reprinted in Muir-Thomson, p. 318.

most mysterious poem—a poem without which we would not be as interested as we are in the others—does so, in a few brief but indelible strokes that take much of their drama from his general habit of restraint. "They fle from me" pivots on an extravagant assertion about sexual love and the world of dreams.

The poem has been extensively discussed, but I do not think justice has been done to the force of its key line: "It was no dreme: I lay brode waking" (80R/37MT.15). A dream would be the inferior state; a firm stand on the side of the real is no more than we would expect from Wyatt. Yet the affirmation has to be made because the experience in question could be mistaken for a dream, that state in which things happen that do not happen elsewhere:

> Thancked be fortune, it hath ben othrewise
> Twenty tymes better; but ons in speciall
> In thyn arraye after a pleasaunt gyse
> When her lose gowne from her sholders did fall,
> And she me caught in her armes long and small;
> Therewithall swetely did me kysse,
> And softely said dere hart, how like you this? (8–14)

There are few enough references to women's clothing and the female body anywhere in Wyatt, and nothing like this. Even when he seizes a woman's glove and exposes her hand, the foreground is still that of male banter and complaint. Here the falling of the gown and the sight of those shoulders and arms effectively render him speechless; the words he remembers being said are not his. Other writers do not share Wyatt's hesitancy about such descriptions, and he could draw on precedents from a range of different contexts. Dido's "longe armes and smalle" are praised in an un-Vergilian *blason* of her beauty in one of the first books printed in England, William Caxton's *Eneydos*.[55] Charles d'Orléans remembers or imagines his own lady:

> The smylyng mouth and laughyng eyen gray,
> The brestis rounde, and long, smal armys twayne,
> The hondis smoþe, the sidis strei3t & playne,
> Yowre fetis lite, what shulde y ferþer say? (4137–40)[56]

---

[55] Caxton's *Eneydos*, ed. W. T. Culley and F. J. Furnivall, p. 113, translating from an anonymous French *Livre des Eneydes* printed at Lyon in 1483.

[56] I quote from Arn's edition; the parallel is noted by H. A. Mason, *Sir Thomas Wyatt*, p. 126. Mason also cites "They flee fro me. They dar not onys abide" (1347; from the ballade "O Swete Thought, y nevyr in no wise"), an even more uncanny point of contact, although "they" in this case are Displeasure, Woe, and Heaviness (p. 122); the possible connection is explored by Leonard E. Nathan, "Tradition and Newfangleness." Some catalogues of the female body in the Welles anthology give even more dramatic evidence of how unguarded some poets could be in this line:

Here the sight is being rehearsed as a stay against absence ("Hit is my craft, when ye are fer away, / To muse þeron, in styntyng of my payne"; 4141–2). Wyatt implies, though, that his vision should make us think of the kind of thing that might happen in a dream poem. The Bannatyne manuscript supplies a Scots version of the poem he may well have had in mind:

> Hir hair wes lyk þe oppynnit silk
> Ane mantill of luve our me scho spred
> And with hir body quhyt as milk
> Vnto my bed scho maid a braid
> Softly talkand to me scho said
> Be ȝe on sleip / And I said nay
> hir chirry lippis to me scho laid
> Bot quhen I walknyt scho wes away
>
> Than in my armes I did hur brace
> With gudly wordis scho said to me
> O ser how lyk ȝe this solace
> content ȝe this tell me q sche
> I said maistres ȝes verrelie
> No thing to pleiss me bettir may
> Nor with ȝour persone evir to be
> Bot quhen I walknyt scho wes away (286.16–31)[57]

Even if it does not give a window to Wyatt's specific source, the Scots poem allows us to see how extreme a claim Wyatt is making. One speaker remembers saying he was awake while he was actually dreaming; he now knows that that conviction is no guaranty of its own truth. Wyatt's contrary affirmation has to my knowledge no parallel in late medieval lyric; you can find its like in Constantin Cavafy addressing Mark Antony in his moment of desolation:

> Πρὸ πάντων νὰ μὴ γελασθεῖς, μὴν πεῖς πὼς ἦταν
> ἕνα ὄνειρο, πὼς ἀπατήθηκεν ἡ ἀκοή σου·
> μάταιες ἐλπίδες τέτοιες μὴν καταδεχθεῖς.

> hur pappys were ronde and ther to ryght praytye
> hur armys sclender and of goodly bodye
> hur fyngers smale and þerto ryght longe
> whyt as mylke with blewe vaynes amonge
> 13.123–6 = Stephen Hawes, *The Pastime of Pleasure* 3863–6

---

[57] *The Bannatyne Manuscript*, ed. W. Tod Ritchie, 3: 308–9. (I once thought "Nor" in l. 30 should be "Bot," but it makes sense as a Scots usage for "than"; I am indebted to Tony Spearing for pointing this out.) The possible connection with Wyatt was first noted by Frankis, pp. 235–6. See also one of the dream poems in the Welles manuscript: "nay sir quod she as towchyng thys case / I pardone yow my owne dere harte anon / with þat I toke hur Softely and swetly dyd hur basse" (36.21–3; "dere harte" is repeated in l. 25).

Above all, don't fool yourself, don't say it was a dream, your ears deceived you: don't degrade yourself with empty hopes like these.[58]

Calling what has been lost a dream, an illusion, is the lesser response.

What has been lost is in the first accounting the world of promiscuous excitement and gratification recalled in the first stanza:

> They fle from me that sometyme did me seke
> With naked fote stalking in my chambre.
> I have sene theim gentill tame and meke
> That nowe are wyld and do not remember
> That sometyme they put theimself in daunger
> To take bred at my hand; and nowe they raunge
> Besely seking with a continuell chaunge. (1–7)

There are many women in the speaker's memory of sexual pleasure. That memory is out of key with Wyatt's usual stance of proud fidelity, but the multiplicity of those lost partners helps set the dreamlike quality unique to this poem: "the heart's desire being fulfilled by a stealthy grace appearing as easily as thought."[59] That ease has much to do with a reversal of expected roles: the male speaker as the passive one, the female as the predator. Yet when they close, the roles reverse again: the seeming predators "put theimself in daunger / To take bred at my hand." The gender politics of this has troubled modern commentators; Greenblatt sees in the speaker's behavior "the almost infantile passivity that is the other side of manly domination,"[60] and traces a thread of male aggression running through the apparent reversals. Eagerness to detect and expose a perverse erotic paradigm can, however, misrepresent the sweetness in the speaker's memory, where sexual love is the common ground on which hunting and waiting dissolve into each other, and tension turns into pleasure. This is not some special perversity of Renaissance court life but Venus at work: would-be partners skillfully finding their way to mutual satisfaction.

What might make one think it was a dream, however, is not so much the sweetness as the way it disappeared; the main force of l. 15 is directed at the fugitive character of the remembered happiness. If it was a dream, it was bound to end, and soon. To assert that it was real is to assert that it had something sterner to it, some capacity for steadfastness. In that sense, the first stanza, dominated by references to flight, is effectively conceded to the world of dreams; but there is no fleeing in the second stanza, and it is this special instance that calls forth the speaker's bold

---

[58] "The God Abandons Antony," in C. P. Cavafy, *Collected Poems*, ed. George Savidis, trans. Edmund Keeley and Philip Sherrard, pp. 60–1.
[59] Arnold Stein, "Wyatt's 'They Flee from Me,'" p. 39.
[60] Greenblatt, *Renaissance Self-Fashioning*, p. 152; see also Michael McCanles, "Love and Power in the Poetry of Sir Thomas Wyatt."

affirmation. Yet even as he makes it, the scene of leave-taking returns to him, and the poem moves to its uneasy conclusion:

> But all is torned thorough my gentilnes
> Into a straunge fasshion of forsaking;
> And I have leve to goo of her goodeness,
> And she also to use new fangilnes.
> But syns that I so kyndely ame served,
> I would fain knowe what she hath deserved. (16–21)

We seem to be hearing an oblique report of a conversation in which the lovers agreed not to continue their affair, though it is an agreement to which the speaker acceded without really assenting or even understanding. "I have leave to goo of her goodeness" recalls her own statement of how things were to be, a statement phrased as a gesture of magnanimity. That gesture was mirrored by his own "gentilnes": his final act of passivity was not to argue with her, not to tell her why she should stay. Phrasing it the way he does—"all is torned thorough my gentilnes"—initially puts the blame for their parting on himself, but he ends asking about her share and its consequences: "I would fain knowe what she hath deserved." If it was not a dream, it did not have to end, and it is therefore someone's decision, someone's fault that it did.

The last stanza is awash in ironic bitterness; "kyndely" is deeply sarcastic, and "gentilnes" not much less so. The speaker's own profession of responsibility is darkly shaded, and there is no question where he would like to place the real guilt. The last line has a menacing bass to it: "a bullying and vague threat figured by the poet's inability to find the words to say or the form to express his rage."[61] Yet that inability also compromises the menace; in other poems Wyatt has no trouble finding words for his anger, but here it is muted and smoky rather than confident and aggressive. Some later variants in the last lines dissipate what Peter Murphy calls "their expressive dead rhythm."[62] In the text in the Devonshire manuscript, the last line gives the poem an addressee for the first time: "but sins that I so gentillye am served / what think you bye this that she hat deserved."[63] The speaker now feels he is in a company that can endorse his sense of grievance. When the poem is first printed some two decades later, the ironic adverb is replaced with something more straightforward, and the outrage is sharper and more impatient, a lot easier to categorize: "But, sins that I unkyndly so am served: / How like you this,

---

[61] Estrin, p. 94. Shulman, pp. 188–9, suggests that Wyatt's poem may have played its role in Anne Boleyn's fall; I suspect other critics have assumed as much, though I do not remember anyone else saying it openly.

[62] Peter Murphy, *The Long Public Life of a Short Private Poem*, p. 132.

[63] *Social Edition*, p. 299. For an appreciation of the Devonshire text on its own terms, see Murphy, pp. 28–33, and Deborah C. Solomon, "Representation of Lyric Intimacy in Manuscript and Print Versions of Wyatt's 'They Flee from Me.'"

what hath she now deserved?" (Tottel 52R/57M). This is how a man might vent to a sympathetic tapster and whoever else might be drinking in his vicinity. The speaker in the original, by comparison, genuinely does not know the answer to his posed question or who might answer it, cannot say to what tribunal the woman might be accountable. His uncertainty makes the brave claim of l. 15 all the more extravagant and isolated.

We of course do not know what we do not know about the encounter recalled in the second stanza; the way is certainly open for second guessing: "the elements of that event can be interpreted, seen, and heard, in ways quite different from the narrator's. The lady's words can be triumphant, cynical, knowing, suggestive—they may represent many feelings other than affection, loyalty, passion, or the dream of true love which the narrator goes on to insist was no dream."[64] Almost any way our imaginations elect to play the scene will be conditioned by the simple and accurate implication of the first stanza, that there is something inherently capricious and evanescent about sexual interest, that it has a nearly limitless capacity for shifting its attention. "Charm'd love endures but whilst the charme doth last," as a later poet will advise a fellow sonneteer.[65] It may be sufficient to assign the woman no more malevolence than an acceptance of that fact. That acceptance would itself be compelling grounds for saying to her lover, as Greenblatt imagines her doing, "Dear heart, what did you expect?"[66] The man got it into his head that this time was different, and cannot believe she did not feel so herself; but she shows no signs that she did, and for all practical purposes that is an end on it. He passionately wants to defy that condition without having any real idea of what it would mean or take to do so.

Four centuries of erotic literature, transmitted to Wyatt with a new sense of authority as Petrarchism though reaching him through other channels as well, provided models for the proud and opulent sustenance of one-sided desire. There are poems of his, such as "It was my choyse," in which that heritage speaks with almost unparalleled confidence. In "They fle from me," though, that confidence cannot find its footing in territory that the tradition generally and Petrarch most decisively avoids: the aftermath of sexual love. There has been in this case, and in many others, no disdain on the woman's part. Desire has been gratified, and the question now is what happens next? What Wyatt responded to in Petrarch and his kin is a dream of constant devotion transcending circumstance, and he bestowed that dream on the circumstance most significantly absent in Petrarch. In places, such as "If waker care," the result is an interesting, beguiling category mistake. In "They fle from me," it is a baffled romantic extremity not quite like anything that European love poetry had yet seen.

---

[64] Donald M. Friedman, "The Mind in the Poem," p. 9.
[65] William Percy, *Coelia*, sig. Di$^r$. So also Shulman, on the import of Wyatt's poem: "fleeing is not the enemy of seeking, but its heir" (p. 279).
[66] Greenblatt, *Renaissance Self-Fashioning*, p. 151.

# 2
# George Gascoigne

During his lifetime and for fifteen years after his death Wyatt's poems circulated primarily in manuscript.[1] The Egerton manuscript, partly in the poet's own handwriting (like, as it happens, one of the manuscripts of Petrarch's *Canzoniere*), possibly represents some stage in Wyatt's sense of what the canon of his poetry should be; he appears to have taken it with him when he traveled. Most contemporary readers of his poems would have read them in manuscripts that circulated more widely, with Wyatt's poems mixed in with poems by others or without any identified author, often accompanied by marginal comments and responses (some of them poems themselves). The Devonshire manuscript is the great instance of this, offering glimpses of the elite circle which was this poetry's intended audience. Yet even while Wyatt was alive someone thought his poems should reach the wider, more impersonal audience of print, and several were apparently published in a book entitled *The Courte of Venus*.[2] No copy survives intact. Three fragmentary copies appear to be of three different editions: the first ca. 1537–39, the others 1547–49 (this one with the subtitle or alternative title *A Boke of Balettes*) and 1561–64. Collectively they include thirteen lyric poems and the last ten lines of another, all broadly similar in manner and content. No poems are identified by author in the pages that we have. Four of the lyrics are securely attributable to Wyatt from other sources, at least three more are usually accepted as his, and the case can be made for several others. It is possible that the lyric section of the collection was entirely, if anonymously, a selection from Wyatt. The existence of at least three editions (from three different printers) over a quarter of a century suggests that the raggedness of its survival was not a matter of readerly disinterest; indeed it seems to have been not obscure but notorious. In 1550, a book of metrical translations from scripture began with a denunciation of "what soever he was that made the courte of Venus or other bokes of lecherous Ballades, the whyche have bene a greate occasion to provoke men to the desyre of synne."[3] In 1565 the author, John Hall, pressed his attack further with *The Courte of Vertue*, a book of

---

[1] Stamatakis provides an up-to-date account of them in *Sir Thomas Wyatt and the Rhetoric of Rewriting*, pp. 213–24.
[2] For what is left and known, see *The Court of Venus*, ed. Russell A. Fraser. The state of the evidence permits skepticism as to whether the earliest edition, published during Wyatt's lifetime, contained poems of his; see Charles A. Huttar, "Wyatt and the Several Editions of *The Court of Venus*." If, however, 237R/262MT is indeed Wyatt's, it did.
[3] John Hall, *Certayn chapters taken out of the Proverbes of Salomon*, sig. Av$^v$.

lyric poems of moral instruction and exhortation that refute its antonymic precursor in its own mode. Some poems are pointed rewritings of profane love poems, with Wyatt one of the identifiable targets. "My lute awake! perfourme the last / Labour that thou and I shall wast" (109R/66MT.1–2) becomes "My lute awake and prayse the lord, / My heart and handes therto accord," with the same stanza form though going on almost twice as long.[4] The strategy was well established on the continent; *Il Petrarcha spirituale*, a poem-by-poem rewriting of Petrarch's *Canzoniere* by a Franciscan friar named Girolamo Malapiero, was published in Venice in 1536 and went through eight editions.

By the time of *The Courte of Vertue*, Hall and those of his mind had a more durable publication to deplore. Richard Tottel's *Songes and Sonettes*, published in 1557, is sarcastically remembered in Hall's subtitle: *Contaynynge Many holy or spretuall songes sonettes psalmes ballettes* .... Tottel's first edition proved to be the first of eleven over the next thirty years. The second followed quickly, with changes and rearrangements. The removal of some poems of possibly illicit love by, of all people, the young Théodore de Bèze (later Calvin's successor at Geneva) may have been in response to or anticipation of criticism from morally sensitive readers. Their excision scarcely softens the emphasis on secular love poetry. It is this for which, as the second edition is regularly reprinted without significant alteration, the anthology is mainly remembered; four decades later, in *The Merry Wives of Windsor*, a worried young wooer in need of assistance speaks of it as essential equipment in the business of courtship: "I had rather than forty shillings I had my book of songs and sonnets here" (1.1.199).[5] There are many poems not about love, but they tend to be toward the back. Until we get to the headings of the individual poems, the para-texts say nothing about their content. It is their style that Tottel praises to his readers, as well as his own role in making them available; it is his intent "to publish, to the honor of the Englishe tong, and for the profit of the studious of Englishe eloquence, those workes which the ungentle horders up of such treasure have heretofore envied thee." There are readers who may find the very virtues of the poems alien: "parhappes some mislike the statelinesse of stile remote from the rude skill of common eares." But Tottel assures them the taste of this alien world is worth the trouble of acquiring: "I exhort the unlearned, by reding to learne to be more skilfull, and to purge that swinelike grossenesse, that maketh the swete majerome not to smell to their delight." What looks like the main selling point, though, is the identity of the two main authors in the collection: "the noble earle of Surrey, and ... the depewitted sir Thomas Wyat." The first two-fifths of the volume are given over to two sections identified as the works of these

---

[4] Wyatt's poem is 109R/66MT; see *Court of Venus*, pp. 114, 119–20. For Hall's poem, see *The Court of Virtue*, ed. Russell A. Fraser, pp. 169–72.

[5] There is evidence that Shakespeare may have owned a copy of a third printing in 1557, at least long enough to give it as a gift; see John F. Fleming, "A Book from Shakespeare's Library Discovered by William Van Lennep."

two poets: twenty-six poems attributed to Surrey, followed by 101 attributed to Wyatt (forty-one and ninety-six respectively in the second edition). Surrey's name is also on the title page: *Songes and Sonettes, written by the ryght honorable Lorde Henry Haward late Earle of Surrey, and other.* Wyatt and Surrey were men of rank, and still famous more than a decade after their deaths. Tottel's collection beckons with access to the highest circles of society, previously out of reach of the general population—"the disclosure of a whole way of life, a way of thinking, a whole world that had been unavailable before, closed off within the walls of the court and within the covers of personal books."[6]

But the two names also count because we are moving into an environment where poetry—poetry in the vernaculars, not just Latin and Greek—is itself recognized as a source of fame for its author and the author's nation. The movement, not detectable in Wyatt's own poetry, is visible in elegies prompted by his death; when Surrey praises the older man for "that lively brayn" within which "some work of fame / Was dayly wrought to turne to Britaines gayn," he is thinking of "A hand that taught what might be sayd in ryme; / That reft Chaucer the glory of his wit" (28.6–7, 13–14).[7] This cult of patriotically competitive literary fame is part of Petrarch's legacy, and Petrarch is a presence in Tottel's collection in other ways as well. Some of this presence is in the anonymous entries: a pair of sonnets in praise of Petrarch and Laura (218–19R/188–9M), a reconfiguring of the rarely translated *Canzoniere* 23 (185R/154M; see Appendix B), brief translated passages from the *Canzoniere* embedded in original poems; the second edition adds translations of *Canzoniere* 1 and 3 into fourteener sonnets (276–77R/226–27M; fourteen lines of fourteen syllables). A poem on one mistress Bays (304R/264M) mimics Petrarch's use of the laureate symbolism (symbolism Wyatt scants when he comes across it). Petrarch's most consequential presence, though, is right at the beginning of the volume, in the two blocks of poems attributed to Surrey and Wyatt. Six of Surrey's poems and twenty-two of Wyatt's are wholly or substantially translations or identifiable imitations of poems from Petrarch's *Canzoniere*; all of them are retained in the second edition. At least as important, if not more so, is that both Surrey and Wyatt translate form as well as content. Four of Surrey's poems and seventeen of Wyatt's are sonnets of Petrarch's rendered into English in a recognizable version of the fourteen-line sonnet form; in another case, Surrey turns a fourteen-line Petrarchan *ballata* into an English sonnet (13R/13M), and in yet another a nine-line Petrarchan *madrigale* that we know from the Egerton manuscript Wyatt had originally translated as a fifteen-line *rondeau* is turned by editorial intervention—Tottel's or someone else's—into another sonnet (69R/74M). Another ten of the poems attributed to Surrey and nine attributed to Wyatt are also sonnets, original

---

[6] Peter Murphy, *Long Public Life*, p. 41.
[7] Text and references for Surrey's poems are from the edition of Emrys Jones. Publishing the elegy shortly after Wyatt's death in 1542 was part of the statement being made; see W. A. Sessions, *Henry Howard, the Poet Earl of Surrey*, pp. 245–59.

or translated from some other continental poet. If there were any sonnets or, for that matter, Petrarchan translations in *The Courte of Venus*, the surviving pages show no trace of them; the sonnets in Tottel's *Songes and Sonettes* are, as far as we can tell, the first English sonnets committed to print, and there are a lot of them. Whoever assembled Tottel's collection from the poetry of the court of Henry VIII made a decision to give prominence to Wyatt's ambition to bring Petrarchan lyricism into English and to Surrey's choice to follow the older man's lead. That editorial decision may or may not have seemed obvious, even inevitable—Petrarch had recently been put before the anglophone reading public as a love poet with the printing of another work from Henry's time, Lord Morley's verse translation of the *Trionfi*[8]—but it was momentous. Tottel's volume suggests a narrative for English literary history in the first half of the sixteenth century that is scarcely altered three decades later in Puttenham's formulation of it: "Sir *Thomas Wyat* th'elder & *Henry* Earle of Surrey were the two chieftaines, who having travailed into Italie, and there tasted the sweete and stately measures and stile of the Italian Poesie as novices newly crept out of the schooles of *Dante Arioste* and *Petrarch*, they greatly polished our rude & homely maner of vulgar Poesie, from that it had bene before, and for that cause may justly be sayd the first reformers of our English metre and stile."[9]

None of the Petrarchan translations and imitations in Tottel's anthology is identified. It may be going too far to say that he expected his readers to recognize them, but his introductory note assumes a general familiarity with "the workes of divers Latines, Italians, and other" whose poetry, "yea & in small parcelles [i.e., lyric poetry], deserveth great praise," and he could not have had any serious thought of concealing his English poets' sources. By midcentury, Petrarch's name was appearing in print with increasing frequency.[10] In learned circles he had long been known for his Latin prose, particularly *De remediis utriusque fortunae* [On the Remedies for Both Kinds of Fortune], an immense (and repetitious) collection of dialogues about various kinds of pleasures and sorrows. There had been a partial translation into Middle English; Katherine of Aragon asked Wyatt to translate it, though he begged off. A complete translation of *De remediis* by Thomas Twyne appeared in 1579. Citations and quotations of the dialogues continue through the next century; a denunciation of dancing—"*Petrarch* calls it the *Spur of Lust*, and the Circle where the Devil stands Laughing in the Center"[11]—has an especially long life. Briefer but more powerful enhancement of Petrarch's English visibility comes from his *Liber*

---

[8] For Morley the *Trionfi* is a love poem, of a piece with the *Canzoniere*: "these syxte wonderfull made triumphes all to the laude of hys Ladye Laura, by whome he made so many a swete sonnet"; *Lord Morley's Tryumphes of Fraunces Petrarcke*, ed. D. D. Carnicelli, p. 77. Laura's name is never actually used in the *Trionfi*, but Morley repeatedly inserts it.

[9] Puttenham, *Arte*, p. 60 (1.31).

[10] See Jackson Campbell Boswell and Gordon Braden, *Petrarch's English Laurels*, from which much of the following information and some of the translations are taken.

[11] N. H., *The Ladies Dictionary*, p. 159.

*sine nomine*, a set of letters denouncing the Avignon papacy. Their ferocity gets Petrarch included in the *Catalogus testium veritatis* [Catalogue of Witnesses to the Truth] of Mathias Flacius Illyricus (Strasbourg, 1562), a widely circulated gathering of pre-Reformation criticism of the Roman church; John Jewel cites Petrarch in his defenses of England's new version of Protestantism (*An Apology of the Church of England*, 1562; *A Defense of the Apology*, 1567), as does John Foxe in his *Ecclesiastical History* (1570). Such citations become commonplace. Petrarch's fellow spirits are sometimes ecclesiastical (Bernard of Clairvaux, Marsiglio of Padua, Savonarola, Wycliffe), sometimes literary (often Dante, who put popes, more than one, in hell; also Boccaccio, Mantuan). Passages from the *Liber sine nomine* are translated into English verse in the early seventeenth century.[12] Petrarch's vernacular works also play their part; the Avignon sonnets in the *Canzoniere* (136-8), often censored in Catholic countries, become popular with English translators, and up to 1700 *Canzoniere* 138 ("*Fontana di dolore*") is the most frequently translated poem from the sequence.[13] Its author is for many English readers "*Franciscus Petrarcha* ... who called Rome the whore of Babilon, the mother of errour, the Temple of Heresie, &c."[14]

Such *bona fides*, when it becomes relevant, could only strengthen English interest in Petrarch and his works, but it is not in the open air when Tottel first publishes his anthology under a Catholic monarch. The *cachet* to which he appeals is literary, a matter of language and style, and has a longer history. In the first half of the sixteenth century John Leland makes a similar gesture toward continental precedent as a way of praising Chaucer:

> Praedicat Aligerum meritò Florentia Dantem,
>    Italia & numeros tota (Petrarcha) tuos:
> Anglia Chaucerum veneratur nostra poetam,
>    Cui Veneres debet patria lingua suas.[15]

Florence rightly commends Dante Alighieri, and all of Italy your verses, Petrarch. Our England venerates the poet Chaucer, to whom his father tongue owes its charms.

It is not an eccentric judgment. John Bale makes it in 1548 in sober prose in an immense scholarly catalogue of British writers: "*Galfridus Chaucer ... poeta lepidus erat. Ac talis apud suos Anglos, quales olim fuere apud Italos, Dantes & Petrarcha. Patrii sermonis restaurator, potius illustrator (& merito quidem) habetur*

---

[12] George Lauder, *The Popes New-Years Gift*, sigs. B3ʳ-C1ʳ; reprinted in *The Anatomie of the Romane Clergie*, pp. 15–19.
[13] See Boswell and Braden, p. 4.
[14] *An Abridgement of the Booke of Acts and Monumentes of the Church ... by Timothe Bright*, p. 257.
[15] John Leland, *Principum, ac illustrium aliquot & eruditorum in Anglia virorum, encomia*, p. 80.

*adhuc primus"*[16] [Geoffrey Chaucer ... was an elegant poet, and to his English people what Dante and Petrarch had been to the Italians. He continues to be thought of—and rightly so—as the first to have rejuvenated his native language, or rather, the first to have brought renown upon it]. The claim about the place of Dante and Petrarch in Italian literary history is common wisdom, and the assertion that a similar place in English literature is occupied by Chaucer—who writes about Petrarch, translates from him, and may even have met him in person—is a trope in Chaucer's reception almost from the start. It is a trope nurtured by a felt need for someone to fill that slot: if English has its Petrarch (Dante gets less traction in this regard), that would validate England's own still dubious cultural ambitions and reflect well on all English writers. But tenancy of that slot is not necessarily stable; linguistic and generational change keeps opening it up, and in 1542 Leland rewrites his own epigram with a more recent candidate:

> Bella suum merito iactet florentia Dantem.
> Regia Petrarchae carmina Roma probet.
> His non inferior patrio sermone Viatus
> Eloquii secum qui decus omne tulit.[17]

Let fair Florence rightly boast of its own Dante. Let Rome praise the regal poems of Petrarch. Wyatt, who wins every prize for eloquence, is not inferior to these in his father tongue.

Tottel's anthology comes close to being the documentation for this claim, that Wyatt is the English Petrarch, though it also in effect announces an ongoing competition for that title.

*

Sixteen months after the publication of Tottel's volume, Henry VIII's daughter Elizabeth became queen of England. Among those attending at her coronation two months later was George Gascoigne, then in his twenties. His father was entitled by land holdings in Bedfordshire to be almoner at such proceedings, but was ill and sent his son instead. Father and son were both MPs; George had attended Cambridge and in 1555 had been admitted to Gray's Inn. He was positioned, in other words, in the lower echelons of England's privileged ranks, with prospects of advancement but no assurance of it. What followed has come down to us as an almost comic story of bungled opportunities. He never practiced law, failed as a farmer, made an expensive but fruitless attempt to succeed at court, went to jail for debt, entangled himself in lawsuits with his brother and was disinherited by his

---

[16] John Bale, *Illustrium Maioris Britanniae scriptorum ... summarium*, fol. 198[r].
[17] John Leland, *Naeniae in mortem Thomae Viati*, sig. Aiii[v].

mother, married a wealthy widow who turned out to be married to somebody else, signed on as a mercenary in the Netherlands, and ended up a Spanish prisoner for four months. He blundered almost fatally when, performing before the Queen at Kenilworth in 1575, he mishandled a prop he was brandishing ("an Oken plant pluct up by the roots") and sent part of it flying in her direction. The queen's horse reared, but, according to eyewitness testimony, "az the footmen lookt well too the hors ... no hurt no hurt quoth her highnes Which woords I promis yoo we wear all glad too heer," and a very relieved Gascoigne with the others could behold "the benignitee of the Prins."[18] Despite (or just possibly because of) the incident, Gascoigne did the next year begin to receive assignments of royal service, reporting to Burghley and Walsingham about developments on the continent. His way at last seemingly clear, in 1577 he suddenly took ill and died, in his early forties. The slapstick consistency of this record should make us suspicious, since, aside from the last part, our main source for most of it is Gascoigne himself. We have independent confirmation for some details, but much of it is derived from Gascoigne's fondness for telling the story of his life and shaping that story to his own ends. Gillian Austen is right, I think, to say that in his account of the sack of Antwerp, published anonymously in 1576 but now well attested as his, Gascoigne "effectively subverts the claim of this text to be non-fiction"[19] by the obvious artfulness of the pamphlet's most memorable moment:

> For by that time I came on the farder syde of the Bource, I might see a great trowpe comming in greater haste, with their heads as close togeather, as a skoule of yong frye, or a flocke of Sheepe: Who met me on the farder side of the Bource, toward the market place: And having their leaders formost ... bare me over backwardes, and ran over my belly and my face, long time before I could recover on foote. At last when I was up, I looked on every syde, and seeing them ronne so fast, began thus to bethinke me. What in Gods name doe I heare which have no interest in this action? synce they who came to defend this town are content to leave it at large, and shift for themselves: And whilest I stoode thus musing, another flocke of flyers came so fast that they bare me on my nose, and ran as many over my backe, as erst had marched over my guttes. (594–5C)

Gascoigne deftly turns whatever actually happened in that flurry of crowd chaos into a short, sharp version of, yet again, the story of his life.

---

[18] Robert Langham, *A Letter*, ed. Roger Kuin, pp. 45–6. Gascoigne improvised a change in the program to accommodate what had happened, though the new script was never performed; see Gillian Austen, *George Gascoigne*, pp. 120–6. Another description of the entertainments, published anonymously in 1576 but included in Gascoigne's posthumous *Whole Woorkes* in 1587, airbrushes the mishap. On the various accounts, see Janette Dillon, "Pageants and Propaganda"; Elizabeth Goldring, "Gascoigne and Kenilworth." A letter home by the Spanish ambassador reporting an assassination attempt against Elizabeth could be a confused rumor prompted by Gascoigne's blunder.

[19] Austen, p. 192.

That sort of thing is of course what writers do, and not the least important of Gascoigne's problematic ambitions was literary—indeed, laureate. These are manifested in a remarkable drawing that Gascoigne submitted to the Queen as a New Year's gift at the beginning of 1576 with the manuscript of translations into several languages of a story that had been the subject of an entertainment for her at Woodstock. An accompanying sonnet partly describes and interprets what is depicted:

> Beholde (good Quene) A poett with a Speare
> (straundge sightes well markt are understoode the better)
> A Soldyer armde, with pensyle in his eare
> with penn to fighte, and sworde to wryte a letter. (473C)

The poet-soldier is kneeling before the seated Elizabeth, looking her "full in the face."[20] He wears a sword and holds a spear in his left hand, while offering her a book with his right; a pen is indeed tucked behind his left ear. Descending allegorically through a hole in the ceiling, a cubit arm suspends a tablet inscribed *Tam Marti quàm Mercurio*, "As for Mars, so for Mercury," which Gascoigne had by then taken as his personal motto. The phrase proclaims Gascoigne's parallel careers in war and literature; it is a mythological encryption of a key phrase from Petrarch's coronation oration, *tam bello quam ingenio*, "as for war, so for wit," encapsulating Petrarch's central argument that the achievements of great poets are like those of victorious generals.[21] The connection to Petrarch is not casual; perhaps the most eye-catching feature of the drawing (unmentioned in the sonnet) is there below the tablet but above Gascoigne's head: a laurel crown hovering halo-like in mid-air. (Someone has colored it green.) A couplet of poulter's measure at the end of the manuscript is even more explicit: "Yf god wolde deigne to make, a *Petrarks* heire of me / the coomlyest Queene that ever was, my *Lawra* nedes must be" (510C). The fealty to Elizabeth entails serious literary ambition.

That ambition showed itself as early as Gascoigne's time at Gray's Inn, where in 1566 his translations of two contemporary Italian plays were performed in the kind of productions that made the Inns of Court an early center for the London theater (*Gorboduc* had premiered at the Inner Temple in 1561). In 1573 Gascoigne took the step of publishing his own book, *A Hundreth Sundry Flowres*; it contained

---

[20] Austen, p. 140. Austen stresses the poet's boldness in this "fantasy of a private audience with Elizabeth ... a far more private encounter than he could ever hope to achieve in life, since there is not an attendant in sight. That he represents himself with an unbound sword in such a private situation is especially audacious" (p. 141).

[21] Carlo Godi, "La 'collatio laureationis' del Petrarca," p. 26. The oration was not published during the Renaissance, but the relevant phrasing shows up in the diploma presented to Petrarch at the laureation ceremony and printed with his collected works in the sixteenth century: e.g., p. 1255 in the third volume of the 1554 Basel *Opera omnia*.

poems with occasional prose commentary, a prose tale containing poems, and the texts of the two dramatic translations. Some of the poems are attributed to "sundry gentlemen" not identified by name, but we are now confident that, aside from some collaboration on one of the translations, a third party epilogue to that translation, and possibly the introductory note from the printer, Gascoigne wrote everything himself (including several poems with a female speaker); he is actually a "self-anthologist."[22] For a poet to publish a substantial book of his own work was not unprecedented—Barnabe Googe had recently done so (1563), as had George Turbervile (1567)—but it was still a brave move, lightly shielded by a pretense of "encoded gentlemanly amateurism,"[23] with an immodestly formulated goal: "our native countrimen" have not "in their verses hitherto (translations excepted) delivered unto us any such notable volume, as have bene by Poets of antiquitie, left unto the posteritie" (143P). More practically, it was likely a try, after disappointments elsewhere, at a career possibility that certainly made more sense in the 1570s than it had before, and one for which Gascoigne had reason to think he had some talent. But it did not break the pattern that, on the evidence of some of the poems, he could already see shaping his life.

The actual publishing was chaotically entangled with Gascoigne's flight from his English debts to his ill-starred military career in the Netherlands; the collection's longest poem appeared incomplete, breaking off mid-stanza with an embarrassed note. When it did come out, the book ran into a buzzsaw. Details are elusive (as usual, Gascoigne is almost our only source), but apparently it caused "the scandalizing of some worthie personages" (362–3P) because they saw themselves or people they knew in its representations of sexual misbehavior among the privileged.[24] One of these is moderately graphic: "the words are cleanly (although the thing ment be somewhat naturall)" is how the printer puts it (3P). Gascoigne's response was to rearrange and slightly rewrite the collection, come up with the rest of the unfinished poem, add some new ones (as well as a practical short guide to poetry writing), and issue the result two years later as *The Posies*, with a triptych of prefaces in which the author both defends and disowns his previous publication. "I delight to thinke," he says, that his case resembles that of "the reverend father Theodore Beza," who also published some questionable poems in his youth (361P). As for his own poems, he got no money out of them ("I never receyved of the Printer, or of anye other, one grote or pennie for the firste Copyes of these Posyes"; 360P), and he also forswears any laureate aspirations: "I chalenge not

---

[22] Matthew Zarnowiecki, *Fair Copies*, p. 48.
[23] Wendy Wall, *The Imprint of Gender*, p. 245.
[24] Various suggestions as to who these people might be are summarized by Austen, p. 75. On Gascoigne and censorship, see Cyndia Susan Clegg, *Press Censorship in Elizabethan England*, pp. 103–22. There is no evidence that *Flowres* was actually "called in" (the records for the relevant years have been lost), though it is part of the story of Gascoigne's life that *Posies*, which ostentatiously presents itself as purging the causes of offense in *Flowres*, was; fifty copies were confiscated by the Stationers' Company in 1576.

unto my selfe the name of an English Poet" (360P). His intention in publishing is a moral one, to turn the follies of his own youth to account: "bicause I have (to mine owne great detriment) mispent my golden time, I may serve as an ensample to the youthfull Gentlemen of England, that they runne not upon the rocks which have brought me to shipwracke" (368P). In any case, the author is a different person now: "a man of middle yeares, who hath to his cost experimented the vanities of youth, and to his perill passed them: who hath bought repentance deare, and yet gone through with the bargain" (364P). Gascoigne casts himself (as he sometimes had in *Flowres*) in the role of the reformed prodigal, a common one for Elizabethan writers of his and the next generation, one that paradoxically helped to establish a professional literary world in London.[25] This role dominated Gascoigne's literary production for the remaining two years of his life.

The self-consciously edifying works subsequent to *Posies* now fill out the second volume of Gascoigne's *Collected Works*; it is by far the less visited volume.[26] *The Steele Glas*, published in 1576, has claimed a place in literary history as the first original blank verse poem in English, and also as England's first formal verse satire on the classical model. After a mythic introduction invoking the story of the nightingale, it becomes an earnest complaint about contemporary morals, surveyed class by class and occupation by occupation, with less in the way of entertainment value than any particular classical exemplar: "A tale ... which may content the mindes / Of learned men, and grave Philosophers" (143C). The same volume contains a kind of continuation in rhyme, *The Complaynt of Phylomene*, more personal in its protestations:

> Beare with me (Lord) my lusting dayes are done,
> Fayre *Philomene* forbad me fayre and flat
> To like such love, as is with lust begonne.
> The lawful love is best, and I like that. (206C)

*The Glasse of Governement*, published the previous year, is a prose drama which Gascoigne calls "a figure of the rewardes and punishmentes of vertues and vices" (5C). It is modeled on neo-Terentian prodigal son comedies then circulating in humanist circles, though Gascoigne provides a conclusion more punitive than redemptive.[27] In the last act, one of the quicker-witted elder sons is executed for robbery and the other charged with fornication and "so sore whipped that I feare

---

[25] See Richard Helgerson, *The Elizabethan Prodigals*, especially pp. 6–7.
[26] On these works see C. T. Prouty in *George Gascoigne*, pp. 180–8, 239–77; and with updated scholarship, Austen, pp. 103–5, 134–79, 196–212. *The Steele Glas* does have its admirers; see for instance Richard C. McCoy, "Gascoigne's '*Poemata castrata*,'" pp. 48–51; Syrithe Pugh, "Ovidian Reflections in Gascoigne's *Steel Glass*." *The Glasse of Governement* has also attracted respectful attention: Adhaar Noor Desai, "George Gascoigne's 'Patched Cote'"; Linda Bradley Salamon, "A Face in 'The Glasse.'"
[27] A catalogue in Charles H. Herford's *Studies in the Literary Relations of England and Germany*, pp. 162–3, efficiently establishes both Gascoigne's indebtedness and his distinctiveness.

hee be dead ... not able to stir either hande or foote" (87C). The two younger sons, slow of study but diligent, listen to their fathers and prosper in good and honorable employment (which for one of them involves witnessing his waistrel brother's death). *A Delicate Diet, for Daintiemouthde Droonkardes*, which appeared in 1576, is a temperance screed, enlivened at times by the half-cryptic Elizabethan fast-talking that is one of Gascoigne's signatures ("of a *Spanish* Codpeece, we make an English footeball: of an *Itallyan* waste, an English Petycoate: of a *French* ruffe, an English Chytterling ... and of a *Turkie* bonnet, a Copentank for *Caiphas*"; 466C).[28] The volume is a by-product of the longest of these works, published the same year: *The Droomme of Doomes Day*, which offers translations from "a small volumne skarce comely covered, and wel worse handled" that Gascoigne says turned up "amongest some bookes which had not often felte my fyngers endes in xv. yeares before," in which "I founde sundrye thinges (as mee thoughte) wrytten with suche zeale and affection, and tendinge so dyrectly unto the reformacion of maners, that I dyd not onley (my selfe) take great pleasure in perticuler reading thereof, but thought them profitable to be published for a generall commoditie" (212–13C). Gascoigne organizes the texts into a three-step program of moral instruction. The first part has been identified as coming from Innocent III's *De miseria humanae conditionis*; the other originals have (perhaps for lack of interest) not been traced. Specific injunctions include warnings against merriment—"if Christ doe threaten everlasting dampnation to them which laugh [Luke 6:25], who is he that dare in this lyfe be carelesse, light mynded, or jocunde?" (418C)—and dancing: "Neyther dyd God lend us our feete to the ende that we should exercise them in trypppinge lyke goates & kyddes" (419C). There was enough of a market for a second edition in 1586.

The last of Gascoigne's reformed works—the poem indeed with which his literary career ends—tempts the modern reader who makes it that far into seeing fissures in the enterprise they represent. *The Grief of Joye* announces its grave purpose at the start: "There is a griefe, in everie kind of joye. / That is my theame, and that I meane to prove" (519C). The first of four "songs" in rhyme deals with the treacherous pleasures of youth, with which the speaker is all too familiar:

> How many tymes, have I beheld the race,
> Of reckles youth, with sondrie greeves disgrast?
> How many Joyes have I seene fade apace,
> When in theire roomes, repentance hathe byn plast? (524C)

---

[28] According to the *OED*, it makes a mark in literary history with the first documented use of "metamorphose" as an English verb (461C, 464–5C), at least half a decade before Philip Sidney (*Astrophil and Stella* 44.14); Gascoigne also apparently coins the noun "metamorphoser" (463C), which did not take.

He announces categories for the remaining three songs—"Bewtye, strength, Activity"—but the somber dignity of the first song is flustered immediately as he starts on the second:

> Muse: plaie thy parte / & fend thy head from blowes /
> I see a swarme, which coome thee to assayle,
> Ne canst thow well, defend so many foes,
> Yf harte wax feynt, or courage seme to quayle /
> Behold, beholde, they come, as thyck as hayle,
> And threat to pluck the tongue owt of thy jawes,
> Which darest presume, to clapp on such a clawse / (526C)

The assailants are a regiment of women outraged at the news that the poet is going to write against Beauty, and he must drop everything to mollify them one by one, beginning with the queen, proceeding through quite a few ladies of the court (identified by their initials),[29] and then some of the women in his own real or imagined life (identified by names Gascoigne gave them in his poems, including a "Livia" we have not heard of before). He is, he tries to make clear, certainly not attacking *them*, nor really attacking Beauty itself, but rather the vanity that can attend it; he is not even singling out the female gender ("I never yet, coulde woman see more vayne, / Then many men, which passe in Courtly trayne"; 535C). By the end of the second song he has recovered his moralist's footing, though as he begins the third, on Strength, the project has become "this weary work" and is about to become more so because of what the First Sex is going to make of this part:

> And now beholde, how men (yea men of might)
> Prepare likewise, to beare my muse adowne,
> Because yt dares, presume for to endight,
> That might (which weares of manhood styll the crowne)
> Shoulde subject bee, to fortunes greevous frowne /
> Or for I dare, avowe that force and strenghte,
> Begynne with Joy, and ende with griefe at lengthe. (540C)

The male caucus proves less of a distraction than the female, though as we move into the fourth song on Activity, another kind of weariness seems to overtake the project. This category proves to be a grouping of smaller categories, signaled in the margins as the poet gets to them: music-making, dancing, various gymnastics ("Leaping, roonyng, vaultyng &c. &c."), wrestling, horse riding. The miscellany

---

[29] See Prouty, *George Gascoigne*, pp. 325–8.

of this, together with the increasing brevity of the entries, dissipates the moral urgency of the polemic. With the last topic, the poem suddenly stutters to a close:

> For sett asyde, the danger of a fall,
> (Which so maye chance, that (woulde we ride or no,)
> Agaynst owre wylles, at last wee must or shall,
> When withe a broken legg wee cannot goe)
> I can rehearce yett many myschieves mo,
> And sundry greeves, thatt &c. &c. (557C)

To which is appended the least edifying of explanations: "Left unperfect for feare of Horsmen." Exit, pursued by the cavalry.

Gascoigne, who says he worked on the poem while traveling on assignment, may have simply run out of time. The work was intended as another New Year's gift for Elizabeth, to be presented in manuscript form on the first day of 1577, and its author may have been unwilling to lose his sweat. He submitted what he had, garnished (in case Elizabeth or someone really did read through to the end) with an apologetic joke. It is a joke, however, that rhymes with interruptions that have already nosed their way into the poem; their cumulative implication is that the enterprise of using an almost Puritan agenda of moral reform as a vehicle for "advauncement by vertue" (361P)[30] is coming apart at the seams. What survives is the poet's own laureate aspiration. At the outset he identifies the succession in which he wishes to see himself:

> Even so my selfe, (who sometyme bare the bookes,
> Of suche as weere, greate Clerkes and men of skill)
> Presume to thinke, that everie bodie lookes,
> I shulde be lyke, unto my teachers still
> And thereupon I venter my good will
> Yn barreyne verse, to doe the best I can,
> Lyke *Chaucers* boye, and *Petrarks* journeyman. (517C)

"Boy" and "journeyman" are appropriately modest titles, and Gascoigne follows through on that modesty:

> But if some Englishe woorde, herein seme sweet,
> Let *Chaucers* name, exalted be therefore, /
> Yf any verse, doe passe on plesant feet,
> The praise thereof, redownd to *Petrarks* lore / (518C)

---

[30] The phrasing is not unconsidered; one of the fathers in *The Glasse of Governement* sets out the theory early in the play: "if I be not deceyved, *Al desire of promotion* (*by vertue*) is godly and Lawfull, whereas ambition is commonly nestled in the brestes of the envious" (9–10C).

Yet the protestation itself signals that literary fame is indeed on Gascoigne's mind, and the filiation he hopes to claim is not a modest one. The citation of Petrarch is somewhat more to the point than that of Chaucer. Gascoigne alerts Elizabeth to the way in which the whole work is a Petrarchan homage: "Towching the *Methode* and *Invention*, even as *Petrark* in his workes *De remediis utriusque fortunæ*, doth recoumpt the uncerteine Joyes of men in severall dialogues, so have I in thes *Elegies* distributed the same into sundrie songes" (514C). Gascoigne is revisiting the royal request on which Wyatt passed fifty years earlier. *De remediis* is indeed the work of Petrarch's most congenial to an agenda of moral austerity; Gascoigne makes it more so by ignoring its second half, the comparatively cheerful part about not being upset at bad fortune. What he provides is not a translation, but it does appropriate some of Petrarch's specific topics and arguments (you may be able to run really fast, but not as fast as a rabbit [*Rem.* 1.6]) and is at times a close paraphrase.[31] Petrarch is an openly acknowledged authority and resource in the literary change of direction of Gascoigne's last years.

\*

But those are not the years that now matter. If *The Grief of Joye* is the most interesting of Gascoigne's last works, that is (perversely) because of its antic self-demolition, which recalls the impenetrable gamesomeness of *The Hundreth Sundrie Flowres*, the volume (together with unfinished business piling over into *Posies*) that has kept Gascoigne on our reading list. Petrarch is a presence in *Flowres* as well, but not so overtly declared and manifested, and also, unsurprisingly, grounded not in *De remediis* but in the part of Petrarch's *oeuvre* by which poets have usually been most engaged. Gascoigne's own copy of an annotated edition of the *Canzoniere* has survived, with his signature on the title page.[32] The signature appears to be genuine, but there are no marginalia or other cues as to what caught Gascoigne's attention in the poems or in the body of commentary which they had accumulated by the later sixteenth century (and indeed no evidence that the book had been heavily used). The title page of *Flowres* describes its contents as "Gathered partely (by translation) in the fyne outlandish Gardins of Euripides, Ovid, Petrarke, Ariosto, and others," though that could be the printer improvising for his absent author; no single poem in the book can reasonably be described as translating a poem of either Ovid or Petrarch. Petrarch's name is never mentioned again. In the book's original compositions ("out of our owne fruitefull Orchardes in Englande," as the title page has it) there are distinctly Petrarchist moments—"My hope such frost, my hot desire such flame, / That I both fryse, and smoulder in the same" (262P)—and a few allusions to specific lines in

---

[31] See Robert Coogan, "Petrarch's *De Remediis* and Gascoigne's *Griefe of Joye*." For attempts to take the poem more seriously than I do, see Austen, pp. 196–212; and, expanding on the citation of Chaucer, Kevin Laam, "'Lyke Chaucers Boye.'"

[32] *Il Petrarcha con la spositione di Giovanni Andrea Gesualdo* (Venice, 1553); see Pigman, 465P.

the *Canzoniere*. "But one which knowes the cause of myne unrest, / And saith, this man is (for my life) in love" (345P) comes directly from "*Di pensier in pensier*" (*Canz.* 129.12–13). A riddling metaphor in which some commentators have intuited a contrast between Laura and a possible rival (*Canz.* 105.14–15) turns up in *Posies* in a woman's appeal to get back into the grace of the lover she had jilted:

> She furder sayde that all too true it was,
> Howe youthfull yeares (and lacke of him alone)
> Had made hir once to choose out brittle glasse,
> For perfect Gold (393P)

The famous *concetto* of *Canzoniere* 189, which Tottel made available in Wyatt's translation, provides a four-line opening for a poem of Gascoigne's:

> A cloud of care hath covred all my coste,
> And stormes of stryfe doo threaten to appeare:
> The waves of woo, which I mistrusted moste,
> Have broke the bankes wherein my lyfe lay cleere
> (161P; lines quoted by Puttenham)[33]

A complex eleven-line stanza that Gascoigne uses on three provocatively chosen occasions (169–71P, 290–3P, 349–51P) may have been inspired by Petrarch's *canzoni*. Gascoigne himself is modestly boastful about it ("for the order of the verse, it is not common"; 171P); it represents the most serious attempt so far to reproduce the prosody as well as the content of that ambitious form in English.[34]

Gascoigne's most significant contribution to English Petrarchism, though, comes at a level above that of the individual passages or poems. He is the first to follow in English the Petrarchan precedent of love poems in definite sequence. Aside from some grouping by verse form, the poems of Wyatt and Surrey come down to us in no particular order; topical references can date a few of them, but otherwise there is no compelling evidence for sequencing them chronologically or thematically. In 1560 Anne Vaughan Lock publishes, anonymously, a verse paraphrase of Psalm 51 as a sequence of twenty-one sonnets, but it will be a while before that form is used by an English-language poet for a full-blown love story in the Petrarchan mode. In *Flowres* Gascoigne prints three short chains of "Sonets in sequence," with internal formal connections so that each reads as a single continuous text (149–51P, 256–7P, 278–81P).[35] The headnote to the longest,

---

[33] Puttenham, p. 188 (3.18).
[34] Pigman suggests it specifically imitates the stanza in *Canz.* 23 (577P).
[35] On these, see William O. Harris, "Early Elizabethan Sonnets in Sequence." The earliest known instance in English is a pair of linked sonnets by Wyatt (34R/238MT); they appear in Tottel

a chain of seven, announces that it resulted from a challenge to write on the theme *Sat cito, si sat bene*;[36] to meet that need, Gascoigne broaches what becomes the great theme of his poetry, the repeatedly cautionary experience of his own biography:

> In haste post haste, when fyrste my wandring mynde,
> Behelde the glistering Courte with gazing eye,
> Suche deepe delyghtes I seemde therin to fynde,
> As myght beguyle a graver guest than I. (278P)

It is already obvious how things will end. The last line of the last poem completes the *corona* structure by recasting the first line with changes that indicate achieved enlightenment—"*No haste but good*, where wysedome makes the waye" (281P)—though the circularity also suggests what turns out to be the case, that this experience is one which the poet will have to go through again and again. The seven sonnets cover the speaker's attempt at being a courtier, which comes to grief when he exhausts his finances trying to keep up with the wardrobe requirements ("the blazing badge of braverie"; 279P) without having anything in particular to show for it. There is an erotic hum in the air:

> The wanton worlde of yong delightfull yeeres,
> Was not unlyke a heaven for to beholde,
> Wherein did swarme (for every saint) a Dame,
> So faire of hue, so freshe of their attire,
> As might excell dame *Cinthia* for Fame,
> Or conquer *Cupide* with his owne desire. (278P)

But the allure is diffused, as in the first stanza of "They fle from me," not centered on any particular woman. A nearby poem in the *Flowres*, "Gascoigne's praise of his Mystres," assures the ladies he addresses that "she doth passe you all, as much, as *Tytan* doth a star"—indeed, "she *Helene* staines for hue, / *Dydo* for grace, *Cressyde* for cheere, and is as *Thisbye* true"—and then discloses the allegory: "if you furder crave, to have hir name displaide, / Dame *Favor* is my mistres name, dame *Fortune* is hir maid" (271P). The equation works for "In haste post haste"; all the seductive delights of "the glistering Courte" are just constituent parts of an exhilarating prospect of advancement: "all was good that myghte be got in haste, / To prinke me up, and make mee higher plaste" (279P).

---

(101R/105M), and the practice was imitated and elaborated by several poets over the next two decades. Romeo and Juliet have improvised their way one quatrain into the second sonnet of such a sequence before they are interrupted (*Romeo and Juliet* 1.5.93–110).

[36] Fast enough if good enough; discussed by Erasmus in his long entry on *Festina lente* (*Adagia* 2.2.1).

Some version of that allegory can and has been asserted for a wide range of Petrarchist love poetry, and indeed of Petrarch's Occitan predecessors. Gascoigne is unusual in making it so overt, to the extent of reducing the women in the story to a crowd of supernumeraries. This is one reason I think it can be helpful to talk about him as a Petrarchan poet even when (as in what is now his most famous poem, discussed later) neither fleshly nor Platonic love is the manifest subject. Still, three of his most substantial works keep within traditional lines by dealing with a man consumingly enamored of a woman ultimately cold to his passion for her. His love and suffering are expressed in lyric poems, some of them sonnets, though these lyrics are presented in their narrative context: somewhat on the pattern of Dante's *Vita nuova*, except that the narrator and the lover are not the same person—or at least not exactly, though by the last of these works Gascoigne is being openly coy (a specialty of his) about the connections between first and third person. The narrative frame in the second two works is in verse; that in the first has given Gascoigne his place in the history of English prose fiction.

*The adventures of Master F. J.* (the running head at the top of the page) deserves that place, but does not exactly present itself that way, and is something odder and more improvised than, say, an English-language novella (which is what Gascoigne turns it into in *Posies*). We almost do not notice when it starts; formally it is the opening exhibit in an anthology of "divers discourses and verses" (141P), and begins off-handedly as one "G. T." (like his friend "H. W." quietly edited out of existence in *Posies*) is explaining how he came into possession of them and got them into order:

> When I had with no small entreatie obteyned of Master *F. J.* and sundry other toward young gentlemen, the sundry copies of these sundry matters ... I did with more labour gather them into some order, and so placed them in this register. Wherein as neare as I could gesse, I have set in the first places those which Master *F. J.* did compyle. And to begin with this his history that ensueth, it was (as he declared unto me) written uppon this occasion. The said *F. J.* chaunced once in the north partes of this Realme to fall in company of a very fayre gentlewoman whose name was Mistresse *Elinor*, unto whom bearinge a hotte affection, he first adventured to write this letter following. (144–5P)

As it happens, this "thriftlesse Historie" (215P) takes almost ninety pages to play out. G. T., at one point, senses that something is getting out of hand—"I doe dwell overlong in the discourses of this *F. J.* especially having taken in hand only to copie out his verses" (152P)—but still follows through as the prose sections get longer and longer. When we reach the end, G. T. does move on to (supposedly) other authors, declaring with some weariness that "henceforwardes I will trouble you no more with such a barbarous style in prose, but will onely recite unto you sundry verses written by sundry gentlemen, adding nothing of myne owne" (216P). The change is less than that makes it sound. G. T. had reported at the start that the writers "did alwayes with the verse reherse unto me the cause that then moved them to write" and that he found his appreciation of each item was enhanced "being considered by the very proper occasion whereuppon it was written" (145P), and he never stops drawing on this information. It mimics (with, paradoxically, more authority) the unstoppable biographical speculations that crowded into the annotations in Renaissance editions of Petrarch's sequence, such as the one we know Gascoigne owned.

All of the poems have expository titles like those in Tottel, and there is often more than that. One run of entries (conceivably outtakes from some earlier or alternative version of F. J.'s story)[37] becomes an ongoing narrative of flirtation in challenging circumstances (229–32P). An exchange of looks between "G. G." and "a Gentlewoman whom he liked very well, and yit had never any oportunity to discover his affection," leads to an exchange of written messages (his in four stanzas of rhyme royal, hers a swift bit of prose that he admires for showing her "quick capacity"), and shortly to a scene out of Ovid's *Amores* where more of the story slips into view:

> for a further profe of this Dames quick understanding, you shall now understand, that soone after this answer of hirs, the same Author chaunced to be at a supper in hir company, where were also hir brother, hir husband, and an old lover of hirs by whom she had bin long suspected. Nowe, although there wanted no delicate viands to content them, yit their chief repast was by entreglancing of lookes.

Everybody knows something is going on and nobody says anything about it, so the prospective new lover takes point. "G. G. knowing that after supper they should passe the tyme in propounding of Riddles, and making of purposes: contryved all this conceipt in a Riddle as followeth," and comes out with an appropriately cryptic rhymed stanza. When none of the other men follow up on it, the woman, observing "your dark speech is much too curious for this simple companie," propounds a comparably riddling response, also in rhyme, and G. G. "held himselfe herwith contented." The contentment proves transient: "afterwardes when they were better acquainted, he chaunced once (groping in hir pocket) to find a letter of hir old lovers," and the narrative gears up for further vexing developments. Gascoigne's anthology, as Richard Helgerson puts it, operates on "the presumption that poems like these do inevitably have occasions; that they are an integral part of the courtly conversation that goes on between lover and mistress, friend and friend, hopeful job seeker and potential patron; that they are ... ordinary rather than fictive speech acts."[38] The play between the collected texts and the

---

[37] See Zarnowiecki, pp. 58–60.
[38] Helgerson, p. 45.

narrative that connects them is one of the most enticing things about this part of the *Flowres*: the poems and occasional letters, sometimes baffling or trivial if read in isolation, become intelligible and important within the story in which they figure, where they also function actively as part of the way in which things happen in this world of sundry gentlemen and gentlewomen on the make. Gascoigne's artful depiction of that world—almost a reenactment—is one of his main literary achievements.

*The adventures of Master F. J.* transcribes twenty-one handwritten documents that figure in the plot.[39] These include fourteen poems by F. J. (including five stand-alone sonnets and a linked sequence of three sonnets) and two prose letters; there are also four prose letters by Mistress Elinor, and it seems in the spirit of things to include the one-word message—"Contented"—that she wears in her cap at dinner after she and F. J. have first become lovers (172P). Each of these documents is specifically contextualized in the ongoing story. Identifying their handwriting is at several places important to the plot ("Contented" is in Elinor's own, distinctively feminine script). Reference is also made to other texts discreetly missing: notably a cache of poems by F. J. that he withholds from G. T. for being "sauced with a taste of glory" (178P) in the afterglow of his success as a seducer, as well as what sounds like an eleventh-hour request for sex "to recomfort his dulled spirits" (211P) after he has been superseded. In general these documents are delivered as communications between F. J. and Elinor, either in person or by messenger (in two cases F. J. sings his poem to a lute accompaniment), though F. J. could be understood to have written a couple of the poems just for his own satisfaction. Occasionally the physical transmission of the document gets dicey:

> Walking in a garden among divers other gentlemen and gentlewomen, with a little frowning smyle in passing by him, she delivered unto him a paper, with these words. *For that I understand not (quote shee) th'intent of your letters, I pray you take them here againe, and bestow them at your pleasure.* The which done and sayde, shee passed by without change either of pace or countenaunce. F. J. ... in great rage began to wreake his mallice on this poore paper, and the same did rend and teare to peeces. When sodenly at a glaunce he perceaved it was not of his owne hande writing, and therewithall abashed, upon better regard he perceyved in one peece therof written (*in Romaine*) these letters *SHE*: wherefore placing all the peeces therof, as orderly as he could, he found therin written, these few lynes herafter followinge .... (146–7P)

These supposedly private communications sometimes get leaked to the general populace of the great house where all the action takes place; by the end of the

---

[39] The choreography of these documents within the narrative is given close and interesting attention by Alan Stewart ("Gelding Gascoigne"), though his increasingly complicated argument eventually pivots on a tricky claim that Elinor's secretary is the primary addressee of one of F. J.'s letters.

story everyone, with the possible exception of Elinor's inconsequential husband, seems to know what is going on. Artful sexual pursuit is the major pastime on view, for spectators as well as players.

A conviction about the effectiveness of poetry in wooing is part of the lore and at least to some extent the experience of Renaissance culture.[40] In *Posies* Gascoigne, eager to deny that *F. J.* is some kind of English *roman à clef,* insists it is a translation from a non-existent Italian *novella*, but in another part of his anxious self-defense he inadvertently affirms the realism of its most literary feature: "out of all doubt, if ever I wrote lyne for my selfe in causes of love, I have written tenne for other men in layes of lust" (370P). That ratio may be an exaggeration, but someone with Gascoigne's gift for prompt and fluent invention might well be importuned by the less talented for practical assistance.[41] He cannot resist implying that his clientele had no call to be disappointed: "in wanton delightes I helped all men" (371P). This may be the truth inside his pretense that the poems in *Flowres* came from multiple authors: they went to multiple customers. F. J. writes all his own material, but an aura of the transactional nevertheless envelopes the proceedings. Elinor sometimes writes and transcribes her own replies to him, but sometimes relies on the male secretary who is her once and future lover. The agenda is recognized from the start as promiscuous adulterous sex, and F. J. achieves that goal less than halfway through the story and without any remarkable suspense. The libidinous ambience resembles that of Henry VIII's court as implied, with far less narrative confirmation, by Wyatt's love poems; in neither environment is a woman's virtuous unattainability central or likely, except for tactical purposes. But Gascoigne's world was lower on the social scale than Wyatt's, less tense because there was less at stake; the real-life danger to the author was not death but humiliation and disgrace, imprisonment not in the Tower for treason but in jail for debt. F. J.'s most grievous punishment is to find himself the butt of an in-joke: "The Lady seemed little to delight in his dallying, but cast a glance at hir secretary and therwith smyled, when as the Secretary and dame *Pergo* burst out into open laughter" (213P). The dissonance between context and the hyperbolic emotions of the Petrarchan rhetoric the lover employs alters accordingly. F. J.'s way with that rhetoric has its own un-Petrarchan archness: "consideringe the naturall clymate of the countrie, I must say that I have found fire in frost" (145P). This from his first letter to Elinor. One

---

[40] See Ilona Bell, *Elizabethan Women and the Poetry of Courtship*, especially pp. 53–99. Concrete evidence is thinner than we would like, though a manuscript by the musician Thomas Whythorne, writing in the mid-1570s, presents as autobiographical fact several detailed flirtations through poetry; his adventures in love begin when a young woman leaves some verses in her own hand for him in the strings of a guitar, and he after some thought responds in kind. James M. Osborn edited the work in two editions, the second sparing the reader Whythorne's experimental orthography. On Whythorne and Gascoigne, see David R. Shore, "Whythorne's *Autobiography* and the Genesis of Gascoigne's Master F. J."

[41] Gascoigne had an attention-getting talent for composing fluent verse on assignment in the pressure of the moment, and was glad for his readers to hear about it (274–82P, 102C).

of his poems mimics the famous *incipit* of *Canzoniere* 23—"*Nel dolce tempo de la prima etade*"—and follows with its own narrative of a life-changing *innamoramento*, but rapidly dissipates any grandeur that the quotation may trail with it from Petrarch:

> In prime of lustie yeares, when Cupid caught me in
> And nature taught the way to love, how I might best begin:
> To please my wandring eye, in beauties tickle trade,
> To gaze on eche that passed by, a carelesse sport I made.
> With sweete entising bayte, I fisht for many a dame,
> And warmed me by many a fire, yet felt I not the flame:
> But when at last I spied, the face that pleasde me most,
> The coales were quicke, the wood was drie, and I began to toste.
> (159P)

The offhanded monosyllabic diction ("trade," "sport," "bayte," "fisht," "toste") decorates the big change in the story. Far from spending his young manhood blessedly free from desire, F. J. used his time to work up his skills as a sexual predator; he was training for the main event. He sings this poem as a song twice in the story, the second time a command performance for Elinor. There is no reason to think she is displeased by what she hears.

Successful seduction being more or less a given, the real focus of Gascoigne's narrative is on the end of the affair. For that, he has a surprise that is one of two places where he genuinely makes his mark as a writer. Here too it is helpful to remember Wyatt, also writing Petrarchist love poetry for an un-Petrarchan story, and often seeming to be writing of the end of a consummated affair. He does so bitterly and repetitiously, with a one-sided sense of betrayal by the woman, except that in one case—"They fle from me"—he finds in that anger unreckoned depths that yield his most memorable poem. In F. J.'s far more clearly articulated story, it is unambiguously the woman who decides that the affair is over and replaces the current lover with another (or others). There is a particular twist here that shows up elsewhere in Gascoigne's work: F. J. is displaced not by a new favorite but by a man who had been in the picture from the start. Gascoigne's literary interest in that circumstance could have something to do with his own experience finding that the woman he had married already had a husband (or at least someone who considered himself her husband), but we do not know enough about the situation to do more than imagine.[42] It is certainly a circumstance that adds a new

---

[42] For what we know, see Prouty, *George Gascoigne*, pp. 293–304. Elizabeth Bacon, first married to William Breton, was widowed in early 1559 and later that year married Edward Boyes; for unknown reasons she considered the marriage invalid and in 1561 married Gascoigne; Boyes tried to assert his claim as her husband, but the court eventually agreed with Elizabeth and issued some kind of divorce decree (what would now be called an annulment); Elizabeth and George remarried sometime

level of humiliation to an already bad shock, and plays an important role in F. J.'s behavior in the last segment of his adventures. He had been intuitively jealous of Elinor's secretary since he recognized that her first written message to him was the work of a professional. The secretary was shortly off to London, and F. J. "thought good now to smyte while the yron was hotte, and to lend his Mistresse such a penne in hir Secretaries absence, as he should never be able at his returne to amende the well writing therof" (154P). Renewing his rebuffed advance, he attracted enough attention to have his initial intuition explicitly confirmed by Frances, another lady of the house (and F. J.'s "kinswoman"; 164P) who had taken her own interest in F. J. and tried to warn him off his pursuit of "the most unconstant woman lyving" (164P). That advice is no more successful than it usually is, and after their Moonlight Banquet he and Elinor "passed many dayes in exceding contentation, and more than speakeable pleasures" (178P). The return of Elinor's husband (the first we have seen of him) disturbs this contentation not a bit, and F. J. writes a taunting sonnet about him. But the reappearance of the secretary undoes him, and he takes to his bed, accompanied by stern words from the narrator about what happens to lovers when "they suffer this venemous serpent jelousie to creepe into their conceipts" (181P). His collapse is tactically shrewd insofar as it brings Elinor to his bedside and eventually moves her to reassure him of her devotion and to start taking off her clothes, but her display of generosity undoes him in another way, spurring a guilty confession: "F. J. as one not maister of him selfe, gan at the last playnly confesse howe he had mistrusted the chaunge of hir vowed affections: Yea (that more was) he playnly expressed with whom, of whom, by whom, and too whom shee bent hir better liking" (197P). The effect on Elinor is explosive; she "began nowe to take the matter whottely, and of such vehemency were hir fancies, that shee now fell into flat defiance with F. J. who although he sought by many faire wordes to temper hir chollerike passions, and by yeelding him selfe to get the conquest of an other, yet could hee by no meanes determine the quarrell" (198P). F. J. deals with the situation by raping her on the spot: "having now forgotten all former curtesies, he drewe upon his new professed enimie, and bare hir up with such a violence against the bolster, that before shee could prepare the warde, he thrust hir through both hands, and etc. wher by the Dame swoning for feare, was constreyned (for a time) to abandon hir body to the enemies curtesie."

---

between 1563 and 1566. Prouty reports no references to her in official records after 1568 (p. 86), but George Whetstone's verse elegy on Gascoigne has her present at his deathbed, addressed as "My loving wife" (*Remembraunce ... of George Gascoigne*, sig. Biii[r]). Their son William died on Sir Francis Drake's expedition in 1585. The apparent durability of the marriage interferes with any simple identification of Elizabeth Gascoigne with the steadfastly unreliable female figures in her husband's writing, but the drama of their early history may well have left its trace. Prouty denies Elizabeth any connection with Ferenda (*George Gascoigne*, pp. 86–7), but thinks she is the coded subject of a poem in *Flowres*, "I cannot wish thy griefe, although thou worke my woe" (223–4P; Prouty, ed., *George Gascoigne's A Hundreth Sundrie Flowres*, p. 262). "Eyther a needelesse or a bootelesse comparison betwene two letters" (253–4P) unquestionably refers to the rivalry between Gascoigne and Boyes.

The way G. T. tells it, Elinor takes this more or less in stride—"having nowe recovered hir chamber (bicause shee founde hir hurt to be nothing daungerous) I doubt not, but shee slept quietly the rest of the night"—in part because F. J. has now greatly simplified any serious decision she may have been facing. She has, we learn, been avoiding her secretary's attempts to resume their liaison—"it was long time before he could obtayne audience"—but now in short order relents and is glad she did: "the *Secretary*... did now prick such faire large notes, that his Mistres liked better to sing faburden under him, than to descant any longer upon F. J. playne song" (199P). F. J.'s story from here on is mostly one of denial. He nurses a hope that he can persuade Elinor "to pardon his presumption, and lovingly to embrace his service in wonted maner," but, as G. T. puts it, "he was far deceyved, for she was in another tewne" (210P). F. J. is now the one who has trouble obtaining audience. When, with Frances's help, he does manage to do so, he pleads his case at such wordy length that Elinor, just to get rid of him, "pretended to passe over all old grudges, and thenceforth to pleasure him as occasion might serve" (211P). But that occasion proves "so long in hapening" that F. J., "forced to use his pen again as an Ambassadour betwene them," sends her a blunt demand that receives an equally blunt reply—"eyther learne to frame your request more reasonably, or else stand content with a flat repulse"—in, of course, the secretary's handwriting. Another ill-considered visit leads to open humiliation, and for a last sonnet he turns (like the hoodwinked Claudio two decades later in *Much Ado about Nothing*: "Out upon thee seeming, I wil write against it" [4.1.56]) to satire against the female sex: "For yet was never good Cat out of kinde: / Nor woman true" (213P). Determined to be done with all the lying, he returns to confront her finally and righteously with the manifest evidence of her faithlessness—and gets what might well be the surprise of his young life: "he ... could not be quiet untill he had spoken with his Mistresse, whom he burdened flatly with this despitefull trechery: and she as fast denied it, untill at last being still urged with such evident tokens as he alleged, she gave him this bone to gnawe uppon. And if I did so (quod she) what then? Whereunto F. J. made none answere" (214P). He is amazed, and knows not what to say.

He does have one more poem in him, though we are not told he sends it to anyone. It is a riff on Elinor's last words—"And if I did what then? / Are you agreev'd therfore?"—that ends with a fantasy of future joy at the fate of his current tormenters: "Then will I laugh and clappe my hands, / As they do now at mee" (215P). That is an ending we might expect from Wyatt, cauterizing the end of the affair with vengeful laughter.[43] But it is Elinor's rhetorical question, coming as if out of nowhere just when F. J. is certain he at last has penetrated all the veils and has

---

[43] F. J.'s last poem is singled out for praise by M. R. Rohr Philmus, both for its own virtues and as the climax of F. J.'s progress from a derivative Petrarchism to "the difficult simplicities" of "the native plain style"; Rohr Philmus sees that progress as the real plot of *Adventures*, which he reads as a *Künstlerroman*. See "Gascoigne's Fable of the Artist as a Young Man," especially pp. 20–2.

her cornered, that sticks in the memory, giving Gascoigne's story its literary distinction. For it *is* a rhetorical question; the very fact that she asks it means that it has no answer, and F. J. knows it. She has been more or less playing along with the hypocrisy whereby a sexually active woman behaves as if she would feel terminally shamed were her unchastity openly acknowledged, but down where it counts she could not care less. She also rejects without fuss any notion that her yielding to a man somehow grants him an ongoing privilege, or for that matter any kind of standing. In one of his more desperate poems F. J. may be trying to deploy such a premise—"Where would is free before, there could can never fayle" (212P)—since without it he actually has little if any leverage as far as getting back into her bed is concerned; but if she does not see it, then it is indeed not there. There is a feminist cast to this self-possession, a rejection of the traditional double standard for sexual behavior, but it is not a radical feminism; it is straightforwardly reliant on Elinor's social rank (securely above F. J.'s) and the compliance or cluelessness of her shadowy husband and only slightly less shadowy father-in-law. But it is radical enough in its way. Courtship and seduction draw on creative resources of attentiveness and expectation that are the most intensely and intimately imaginative activity that most people ever experience. And in this case the immense elaborated web of that activity, whose step-by-step growth G. T. has expended so much time and effort charting for us, suddenly simply does not exist, like a masque leaving not a rack behind. The consuming passion between F. J. and Elinor not only does not last, it does not even die or fade into memory; it disappears. End of story.

*

After this abrupt conclusion, *Flowres* turns to the previously announced program of presenting an anthology of headnoted poems by various authors. The running head in the printed volume becomes *The devises of sundry Gentlemen*, but before long the fiction of multiple authorship vanishes and Gascoigne's authorship is openly acknowledged with titles like "Gascoignes good morrow," "Gascoignes good nyghte," "Gascoignes councell to *Douglass Dine*," etc. At the end, though, we find, "to recomfort you and to ende this worke" (329P), another extended narrative containing love poems by the lead character, named in a new running head, *Dan Bartholmew of Bathe*. This one turns out to be a story that has no end. Twice.

The first time may be accidental. We are offered a series of interleaved texts by two carefully distinguished authors. Those in rhyme royal are by a "Reporter" who is a close friend of the title character (who shares his first name with a close friend of Gascoigne's, Bartholomew Withypoll, the addressee of an entry in *Flowres* [295–9P]); the others, supposedly written by that character, are in various meters, with heroic quatrains for the longer narrative passages. In 1573, one of the Reporter's sections is printed out of sequence, with a headnote saying where it "should have bin placed" (336P). In 1575 this is given in its proper place, and a new poem and a poem from earlier in *Flowres* (247–8P) are inserted at an early point in the sequence as poems by Bartholmew. Most importantly, in *Flowres* the last poem by the Reporter is, as its headnote warns us, "unfinished" (356P), and obviously so. It breaks off the way *The Grief of Joye* will four years later, interrupting the moral lesson that his friend needs to learn:

> Tell him that reason ought to be his rule,
> And he allowed no reason but his owne,
> Tell him that best were quickly to recule,
> Before all force by feare were overthrowen,
> And that his part. etc. (358P)

A note (presumably from G. T., though those initials do not appear) explains, "I have not (hitherto) recovered a full ende of this discourse, the author thereof being more curious in deliverie of the same, than he hath bene hithertofore in any other of his doings," but also expresses the opinion that what is here "amounteth to a good rounde vollume, the which some would judge worth the Imprinting." It is hard to resist the theory that the incompletion of the sequence is part of the chaos connected to the publication of that volume and its real author's departure to the wars.

It also seems, on the face of it, one of the less important parts. The verse narration in the sequence is much less circumstantial than the prose in *F. J.*, less clear about exactly what happened and who was involved, with some vaguenesses and inconsistencies (particularly regarding the age and erotic experience of both Bartholmew and the Reporter). But the general lines are drawn with a deliberately mythic boldness. The story is that of Batholmew's unhappy love affair with a woman who is the allegorical embodiment of female faithlessness: "of hir cage Inconstance kept the keyes / And Change had cast hir honoure downe in dike: / Since fickle kind in hir the stroke did strike" (331P). The Reporter gets to decide what to call her: "since I must a name to hir assigne, / Let call hir now *Ferenda Natura.*" The Latin title resembles the mottos posted at the end of the individual poems to identify their authors; according to the Reporter, this one means "dame *Nature* beares the blame," though the Latin gerundive is passive and in *Posies* (443P) the Green Knight will phrase it that way: Nature which is "to be borne" (as if the question of blame were irrelevant). Nature in either case means woman's nature according to traditional gender theory: "*varium et mutabile semper / femina*" (Vergil, *Aeneid* 4.569–70; always a variable and changeable thing, woman). She is "Ferenda" for short. Describing her, the Reporter momentarily seems to be defying Petrarchan precedent, as Shakespeare will later do: "First for hir head, the heares were not of gold" (330P). There is a sonnet along that line nearby in *Flowres* (228P), "written in prayse of the brown beautie," scorning the cosmetic falsities of "pampred beauty" and concluding "A lovely nutbrowne face is best of all." The *blason* of Ferenda, however, turns out to be not counter-Petrarchan but hyper-Petrarchan:

> the heares were not of gold,
> But of some other metall farre more fine,
> Whereof each crinet seemed to behold,
> Like glistring wiers against the sun that shine,
> And therewithall the blazing of her eyne,
> Was like the beames of *Tytan*, truth to tell,
> Which glads us all that in this world do dwell. (330P)

This mistress's eyes are very much like the sun, and more so.

Where she does break with Petrarchan precedent is in being attainable. In seemingly short order (though, we are told, "with mickell payne") Bartholmew "procured / The calme consente of hir unweldie will" (332P) and she becomes his mistress in the modern sense of the term. His emotional and carnal happiness is both hyperbolic and cunningly managed; the Reporter's depiction of it oddly anticipates the unfallen life of Adam and Eve in Milton's Eden:

> The lingring dayes he spent in trifling toyes,
> To whette the tooles whiche carved his contente,
> The poasting nightes he past in pleasing joyes (332P)

Bartholmew writes a celebratory poem to let the world know:

> Then lovers by your leave, and thinke it nothing straunge
> Although I seeme with calme content, in Seas of joye to range:
> For why, my sailes have found both wind and waves at will,
> And depths of all delights in hir, with whome I travell still (335P)

"These vaunting verses" (336P) come, unsurprisingly, before a fall. (The Reporter indicates that there are more of them he could have included; in *Posies* two other "triumphes" are there for us to read.) Before long, "The Saint he serv'd became a craftie devill, / His goddesse to an Idoll seemed to chaunge" (336P), and he withdraws to Bath, where the Reporter witnesses him in a far more familiar Petrarchan state:

> I sawe him there with many moanes dysmayde,
> I saw him there both fryse and flashe in flame,
> I saw him greev'd when other made good game (337P)

And we come to "Dan Bartholmews Dolorous discourses," the showcase aria of the sequence.

Addressing Ferenda, Batholmew makes reference to what brought him to his current state:

> Myne absent thoughts did beate on thee alone,
> When thou hadst found a fond and newfownd choyce:
> For lacke of thee I sunke in endlesse mone,
> When thou in change didst tumble and rejoyce. (340P)

He gets elusively more specific with references to a mysterious "Admyrall" (341P) and some kind of judicial proceeding where Ferenda testified that it was actually Bartholmew who corrupted her, making her betray some prior loyalty:

> whyles in toyle, this lothsome life I leade,
> Camest thou thy selfe the fault for to confesse,
> And downe on knee before thy cruell foe,
> Didst pardon crave, accusing me for all,
> And saydst I was the cause that thou didst so,
> And that I spoon the thread of all thy thrall. (341P)

Mainly he talks about how he is now that she has shown herself to be "of *Cressides* kynde" (340P) and left him for someone else—about the wretched reclusive life he leads, his emotional collapse, the decay of his health in the midst of supposedly healing waters:

> I take my sheete, my slyppers and my gowne,
> And in the *Bathe* from whence but late I came,
> I cast my selfe in dolors there to drowne.
> There all alone I can my selfe conveye,
> Into some corner where I sit unseene,
> And to my selfe (there naked) can I saye,
> Beholde these braunefalne armes which once have beene
> Both large and lustie, able for to fight,
> Nowe are they weake, and wearishe God he knowes,
> Unable now to daunt the foule despight
> Which is presented by my cruell foes. (343P)

He turns again, not very confidently, to poetry ("Beare with my muse, it is not as it was"; 347P) and switches from "this folish riding rime" to other meters to give lyric voice to his misery, including two poems presented as quasi-legal documents: a "libell of request exhibited to Care" in the *canzone*-like form that F. J. uses to celebrate his conquest of Elinor (349–51P), and a "last will and Testament" in poulter's measure (353–5P).[44] After these, there is nothing left to do except die:

> My weary tongue can talke no longer now,
> My trembling hand now leaves my penne to holde,
> My joynts now stretch, my body cannot bowe,
> My skynne lokes pale, my blood now waxeth colde.
> And are not these, the very pangs of death? (355P)

A final sonnet entitled "His Farewell" (356P), and we hear no more from him.

His disease is infectious. The Reporter is there with him, hoping to do some good:

> The force of friendship bound by holy oth,
> Did drawe my will into these croked wayes,
> For with my frend I went to *Bathe* (though loth)
> To lend some comfort in his dolie dayes,
> The stedfast friend sticks fast at all assayes (357P)

But friendship is no help:

> By proofe I found as you may well perceive,
> That all good counsell was but worne in wast,
> Such painted paines his passions did deceive,
> That bitter gall was mell to him in tast,
> Within his will such rootes of ruine plast (357P)

And in his ineffectiveness the Reporter is whelmed in a despair as crushing as his friend's:

> I am that man whome destenies ordeine,
> To beare each griefe that groweth on the mold,
> I am that man which prove unto my paine,
> More pangs at once than can with tong be told,
> I am that man (hereof you may be bold)
> Whome heaven and earth did frame to scoffe and scorne,
> I, I am he which to that end was borne. (357P)

---

[44] Gascoigne's legal training has attracted interesting recent attention: Lorna Hutson, *The Invention of Suspicion*, pp. 185–216; Michael Hetherington, "Gascoigne's Accidents."

He is rehearsing the wise advice that did neither Bartholmew nor himself any good when the text in *Flowres* cuts off. What is there left to tell but Bartholmew's seemingly imminent death? It would almost be superfluous to do so; you could almost convince yourself that the ragged termination is deliberate, part of the point.

Two years later, though, we have a completed version of the sequence, straightened out and amplified in the earlier part and with the Reporter's fragmentary stanza finished off and another fifty-five stanzas following it. Just as Bartholmew's story is at the very point of ending ("at the last he gan in deede to dye"), a melodramatic messenger arrives on horseback ("Upon the stones a trampling steede we heard"; 388P), bearing a letter from Ferenda, written (we are told) in her own blood, confessing her guilt and begging for Bartholmew to come to her in London. The sight of it almost finishes him off, but when he reads it he is recalled to life and decisiveness:

> feelingly he banished his bale,
> Taking herein a tast of remedy,
> By lyte and lyte his fittes away gan flye.
> And in short space he dyd recover strength,
> To stand on foot and take his horse at length. (392P)

"So," the Reporter continues, "we came to London both yfere," though the *camaradarie* masks the fact that our narrator does not for a second think Ferenda has changed her ways. He keeps that opinion to himself—out of kindness to his friend, of course, though he generalizes the principle behind it in an unexpected way: "he that hath not all thinges as he would, / Must winke sometimes, as though he dyd not see, / And seeme to thinke things are not as they bee" (391P). This looks like an awed reflex to the power he is watching Ferenda exercise: "These *Courtisanes* have power by pretence / To make a Swan of that which was a Crowe, / As though blacke pitche were turned into Snowe" (393P). Events seem to prove him right about Ferenda's nature. For a while Bartholmew "seemde to bathe in perfect blisse againe," but "could *Ferenda* never more forget, / The lease at large where she hir flinges had set, / But rangde againe, and to hir byas fell" (395P). This time around "*Dan Bartholmew* perceyvde it very plaine" and instead of relapsing into despair tries something new:

> His lustlesse limmes which wonted were to syt,
> In quiet chaire, with pen and paper prest,
> Were armed nowe with helme and harnesse fyt,
> To seeke adventures boldly with the best,
> Hee went to warres that wont to live in rest. (395–6P)

This might seem like a positive development, but the Reporter is past feeling celebratory, and shadows his conclusion with a sense that we have not heard the last of Ferenda and her like: "I do beleeve, / That once againe he wyll bee amorous, / I fere it muche by him that dyed for us" (396P). The completed sequence leaves us with the implication that what is to come will be a story of endlessly repetitive misadventure—even with the suspicion that Bartholmew's military career is just another version of his love life, folly pursued by other means.

*

This implication is clinched when Gascoigne explicitly links Bartholmew's story forward to the new sequence later in *Posies*: he becomes the Green Knight. That starts out as a mere analogy; Bartholmew choses green as one of his martial colors, and the reader who queries the Reporter's take on him is told, "but reade the greene Knights heavy plaint" (396P), which comes later in *Posies*. But immediately Gascoigne pulls the kind of fast one we learn to expect:

> *Bartello* he which writeth ryding tales,
> Bringes in a Knight which cladde was all in greene,
> That sighed sore amidde his greevous gales,
> And was in hold as *Bartholmew* hath beene.
> But (for a placke) it may herein be seene,
> That, that same Knight which there his griefes begonne,
> Is *Batts* owne Fathers Sisters brothers Sonne. (396–7P)

Gascoigne deploys a flirtatious gambit that F. J. uses on Elinor (166P) to equate Bartholmew with the Green Knight, while turning both of them into fictional characters in the work of the non-existent Italian writer (the Bandello of the bordello) whom Gascoigne confects to be the author of the newly Italianized "Fable of *Ferdinando Jeronimi and Leonora de Valasco*." (In due course Ferenda will address the disconcerted speaker of *The Grief of Joye* as "Bartholomew" [530C].) Even readers slow to sense that all these jilted males are in one way or another *personae* for Gascoigne himself (who tells us elsewhere in *Posies* [423P] that in Holland he was *die groene Hopman* [the Green Captain]) should get the point now, and understand why Bartholmew and the Reporter do everything together.

The relationship between protagonist and commentator is even more intimate in the Green Knight's sequence, *The Fruite of Fetters*. It begins with a first-person lament for "my time (ay me) in prison pent" (439P) as a kind of death-in-life: "Lo thus I live in spite of cruell death, / And die as fast in spite of lingring life" (441P). We are sixteen stanzas into it before, in the absence of quotation marks, we get any signal that the poet is not the speaker: "So sighed the knight of whome *Bartello* writes, / All cladde in Greene, yet banisht from delights" (442P). The two voices continue to alternate, though they are not cleanly distinguished by verse form (as they are in *Dan Bartholmew*) and sometimes nestle into the same stanza or couplet. Late in the sequence their two lives dovetail into the present tense:

> I saie his lottes and mine were not unlike:
> He spent his youth (as I did) out of frame,
> He came at last (like me) to trayle the pike,
> He pynde in pryson pinchte with privie payne,
> And I likewise in pryson still remayne. (449P)

Within the sequence's swirl of self-consciously "strange conceytes" (445P), the prison is both literal, the absurd finale to Gascoigne's own military career, and figurative, part of a determined attempt to extract some lesson from his experiences:

> Came crabbed Chance and marred my merry marte:
> Yea, not content with one fowle overthrowe,
> So tied me fast for tempting any mo.
> She tied me fast (alas) in golden chaines,
> Wherein I dwell, not free, nor fully thrall (440P)

Gascoigne's tendency to let his tropes run away with themselves can both obscure the narrative line and seem distractingly specific. A commonplace and seemingly casual metaphor for early manhood as a frisky colt in need of management—"When rash unbridled youth had run his recklesse race"—turns out to be just the start of a comparison that is maintained for twenty lines, working up to a climax that is unproblematic as far as horse training is concerned but not at all transparent on the human side:

> I kepte him still in harte
> And founde a pretie provander appointed for his parte,
> Which once a day, no more, he might a little tast:
> And by this diet, made I youth a gentle jade at last. (444P)[45]

(What *does* that mean? A strict once-a-day regimen of masturbation?) The larger narrative arc carries over from *Dan Bartholmew*. There is a bad early experience with a previously unattested Cosmana who betrayed the Green Knight and *may* have died (or is that metaphorical?), followed by Ferenda in recognizable form ("*Ferenda* changde for new: / *Ferenda* did hir kinde"; 443P). Fleeing disaster in

---

[45] We have a personal letter to Nicholas Bacon (Elizabeth Gascoigne's kinsman) in which Gascoigne lets the same metaphor run on in a similar way in direct reference to himself, without *persona* protection, ending in this case with a right raucous appeal for funds: "withowte some spedye provysione of good provender I shall never be able to endure a longe jorneye, and therfore am enforcede to neye and braye unto your good Lordship and all other which have the keye of Her Majesties storehowse"; *The Papers of Nathaniel Bacon of Stiffkey*, vol. 2, ed. A. Hassell Smith and Gillian M. Baker, p. 3. See Austen, pp. 213–15, who also discusses the emblematic device that accompanies the letter.

love, he goes off to war, where for a while he finds a happiness that sounds surprisingly erotic: "I bathed still in blisse, I ledde a lordly life, / My Souldiers lovde and fearde me both, I never dreaded strife" (445P). But that has ended badly too—and when the Knight comes to say how, the poem takes its most bizarre turn, into something very specific and wildly figurative at the same time.

He makes some to-do about setting it up: "No blasing beautie bright, hath set my heart on fire, / No ticing talke, no gorgeous gyte, tormenteth my desire," and so on for several lines before he reveals the "strange affect" that has undone him this time:

>     since I have begonne (quoth he) to tell my griefe,
> I wil nought hide, although I hope to finde on great reliefe.
> And thus (quoth he) it is: Amongst the sundrie joyes
> Which I conceivde in feates of warre, and all my Martial toyes,
> My chaunce was late to have a peerlesse firelock peece,
> That to my wittes was nay so like, in *Turkie* nor in *Greece* (446P)

So this is about a gun. He first says "it be not lost" and he is simply "shut from sight therof" (446P), but within a few lines, "My peece, my locke, and all is lost, and I shall never see / The like againe on earth" (447P). The description of this now absent wonder is rapturously physical—"A peece so cleanly framde, so streight, so light, so fine, / So tempred and so polished, as seemeth worke divine" (446P)—and goes on in the same style and with a touch of the same phrasing as the earlier *blason* of the women who no longer rouse the Knight's admiration and desire: "No bodies finely framde, no haggarde Falcons eie, / No ruddie lip, no golden locke..." (446P). His feelings for his peerless firelock piece mimic his feelings for Cosmana and Ferenda, and as Gascoigne keeps going he animates the rude pun a modern reader might think an anachronistic distraction, but which is right there in sixteenth-century English: piece as a portable firearm (*OED n.* 15b) and piece as a sexualized woman, a piece of flesh (9b). The second was not necessarily as degrading in early modern usage as it is now, but it certainly could be: "He like a puling Cuckold would drinke up, / The lees and the dregs of a flat tamed peece" (*Troilus and Cressida* 4.1.62–3). The Knight's gun is, or at least was, his mistress, the metallic vagina where he has garnered up his heart—though as his lament goes on the physical specifics of his beloved inevitably keep suggesting, sometimes painfully, the operations of the male genitalia:

>     A peece whose locke yet past, for why it never failde,
>     And though I bent it night and day, the quicknesse never
>         quailde...
>     A peece which shot so well, so greatly and so streight,
>     It neyther bruzed with recule, nor wroong with overweight.
>         (446P)

Both instrument and symbol for phallic dominance, the peerless firelock piece was everything, and with it "lost" (captured? stolen? confiscated? misplaced? broken?) the Knight is nothing. This is a bit much for the onlooker to digest, and when the poet takes over again he is scratching his head: "Thus have you heard the green Knight make his mone, / Which wel might move the hardest heart to melt: / But what he ment, that knewe himselfe alone" (448P). The poet decides to have a go at it, though he is not off to an impressive start: "by like, some peerlesse peece it was, / That brought him so in raging stormes to passe." The matter is pursued in a seriously literal-minded way: maybe it was a kind of gun the poet had heard about, used by people "neare the *Alpes*,"

> wherof the very ball
> Is bigge of bulke, the peece but short to see:
> But yet it shootes as farre, and eke as fast,
> As those which are yframde of longer last. (448P)

They are, he remembers, called "petronels" (449P)—indeed the name of a sixteenth-century firearm, a kind of hybrid pistol and rifle, though one with an unusually long barrel (along the lines of a Buntline Special) rather than an unusually short one. He suggests an etymology from "the Stone [*petra*] wherewith the locke doth strike" (449P), but he happens to be wrong about that too.[46] A reader of *The Grief of Joye* will notice in Gascoigne's catalogue of the women in his life two Petronellas (Petronella de Alquemade and Petronella van Schonhoven, according to marginal notes; 531–2C); one of these may (or may not) be the woman whose love letter to *die groene Hopman* caused him so much trouble in the Netherlands (422P). The signifiers refuse to alight.[47]

Looking for closure, the poet stops talking about guns and turns to the good that might come from a young man's prison experience, literal and metaphorical—the "fruite in fetters" (449P) that gives the sequence its title. He floats another "strange conceyt, and yet a trustie truth":

> there is no kinde of ground,
> That yeeldes a better croppe to retchlesse youth,
> Than that same molde where fetters serve for mucke,
> And wit stil woorkes to digge up better lucke. (450P)

---

[46] The correct etymology is French, from *poitrine*: the gun was held against the chest when fired. The narrator's ignorance is likely part of the joke.

[47] The best discussion of the Knight's fantasia is by Catherine Bates, *Masculinity and the Hunt*, pp. 129–37. She goes beyond the more or less obvious innuendos to coax "an exciting and highly perverse scenario of, at the very least, male homosocial desire" (p. 136) out of references to the gun's possible circulation among other soldiers. Her most significant predecessor commenting on the sequence, Felicity A. Hughes, seems wary of getting into any of this and hurries past it: "Gascoigne has *got to be* joking" ("Gascoigne's Poses," p. 10).

But that valuable crop is prey to an invasive species, "a kinde of Tares, / Which are vile weedes, and must be rooted out" (450P), though fortunately "this weede [is] an easie thing to spie" (451P). Gascoigne here employs the taxonomy of flowers, herbs, and weeds that provides the edifying new structure for the 1575 volume; we are now deep into the last of those, and beholding the most dangerous of the weeds: "Men call it Fansie" (451P). The term "fancy" had regularly been named in *Dan Bartholmew* as a driver in the protagonist's actions ("Then mighte you see howe fansie fedde his mynde"; 333P); the word, a contraction of "fantasy," merges senses of imagination (*OED n.* 4a) and desire (8b) in a diagnostic spirit. Now, in "The greene Knights farewell to Fansie" (452–3P), the Knight, taking the poet's advice, conducts an audit of everything he has set his mind to in his life, and pronounces each effort a project of fancy, and each effort a failure. Love and war are first and last among these, but there are eight altogether, each allotted three couplets of poulter's measure, reaching past anything we have been told of Bartholmew and the Knight into Gascoigne's own biography, and likely beyond into some inclusive portrait of Renaissance Man as versatile loser. The speaker has tried to be a lover, a courtier, a farmer, a hunter, a poet, a musician, an experimental horticulturist ("To plant straunge countrie fruites, to sow such seedes likewise, / To digge and delve for new found rootes, where old might wel suffise"), and a soldier. Each endeavor leads to the same refrain: "And since I finde my selfe deceyved, *Fansie* (quoth he) *farewell*"; "But since I see how vayne it is, *Fansie* (quoth he) *farewell*," etc. He looks toward "comfort of Philosophie" and resolves to stop trying and leave it to God: "since I must accept, my fortunes as they fall, / I say God send me better speede, and *Fansie now farewell.*" It is a comprehensive and uncompromising self-assessment, rejecting not only every genre of folly the poor man can think of but also the fatal disposition that is the root of them all. One assumes the observing poet must be pleased.

Yet he, or at any rate someone, is not. The sequence promptly concludes with its only sonnet, entitled "Epilogismus" (453–4P), in which the Knight's reformation is called out as a fraud:

> See sweete deceipt, that can it self beguile,
> Behold selfe love, which walketh in a net:
> And seemes unseene, yet shewes it selfe therewhile,
> Before such eyes, as are in science set.
> The Greene knight here, leaves out his firelocke peece
> That Fancie hath not yet his last farewell.

The Knight renounces everything except the one thing which is everything. The peerless firelock piece is simultaneously a specific object of fanciful desire and the underlying priapic principle of such desire in all manifestations. The Knight is not really giving up anything, and in composing a poem—one of his more entertaining poems, and, as it happens, for publication—that enacts his conspicuous renunciation of his many ambitions he is indulging the fifth ambition on this particular list. There is a moral hazard here from which it is not so easy to extricate himself (other poets have written more thoughtful poems about it). The sonnet writer finishes off by warning his readers to be careful whom they listen to— "When Foxes preach, good folke beware your geese"—and voicing empathetic skepticism about anyone's cleverness: "The mounting kite, oft lights on homely pray / And wisest wittes, may sometimes go astray." As for the Green Knight, we are left with the expectation that what is to come will, perhaps after some pause, be more of the same. He will always be gamely picking himself up and heading on to the next predictable disaster. It is the story of his life—a joke of which that is the punchline.

\*

That is a smart way to end it, a conclusion in which nothing is concluded, and reason to keep *Posies* on the reading list despite the modern preference for *Flowres*. Life goes on *because* men are fools, a proposition that might be dismaying, even tragic, if it were not so funny and sometimes heartening. Much of what is acute and appealing about Gascoigne's work comes to a focus in the last two poems in *Fetters*. But that's not all there is to it, and Gascoigne's disposition of the Green Knight's case, however well executed, is not as memorable or compelling as an earlier treatment of his own case, in the other poem where, and with considerably less literary masking, he tells us the story of his life, "Gascoignes wodmanship." Yvor Winters, in the essay that restored Gascoigne to twentieth-century visibility, called it "Gascoigne's greatest poem."[48] I do not dispute that judgment, though I have different grounds for it from Winters, for whom Gascoigne was valued as one of the masters of the "plain style" which was eventually eclipsed in English poetry by the enfeebling decorativeness of "the Petrarchist moment." I am of course offering a different narrative, and while a commitment to colloquial directness—which is indeed at times, as Winters has it, a moral commitment—is a serious component of Gascoigne's writing, I think "Wodmanship" achieves its greatness precisely when, toward the end, its plain-speaking yields something unexpected and mysterious, a "figure [that] I fynde within my head" (316P) that critics have admired but never really unraveled. It is not the same as Elinor's "what then?" but it is at that level: Gascoigne's other sublime moment.

In *Flowres* the poem comes with an unusually full headnote:

Gascoignes wodmanship written to the Lord Grey of wilton uppon this occasion, the sayde Lord Grey delighting (amongst many other good qualities) in chusing

---

[48] Winters, *Forms of Discovery*, p. 17.

of his winter deare, and killing the same with his bowe, did furnishe master Gascoigne with a crossebowe cum Pertinenciis, and vouchsafed to use his company in the said exercise, calling him one of his wodmen. Now master Gascoigne shooting very often, could never hitte any deare, yea and often times he let the heard passe by as though he had not seene them. Whereat when this noble Lord tooke some pastime, and had often put him in remembrance of his good skill in choosing and redinesse in killing of a winter deare, he thought good thus to excuse it in verse. (312P)[49]

We have no reason to doubt the general accuracy of this account of the poem's origin.[50] Gascoigne dedicated several works to Grey, a newly installed Knight of the Garter, owner of a large estate about twenty miles from the Gascoigne family home in Bedfordshire, and would have been a credible candidate for the appointment that three years after his death proved important to the career of Edmund Spenser, then a poet of more modest credentials, when Grey became Lord Deputy of Ireland and needed a secretary. In "Wodmanship" Gascoigne keeps deferentially referring to himself as "your wodman" and makes clear that he could really use some help with his affairs. It is an extremely odd job application; like the Green Knight in his "Farewell," Gascoigne stresses his failure in everything he has set his hand to. The list here and the Knight's overlap but are not the same. In general the Knight's is the more comprehensive (including indeed deer hunting); the catalogue in "Wodmanship" lacks five of the items on that list, including two whose absence seems particularly striking: love and poetry. On the other hand, the Knight makes no reference to any time at university or the Inns of Court, while Gascoigne puts those two educational experiences at the head of his parade of disappointment. The shakiness of his newest enterprise provides the starting point:

> My worthy Lord, I pray you wonder not,
> To see your wodman shoote so ofte awrie,
> Nor that he stands amased like a sot,
> And lets the harmlesse deare (unhurt) go by,
> Or if he strike a doe which is but carren,
> Laugh not good Lord, but favoure such a fault,
> Take well in worth, he wold faine hit the barren.
> But though his harte be good, his happe is naught (312-13P)

---

[49] On this conceit and its relation to actual hunting, see Bates, *Masculinity and the Hunt*, pp. 111-14. Lord Grey's hunt appears not to have been the strenuous hunt *par force de chiens* but the easier variety "in which the animals were driven before fixed standings from which the hunters would take their shots" (p.112)—a distinction relevant to the poem.

[50] The vicissitudes of Gascoigne's relationship with Grey are traced by Meredith Anne Skura, *Tudor Autobiography*, pp. 188-93. Grey's fortunes in the game of courtly favor were variable; by the end of 1573 he was in disgrace with the Queen and confined to the Fleet—apparently because of a dispute over, as it happens, hunting rights—and not released until 1575 (see Pigman, 662P).

Those last four lines add something to the conceit set out in the headnote, and bring with it an interpretive *crux* that G. W. Pigman has highlighted (664P) and for which I do not have a clean solution: what exactly is a "carren [carrion] doe"? The opposition with "barren" suggests that it was hunter's slang for a pregnant doe, and that is the gloss that until Pigman appears without comment in almost all annotated editions of the poem. Pigman, searching carefully and over many years, could find no such usage in English Renaissance hunting texts or other sources, but did find places where "carrion" and "barren" are paired in contexts where fecundity is not an issue, and the former term just means "worthless." The context in "Wodmanship" strictly requires only that meaning: Grey's woodman almost never actually kills a deer, and when he does it is one that is not of use. On the other hand, Gascoigne has a way of using oddball slang and proverbs not attested elsewhere, and he comes across as the kind of writer who would actively enjoy making them up; and also, the more important *crux* at the end of the poem has to do precisely with a dead doe's maternal function. It would make sense for the poet to set that up now, though it is not needed in this part of the poem for formulating, like the Green Knight in his "Farewell," the thematic unity of his sorry life:

> I crave your Lordships leave,
> To tell you playne what is the cause of this:
> First if it please your honour to perceive,
> What makes your wodman shoote so ofte amisse,
> Beleeve me *Lord* the case is nothing strange,
> He shootes awrie almost at every marke,
> His eyes have been so used for to raunge,
> That now God knowes they be both dimme and darke. (313P)

It apparently helps to keep himself in the third person as he works through the details. There is an allusion to his time in college (he "shotte sometimes to hit Philosophie"), then a longer passage about his attempt to study law ("in the end, he proved but a dawe, / For lawe was darke and he had quickly done"), then yet a longer one on his try to be a courtier:

> From thence he shotte to catch a courtly grace,
> And thought even there to wield the world at will,
> But out alas he much mistooke the place,
> And shot awrie at every rover still. (313P)

This is the game Gascoigne is returning to when he makes his pitch to Lord Grey, though with a change of venue and strategy. The earlier pursuit of high-profile advancement, like that in the seven-sonnet *corona* earlier in *Flowres*, is recalled as a frontal assault through stylish self-advertising ("His bumbast hose, with linings manifold, / His knit silke stocks and all his queint aray"; 314P) that yielded not much more than financial exhaustion: "Then (all to late) he found that light expence, / Had quite quencht out the courts devotion." And so on to the next bright idea: "now behold what marke the man doth find, / He shootes to be a souldier in his age ...." At least as warrior-for-hire someone would presumably be paying *him*, but it did not work out that way. Gascoigne did not even know at this point the full extent of his military misfortunes and disillusion with that life; they would provide rich material in *Posies* for "*Dulce Bellum Inexpertis*," a lengthy poem (also dedicated to Lord Grey) that takes its title from a famous anti-war essay by Erasmus (*Adagia* 4.1.1). Here what eats at Gascoigne is that he could not make any money at it:

> He trusts the power of his personage.
> As though long limmes led by a lusty hart,
> Might yet suffice to make him rich againe.
> But flussing [Flushing] fraies have taught him such a parte,
> That now he thinks the warres yeld no such gaine. (314P)

On this note he appeals to his prospective patron for help:

> And sure I feare, unlesse your Lordship deigne
> To traine him yet into some better trade,
> It will be long before he hit the veine,
> Whereby he may a richer man be made. (314P)

But then something starts to shift in this parade of ineptitude—a shift we might well have expected. When he gets into the details, his incompetence begins to sound like something else: "He cannot stoupe to take a gredy pray / Upon his fellowes groveling in the streetes" (314P). That is, he could not bring himself to rob grievously wounded comrades crying out for help—a disability that testifies to simple human decency on his part at the same time that he is implicitly reporting on behavior that he *did* observe in the Netherlands, and more generally telling us what as far as he can tell it takes to turn a good profit from a military career. By a stratagem possibly picked up from Wyatt's verse letter to John Poins (149R/105MT.19ff: "I cannot frame my tonge to fayne..."), Gascoigne's supposedly shamefaced apology for himself becomes a sharp, righteous satire on the world in which he is being asked to succeed. Once started, the line of thought takes hold:

> Alas my Lord, while I do muze hereon,
> And call to mynde my youthfull yeares myspente,

> They give mee suche a boane to gnawe upon,
> That all my senses are in silence pente. (315P)

With a favorite bit of streetwise diction (Elinor's "what then?" was a bone for F. J. to gnaw upon) Gascoigne begins to find a more comfortable level of vernacular confidence. Suddenly he is speaking of himself in the first person, and the veneer of humility evaporates:

> Yet therewithall I cannot but confesse,
> That vayne presumption makes my heart to swell,
> For thus I thinke, not all the worlde (I guesse,)
> Shootes bet than I, nay some shootes not so well. (315P)

The poem returns to Gascoigne's education, humanist and legal, to affirm his success in learning its lessons. Even his unhappy time at court was training he turned to account: "The craftie Courtyers with their guylefull lookes, / Muste needes put some experience in my mawe" (315P). The story is not just one of his own falling short; success in others begins to look like a badge of shame:

> some that never handled such a bow,
> Can hit the white, or touch it neare the quicke,
> Who can nor speake, nor write in pleasant wise,
> Nor leade their life by *Aristotles* rule,
> Nor argue well on questions that arise,
> Nor pleade a case more than my Lord Maiors mule,
> Yet they can hit the marks that I do misse,
> And winne the meane which may the man mainteine (315P)

The perverse paradox of unrewarded merit is at the root of his seemingly daft inability to get with the hunt:

> Nowe when my mynde dothe mumble upon this,
> No wonder then although I pyne for payne:
> And whyles myne eyes beholde this mirroure thus,
> The hearde goeth by, and farewell gentle does (315–16P)

The poem could end more or less here, or perhaps with further explication of the argument that seems about to be on the table: the world in which Gascoigne is expected to contend is one which systematically rewards the wrong kind of people. Humanist education (then and now) is resourceful at nurturing a conviction that your failure to master certain worldly skills is evidence of your seriousness and moral superiority,[51] and Gascoigne is poised to reap that benefit from his studies—but he swerves instead into something stranger.

The pivot is the poem's first mention of poetry: "Let me imagine in this woorthlesse verse ..." (316P). Despite its worthlessness, poetry is not on Gascoigne's list of failed careers, or at least not yet; at the time of "Wodmanship," both fictional and compositional, that would in simple fact be premature. And that exemption looks to be enough for the poet to trust where his poem somehow wants to go. Jane Hedley registers a sense that Gascoigne suddenly seems to be breathing something like the air of Sidney's *Defence of Poesie* at its most heady:

> The decision to depart from the givens of the poem's occasion and invent an emblematic occurrence which remains somewhat taciturn and defiant of "playne paraphrase" looks like a discovery of the poet's power to make "things ... better than nature bringeth forth ... not enclosed within the narrow warrant of her gifts, but freely ranging only within the zodiac of his own wit."[52]

The unexpected image surfacing within Gascoigne's self-absorption takes us in short order to the poem's eerie and sudden conclusion:

> Let me imagine in this woorthlesse verse:
> If right before mee, at my standings foote
> There stood a Doe, and I shoulde strike hir deade,
> And then shee prove a carrion carkas too,
> What figure might I fynde within my head,
> To scuse the rage whiche rulde mee so to doo?
> Some myghte interprete by playne paraphrase,
> That lacke of skill or fortune ledde the chaunce,
> But I must otherwyse expounde the case,
> I saye *Jehova* did this Doe advaunce,
> And made hir bolde to stande before mee so,
> Till I had thrust myne arrowe to hir harte,
> That by the sodaine of hir overthrowe,
> I myght endevour to emende my parte,
> And turne myne eyes that they no more beholde,

---

[51] A nineteenth-century example, from a Parisian garret: "Juste and I could see no place for us in the professions our parents insisted we should pursue. ... Today talent needs the kind of luck that favors the incompetent; in fact, if a skilled man rejects the vile arrangements that bring success to rampant mediocrity, he will never get on at all"; Honoré de Balzac, "Z. Marcas" (1840), in *The Human Comedy: Selected Stories*, ed. Peter Brooks, trans. Linda Asher et al, pp. 201–2.

[52] Jane Hedley, "Allegoria: Gascoigne's Master Trope," p. 156. She is quoting from Sidney, *A Defence of Poetry*, ed. Jan van Dorsten, pp. 23–4.

> Suche guylefull markes as seeme more than they be:
> And though they glister outwardely lyke golde,
> Are inwardly but brasse, as men may see (316P)

Again, we might be done; but then, astonishingly:

> And when I see the milke hang in hir teate,
> Me thinkes it sayth, olde babe now learne to sucke,
> Who in thy youthe couldst never learne the feate
> To hitte the whytes whiche live with all good lucke. (316P)

Winters singles out the conclusion as "the greatest passage in the poem,"[53] and quotes the last twenty-six lines. Having done so, he has nothing more to say about it except that it expresses "Christian pessimism, or disillusionment with the world"[54]; the implication is that in its plain-style way it needs no further explication. Gascoigne does offer up an overt lesson, about not being fooled by glittering externals but seeing things for what they truly are—but that in itself does not make the poem stand out within the morally earnest poems of the later sixteenth century, and the presentation of that message is only part of what is happening in these lines. Subsequent commentary has tended to follow Winters in assuming that the ending largely speaks for itself, but I think that has been more a matter of hope than of conviction. Critics note the visual pun equating the milk in the teat of the dead deer with the archery target that has been part of Gascoigne's ruling conceit from the start—mother's milk is life's bull's eye, the white prize—but otherwise, despite the climactic placement of that equivalence, as if it were the long-withheld solution to a mystery, no one has too much to say about lactation. But it is highly uncharacteristic of Gascoigne, a writer who despite his vigorous interest in sex is seldom very sensuous, and certainly not like this: a brief but unforgettable recapture of the sense of unstinting, overwhelming nurture that is among the first experiences a lucky newborn has of external reality. It is the sort of thing we more likely expect from the lush "Petrarchist moment" that Winters excoriates—from, for instance, Sidney's Astrophil celebrating the beauty of the woman he hopelessly and extravagantly desires: "if (both for your love and skill) your name / You seeke to nurse at fullest breasts of Fame, / Stella behold, and then begin to endite" (*Astrophil and Stella* 15.12–14).[55] "Wodmanship" ends with a sudden feel that we have crossed over into new territory, only to leave us just as suddenly to make of it what we can: "Thus have I tolde my Lorde, (God graunt in season) / A tedious tale in rime, but little reason" (316P). I think we are meant to experience the conclusion of the

---

[53] Winters, p. 18.
[54] Winters, p. 19.
[55] One of a "cluster of images of lovers as suckling children" in Sidney's poetry; see Katherine Duncan-Jones, *Sir Philip Sidney*, pp. 8–9.

poem as an abrupt and meaningful shift of stylistic register, and any satisfying reading of the poem needs to acknowledge that shift.

The only extended attempt I know to unpuzzle the poem's ending is that of Jonathan Crewe in his *Trials of Authorship*.[56] Crewe reads the poem in relation to the problematics of male competitiveness within the later Tudor court. As a poet, Gascoigne struggles, for the most part unsuccessfully, with the "inherently masculinist, overdisciplined forms" (p. 118) inherited from Wyatt and Surrey, whose poetic prestige, whatever the mixed record of their other ambitions, was secured by Tottel. In "Wodmanship" all ambitions are assimilated to the very male, "toxophilic" figure of the hunt in which Gascoigne simply cannot do right; that figure stands for the authoritative values by which masculine success and failure are adjudicated in the world. For much of the poem, as Crewe puts it, Gascoigne mobilizes a "countercultural discourse" (p. 134) in which the hunt itself is denied such authoritative status. There is good if slightly clandestine evidence elsewhere for Gascoigne's complicated attitude towards the aristocracy's signature sport,[57] but in "Wodmanship" he never gets as far as criticizing the hunt as such; the most he says is that many of the winners do not deserve their prizes. When he seems perhaps about to go further, he switches track to his strange vision of the dead doe. Crewe takes this to be a peremptory reaffirmation of official values—"the dominant oedipal scenario" (p. 135)—through the direct intervention of Jehovah, God of the patriarchs. "Never for a moment having departed from it, the ending of the verse text enacts the eventual return of/to the 'classic' script" (p. 136), though Crewe also admits that it is an "imperfectly elicited master script" (p. 139), announced in three "incompatible readings":

(1) his hitting the doe is simply a further instance of his perverse misfortune in a world governed by fortune, since even the mark he hits is the wrong one; (2) the doe is a heuristic device employed by "Jehova" to teach the speaker once and for all to stop aiming at unworthy marks implying false values; (3) that the truly instructive emblem is the maternal-feminine one of the *carren* doe, which may teach the speaker about sources of power and nourishment to which he had better attach himself for the duration of his limited future. (pp. 137–8)

The third obviously is the most important, though also the most cryptic. As a "maternal-feminine" (p. 138) emblem the dead deer is associated with the

---

[56] Zarnowiecki's brisk recent attempt seems to me too ingenious for its own good (it involves retaining the f-like long s in "sucke") and bland in its final twist: "what comes out of his failures at traditional professions is poetry itself" (p. 68).

[57] Gascoigne's anonymously published translation of a French treatise on hunting, *The Noble Arte of Venerie or Hunting* (1576), amplifies his source with four poems of protest spoken by hunted animals. See Bates, *Masculinity and the Hunt*, pp. 141–4; also Rob Wakeman, "Shakespeare, Gascoigne, and the Hunter's Uneasy Conscience." The fullest treatment of the translation is now that of Austen, pp. 105–15, though her emphasis is on the translator's well-informed enthusiasm for the sport.

anti-masculinist discourse that Gascoigne has been trying to assemble, and also with the fact that unlike his intimidating predecessors Gascoigne is working under a female monarch (who, despite his modest history with her, is never referenced in the poem). Crewe does not emphasize either matter in this summary, but they are important in the argument that gets him there. These encumbrances are presumably the reason that even Jehovah can only manage a blurred reassertion of his power, which reimposes masculine authority in the end (seemingly having the last word) by directing the poet to feminine nurture. The paradox is resolved through a complicated transaction centered on the killing of the deer: "The Doe's being offered as a virtual scapegoat for the speaker's guilty desire ... seemingly arrests his rage before any of it can be turned against the lawgiver Himself. At the same time, any prohibitive power of the woman (*diva virago*, phallic mother) is reconstrued as a function of the father's possession and investment of her" (pp. 138–9). That is trying to do a lot in two sentences; it is a hurried and cluttered resolution to the bind the interpreter has gotten himself into. The poem it describes sounds like the confused victim of its own conflicting agendas.

Crewe gets key elements in play as no other critic has risked doing. He is right that the final vision marks yet another change in the poem's direction; the excusing that Gascoigne has begun to do for his bad archery is interrupted and reproved by the poem's conclusion. The rebellious egotism that has been bestirring itself in the poem—Crewe calls it "the intolerably narcissistic subject of an interminable satiric diatribe against the world" (p. 134)—is halted when it moves into the open. Michael Hetherington catches this dimension of the poem's ending economically: "it surrenders petition for prayer, agency for humility."[58] We do not just return to the pragmatic career counseling against which the poem had been implicitly fighting. The alternative is imaged as an acceptance of infantile dependence on maternal nurture ("now learne to sucke"), which in psychoanalytic terms is not so much a disciplining of the speaker's narcissism as a reversion from its secondary to its primary form. Gascoigne has laid the ground for this turn by making the archery targets female from the start, but he waits until the last moment to spring the trap. The preparation is even more adroit if "carren" does mean "pregnant." Among the objections Pigman raises against that meaning is precisely that the doe at the end is lactating and mammals lactate *after* giving birth, but Gascoigne is not necessarily constrained by the rules of real-world biology—the doe in question is specifically identified as an imagined doe—and in any case there is within the conceit a dark logic to the transition. The doe has given birth precisely by dying (her death is that birth) and with that oxymoron the nourishment begins to flow. There is an air of redemptive sacrifice to this conclusion, and a christological reading might seem the historically appropriate one.

[58] Hetherington, p. 40.

Without exactly dismissing that dimension, I have a different sense of where we are at the end of the poem. The creature who dies this redemptive death is, as the poet says, a figment of his own imagination. What he kills is his own creation, a kind of suicide—and doing so, unaccountably, is a source of uncanny comfort. I think what happens emotionally is that on a deep level the speaker gives up: not with the comic, resilient embarrassment with which Gascoigne meets failure elsewhere in his writing (and apparently in his life), but simply, quietly, gives up. This is not necessarily secure emotional information about the poet's own emotional career. "The greene Knights farewell to Fansie" two years later is probably a more accurate account than "Wodmanship" of Gascoigne's affective biography; it is certainly more realistic. But "Wodmanship" is the greater poem, and that is because it offers the prospect of a far purer abnegation, and of a blessedness that can come with just letting go.

Ronald Johnson, in a less ambitious reading than Crewe's, almost gets it: "The poet is to suck at the carrion doe's teat, thereby himself becoming all that she stands for—something wasted and unwanted! ... He must learn to accept his futile life—nothing more."[59] Except that that is to miss almost everything. The discovery to which the poem wants to testify is that truly giving up can be an unexpected, enthralling source of nurture and peace, with a richness not known to the arid pride of Stoic endurance, with which it might be confused. My reference point here is well outside the sixteenth century; a graduate student suggested it to me decades ago. It comes from a more intense and systematic connoisseur of worldly disinvestment, Emily Dickinson, at the conclusion of what for her is a love poem, the one that begins, "I cannot live with You— / It would be Life."[60] After running through the iron logic of love's impossibility, she ends:

> So we must meet apart—
> You there—I—here—
> With just the Door ajar
> That Oceans are—and Prayer—
> And that White Sustenance—
> Despair—

Something like that is the white sustenance the speaker in "Wodmanship" finds in the imagined milk of the slain doe. Another nineteenth-century poet scornfully calls despair "carrion comfort." For Grey's woodman, that turns out to have been his true target all along.

---

[59] Ronald C. Johnson, *George Gascoigne*, p. 69.
[60] Poem 706 in *The Poems of Emily Dickinson: Variorum Edition*, ed. R. W. Franklin, from which I quote. The manuscript preserves "exercise" and "privilege" as alternative readings for "Sustenance"; the adjective was searching for its noun, and chose the one that brought out the hint of maternal nurture. That hint vanishes in early printed editions when "White" is attenuated to "Pale."

# 3
# Philip Sidney

Gascoigne's *Posies* opens with a large number of commendatory poems in English, Latin, and French, as well as a prose contribution in Italian. The last is attributed to a mysterious "M. A. Perugino," one of the English poems is attributed to the printer (Richard Smith or Henry Bynneman, depending on how you interpret the title page); other authors are identified by initials. Even by sixteenth-century standards, this onslaught of laudation approaches overkill. The precedent of G. T., H. W., and their more anonymous fellows in *Flowres* is hard to forget; Pigman "cannot shake the suspicion" that Gascoigne himself wrote some if not most of them (P698). The poem supposedly from the printer (C29, P381) may be even more devious than that. It inscribes Gascoigne in the illustrious company of those who "by writing purchast fame," in an arc from Chaucer through Gower, Surrey, and Wyatt, to "Old *Rochfort*" who "clambe the Stately Throne, / Which *Muses* holde, in *Hellicone*." That would be (?!) George Boleyn, Viscount Rochford, Anne Boleyn's brother, beheaded with her on a morals charge in 1536 long before he was old, not known as the author of any surviving poem.[1] The anticlimax could be slapstick ineptitude from an inexperienced praise singer (never a profession strong on quality control). It could also be another of Gascoigne's hangdog jokes about how his scramble for the laurel is likely to end up. That would be just like him.

Some of the poems are what they are said to be. T. Ch. is probably Thomas Churchyard, and G. W.'s thirty-four lines in poulter's measure can be confidently attributed to George Whetstone, Gascoigne's most visible literary disciple; Gascoigne did not need to invent him. The year after *Posies* Whetstone published *The Rocke of Regard*, a poetic miscellany with an avowed intent similar to that of the *Posies*: "it importeth necessarie matter of direction, for unstayed youth, who having the raines at libertie, are so hote in expence, as that they be many time surfited with incumberances, yea, tyred out right with prodigalitie, before they be brought into any perfect order of spending."[2] A "discourse of Rinaldo and Giletta," said to be "first written in Italian by an unknowne authour,"[3] is actually the first generic offspring of *The adventures of Master F. J.*, a prose narrative containing nine poems by

---
[1] "My lute, awake," now confidently assigned to Wyatt (109R/66MT), is attributed to George Boleyn in Harington's *Nugae Antiquae* 3: 286–7, possibly on the authority of what are now lost pages of the Arundel manuscript; see Hughey, *Arundel Harington Manuscript* 1: 24–5.
[2] George Whetstone, *The Rocke of Regard*, sig. ii[r].
[3] Whetstone, *Rocke*, p. ¹23.

the hero and three letters by the heroine. Keeping the theme of "the inconveniencies of jealousie,"[4] Whetstone reconfigures the story as one of virtuous chivalric love ending happily in marriage, though that ending comes with a snappy mercenary flourish very much in Gascoigne's manner: "The marriage rites solemnly pronounced, these faithfull lovers repaired to *Bologna* castle, where ... for to worke satisfaction for their long miseries, there wanted nothing, that coyne, cunning, or credit might compasse."[5] Dan Batholmew and the Green Knight reappear as "P. Plasmos," whose versified "Inventions ... touching his hap and hard fortune" are presented with commentary and narrative context by an observing "reporter." His utterances are at times exultant—he has (like Bartholmew) his "triumphe," and also a gleeful poem "in praise of his Purse"—but regret and repentance dominate. His final poem is a "farewell to folly" which descends from the Green Knight's "farewell to Fansie": "Farewell you fading joyes, / Which fancie forst me love."[6]

Whetstone's imitation becomes impersonation the next year in his *Remembraunce* of Gascoigne, a biographical verse elegy that for 294 of its 362 lines is spoken, without interruption, by Gascoigne himself on his deathbed. "And is there none, wil help to tel my tale," he begins (without introduction), but quickly answers his own question: "Yea *Whetston* thou, hast knowen my hidden hart / And therfore I conjure thee to defend: / (when I am dead) my life and godly end."[7] The poem may add some details to our knowledge of Gascoigne's life. Scholars are wary of accepting its testimony too literally, though there is no evidence specifically contradicting it, and no particular reason to doubt Whetstone's claim to a close friendship that would motivate and entitle him to be the custodian of Gascoigne's reputation. Whetstone has Gascoigne confess his youthful follies, stress the genuineness of his repentance and reformation, lay some of his misfortune on the spite and ignorance of others, and die affirming a dark view of human nature ("And what is man? Dust, Slime, a puf of winde"), loving devotion to his monarch and his family, and a secure Christian faith:

> My soule I first, bequeath Almighty God,
> and though my sinnes are grevous in his sight:
> I firmly trust, to scape his firy rod,
> When as my faith his deer Sonne shall recite.[8]

---

[4] Whetstone, *Rocke*, sig. ii^v.
[5] Whetstone, *Rocke*, p. ^1 61.
[6] Whetstone, *Rocke*, p. ^2 102. Another character, Dom Diego, also has a "triumphe," as well as, in further mimicry of Bartholmew, a "dolerous discourse." One "false Frenos" has a "complaint" in a sequence of four sonnets on Gascoigne's model.
[7] Whetstone, *Remembraunce*, sig. Aii^r.
[8] Whetstone, *Remembraunce*, sigs. Aiiii^v, Bii^r, Bii^v.

When Whetstone finally enters the poem in his own voice, he shifts attention to Gascoigne's literary legacy:

> by such death, two lyves he gaines for one,
> His Soule in heaven dooth live in endles joye
> His woorthy woorks, such fame in earth have sowne,
> As sack nor wrack, his name can there destroy.[9]

Whetstone does what he can to rise to a resonant conclusion, possibly hoping for an effect like that at the end of "Wodmanship": "once in earth, his toyle was passing great: / And we devourd the sweet of all his sweat."[10] That would now qualify for *The Stuffed Owl*, but the intended message is serious and indeed valid: Gascoigne's readers can encounter an unexpected *dulce* inside his catalogue of worldly failure and moral earnestness.[11]

Despite that parting shot, the work Whetstone's Gascoigne singles out as "that which should be praisd aboove the rest" is of all things "My Doomes day Drum,"[12] and as promotion of Gascoigne's literary stock for the last decades of the Elizabethan age Whetstone's poem is an unpromising start to what proves a modest record. *A Remembraunce* survives in a single copy. Six glum stanzas from it ("What is this world, a net to snare the soule ...") are inserted into *The Paradyse of Daynty Devises* from 1580 onward as the work of "G. G."[13] *The Tears of Fancie*, a sonnet sequence by "T. W." published in 1593, silently appropriates several of Gascoigne's poems as its own.[14] An edition of Gascoigne's *Whole Woorkes—The Posies*, with *Certayne Notes of Instruction* subtracted and *The Steele Glas, The Complaynt of Philomene*, and the text of the Kenilworth entertainment added—appears in 1587, and is the last such publication until the nineteenth century. Gascoigne regularly turns up in enthusiastic audits of England's growing literary achievement, if only as a name to pad the roster:

> these are the most passionate among us to bewaile and bemoane the perplexities of love, Henrie Howard, Earle of Surrey, Sir Thomas Wyat the elder, Sir Francis Brian, Sir Philip Sidney, Sir Walter Rawley, Sir Edward Dyer, Spencer, Daniel, Drayton, Shakespeare, Whetstone, Gascoyne, Samuell Page, sometimes Fellowe of Corpus Christi Colledge in Oxford, Churchyard, Bretton.[15]

---

[9] Whetstone, *Remembraunce*, sig. Biiii^v.
[10] Whetstone, *Remembraunce*, sig. Biiii^v.
[11] "We may well imagine our author straining here for a provocative conceit, an inevitable phrase, some deathless expression to bestow in parting on his immortal friend, the dead man. ... The pity of it is that those really *were* rather good lines in 1577"; Thomas C. Izard, *George Whetstone*, p. 230.
[12] Whetstone, *Remembraunce*, sig. Aiii^v.
[13] *The Paradise of Dainty Devices*, ed. Hyder E. Rollins, pp. 119–20.
[14] Even within a literary culture where *imitatio* has a central and honored place, these count as plagiarism. See Janet G. Scott, *Les Sonnets élisabéthains*, pp. 65–8.
[15] From Francis Meres, *Palladis Tamia* (1598); *Elizabethan Critical Essays*, ed. G. Gregory Smith 2: 320–1.

In 1589 Puttenham singles out "*Gascon* for a good meeter and for a plentiful vayne" and quotes his poetry to illustrate particular poetic tropes, usually without attribution and not always with approval.[16]

Gabriel Harvey left maginalia that are the most detailed record we have from one of Gascoigne's readers in the decade or so after his death. His reputation as a reformed prodigal still commanded respect, but had something comic to it: "Lewd Gascoigne, when all was prodigally spent, thowght to repayre himselfe by magnanimity & Industry: as he professed to My L. Gray of Wilton. he acknowledgith his loytering & lubbering, when the sonne shyned in the Maymoone of his youth: & therfore was now striving to load the Cart, even when it rayned."[17] Harvey's judgment on him as a writer is mixed: "He doth prettily well: but might easely have dun much better."[18] What is most interesting about him is his energetic confusion:

> Sum vanity: & more levity: his special faulte, & the continual causes of his misfortunes. Many other have maintained themselves gallantly upon sum one of his qualities: nothing fadgeth with him, for want of Resolution, & Constancy in any one kind. ... It is no marvell, thowgh he had cold successe in his actions, that in his studdies, & Looves, thowght upon the Warres; in the warres, mused upon his studdies, & Looves.[19]

Harvey is probably behind E. K.'s mixed appreciation in *The Shepherdes Calender* (1579): "Ma. George Gaskin a wittie gentleman, and the very chefe of our late rymers, who and if some partes of learning wanted not (albee it is well knowen he altogyther wanted not learning) no doubt would have attayned to the excellencye of those famous Poets."[20] Appreciation fades in the seventeenth century. "Among the lesser late Poets, *George Gascoign's* Works may be endur'd," writes Edmund Bolton in his *Hypercritica* (ca. 1618).[21] Fifty years after Gascoigne's death, he and his generation have all but lost their place in literary history in Michael Drayton's account of English poetry so far:

> *Gascoine* and *Churchyard* ...
> In the beginning of *Eliza's* raine
> Accoumpted were great Meterers many a day,
> But not inspired with brave fier; had they

---

[16] Puttenham, *Arte*, p. 63 (1.31). Willcock and Walker list the quotations on pp. 324–5.
[17] *Gabriel Harvey's Marginalia*, ed. G. C. Moore Smith, p. 189.
[18] *Gabriel Harvey's Marginalia*, p. 168; Harvey is here specifically talking about *Certayne Notes*.
[19] *Gabriel Harvey's Marginalia*, pp. 166–7.
[20] *The Yale Edition of the Shorter Poems of Edmund Spenser*, ed. William A. Oram et al, p. 197; "those famous Poets" are Ovid and others who had written about Philomela. William Webbe defers to E. K.'s judgment in *A Discourse of English Poetrie* (1586); Gregory Smith 1: 242.
[21] *Critical Essays of the Seventeenth Century*, ed. J. E. Spingarn 1: 110.

86   PETRARCHAN LOVE AND THE ENGLISH RENAISSANCE

>    Liv'd but a little longer, they had seene
>    Their workes before them to have buried beene.[22]

A more important dismissal may have come sooner, and been the more powerful for being invisible. There is no mention of Gascoigne in Philip Sidney's *Defence of Poesie*, which becomes the most famous essay of literary criticism of the English Renaissance (easily outclassing *Certayne Notes of Instruction*). Primarily theoretical (as against the nuts-and-bolts practicality of *Certayne Notes*), it nevertheless addresses the contemporary literary scene before it is done, and Gascoigne is not there. That absence, Katherine Duncan-Jones argues, is "noticeable."[23] Sidney was present at Kenilworth; a woodcut of the assembly of the hunt during those festivities may indeed portray both Gascoigne and the twenty-year-old Sidney in the same frame.[24] Duncan-Jones suspects Sidney, newly returned from the continent, would have found at least some of the entertainments "excruciatingly inane and provincial," and at the commissioned poetry he was hearing—most prominently Gascoigne's—"must have thought again and again how much better it could all be done."[25] Among the set pieces performed by Gascoigne in his unfortunate wild man role was the first known echo poem in English. One of Sidney's earliest compositions was his own echo poem; Duncan-Jones thinks it may have been a rivalrous response to an original that "left plenty of room for improvement," even an attempt to usurp Gascoigne's place in Elizabeth's favor if it was drafted quickly enough to be performed at her birthday celebration less than two months later.[26] When Gascoigne died in 1577, after what indeed could have looked like "a brief career as England's leading court poet," Sidney might not have "felt much regret at his passing," but rather sensed an opportunity: "Someone else was now needed to write and devise court entertainments for Leicester and the Queen, and indeed Sidney's new brother-in-law ... the Earl of Pembroke."[27] Omitting Gascoigne from the *Defense* would be one move in availing himself of this opportunity.

As an origin story for Sidney's serious turn to poetry on returning home this is speculative but plausible, and consistent with what did happen. If there was any possibility of Gascoigne's name becoming the guiding light for Elizabethan poetry, it was eclipsed by Sidney's. Sidney had blinding advantages of family and status; and if his aristocratic pedigree was a bit tattered and the expected marks of royal favor, such as his knighthood, were sluggish in arriving, his uncanny talent for impressing almost everyone he met was in play from the start, well documented in connection with his European travels. (He was granted a French

---

[22] Drayton, "Epistle to Henry Reynolds" (1627); Spingarn 1: 136.
[23] Duncan-Jones, *Sir Philip Sidney*, p. 138.
[24] *The Noble Arte of Venerie or Hunting*, p. 90. On the identifications, conjectural but credible, see Austen, p. 109, and Duncan-Jones, *Sir Philip Sidney*, p. 94.
[25] Duncan-Jones, *Sir Philip Sidney*, pp. 97, 98.
[26] Duncan-Jones, *Sir Philip Sidney*, pp. 98–9.
[27] Duncan-Jones, *Sir Philip Sidney*, p. 138.

title of nobility—"Baron de Sidenay"—in 1572, and often so addressed by letter-writers: "*illustris et generose domine comes*," etc.) Any blemishes to his reputation were rendered dramatically irrelevant by his death in the Netherlands in 1586 from a battle wound. One of very few men of rank to die such a death in Elizabeth's reign, he became a national hero, honored with a spectacular funeral and an unparalleled outpouring of lament in verse and prose. One contributor was indeed Whetstone, whose poem on Gascoigne had proved to be the first of six biographical verse elegies—the last, published in 1587, being of Sidney. Sidney's military career receives the most emphasis, and necessarily so; at this point Whetstone, like most of the English public, would have known Sidney's literary efforts mainly by report, and is not entirely sure what they are ("What be his workes, the finest wittes doe gesse"). In addition to "His *Archadia*, unmacht for sweete devise" (still in manuscript) and the partial translation of Philippe de Mornay's *Trewnesse of the Christian Religion* (printed with Arthur Golding's completion in 1587), Whetstone cites "The Shepherds notes, that have so sweete a sounde," by which he appears to mean *The Shepheardes Calender* (printed anonymously, with a dedication to Sidney).[28] But however hazily perceived, Sidney's literary achievement is still an urgent part of the picture, as Whetstone affirms in his allegorized representation of Sidney's funeral:

> Whom to revive, *Mars and the Muses* meete,
> In Armor faire, his hearse, the[y] have arayde:
> And on the same, a robe downe to the feete,
> About his Healme, a Lawrell wreath is brayde.
> And by his Swoord a Silver penne is layd.[29]

*Tam Marti quam Mercurio*, Gascoigne's self-bestowed motto, is recrafted by his own friend and elegist to be bestowed on the new champion.

\*

Whetstone gives no sign of being aware—why would he be?—of the work which makes good on the literary boast of his elegy. *Astrophil and Stella* is a literary landmark for several converging reasons. It is the place where over a half century's collective work introducing strict metrical form into modern English finally hits its stride—not just fluent "regularity" (Gascoigne managed that, for pages at a time,

---

[28] Whetstone, *Sir Phillip Sidney*, sig. B2ᵛ.
[29] Whetstone, *Sir Phillip Sidney*, sig. B1ᵛ. On Whetstone's elegy and the wider popularity of the topic of Mars and the Muses in praises of Sidney, see Lisa M. Klein, *The Exemplary Sidney*, pp. 39–46. As she points out, its history (with a slight change of personnel) reaches into the seventeenth century and the New World, where Anne Bradstreet writes "An Elegie upon that Honourable and renowned Knight, Sir *Philip Sidney*": "*Mars* and *Minerva* did in one agree, / Of Armes, and Arts, thou should'st a patterne be"; *The Tenth Muse*, p. 191.

and made it look instinctive), but a dynamic interplay between rigor and energy. John Thompson's classic account remains authoritative:

> Sidney discovered how to maintain a maximum tension between the language of the poem and the abstract pattern of the metre; the language is colloquial, with the full resources of speech, and the pattern is strict; the two are bound together in a state of mutual strain according to a set of conventions. The development that began with Wyatt's interest in the sounds of speech and continued through the poets who subjected these sounds of speech to the metrical pattern, distorting them in the process, came to a conclusion in the poetry of *Astrophel and Stella*. There the basic system of using metre and language was established for the English poetry of the three centuries that followed.[30]

This achievement comes with a new versatility in poetic form. Inspection shows *Astrophil and Stella* taut with formal decisiveness, especially regarding the sonnet. There are no feminine rhymes in the sonnets in the sequence, though they are regularly used in the "songs" eventually interspersed among them.[31] The default rhyme scheme for English sonneteers had been Surrey's: three independent quatrains and a couplet. All but a handful of Gascoigne's sonnets fit this pattern without fuss; it is the form he sketches in *Certayne Notes*. In *Arcadia* and the poems collected as his "Certain Sonnets" about half the sonnets have this form, though he also tried his hand at a more demanding pattern resembling the one that Wyatt (also, as it happens, unmentioned in the *Defense*) crafted for his sonnets: a unified octave using two rhymes to form two quatrains (ABBA ABBA or ABAB ABAB), followed by a sestet that switches to different rhymes for a third quatrain and then an independent couplet. For *Astrophil and Stella* Sidney made a decision to work exclusively with the latter, though with some experimenting in the sestet.[32] Of that sequence's 108 sonnets, twenty-three do not end with a couplet; twenty of those invert the pattern so that the couplet comes immediately after the octave and before the third quatrain—a very common pattern in sonnets of the Pléiade—and others play with other possibilities. In one virtuoso performance (89) only two words are used to end the individual lines, in partly syncopated alternation throughout the poem (ABBA ABBA ABABAB). Varying things along

---

[30] Thompson, *The Founding of English Metre*, p. 156.
[31] Ringler suspects the presence of "some privately formulated and as yet unexplained principle of decorum" (p. lvi). Either by precept or example Philip communicated the principle to his younger brother Robert, who observed it in his own poems; see P. J. Croft, ed., *The Poems of Robert Sidney*, p. 20. The custom was passed on to Robert's daughter Mary; see Chapter 4. Despite the terminology (which Sidney uses in his *Defense* and which comes from the French), practice here has less to do with anything connected to gender than with opportunities for rhyme presented by the languages involved; see Walter Cohen, *A History of European Literature*, pp. 201–11.
[32] See R. G. Whigam and O. F. Emerson, "Sonnet Structure in Sidney's 'Astrophel and Stella.'" Sonnet 5 becomes in modern pronunciation an "English" sonnet, but "serve" / "swerve" // "carve" / "starve" were straightforward rhymes in the sixteenth century.

another axis, six sonnets (including, notoriously, the first) are in iambic hexameter (like French alexandrines) rather than the expected pentameter. The formal variation is not as relentless as in Sidney's psalm translations, which his sister Mary finished with the same regimen, whereby each poem employs a different stanza form (or for that matter in the songs, which also never repeat a stanza form); but the ethos is the same, a sustained exploration of formal possibilities within well-defined constraints.

The yield of this experimentation is not uncertainty or tentativeness, but an unprecedented sense of controlled drama in how those fourteen lines play out. The first sonnet in *Astrophil and Stella* opens *in medias res*—"Loving in truth, and faine in verse my love to show"—and rises through swiftly articulated stages of aspiration ("Pleasure might cause her reade ... Knowledge might pitie winne ...") and frustration ("words came halting forth ... helplesse in my throwes ...") toward what you quickly catch on is going to be some carefully withheld pay-off. And so it is: "Foole, said my Muse to me, looke in thy heart and write." Time and again in the sequence a sonnet moves by sometimes deceptive steps to a kind of punchline.[33] Readers come to expect it, and read toward it, knowing they will not really know what is going on until the poet shoots that last bolt. To some extent the English predilection for ending a sonnet with a couplet encourages this dynamic. In one of Surrey's best-known sonnets, "The soote season," we can almost see the rhyme scheme significantly rebalancing a Petrarchan original. Surrey is working from "*Zefiro torna*" (*Canz.* 310), one of Petrarch's most imitated poems, in which the joys of spring are set against the all-consuming despair of the lover. In the Italian poem, though, the former and the latter are rigorously separated into the octave and the sestet, while in English the now Chaucerian spring expands to fill the three quatrains with carefully catalogued description, and the lover's misery is held back until the couplet, and within that until the last two words: "And thus I see among these pleasant thinges / Eche care decayes, and yet my sorow springes" (Surrey 2.13–14). Yet the effect of that shift is more elegiac than dramatic or disruptive (April landscape, with melancholy lover in the lower right corner), and in other cases the final couplet can simply recap the conceit of the three quatrains without adding anything new: "That ship, that tree, and that same beast am I, / whom ye doe wreck, doe ruine, and destroy" (Spenser, *Amoretti* 56.13–14). The sonnet punchlines in *Astrophil and Stella* are different, and do not necessarily harmonize with the rhyme scheme, whose "formalities," as David Kalstone puts it, are apt to "conceal rather than reveal" the actual movement of the poem.[34] Sonnet 1 is only the first instance of a zinger slicing a final couplet cleanly in two. Astrophil's way of craning towards something unrevealed that is going to

---

[33] I turn out to have precedent for this term: see Ann Romayne Howe, "*Astrophel and Stella*: 'Why and How,'" p. 158, and A. C. Hamilton, "Sidney's *Astrophel and Stella* as a Sonnet Sequence," p. 60.

[34] David Kalstone, *Sidney's Poetry*, p. 123.

happen in about fourteen lines imparts a tension and impatience that do much to characterize him, a lover unlike any that English poetry had yet seen. They also feed into one of the sequence's least honored but most distinctive strengths, its narrative force. Despite C. S. Lewis's frequently cited assertion, made in discussing *Astrophil and Stella*, that "the sonnet sequence ... is not a way of telling a story,"[35] it is also widely acknowledged that in comparison with others of the genre Sidney's sequence "contains a high concentration of narrative."[36] I wish to argue that even more emphatically; Sidney's narrative, whose forward drive makes sense of a lot of its supposed inconsistencies, has yet to be set out as clearly as it deserves.

That *Astrophil and Stella* is a sequence is itself momentous.[37] The "sonnets in sequence" of Gascoigne and others, whatever their virtues and interest, do not bestow on English what was already well established on the continent as one of the century's prestige literary genres: the authorially ordered (often numbered) sequence of lyric poems, primarily sonnets, on the great Petrarchan theme of unreciprocated love. This lack had become something of a sign of England's cultural belatedness. Gascoigne's attempts in presenting the adventures of F. J., Dan Bartholmew, and the Green Knight were in his own eccentric mode. In the decade after his death two somewhat more orthodox efforts (both as it happens dedicated to Sidney's sometime antagonist, the Earl of Oxford) appeared in print. In 1584 John Soowthern[38] published *Diana*, a sequence of thirteen numbered sonnets (all structured in the French manner as quatrain-quatrain-couplet-quatrain) interspersed with six elegies (in, more or less, fourteeners) and concluded with a tripartite "Pindaric" ode, as the centerpiece of his *Pandora*, "probably the worse volume of verse ever printed in English."[39] Its ineptitude is the stuff of legend, worthy of Bottom the Weaver's writing sample for a Master of Fine Arts program:

> And as sylver *Pheb*, is the aster, most clare:
> So is thy beauty the beauty, the most rare.
> Wherefore I call thée *Dian*, for thy beautee,
> For thy wisedome, and for thy puissaunce Celest.

---

[35] Lewis, *English Literature in the Sixteenth Century*, p. 327.

[36] Roger Kuin, *Chamber Music*, p. 62.

[37] The conceptual and even authorial unity of *Astrophil and Stella* has been challenged—e.g., by Rudolph P. Almasy, "Stella and the Songs," with calls to re-do Ringler's assessment of the manuscripts—but the challenge remains speculative. I do not dispute that individual poems in the sequence may have been composed separately and later included in the sequence (see n. 82).

[38] Probably John Southern, under which name he appears in *ODNB*, though his existence is attested only by his one publication.

[39] Michael R. G. Spiller, *The Development of the Sonnet*, p. 103. Most of the recent interest in Soowthern's volume has been due to the presence in it of a sonnet attributed to Elizabeth I and four sonnets and two quatrains attributed to Anne Cecil, Burghley's daughter and the Earl of Oxford's wife; see Ellen Moody, "Six Elegiac Poems, Possibly by Anne Cecil de Vere, Countess of Oxford"; Steven W. May, "The Countess of Oxford's Sonnets: A Caveat."

And yet thou must be but a Goddesse terest:
And onely because of thy great crueltée.[40]

Without naming him, Puttenham spends two pages attacking Soowthern for his "peevishly affected" Gallicisms and his unacknowledged borrowings ("*pety larceny*") from Ronsard.[41] Two decades later Drayton unexpectedly praises "Southerne" as a predecessor "who me pleased'st greatly" in the writing of bardic odes.[42] Other than that he makes no discernible mark.

Thomas Watson's *Hekatompathia* (*A Hundred Passions*, 1582) has also attracted its share of mockery, but represents a more serious effort, with scansion and diction more firmly under control; Lewis credits the verse with "that graceful movement which was then so new and ... still so far from easy."[43] The title sequence consists of a hundred numbered entries (one to a page), mostly in a sonnet-like format of eighteen lines in three sixains (ABABCC); excise ll. 5–6 and 11–12 (often not hard to do) and they are indeed sonnets.[44] They give little if any hint of specific narrative incident, but there is a macro-narrative of enamorment ("*Cupid hath clapt a yoake upon my necke, / Under whose waighte I live in servile kinde*"; 1) and disillusion. The transition to the latter is decisively signalled by the title "My Love Is Past" for entry 80 (a sober prose explanation of the shape poem that constitutes entry 81, "A Pasquine Piller erected in the despite of Love," which is in turn typographically reconfigured as an acrostic for entry 82). "My Love Is Past" becomes a running head for the rest of the book. Entry 100 is a dismissive epitaph ("Here lyeth Love, of Mars the bastard Sonne, / Whose foolish fault to death him selfe hath donne"), and a Latin translation of *Canzoniere* 365 (fourteen lines but unrhymed, in dactylic hexameter) concludes things. Three more Latin translations from the *Canzoniere* provide entries for the numbered sequence; Watson says there are "many others, which one day may perchance come to light" (6; they have not).

Watson also supplies the individual poems with headnotes ("the most interesting part of the book"),[45] where he summarizes their content and frequently identifies classical and continental sources.[46] Sometimes there is just one, but often they are multiple: "In the first six verses of this Passion, the Author hath imitated perfectly six verses in an *Ode* of Ronsard ... And in the last staffe ... also he commeth very neere to the sense, which *Ronsard* useth in an other place ..." (27).

---

[40] *Pandora*, sig. Bi$^v$.
[41] Puttenham, pp. 252–3 (3.22).
[42] Drayton, *Poemes Lyrick and Pastorall*, sig. B2$^v$ ("Ode 1. To himselfe and the Harpe").
[43] Lewis, p. 483.
[44] I quote from the original edition, with references to entry number in the sequence. The fullest study of the sequence is Cesare G. Cecioni, *Thomas Watson e la tradizione petrarchista*.
[45] Lewis, p. 483.
[46] See A. E. B. Coldiron, "Watson's *Hekatompathia* and Renaissance Lyric Translation," and "Sidney, Watson, and the 'Wrong Ways' to Renaissance Lyric Poetics."

On occasion, Watson takes note of his sources' sources—"This Latine passion is borrowed from *Petrarch* [*Canz.* 164] . ... Wherein he imitated *Virgill*, speaking of Dido [*Aeneid* 4.422ff.]" (66)—the point being that Watson was imitating not only the wording of his authors but also their methods. Aside from one not especially friendly reference to Chaucer (5), those predecessors are from foreign literatures, reaching back to antiquity: French, Italian, neo-Latin, classical Latin, and, with interesting familiarity, ancient Greek.[47] These citations, amplified with marginal notes, amount to a statement about the direction which English poetry should be taking, not nursing its native roots but self-consciously and conspicuously annexing itself to already established European traditions, of which the Petrarchan lyric sequence is a kind of culminating manifestation. The *Hekatompathia* volume presents such a sequence with much of the machinery of its composition openly on display, a do-it-yourself kit for prospective poets.

There is evidence it was indeed so received by some of them, though the ones for whom the evidence is strongest are not an impressive group: the elder Giles Fletcher, Bartholmew Griffin, Richard Lynche, William Smith, and especially the semi-anonymous "J. C.," whose *Alcilia* uses Watson's six-line "staff" as its form.[48] Watson's friendliest modern scholar admits that "The *Hecatompathia* is a museum-piece that should have marked the end of an epoch."[49] As Soowthern's and Watson's Petrarchan sequences made their way into print, the one that actually counted was incubated and circulated for almost a decade in a discreet aristocratic privacy to some extent dictated by the circumstances of its composition. *Astrophil and Stella* can be dated 1581–83 because of biographical events to which it refers. On November 1, 1581 Penelope Devereux, sister to the Earl of Essex and step-daughter to the Earl of Leicester, married Robert, Lord Rich, and details in Sidney's sequence unambiguously identify her in her married state as Stella (sonnets 24 and 37 depend on our knowing her real-life husband's name). The decisiveness of this identification, whatever use you decide to make of it in reading the sequence, is extraordinary.[50] Petrarchism had been accompanied from the start by curiosity as to the real-life identity of the beloved, and also by doubt as to whether such a person actually existed. Petrarch assured a skeptical correspondent that Laura was only too real (*Epistolae familiares* 2.9), but the character of the poetry with which he celebrated her does little to dissipate doubts. A soft consensus has evolved that Laura was in some sense Laurette de Noves, the wife of Count Hugues de Sade, but few identifications of the objects of later Petrarchist

---

[47] Watson's previous publication, the year before, had been a Latin translation of Sophocles's *Antigone*. The annotations in *Hekatompathia* cite and often quote all but one of Sophocles's extant tragedies, varyingly in English, Latin, and the original.

[48] See William M. Murphy, "Thomas Watson's *Hekatompathia*." Shakespeare's Don Pedro in *Much Ado about Nothing* (1.1.261) may be quoting 47.1 from memory, possibly by way of *The Spanish Tragedy* (2.1.3).

[49] Willliam Murphy, p. 428.

[50] See Ringler, pp. 435–47.

love poetry achieve even that modest level of certainty or, for that matter, relevance. Pietro Bembo, a prime authority for the theory and practice of literary Petrarchism in the sixteenth century, candidly affirms late in life the fictiveness of his own love poetry: *"fingo, per aver da rimare,"* I make it up in order to have something to write poetry about.[51] Watson, in a preface "To the frendly Reader" in *Hekatompathia*, refers casually to his sufferings in love as "but supposed"; that sounds as if he assumes we will assume as much, and think no less of his poetry for it.[52] His offhanded, parenthetical remark is consistent with what we see in his headnotes, that the inspiration that matters for him is previous poetry. The case with *Astrophil and Stella* is otherwise.

Sidney put famous indicators to that effect into the text of his sequence. That opening sonnet is about the folly of seeking inspiration for poetry in reading other poets. Elsewhere Astrophil dissociates himself from the crowd of imitative poetasters "that poore *Petrarch's* long deceased woes, / With new-borne sighes and denisend wit do sing" (15.7–8), and brags, "I am no pick-purse of another's wit" (74.8). Gestures like that of course do not necessarily vaccinate against conventionality. Under Sidney's influence they themselves become conventional; Drayton mimics the last of them verbatim (with attribution) in asserting the originality of his own sonnet sequence.[53] They are best taken as part of Sidney's characterization of Astrophil; certainly any reader led by them to expect a run of poems free of the paraphernalia of Petrarchan sonneteering is going to feel cheated. *Astrophil and Stella* is in fact lushly dressed in that *couture*, with an opulence previously unknown in English ("The doore by which sometimes comes forth her Grace, / Red Porphir is, which locke of pearle makes sure" [9.5–6]). When, on the belated publication of the sequence, Sidney was called (as Gascoigne never was) "our English *Petrarke*,"[54] it was the obvious thing to say.

The originality of *Astrophil and Stella* within Petrarchism is not so much in its rejection of tradition as in the use it makes of it. An instance of Sidney's imitation

---

[51] Pietro Bembo, *Lettere*, ed. Ernesto Travi, 4: 163 (letter 1996, dated December 22, 1538).

[52] Watson does alter a time reference in his Latin translation of *Canz.* 364 to fit the facts of his own supposed love story, and draws his reader's attention to the change (90). Cecioni (pp. 124–7) intrepidly identifies Watson's beloved (or at least the *ispiratrice* of his sequence) as the teenaged Frances Walsingham, who the year after the publication of *Hekatompathia* was to marry Sidney. The elder Giles Fletcher, one of Watson's imitators (see n. 48), teases his readers with the notion that his "Licia" is some kind of allegory: "take her to be some *Diana*, at the least chaste, or some *Minerva*, no *Venus*, fairer farre; it may be shee is Learnings image, or some heavenlie woonder, which the precisest may not mislike: perhaps under that name I have shadowed *Discipline*"; *English Works of Giles Fletcher, the Elder*, ed. Lloyd E. Berry, p. 80.

[53] "Divine Syr *Phillip*, I avouch thy writ, / I am no Pickpurse of anothers wit"; Michael Drayton, *Ideas Mirrour*, sig. [A]2ʳ. This particular metaphor does seem to originate with Sidney, but he comes to it by way of the classical satirist Persius and the Pléiade; see Scott, pp. 44–5, and Erik Gray, "Sonnet Kisses," pp. 127–8.

[54] John Harington, *Orlando Furioso*, p. 126 (in the commentary on Book 16). About the same time (and noted by Harington), an anonymous verse epitaph (probably by Walter Ralegh) called Sidney "Scipio, Cicero, and Petrarch of our time"; *The Phoenix Nest*, ed. Hyder Edward Rollins, p. 18.

of a specific Petrarchan original—something he does not do often—occasions one of his most abrupt last-minute reversals:

> Who will in fairest booke of Nature know,
>    How Vertue may best lodg'd in beautie be,
>    Let him but learne of *Love* to reade in thee,
> *Stella*, those faire lines, which true goodnesse show.
> There shall he find all vices' overthrow,
>    Not by rude force, but sweetest soveraigntie
>    Of reason, from whose light those night-birds flie;
> That inward sunne in thine eyes shineth so.
>    And not content to be Perfection's heire
> Thy selfe, doest strive all minds that way to move,
> Who marke in thee what is in thee most faire.
> So while thy beautie drawes the heart to love,
>    As fast thy Vertue bends that love to good:
>    But ah, Desire still cries, give me some food. (71)

Behind this is one of Petrarch's most widely copied sonnets, a compact presentation of Laura at her most idealized and redemptive:

> Chi vuol veder quantunque po Natura
> e 'l Ciel tra noi, venga a mirar costei
> ch' è sola un sol, non pur a li occhi mei
> ma al mondo cieco che vertù non cura;
>
> et venga tosto, perché Morte fura
> prima i migliori et lascia star i rei:
> questa aspettata al regno delli dei
> cosa bella mortal passa et non dura.
>
> Vedrà, s'arriva a tempo, ogni vertute,
> ogni bellezza, ogni real costume
> giunti in un corpo con mirabil tempre;
>
> allor dirà che mie rime son mute,
> l'ingegno offeso dal soverchio lume.
> Ma se più tarda, avrà da pianger sempre. (248)[55]

---

[55] For the popularity of this poem with French and English poets, see William J. Kennedy, *Petrarchism at Work*, pp. 137–8, 245–9, 290–2, 315–16; also Kennedy, *The Site of Petrarchism*, pp. 174–76, where he connects Sidney's "night birds" to the *augelli notturni* in the commentary on *Canz*. 248 by Giovanni Andrea Gesualdo (the commentary we know Gascoigne possessed).

Whoever wishes to see all that Nature and Heaven can do among us, let him come gaze on her, for she alone is a sun, not merely for my eyes, but for the blind world, which does not care for virtue; and let him come soon, for Death steals first the best and leaves the wicked: awaited in the kingdom of the blessed, this beautiful mortal thing passes and does not endure. He will see, if he comes in time, every virtue, every beauty, every regal habit, joined together in one body with marvelous tempering; then he will say that my rhymes are mute, my wit overcome by the excess of light. But if he delays too long he shall have reason to weep forever.

Sidney has singled out a Petrarchan sonnet that in its own way builds to a punchline.[56] Laura is the sun, but suns will set and time is running out; we are less than twenty poems away from the announcement of her death. The conclusion to the sonnet is not exactly a surprise, since Laura's mortality had already been mentioned in the second quatrain; but the solar metaphor had slipped into the background, only to be reasserted in the penultimate line in her *soverchio lume*, which turns out to be the flare of a spectacular sunset. In Sidney's sonnet, the turnaround is far ruder—not a grave reminder of the woman's mortality but a sudden irruption of the speaker's lust. Within the drama of Sidney's poem, the first thirteen lines, which draw both on Petrarch's sonnet and on the sixteenth-century assimilation of Petrarchan love to Neoplatonic philosophy, serve not (as they should in theory) to dissipate that lust but instead enflame, even enrage it until it bursts out in l. 14. The rhythm of that, the signature rhythm of many of the sonnets that Sidney has Astrophil write, becomes on a larger scale the narrative rhythm of most of the sequence. Petrarchist high-mindedness is part of what shapes and even energizes the story of a young man's ungratified and increasingly eager libido.[57]

Indeed, not the least important way in which *Astrophil and Stella* is newly and definitively "Petrarchan" is that here, for the first time in this study, the woman's resolved chastity—a more restrictive and abstract virtue than the fidelity that is paramount for Wyatt and Gascoigne—is assumed from the start and continues to be at the center of the narrative.[58] She will not bed her lover, and this is so clear to him that he is almost too intimidated to try. Wyatt's and Gascoigne's Petrarchan imitations imply an environment of inexplicitly but appreciably different expectations about how things are between men and women. We cannot be sure they

---

[56] There is a sharp-eyed discussion by Spiller, pp. 119–21; see also Kalstone, pp. 117–24, and J. W. Lever, *The Elizabethan Love Sonnet*, 2nd ed., pp. 58–62. Five sonnets later Sidney economically repurposes the metaphor of the setting sun for the bawdy punchline of sonnet 76.
[57] Astrophil's youthfulness is a persistent and subtle thread in Sidney's characterization of him; see Joseph Loewenstein, "Sidney's Truant Pen." The theme of Astrophil as the eternal schoolboy is taken further by Andrew Strycharski, "Literacy, Education, and Affect in *Astrophil and Stella*."
[58] Stella is not without her predecessors in less remembered literature, such as George Turbervile's Pyndara (a *senhal* for the virtuous Countess of Warwick); see Germaine Warkentin, "The Meeting of the Muses."

ever paused to consider the incongruity of what they were doing. Actual sexual behavior in the vicinity of the English court had not necessarily changed much by the 1580s (see Appendix A), but we do not have to read far to realize that Sidney wrote his Petrarchan sonnets for a story much more like that for which Petrarch wrote his—though this one seems to unfold over a matter of weeks or months rather than decades. The result of that greater urgency is a unique enactment of the dynamics of *innamoramento* and attempted seduction, entirely (almost) as lived by the would-be seducer step by step and in the moment. The sonnet sequence turns out to be ideal for telling such a story, foregrounding in a series of miniature dramatic monologues the lover's acute, fiercely observant self-absorption as it mutates across time, with just enough information or implication about the rest of reality for the alert reader to place the obsession in its landscape. To this opportunity, Sidney brought an already well-honed skill as a poet and—possibly—the salutary shock administered to his considerable youthful rectitude by the disorienting experience of falling in love with another man's wife.[59] The rest is literary history.

*

Discussions of *Astrophil and Stella* have tended to take its story for granted, as if it were too simple or even trite to need much thinking about: "Though a narrative is closer to the surface of Sidney's sequence than it is in most others, this narrative is composed of familiar elements: the knight taken by love, kept at a distance by his lady, allowed a kiss, finally separated from her and left complaining fiercely of love."[60] So Kalstone, in general one of Sidney's most perceptive readers, though he becomes less so in a rushed treatment of the last part of the sequence as Astrophil's agenda reaches its crisis (certainly "allowed a kiss" is an oversimplification, if not a simple mistake). There has been, especially in older criticism, some uncomfortableness about that agenda, though even Richard Lanham, perhaps the first critic to be openly unsqueamish on the subject ("He wants to bed the girl"), can get inattentive paraphrasing the action: "The essential cause of the sequence is sexual

---

[59] I suspect life intervened in Sidney's literary career between the idealistic theory of poetry set forth in the *Defence* and the composition of *Astrophil and Stella*. A desire to square the latter with the former has yielded readings of the sequence as didactic instruction in the kind of lover to avoid being. I am drawn to Steven W. May's more straightforward claim that "for all its success as love poetry, Sidney's poetic masterpiece fails to embody his highest literary ideals ... a failure caused ultimately by the fact that his sonnet sequence, unlike his *Arcadia*, was not fictional enough"; *The Elizabethan Courtier Poets*, p. 84. A chronology placing the *Defense* in 1579–80 would make the situation even more straightforward. There is no objective evidence to confirm that date, but none against it either. For arguments that Sidney's own attitudes toward sex and marriage were or at least became less strict than we would expect, see Melissa Sanchez, "'In My Selfe the Smart I Try,'" pp. 6–10.

[60] Kalstone, pp. 105–6. The most thorough treatments of the sequential action in *Astrophil and Stella* are Richard B. Young, "English Petrarke," and, more briefly but sharper on some details, Katherine Duncan-Jones, "Sidney, Stella and Lady Rich."

frustration. He is fain in verse his love to show because Stella will not allow him to show it in a more satisfactory manner."[61] Putting it that way implies that Astrophil has already been rejected by Stella and then turned to poetry as an alternative. But we miss something important in the rhythm of the story, and indeed in the Petrarchism of Sidney's sequence even as it keeps declaring its hostility to Petrarchan precedent, if we assume that Astrophil has turned to poetry after having had some more direct appeal rejected. The poetry—the first topic of which is how hard it is to write poetry—comes before, long before any such appeal. Astrophil's story begins with him talking with his annoyed Muse, trying to deal with the experience of desire in solitude and at a distance.

The prehistory for the first sonnet is given in the second:

> Not at first sight, nor with a dribbed shot
> > *Love* gave the wound, which while I breathe will bleed:
> > But knowne worth did in mine of time proceed,
> Till by degrees it had full conquest got.
> I saw and liked, I liked but loved not,
> > I loved, but straight did not what *Love* decreed:
> > At length to *Love's* decrees, I forc'd, agreed,
> Yet with repining at so partiall lot. (1–8)

That Petrarch fell consumingly in love with Laura when he first saw her that April morning in church was a major part of the legend. Astrophil tells what starts out as a more reasonable, and more realistic, story. There were gradual degrees of acquaintance, beginning casually, then repeated and becoming more serious. The reference to "knowne worth" suggests that the slowness of the process included time for Astrophil to learn what Stella was actually like, and we seem to be moving toward a normal (for want of a better word) and satisfying courtship. But the language shifts to that of force and conquest, and not his conquest of her but Love's conquest of him. At a certain point he falls deeply in love but, we are told, does not act on it, and then consents to that situation, though "with repining at so partiall lot." There is some barrier between what he experiences as his developing closeness to Stella and the ordinary result of such closeness; later we will learn that she is married.[62] Here Astrophil ends the octave complaining about that circumstance, as if it were perverse bad luck (maybe just bad timing); but in the sestet he remembers that repining as merely a last grasp at rationality before he plunged into the cauldron that awaited him:

---

[61] Richard Lanham, "*Astrophil and Stella*: Pure and Impure Persuasion," p. 102.
[62] Young, pp. 20–1, argues that in sonnet 13 Cupid's shield bears the Devereux coat of arms, and that therefore Stella is not yet Lady Rich. If so, she is married by sonnet 24, where Astrophil denounces "that rich foole, who by blind Fortune's lot / The richest gemme of Love and life enjoyes" (9–10).

> Now even that footstep of lost libertie
> Is gone, and now like slave-borne *Muscovite*,
> I call it praise to suffer Tyrannie;
> And now employ the remnant of my wit,
>    To make my selfe beleeve, that all is well,
>    While with a feeling skill I paint my hell. (9–14)

His emotional life is now a boiling paradox, and his newly discovered poetic vocation (the painting is verbal, writer's block a thing of the past) is the celebration of the irrational oxymorons of impossible desire. He has become the English Petrarch.

As if to ward off that kind of talk, he heaps scorn in the next sonnet on poets who imitate other poets ("*Pindare's* Apes"; 3.3); as for his own poetry, "in *Stella's* face I reed, / What Love and Beautie be, then all my deed / But Copying is, what in her Nature writes" (3.12–14). What follows, though, is a run of sonnets that to many readers has seemed derivative and conventional, some of them possibly composed as exercises before Penelope Devereux became a factor. The most egregious of these is Astrophil's description of Stella's face, a specimen of Petrarchism at its most ponderously decorative and artificial: "Queene *Vertue's* court, which some call *Stella's* face, / Prepar'd by Nature's chiefest furniture, / Hath his front built of Alablaster pure …" (9.1–3). The archness of "which some call" feints at being ironic, but the architectural metaphor unfolds in relentless detail; the poem in fact bestows on English literature its first full-dress example of the anatomical Petrarchan *blason*, the tradition's most readily mockable feature.[63] Whatever its genesis, though, the sonnet belongs where Sidney put it in his sequence. We are at a point in the story where Astrophil's connection to Stella is still abstract, intimidated:

> The windowes now through which this heav'nly guest
> Looks over the world, and can find nothing such,
> Which dare claime from those lights the name of best,
> Of touch they are that without touch doth touch,
>    Which *Cupid's* selfe from Beautie's myne did draw:
>    Of touch they are, and poore I am their straw. (9.9–14)

She is, just from that look, without needing to say anything, forbidding, and the man who has come to realize that he is her lover is caught in an absolute power exercised at an icy distance. The metaphor of the poem's punchline is, for Sidney,

---

[63] Sidney's anatomical *blason* is followed by a heraldic *blason* in sonnet 13, one unquestionably linked to Penelope Rich. On these two categories of *blason* and the specific influence of Sidney's examples on English sonneteers, see Laura Friedman, "Displaying Stella."

uncharacteristically unclear,[64] but its implication is not: look, do not touch. She is the riveting center of his attention while firmly separated from him by the authority of Virtue. In the surrounding poems he does not approach her directly, though he does address others: a collective of friends, whom we do not need to be told are male ("Flie, fly, my friends, I have my death wound; fly"; 20.1), and especially one particular friend (if Astrophil is Sidney, this would be Fulke Greville) whose disapproving presence can be felt as early as sonnet 5 and who beginning with sonnet 14 emerges as the confidant who keeps trying to talk him out of it:

> Alas have I not paine enough my friend,
>   Upon whose breast a fiercer Gripe doth tire
>   Then did on him who first stale downe the fire,
> While *Love* on me doth all his quiver spend,
> But with your Rubarb words yow must contend
>   To grieve me worse, in saying that Desire
>   Doth plunge my wel-form'd soule even in the mire
> Of sinfull thoughts, which do in ruine end? (14.1–8)

Responding to his friend's "right healthfull caustiks" (21.1), Astrophil twists and squirms with a variety of moves whose outcome is somehow always the same: "True, and yet true that I must *Stella* love" (5.14). His paralyzed state is hopeless and shameful and necessary.

It is a while (if we measure time with sonnets) before things, slowly, begin to change. An important transition comes unexpectedly, the stealth punchline to a poem mostly devoted to the rest of what is going on in Astrophil's world:

> Whether the Turkish new-moone minded be
>   To fill his hornes this yeare on Christian coast;
>   How *Poles'* right king meanes, without leave of hoast,
> To warme with ill-made fire cold *Moscovy*;

---

[64] Scholarly debate on the conceit begins in the late sixteenth century, when the young Brian Twyne (later an important Oxford antiquary) takes "touch" to be magnetism and complains that "the touch-stone doth not drawe strawe but iron: it hath no like sympathy with strawe: wherefore indeed this touchstone wanteth the touchstone of truth"; James J. Yoch, "Brian Twyne's Commentary on *Astrophel and Stella*," p. 116. There is some confusion here on Twyne's part; though "touch" can indeed refer to magnetism, touchstone is not a synonym for loadstone. Ringler (p. 463) suggests Sidney is thinking of "a glossy black stone ... a form of lignite that has the property of attracting light bodies when static electricity is induced by rubbing" (a phenomenon that turns up in Fulke Greville's *Cælica* 78.3 to explain the behavior of courtiers toward their prince). Sidney's conceit, however, does imply the proper sense of a touchstone in determining true value, even though doing so does not involve action at a distance; in the poem multiple senses are seemingly being punned upon one another and operate simultaneously. Ringler disallows a further suggestion, supported by Lever (p. 77) and others, that the associations of "touchwood" and "touch-hole," having to do with the ignition of explosives and the use of firearms and artillery, are also in play. I find that hard to resist: with those jet-black eyes of hers, she could fire off a cannon by just looking at it.

> If French can yet three parts in one agree;
>> What now the Dutch in their full diets boast;
>> How *Holland* hearts, now so good townes be lost,
> Trust in the shade of pleasing *Orange* tree;
>> How *Ulster* likes of that same golden bit,
> Wherewith my father once made it halfe tame;
> If in the Scottishe Court be weltring yet;
> These questions busie wits to me do frame. (30.1–12)

Sidney's correspondence, which, aside from some expressions of hesitancy about getting married, has nothing to tell us about his love life, richly documents his instinct and talent for holding his own in just this kind of knowing geopolitical speculation:

> Thoughe the peace betwixt the Turke and [the Emperor] is not as yet as fur as it is knowne perfittlie concluded, yet it is thoughte the Turke will rather proceede by sea then this waie. and as the frenche embassadour hathe writtne, means to visite the Popes territorie, perchaunce his conscience moveth him, to seeke the benefitt of the Jubilé. ... The Polakes hartily repente their so fur fetcht election. beinge now in suche case that neither they have the kinge, nor any thing the kinge withe so many other hath promised besides that their is lately sturred up a very dangerous Sedition, for the same cawse that hathe bredde suche lamentable ruines in France and Flandres.[65]

For three quatrains sonnet 30 gives us our most direct look at the world for which we may assume Astrophil, like his creator, was bred and to which he aspired. If the poem stopped here, we could think that after his disorienting and disappointing but not all that unusual experience with love he was returning to his adult competence and responsibilities, which is after all what people mostly do. But that suggestion is a set up. Astrophil has come to understand that his alienation from that world is more profound than he had realized. He keeps up the conversation about the great game, but (being, after all, good at it) he can do so on autopilot. On some deep level where no one else can see, he has turned away, and his poetry has a new addressee: "I, cumbred with good manners, answer do, / But know not how, for still I thinke of you" (30.13–14). It is the first time in the sequence that Stella is spoken of in the second person.

This is not I think an actual address to Stella, not a poem to be sent or read to her. It is an inward thing, and not immediately followed up on; but it is a change of direction whose consequences gradually manifest themselves. The next poem is not addressed to Stella but to the night sky, with presumably nobody else around:

---

[65] Writing to Leicester from Vienna, November 27, 1574; *Correspondence*, ed. Roger Kuin, pp. 345–6.

"With how sad steps, ô Moone, thou climb'st the skies, / How silently, and with how wanne a face" (31.1–2). It is one of Sidney's most famous sonnets, breathing a mood of graceful languor often associated with Petrarchism but actually rare in this usually edgy sequence. There has been some emotional release, some deep surrender to his condition; the caustic friend no longer needs to be answered. The next time Stella appears in the second person is in the sestet of sonnet 35:

> Honour is honour'd, that thou doest possesse
> Him as thy slave, and now long needy Fame
> Doth even grow rich, naming my *Stella's* name. (35.9–12)

The next sonnet begins by addressing her, more directly than ever, with what is phrased as an accusation: "*Stella*, whence doth this new assault arise, / A conquerd, yelden, ransackt heart to winne?" (36.1–2). What just happened? The hyperbolical emotions of Petrarchan poetry often seem to be in reaction to some invisible event. Readers are teased into imagining what it might be; the annotated editions of Petrarch's *Canzoniere* that circulated in the Renaissance are filled with speculations, some quite fanciful and easily mocked. (How do we know Laura is sad about the death of her mother? Maybe her cat died.)[66] Modern critical practice has discouraged such back-formations and tried to focus on the poem as presented; but the strong sequentiality of *Astrophil and Stella* (aided by some artfully placed details) does things to make such narrative reconstructions, such efforts to see around the self-centered speaker, both possible and necessary as we try to place the reaction of the moment in the context of what precedes and what follows. In sonnet 36 the "new assault" that Astrophil is convinced Stella has launched against him turns out—it takes him some lines to get around to mentioning this—to be the sound of her "sweete voice," evoked in some of Astrophil's tumultuous babytalk: "by sweete Nature so, / In sweetest strength, so sweetly skild withall, / In all sweete stratagems sweete Arte can show" (36.9–11). The stress on artfulness strongly suggests singing, with a further hint of Orphic powers in the couplet: "stone nor tree / By Sence's priviledge, can scape from thee" (36.13–14; we will hear more of these powers later in the third song).[67] This would fit: some kind of recital on Stella's part, a more intimate occasion than anything that has been specifically indicated, though still at this point with other people present. Hearing her sing (which he may well never have heard before), Astrophil experiences the beauty of her voice as erotic aggression. The all-important question, which he has to be asking himself despite his choice of words, is whether she actually intended it that way.

Imagining that she did prompts an uncontrolled physical reaction in Astrophil—"My mouth doth water, and my breast doth swell, / My tongue doth

---

[66] Alessandro Tassoni, *Considerazioni sopra le rime del Petrarca*, p. 230.
[67] On Stella's Orphic powers, and the gendered complexities they introduce into the sequence, see Maria Teresa Micaela Prendergast, *Renaissance Fantasies*, pp. 67–85.

itch, my thoughts in labour be" (37.1–2)—introducing a poem excluded from the published text until 1598. Its praise of Stella is inseparable from a barely coded aggression against her husband; she, "though most rich in these and everie part, / Which make the patents of true worldly blisse, / Hath no misfortune, but that Rich she is" (37.12–14). Rich has been mentioned before, and was presumably present from the start, but there is a new agitation here as the rivalrousness in the love triangle becomes more acute. In the first part of the sequence Astrophil seems to have assumed that Rich's possession of Stella was settled, but her "new assault" introduces the prospect that in this competition Astrophil may have an opening and might even prevail. We begin to leave the world of the *Canzoniere* for that of the troubadours. If there is a love triangle in Petrarch's sequence, it is all but invisible; the poems offer no clear evidence as to whether Laura is supposed to be married or not, and expressions of jealousy on the lover's part are very muted. Petrarch's followers are less demure, and it is even argued (with prooftexts from Petrarch) that jealousy is an indispensable component of love,[68] but Astrophil goes farther in this direction than almost any of his brethren. Before he is done, he is openly relishing the prospect of cuckolding Rich: "Is it not evill that such a Devill wants hornes?" (78.14).

In sonnet 41, one of Elizabethan England's most spectacular public arenas for manly competitiveness is the site of the sequence's most complex presentation of Astrophil as a man with a secret. The first eleven lines set things up:

> Having this day my horse, my hand, my launce
> > Guided so well, that I obtain'd the prize,
> > Both by the judgement of the English eyes,
> And of some sent from that sweet enemie *Fraunce*;
> Horsemen my skill in horsmanship advaunce;
> > Towne-folkes my strength; a daintier judge applies
> > His praise to sleight, which from good use doth rise;
> Some luckie wits impute it but to chaunce;
> > Others, because of both sides I do take
> My bloud from them, who did excell in this,
> Thinke Nature me a man of armes did make. (41.1–11)

Sidney appears to be conflating details from different tournaments in which he himself participated. In this fictional one, Astrophil came in first by the unanimous judgment of an international audience, though there is no unanimity of opinion (there never is with spectator sports) as to how he did so. The diverse

---

[68] See *The Blazon of Jealousie*, Robert Tofte's translation of *Lettura di M. Benedetto Varchi sopra un sonetto della gelosia di Mons. Della Casa* (Mantua, 1545). Varchi echoes the second of the thirty-one rules of love formulated by Andreas Capellanus in the twelfth century: "He who is not jealous cannot love" (*The Art of Courtly Love*, trans. John Jay Parry, p. 184 ["*qui non zelat, amare non potest*"]).

explanations themselves discriminate the range of diverse folk making them: the horsey set who think horsemanship is what makes the difference, ordinary townspeople who respect brute force, people who think it is all about skill, people who think it is all about luck, and those whose default explanation for anything is aristocratic heredity. Well before we get there, we know they are all going to be wrong; what made the difference is the thing only Astrophil knows about or cares about:

> How farre they shoote awrie! the true cause is,
>   *Stella* lookt on, and from her heavenly face
>   Sent forth the beames, which made so faire my race. (41.12–14)

It is his secret that has made him the center of uncomprehending attention. Behind this is the chivalric ideal of the knight made invincible by his lady's gaze, though there is no indication here that Astrophil is wearing Stella's colors (whatever those would be) or sending any of the other signals by which the tiltyard warriors of Tudor England did indeed declare their crypto-private allegiances. The determining factor of the day was a connection which no one other than Astrophil perceived or could perceive: the way Stella looked at him.

Did she? We can take Astrophil's word for it that she was there; it is reasonable that she would have been, and he surely checked. From his point of view, his victory itself is evidence that she was watching his performance with particular intent—though his imagining that, if he had enough faith in his own imagination, would have been sufficient to have the same effect. The lady's wordless look, interpreted by her lover, is an important motif in Petrarch's sequence, the occasion for some rare moments of possible grace:

> Conobbi allor sì come in paradiso
> vede l'un l'altro; in tal guisa s'aperse
> quel pietoso penser ch'altri non scerse,
> ma vidil io, ch' altrove non m'affiso. (*Canz.* 123.5–8)

> I learned then how they see each other in Paradise; so clearly did that merciful thought open itself, which no one else perceived, but I saw it, for I fix myself nowhere else.

Yet of course if no one else perceived it, imagination could be delusion, a possibility Petrarch acknowledges even as savors the memory: "*tacendo dicea, come a me parve*" (123.13; in her silence she said, as it seemed to me). Meaningful looks are important in courtship and seduction, but they need to be confirmed by subsequent developments. Astrophil's exhilaration in sonnet 41 follows from the "new assault" in sonnet 36, but is not conclusive. In the following poems he will be watching Stella very closely ("*altrove non m'affiso*") for more definitive signs that he is right about what is now going on.

Three sonnets after the tournament Astrophil, in what sounds for the first time like a one-on-one encounter with Stella, has put things to the test, though with disappointing results:

> My words I know do well set forth my mind,
>     My mind bemones his sense of inward smart;
>     Such smart may pitie claime of any hart,
>     Her heart, sweete heart, is of no Tygre's kind:
> And yet she heares, yet I no pitty find;
>     But more I crie, lesse grace she doth impart. (44.1–6)

Still, finding no pity and receiving less grace do not necessarily constitute definitive rejection. Astrophil may have been more oblique than he makes it seem if he was putting into action the plan he set out in the first sonnet: not trusting to unscripted eloquence, he reads some of his poems to her.[69] Stella's response could be as simple as an objection, shared with many of Sidney's modern critics, to the biographical interpretation of lyric poetry; or, if from her point of view this is coming out of nowhere, she may just be perplexed, at a loss for words, looking to buy time before she reacts. (Perhaps she complimented him on his rhyme scheme.) Astrophil hurries things on to one of his more fanciful conceits, and one you know he does not believe in:

> Alas, what cause is there so overthwart,
>     That Noblenesse it selfe makes thus unkind?
>     I much do guesse, yet find no truth save this,
>     That when the breath of my complaints doth tuch
> Those daintie dores unto the Court of blisse,
>     The heav'nly nature of that place is such,
>         That once come there, the sobs of mine annoyes
>         Are metamorphosed straight to tunes of joyes. (44.7–14)

The argument that ostensibly transforms an unwanted circumstance into yet more praise of the beloved will become a mainstay of Shakespeare's sonnet sequence. That is not really Sidney's way, certainly not Astrophil's. Stella's lover is not done with this.

He keeps up the pressure, and the poems suggest exchanges between them become more frequent and more overt. He repeatedly declares his love for her, she repeatedly puts him by. Discouraged, he makes a show of breaking it off on

---

[69] I agree with Hallett Smith that the poems Stella hears are unlikely to be any of the poems we are now reading; *Elizabethan Poetry*, p. 145. If the sequence were any kind of diary of poems actually composed during the events being dramatized, that story would be considerably less easy to follow than it is—something more like the ragged and uneven narrative that struggles to emerge from Shakespeare's sonnets.

the virtuous grounds his caustic friend used to urge—"I may, I must, I can, I will, I do / Leave following that, which it is gaine to misse. / Let her go" (47.10–12)— but he is in too far: "Soft, but here she comes. Go to, / Unkind, I love you not: O me, that eye / Doth make my heart give to my tongue the lie" (47.12–14). He stages one of his allegories—"A strife is growne betweene *Vertue* and *Love*, / While each pretends that *Stella* must be his" (52.1–2)—which in one of his most shameless punchlines yields an unexpectedly sharp specification of his goal: "Let *Vertue* have that *Stella's* selfe; yet thus, / That *Vertue* but that body graunt to us" (52.13–14). He has perhaps even to himself never before put it quite that bluntly. While he is taking that in, she responds to the extent of not just hearing him out but actually singing his poems for him—

> She heard my plaints, and did not only heare,
> But them (so sweete is she) most sweetly sing,
> With that faire breast making woe's darknesse cleare (57.9–11)

—intentionally or not reenacting the "new assault" from sonnet 36. The situation has become highly fraught, and he pushes the moment, almost or close enough, to its crisis:

> Late tyr'd with wo, even ready for to pine
> With rage of *Love*, I cald my Love unkind;
> She in whose eyes *Love*, though unfelt, doth shine,
> Sweet said that I true love in her should find.
>   I joyed, but straight thus watred was my wine,
> That love she did, but loved a Love not blind,
> Which would not let me, whom she loved, decline
> From nobler course, fit for my birth and mind:
>   And therefore by her Love's authority,
>   Willd me these tempests of vaine love to flie,
> And anchor fast my selfe on *Vertue's* shore. (62.1–11)

The key line, almost slipped past us as she goes on about virtue, is the third: "She in whose eyes *Love*, though unfelt, doth shine." He is now, after more time at close range, confident of how to interpret that look. He has her, and the rest is just a matter of bringing her around to his definition of love:

> Alas, if this the only mettall be
> Of *Love*, new-coind to helpe my beggery,
> Deare, love me not, that you may love me more. (62.12–14)

That confidence is excitingly strengthened four sonnets later with another wordless exchange of looks (also probably in some at least semi-public context) in which the evidence that hers, however fleeting, does indeed mean what he wants it to mean is more objective than anything so far:

> And do I see some cause a hope to feede,
> Or doth the tedious burd'n of long wo
> In weakened minds, quicke apprehending breed,
> Of everie image, which may comfort show?
>    I cannot brag of word, much lesse of deed,
> Fortune wheeles still with me in one sort slow,
> My wealth no more, and no whit lesse my need,
> Desire still on the stilts of feare doth go.
>    And yet amid all feares a hope there is
> Stolne to my heart, since last faire night, nay day,
> *Stella's* eyes sent to me the beames of blisse,
> Looking on me, while I lookt other way:
>    But when mine eyes backe to their heav'n did move,
>    They fled with blush, which guiltie seem'd of love. (66)

He has indeed been keenly aware of the power of obsession to generate fake news, but it can also uncover things only obsession can see. Having the uncanny sense of her eyes on him, he turns to check, and finds out not only that he was right about that, but also that there is something she feels guilty about. She has been caught out, and she blushes—like Marlowe's Hero when she first meets Leander (*Hero and Leander* 181), an involuntary reaction that further arouses Leander and signals that the outcome of their meeting is a foregone conclusion. (In the aftermath of their eventual lovemaking, at the end of the poem, Hero will blush again [801], bringing a "false morne" to the dark bedroom.)[70] A blush is not just a psychological giveaway, it is also intensely physical, a rush of blood to the face, an arousal. This blush, in addition to confirming Astrophil's hopes and intuitions, is also a first sign to readers of what has been going on with Stella all this time, evidence that her feelings, and potentially her actions, are no longer entirely under her own control.[71]

Very soon she comes forward with an extravagant declaration:

> O joy, too high for my low stile to show:
> O blisse, fit for a nobler state then me:

---

[70] On Hero's blushes, see my "Hero and Leander in Bed," pp. 226–8; Tania Demetriou, "The Non-Ovidian Elizabethan Epyllion," p. 58.

[71] The textual evidence that Stella begins to respond in kind to Astrophil's increasingly obvious desire is, I think, clear, though acknowledgment of this has been rare in the critical tradition; Sanchez's article is a great burst of clarity on the "critical disavowal of Stella's sexuality" (p. 4) by a surprisingly wide range of critics, including those who stress Stella's own agency in the sequence. (On Stella's blushes, see pp. 13–14.)

> Envie, put out thine eyes, least thou do see
> What Oceans of delight in me do flow.
>
> ...
>
> For *Stella* hath with words where faith doth shine,
> Of her high heart giv'n me the monarchie:
> I, I, ô I may say, that she is mine. (69.1–4, 9–11)

We are getting something close to a direct quotation from her. She has been from her point of view unstinting in her profession of love, and it probably cost her to make it. There is still a distance between them. Astrophil does not miss that for a second, but he also is not a bit fazed. He senses momentum, and handles the condition she puts on her surrender with the strategic coolness of one of the power figures in those geopolitical conversations:

> And though she give but thus conditionly
>   This realme of blisse, while vertuous course I take,
>   No kings be crown'd, but they some covenants make.
> (69.12–14)

Promise whatever you need in order to become monarch. Astrophil's rising sense of where things are headed feeds into his outcry two poems later: "But ah, Desire still cries, give me some food" (71.14). The temperature is rising, and things are about to enter a whole new phase.

*

This crossing coincides with the entry of the songs into the sequence, at least in the 1598 edition which has become canonical. Proposals have been made for distributing the songs differently, but editors have not accepted them.[72] The lop-sided distribution of the songs, beginning more than halfway through the numbered sequence of sonnets, does make dramatic sense. They change the weather just as the action is escalating into physical contact; new currents of emotion are released, and certain events need to be more directly narrated or enacted, not just implied retroactively. With one important exception, the first-person perspective is kept, but we also get poems where the action unfolds in the present tense, as we read. Our first taste of that comes immediately after sonnet 72, in the second song:

> Have I caught my heav'nly jewell,
> Teaching sleepe most faire to be?
> Now will I teach her that she,
> When she wakes, is too too cruell. (ii.1–4)

---

[72] See Howe, pp. 164–7. Howe's most confident adjustment concerns the fourth song; I address it in Appendix A.

At least one of them is a guest under the same roof as the other. We are not told whether it is day or night, though probably the former; if Stella were just casually or inadvertently napping, that would explain Astrophil's easy access to her and the apparent lightness of her sleep. He does not need long to see the situation as an opportunity in an agenda that despite his possessing the monarchy of Stella's heart still threatens to stall:

> Her tongue waking still refuseth,
> Giving frankly niggard No:
> Now will I attempt to know,
> What No her tongue sleeping useth. (ii.9–12)

His language quickly becomes alarming:

> See the hand which waking gardeth,
> Sleeping, grants a free resort:
> Now will I invade the fort;
> Cowards *Love* with losse rewardeth. (ii.13–16)

He hesitates, but reassembles his resolve by focusing on a more specific goal:

> Yet those lips so sweetly swelling,
> Do invite a stealing kisse:
> Now will I but venture this,
> Who will read must first learne spelling. (ii.21–4)

He will settle for a kiss, easier to get away with than rape, but still an important step toward his wished-for end. The kiss is then indeed stolen, in the space between the stanzas—certainly their first kiss, possibly their first physical contact of any sort.

She responds immediately and, as he knew it would be, angrily, and he quickly retreats. But the adventure, with a curious echo of the punchline to sonnet 1, reconfirms his further intent:

> Oh sweet kisse, but ah she is waking,
> Lowring beautie chastens me:
> Now will I away hence flee:
> Foole, more foole, for no more taking. (ii.25–8)

The following sonnet stays in the present tense to trace the aftermath:

> no scuse serves, she makes her wrath appeare
> In Beautie's throne, see now who dares come neare

>     Those scarlet judges, threatning bloudy paine?
>         O heav'nly foole, thy most kisse-worthie face,
>         Anger invests with such a lovely grace,
>     That Anger' selfe I needs must kisse againe. (73.9–14)

Implying that Stella's anger itself is a turn-on—for him it probably is—Astrophil shamelessly dickers for another kiss. In so doing, he distinguishes himself from another of Sidney's aristocratic lovers, in an episode inserted (probably after the composition of *Astrophil and Stella*) into the revised *Arcadia*. At the beginning of the third book, the heroic service that prince Musidorus, disguised as the shepherd Dorus, has done for princess Pamela and her family moves her "both to pitie him, and let him see she pityed him ... making her owne beautifull beames thawe away the former icinesse of her behaviour."[73] Her change of looks is not lost on Musidorus, and, as soon as they are alone together, "the sudden occasion called Love, & that never staid to ask Reasons leave; but made the too-much loving *Dorus* take her in his armes, offering to kisse her, and, as it were, to establish a trophee of his victorie." It turns out to be a disastrous move; Sidney's description of her response parallels Stella's and borrows Astrophil's phrase for it: "she, as if she had bin ready to drinke a wine of excellent tast & colour, which suddenly she perceived had poison in it, so did she put him away from her ... laying the cruel punishment upon him of angry Love, and lowring beautie, shewing disdain, & a despising disdain." Musidorus's reaction, though, is not wily maneuvering but utter emotional collapse, a psychic implosion: "It was not an amazement, it was not a sorrow, but it was even a death, which then laid hold of *Dorus*: which certainly at that instant would have killed him, but that the feare to tary longer in her presence (contrary to her commandement) gave him life to cary himselfe away from her sight. ... he did not tender his owne estate, but despised it; greedily drawing into his minde, all conceipts which might more and more torment him. And so remained he two dayes in the woods." Musidorus takes hyperbolically to heart what Astrophil pretty much shrugs off.

Musidorus's reaction is the orthodox Petrarchan one. There is little indication in the *Canzoniere* that Petrarch is ever particularly aggressive, let alone physical in his dealings with Laura; but one traumatically memorable incident is cryptically encoded into a particularly important poem in the sequence:

>     Questa che col mirar gli animi fura
>     m'aperse il petto el' cor prese con mano,
>     dicendo a me: Di ciò non far parola.
>     Poi la rividi in altro abito sola,
>     tal ch' i' non la conobbi, o senso umano!
>     anzi le dissi 'l ver pien di paura;

---

[73] Quotations of the *Arcadia* are from *The Countesse of Pembrokes Arcadia*, fols. 244ʳ–5ᵛ.

> ed ella ne l'usata sua figura
> tosto tornando fecemi, oimè lasso!
> d'un quasi vivo et sbigottito sasso.
>
> Ella parlava sì turbata in vista
> che tremar mi fea dentro a quella petra,
> udendo: I' non son forse chi tu credi.
> E dicea meco: Se costei mi spetra
> nulla vita mi fia noiosa o trista;
> a farmi lagrimar, signor mio, riedi.
>   Come non so, pur io mossi indi i piedi,
> non altrui incolpando che me stesso,
> mezzo tutto quel dì tra vivo et morto. (23.72–89)

She, who with her glance steals souls, opened my breast and took my heart with her hand, saying to me: "Make no word of this." Later I saw her alone in another garment such that I did not know her, oh human sense! rather I told her the truth, full of fear, and she to her accustomed form quickly returning made me, alas, an almost living and terrified stone. She spoke, so angry to see that she made me tremble within that stone, hearing: "I am not perhaps who you think I am!" And I said to myself: "If she there unrocks me, no life will be sad or noisome to me: come back, my Lord, to make me weep!" How, I do not know, but I moved my feet thence, blaming no one but myself, a mean, all that day, between living and dead.

This from the so-called *canzone delle metamorfosi*, the longest poem in the *Canzoniere*, and the closest thing to a comprehensive autobiographical narrative of its story. The usual gloss is that the unfamiliar garment is that of ordinary human flesh, which misled Laura's lover, in the wake of what he experienced as a new assault on her part, into approaching her as a potential seducer. This need not have been more than a certain kind of look—unfurling Love's ensign in his face, in the metaphor of *Canzoniere* 140—but it is enough to prompt a devastating rebuke which reduces him to an emotional petrification ("greedily drawing into his minde, all conceipts which might more and more torment him" would serve as a psychological paraphrase). Petrarch begins to find his way out of it by turning to poetry:

> Morte mi s'era intorno al cor avolta
> né tacendo potea di sua man trarlo
> o dar soccorso a le vertuti afflitte;
> le vive voci m'erano interditte,
> ond' io gridai con carta et con incostro:
> Non son mio, no; s' io moro il danno è vostro. (23.95–100)

Death was wrapped about my heart, nor by being silent could I draw it from her hand or give any aid to my afflicted powers. Words spoken aloud were forbidden me; so I cried out with paper and ink: "I am not my own, no; if I die, yours is the loss."

As does Musidorus, who finds it in himself "onely so farre to wish his owne good, as that *Pamela* might pardon him the fault, though not the punishment: & the uttermost height he aspired unto, was, that after his death, she might yet pittie his error." Eventually that ambition "found such friendship in his thoughts, that at last he yelded, since he was banished her presence, to seeke some meanes by writing to shew his sorrow, & testifie his repentance"; he gets hold of "the necessarie instruments of writing" and composes a poem.

Astrophil has been writing poems all along (better poems than what Musidorus manages to come up with), and his response to being angrily arraigned by Stella for stepping over the line involves no agonizing reassessment of what he has been up to. The episode in *Arcadia* may indeed have been inserted to make the point that Musidorus is different from Astrophil, more principled and in that sense worthy of Pamela. In literary terms, Astrophil has left the circuit of Petrarch for that of Janus Secundus (Jan Everaerts), the Flemish neo-Latin poet whose *Basia* (*Kisses*, 1541) sparked a vogue that changed the face of European poetry, not as profoundly as the *Canzoniere* had, but dramatically and in a way that is easy to track. An even younger man than Sidney, Secundus (who died before he turned twenty-five) was a poet of uninhibited physical love. The first book of his *Elegies* is the definitive Renaissance reenactment of a transient Ovidian love affair (with a woman he calls Julia). His *Basia* are neo-Catullan celebrations of the erotic pleasure lips can give; the wittily described kisses are sometimes obvious euphemisms for full sexual pleasure, sometimes confident preludes to it ("Breakefast of *Love*," in Astrophil's words [79.13]; *Basia* ends with an epithalamium). The motif of the stolen kiss, its pedigree reaching back to Catullus (99), is an important one in the poems of Secundus and his numerous imitators, and Sidney's interest in this tradition is firmly attested.[74] He was friends with the elder Janus Dousa (Jan van der Does), one of Secundus's most prominent Dutch imitators and, intriguingly, author of an epigram, published in 1569, entitled "Ad Stellam et Philastrum amantes."[75] From a distance this poetry looks like a vigorous but passing fad, but beginning with the second song it impacts Sidney's sequence in important ways. The Petrarchan lover finds some new utensils in his emotional toolkit:

---

[74] See James Finn Cotter, "The 'Baiser' Group in Sidney's *Astrophil and Stella*"; Alex Wong, *The Poetry of Kissing*, especially pp. 201–9; also Wong, "Sir Philip Sidney and the Humanist Poetry of Kissing."
[75] See Ulrike Auhagen, "*Ad Stellam et Philastrum amantes*." The younger Janus Dousa was also a poet, known as "the Dutch Sidney"; he composed three elegies on Sidney after his death.

In the parts of *Astrophil* which concern the kiss, it is in tone as well as in theme that Sidney draws on Latin models. And that Latin tradition, the Secundan tradition, was part of the mediation of Petrarchism which contributed to Sidney's tonal range and the diverse moods of his hero: solemn and skittish, languid and predatory, droll and despairing, sentimental and sarcastic.[76]

Earlier Astrophil would never have found himself, as he does in sonnet 83, threatening to wring the neck of his lady's pet sparrow out of sheer envious excitement at the freedom with which the bird is allowed to peck at her.

We are not specifically told how Stella responded to the solicitation for a second kiss. Waking up to find herself looking into the eyes of a potential rapist could be a hard experience to get past, though Astrophil did have the decency to run away. The next sonnet attributes fresh poetic inspiration to "*Stella's* kisse" (74.14), phrasing which makes it sound as if she kissed him. Subsequent sonnets radiate a new confidence on the prospective seducer's part. Sonnet 76, the grandest of the hexameter sonnets, enacts Astrophil's arousal at her approach, in which she moves as it were directly at the camera, with electrifying eye contact:

> She comes, and streight therewith her shining twins do move
> Their rayes to me, who in her tedious absence lay
> Benighted in cold wo, but now appeares my day,
> The onely light of joy, the onely warmth of *Love*. (76.1–4)

The effect threatens to become physically overwhelming, but the remedy becomes clearer than ever:

> My heart cries ah, it burnes, mine eyes now dazzled be:
> No wind, no shade can coole, what helpe then in my case,
>  But with short breath, long lookes, staid feet and walking hed,
>  Pray that my sunne go downe with meeker beames to bed.
>  (76.11–14)

Two sonnets later Astrophil imagines cuckolding Rich. And then, another run of kiss poems, more lingering and luscious than their predecessors ("O kisse, which doest those ruddie gemmes impart, / Or gemmes, or frutes of new-found *Paradise*" [81.1–2]). I think the implication is that after the furor over the first kiss, kissing has actually become customary between them—a gratifying development for Astrophil, as Stella crosses an important line from which she had previously

---

[76] Wong, *The Poetry of Kissing*, p. 209.

held back. He is no Musidorus, and she turns out to be no Pamela.[77] His success tempts him into further risks:

> Most sweet-faire, most faire-sweet, do not alas,
> From comming neare those Cherries banish me:
> For though full of desire, emptie of wit,
> Admitted late by your best-graced grace,
> I caught at one of them a hungrie bit;
> Pardon that fault, once more graunt me the place,
> And I do sweare even by the same delight,
> I will but kisse, I never more will bite. (82.7–14)

L. 10 is our strongest evidence that the kisses are now consensual, but Astrophil is too charged up to settle for what he had just been praising so extravagantly. The erotics of biting, going back to Catullus (8.18), are an established topic in Secundan kiss-poetry.[78] Astrophil quickly retreats from his presumption in taking things that far, but he has done that before. His discovery has repeatedly been that transgression provokes Stella's anger and retribution, but when the smoke clears he has gained ground and the transgression becomes the norm. The voice in his head might as well be Ovid's: "*oscula qui sumpsit, si non et cetera sumet, / haec quoque, quae data sunt, perdere dignus erit*" (*Ars amatoria* 1.669–70; whoever has taken kisses deserves to lose what he has been given if he does not take the rest). Astrophil senses that he is getting very, very close.

After the third song, praise of Stella's singing voice, encouraging memories of the "new assault" back in sonnet 36, Astrophil travels to where he will once again be under the same roof with her, with almost unmanageable anticipation: "I see the house, my heart thy selfe containe, / Beware full sailes drowne not thy tottring barge" (85.1–2). Then without warning we are into the fourth song, and an opportunity—the two of them alone, at night, presumably by Stella's compliance, the rest of the house apparently asleep—that brings things to a moment of truth:

> Better place no wit can find,
> Cupid's yoke to loose or bind:
> These sweet flowers on fine bed too,
> Us in their best language woo:
> Take me to thee, and thee to me.
> No, no, no, no, my Deare, let be. (iv.13–18)

---

[77] One seventeenth-century reader, writing into his copy of the *Arcadia* his list of the real-life originals behind Sidney's characters, equated "Ladie Rich" with Philoclea, Pamela's more tender-hearted and compliant sister; see Samuel Fallon, "Astrophil, Philisides, and the Coterie in Print," pp. 186–7. The same identification occurs in a key distantly remembered by one of John Aubrey's informants: "*Brief Lives*," ed. Andrew Clark 2: 250–1.

[78] Wong, *The Poetry of Kissing*, pp. 77–81.

Presented in dialogue, it is one of the most fully narrated moments in the sequence—at least until the almost cinematic cut at the end. Stella's words, the first words directly attributed to her in the sequence, are nine iterations of the same line, repeated to conclude the six-line stanzas in which Astrophil makes his pitch, with rising urgency and ingenuity:

> Your faire mother is a bed,
> Candles out, and curtaines spread:
> She thinkes you do letters write:
> Write, but first let me endite. (iv.37–40)

Stella's verbatim refrain continues to deny him, and familiarity with Sidney's fondness for punchlines gives the reader a good idea what is coming: Stella will continue to say the same thing, but the meaning of what she says will change at the end. After seven stanzas Astrophil's confidence falters, and he takes what may be desperate measures:

> Sweet alas, why strive you thus?
> Concord better fitteth us:
> Leave to *Mars* the force of hands,
> Your power in your beautie stands. (iv.43–6)

He has laid hands on her, and she is fighting back. He had not expected this, and, rather than main force, he tries one last ploy:

> Wo to me, and do you sweare
> Me to hate? But I forbeare,
> Cursed be my destines all,
> That brought me so high to fall:
> Soone with my death I will please thee. (iv.49–53)[79]

Critics have emphasized the bawdy sense of "death" as slang for orgasm, though we should acknowledge that Astrophil is also counting on the literal sense of his prediction. It was part of the lore of Renaissance culture that a man's threat (or offer) of imminent death can be a useful move in winning over a woman. A song of Wyatt's ("Lyke as the Swanne towardis her dethe"; 98R/70MT) takes such a tack. Erasmus includes suicide threats in his catalogue of things a young man might write in a love letter.[80] The second scene in Shakespeare's *Richard III* (a famous challenge to actors) turns on the premise that this tactic can indeed work. Women

---

[79] I follow Ringler's punctuation, but in l. 50 the quartos have the question mark not after "hate" but after "forbeare," which yields perhaps the better sense: Do you swear to hate me unless I hold off?

[80] *De conscribendis epistolis*, ed. Jean-Claude Margolin, in *Opera omnia Desiderii Erasmi* 1.2: 511–12.

are also said to avail themselves of this maneuver, if more obliquely; in the widely read *Historia de duobus amantibus* (1444) by Aeneas Sylvius Piccolomini (later to become pope Pius II), the still chaste heroine secures the unwilling help of a family servant in her adulterous love affair by threatening suicide.[81] Astrophil is reacting in his opportunistic way to the pattern Stella has so steadfastly set up with her replies: in the expectation that she will keep that up, he changes course so as to give that reply an entirely different meaning. No, she does not want him to die (and what else could she say?). With that bit of conversational jujitsu, the poem stops. Then what happens?

\*

The screen, to continue the cinematic metaphor, goes blank. The question of how to fill in that blank is sufficiently complicated to rate separate treatment (Appendix A). The next thing in the sequence is a sonnet expressing bafflement at Stella's "change of lookes" (86.1). Then the torrential fifth song, the second longest poem in the sequence, ninety hexameters of cascading rage from Astrophil against the woman he adored:

> ô my Muse, though oft you luld her in your lap,
> And then, a heav'nly child, gave her Ambrosian pap:
> And to that braine of hers your hidnest gifts infused,
> Since she disdaining me, doth you in me disdaine:
> Suffer not her to laugh, while both we suffer paine:
> Princes in subjects wrongd, must deeme themselves abused.
>
> Your Client poore my selfe, shall *Stella* handle so?
> Revenge, revenge, my Muse, Defiance' trumpet blow:
> Threat'n what may be done, yet do more then you threat'n.
> Ah, my sute granted is, I feele my breast doth swell:
> Now child, a lesson new you shall begin to spell:
> Sweet babes must babies have, but shrewd gyrles must be beat'n.
> (v.25–36)

Stella is "a theefe, a theefe" (43), an "English murdring theefe" (50), "a Tyran" (57), "Rebell by Nature's law, Rebell by law of reason" (63); "A witch I say thou art" (74), "Yet witches may repent, thou art far worse then they" (79), "I say thou art a Devill" (81). Behind all this is not just pain at being rejected but the angry certainty that Stella led him on and then treacherously switched sides: "For wearing *Venus'* badge, in every part of thee, / Unto *Dianae's* traine thou runaway didst flee" (v.70–1). There is textual evidence that the poem predates the circumstances that

---

[81] The lady perhaps got the idea (her humanist author certainly did) from Seneca's *Phaedra* (250–73). See the Latin text with an Italian translation, *Storia di due amanti*, ed. Maria Luisa Doglio, pp. 38–45. For an abbreviated sixteenth-century English translation, printed anonymously ca. 1533, see *The Goodli History of the Ladye Lucres of Scene*, ed. E. J. Morrall, pp. 7–9.

prompted *Astrophil and Stella* and may have been intended as part of the story of Mira and Phillisides in the *Arcadia*.[82] It does come from emotional precincts different from anything that we have yet encountered in Astrophil, and we never hear its like again. But its stunning strangeness has a powerful effect in its present location, making the silence between the fourth song and sonnet 86 even more tumultuous; whatever happened then had an explosive effect, unleasing winds that have not blown before.

The potential for such anger is implicit in the Petrarchan situation from the start, but in the *Canzoniere* it is rarely and barely audible, scrupulously muted. It breaks out openly in subsequent Petrarchists; we see it in Wyatt, though never with this extravagance. The rupture in Sidney's sequence of sonnets continues with four more songs, the longest interruption in the sequence, located just where the story line becomes most critical. Modulation back to what passes for normality begins as the fifth song reveals its punchline:

> You then ungratefull thiefe, you murdring Tyran you,
> You Rebell run away, to Lord and Lady untrue,
> You witch, you Divill, (alas) you still of me beloved,
> You see what I can say; mend yet your froward mind,
> And such skill in my Muse you reconcil'd shall find,
> That all these cruell words your praises shall be proved. (v.85–90)

Stella's response, if any, is not given, but Astrophil almost immediately acts on his side of the proposed bargain. There follow two songs of praise that might be placed almost anywhere in the sequence, but they deliver us to something unprecedented. The eighth song is the sequence's longest poem and only instance of third-person narration (and the only place where the hero's name appears in the text), and what it narrates is the astonishing calm and peacefulness revealed with the passing of the storm:

> In a grove most rich of shade,
> Where birds wanton musicke made,
> May then yong his pide weedes showing,
> New perfumed with flowers fresh growing,
>
> *Astrophil* with *Stella* sweete,
> Did for mutuall comfort meete,
> Both within themselves oppressed,
> But each in the other blessed. (viii.1–8)

---

[82] Michel Poirier, *Sir Philip Sidney*, p. 180; Ringler, p. 484.

There follows a replay of the fourth song with a difference, as it might or should have been played in the first place.[83]

They are once more alone together, as far as they know unobserved. It is day rather than night, and the scene is out of doors rather than in. The opening note is not of challenge and repulse, but of deeply shared emotion, even if it is as yet wordless:

> Wept they had, alas the while,
> But now teares themselves did smile,
> While their eyes by love directed,
> Enterchangeably reflected. (viii.13–16)

John Donne, never keen on imitating other people's poems, tracked this one with some care in "The Exstasie."[84] There is even a hint that in a dreamlike way the wordlessness continues even as the dialogue begins:

> But when their tongues could not speake,
> Love it selfe did silence breake;
> Love did set his lips asunder,
> Thus to speake in love and wonder. (viii.25–8)

(Does "his" in l. 27 refer to Astrophil or Love? The designation of Love as "it" does not, in sixteenth-century usage, answer the question.) The speech that follows begins with escalating praise—"*Stella* soveraigne of my joy, / Faire triumpher of annoy" (viii.29–30)—but rises within a few stanzas to make again (with intruded stage directions) the plea that brought the fourth song to its unseen outcome:

> Graunt, ô deere, on knees I pray,
> (Knees on ground he then did stay)
> That not I, but since I love you,
> Time and place for me may move you.
>
> Never season was more fit,
> Never roome more apt for it;
> Smiling ayre allowes my reason,
> These birds sing: Now use the season. (viii.49–56)

Once again he reaches for her, and once again she puts him by:

> There his hands in their speech, faine
> Would have made tongue's language plaine;

---

[83] On the eighth song as a rewriting of the fourth song, see Margaret Simon, "Refraining Songs."
[84] See George Williamson, "The Convention of *The Extasie*." On the widely read French antecedent (set "*au secret cabinet / D'un delicieux jardinet*"), see John J. O'Connor, *Amadis de Gaule and Its Influence on Elizabethan Literature*, pp. 149–53, 239–41.

> But her hands his hands repelling,
> Gave repulse all grace excelling. (viii.65–8)

In the first printed texts of the sequence in 1591, this is followed immediately by Stella's abrupt departure and the end of the song, with a reassertion of the first-person singular:

> Therewithall away she went,
> Leaving him so passion rent,
> With what she had done and spoken,
> That therewith my song is broken. (viii.101–4)

(Astrophil has been speaking all along, and the willful distinction between Astrophil and the poet evaporates as we watch.) "Therewithall" makes a reasonable transition, but the reference to what Stella had "spoken" indicates something was passed over, as indeed it was. The full text of the song, printed in 1598, includes the seven stanzas of Stella's reply. The most obvious reason for their excision is the connection with Penelope Rich; that connection in itself was not especially secret (sometime in the 1590s John Harington began transcribing the sequence into his family poetry manuscript as "Sonnettes of Sir Phillip Sydneys to the Lady Ritch"),[85] but someone thought aspects of it too sensitive for public exposure. Sonnet 37, which lingers with loathing over Lord Rich's name, was also excised from the 1591 quartos (sonnet 24 for some reason stayed), and the missing speech from the eighth song has Stella declaring more fully than she does anywhere else that she loves Astrophil in return:

> If more may be sayd, I say,
> All my blisse in thee I lay;
> If thou love, my love content thee,
> For all love, all faith is meant thee. (viii.89–92)

This is what he had wanted to hear from the start, presumably the happy ending to this love story. It is an ending that Astrophil's reading in Petrarch might lead him to expect, if he had gotten past the *Canzoniere*; in the *Trionfi* Laura confesses to Petrarch that she had loved him in return almost from the start, but until now had kept it to herself:

> Fur quasi eguali in noi fiamme amorose,
>   almen poi ch'i' m'avidi del tuo foco;
>   ma l'un le palesò, l'altro l'ascose. (*Triumphus Mortis* 2.139–41)

---

[85] No. 223 in Hughey 1: 254. Harington gets as far as the first sonnet.

> Almost equal flames of love were in us, once I had known of your fire; but one of us publicized it, the other hid it.

But this revelation comes in a visionary encounter after Laura's death, when she is assured that his own soul has freed itself from the stain of carnal desire, a freedom which she feels she had a role in bringing about. Stella, in contrast, is all too alive and present and her confession in that sense a bolder thing.[86] Astrophil is learning, however, that like Laura's it comes only, indeed precisely because their story is now over. Stella says what she does as a way of making clear that her refusal is definitive, and made for reasons that are in their way colder than the death now separating Petrarch and Laura:

> Trust me while I thee deny,
> In my selfe the smart I try,
> Tyran honour doth thus use thee,
> *Stella's* selfe might not refuse thee. (viii.93–6)

As Melissa Sanchez points out, Stella here claims for herself the unhappy satisfaction that she thinks remains open to her, that of Petrarchan love: "Stella's 'while' indicates that denying Astrophil's suit, paradoxically, allows her to prove to herself just how much she wants him."[87] Accepting this finality is for Astrophil the price of learning how mutual their feelings are. The contrast between "Tyran honour" and "*Stella's* selfe" dispenses with any distinction between virtuous and sensual love on her part.[88] The problem with taking a lover is not any disinclination from her—at some point, possibly since the fourth song, she has become aware of this—but the very serious worldly danger of betraying herself within the tight weave of the society in which they both must move. Her desire puts her at risk of doing so:

> Therefore, Deere, this no more move,
> Least, though I leave not thy love,

---

[86] Simon, p. 99, takes the conclusion of the eighth song to indicate that the rewriting is taking place within Astrophil's own imagination; I discuss her argument in Appendix A. For a bracing analysis of Stella's voice in the eighth song as legitimately hers, see Sanchez, pp. 11–13.

[87] Sanchez, p. 13.

[88] Thomas Roche, *Petrarch and the English Sonnet Sequences*, gallantly objects to taking ll. 95–6 to mean "I would if I could": "this reading does a disservice both to Stella and to sixteenth-century morality. *Honour* is the operative word; *tyran* is her mere concession to Astrophil's obsession, her grace to the grieving lover" (pp. 229–30). She is chaste but kind, gently deluding Astrophil about her feelings. Andrew D. Weiner, working from premises very close to Roche's, is more attentive to the text: Stella's "unwillingness to yield to Astrophil's appeals must ... be seen as stemming not from love of Astrophil's better self, virtue, or God, but from fear"—primarily "fear of the social consequences attendant upon the discovery of her actions," which "is no more than a false honor consisting in fear for her reputation"; "'In a grove most rich of shade,'" p. 354. The less censorious thing to call it is fear of losing what control she feels she has over her life. Astrophil (and some of Sidney's readers) might want Stella to hazard all for love, but the hazard and choice are hers, and she declines.

> Which too deep in me is framed,
> I should blush when thou art named. (viii.97–100)

Which are indeed her parting words.

With this dismissal comes a new oxymoron:

> When I was forst from *Stella* ever deere,
> *Stella* food of my thoughts, hart of my hart,
> *Stella* whose eyes make all my tempests cleere,
> By iron lawes of duty to depart:
>   Alas I found, that she with me did smart,
>   I saw that teares did in her eyes appeare;
>   I saw that sighes her sweetest lips did part,
>   And her sad words my sadded sence did heare.
>     For me, I wept to see pearles scattered so,
>     I sighd her sighes, and wailed for her wo,
>   Yet swam in joy, such love in her was seene.
>     Thus while th' effect most bitter was to me,
>     And nothing then the cause more sweet could be,
>   I had bene vext, if vext I had not beene. (87)

Things might conceivably stop here, with new emotional gravity on both sides and life going on as it apparently needs to. Astrophil turns out to be still a little young for that. Even before we get to sonnet 87 we hear him reverting to a more one-sided version of what has happened—"*Stella* hath refused me"—and he gets petulant: "No, she hates me, wellaway, / Faining love, somewhat to please me" (ix.21, 41–2). A plot point not quite in focus at the end of the eighth song becomes clear as things continue: Stella does not just deny Astrophil as a lover, but also banishes him from her company. She may have felt forced to take this step by small transgressions like the ones we hear of later: calling out to her as he sees her sail past on the Thames in sonnet 103, bemoaning his fate under her window at night in the eleventh song ("Come no more, least I get anger," she has to tell him [xi.37]), agonizing in sonnet 105 after catching a brief glimpse of her going by in a coach. But there is no real sign that he, who understands their world as well as she does, pushes any of this dangerously; fundamentally he seems to recognize and look for ways to live with his new condition. It is like his condition at the beginning of the sequence: desire at an intimidated distance. The words "absence" and "absent" keep coming up. The difference is that Astrophil has now irretrievably lost something that in the meantime he thought he had gained, the possibility of closer intimacy if he could just summon the nerve.

With that loss Astrophil is, as Young puts it, "transformed into the Petrarchan lover who dominates the remainder of the sequence," indeed "as thoroughly conventional a lover as one can imagine, and Sidney ... as thoroughly conventional a poet."[89] We need not, however, assume that conventionality is inauthenticity, especially since there is a new edge of despair and even derangement:

> Now that of absence the most irksome night,
>   With darkest shade doth overcome my day;
>   Since *Stella's* eyes, wont to give me my day,
> Leaving my Hemisphere, leave me in night,
> Each day seemes long, and longs for long-staid night,
>   The night as tedious, wooes th'approch of day;
>   Tired with the dusty toiles of busie day,
> Languisht with horrors of the silent night ... (89.1–8)

This sonnet has a history of being singled out as the clumsiest poem in the sequence, but I think it is one of the boldest and most effective; it captures wretchedness on the cusp of madness as the unstoppable circadian rhythms of life degrade into an "infernal litany."[90] A final sonnet is less panicky but more relentless in setting out the logic with which Astrophil's emotions cycle in endless self-contradiction:

> When sorrow (using mine owne fier's might)
>   Melts downe his lead into my boyling brest,
>   Through that darke fornace to my hart opprest,
> There shines a joy from thee my only light;
> But soone as thought of thee breeds my delight,
>   And my yong soule flutters to thee his nest,
>   Most rude dispaire my daily unbidden guest,
> Clips streight my wings, streight wraps me in his night. (108.1–8)

He had begun the sequence imagining, and becoming increasingly confident, that if he could only get through to her he would find a way out. But the way out has turned out to be the way back in:

> So strangely (alas) thy works in me prevaile,
>   That in my woes for thee thou art my joy,
>   And in my joyes for thee my only annoy. (108.12–14)

And with that, he has nothing more to say.

---

[89] Young, pp. 81–2.
[90] Roche, p. 199.

# 4
# Sonneteers

If two sonnets in *The Four Foster Children of Desire* (1581) are Sidney's, they are the only works of his to appear in print during his lifetime. He wrote for circulation in manuscript, and the scope of that circulation varied. His letter to Queen Elizabeth advising against marriage to Alençon (1579) was meant to impact public opinion and received what was effectively scribal publication, with multiple copies distributed to select recipients with the expectation of further copying, in apparent coordination with a cruder polemic in print. The first version of *Arcadia* was made available for copying by a select constituency as Sidney was still working on it. Surviving manuscripts, showing revisions made at different stages, secured the work's reputation even before most people had the chance to read it. *Astrophil and Stella*, on the other hand, was kept relatively close (Astrophil's own term; see 34.8). Whetstone had heard of *Arcadia* but not of the sonnet sequence. The most thorough scholar of Sidney's manuscripts thinks there is a "strong possibility" that he gave a copy to Penelope Rich.[1] Mary Sidney and Fulke Greville certainly had access, probably personal copies. In Greville's hands the work provoked the first instance of an ambition shortly to stampede across the English literary landscape: he would write his own sequence.

In the late 1570s and early 80s Greville, Sidney, and Edward Dyer formed a "happy blessed Trinitie" of courtier poets, "one Minde in Bodies three," who exchanged poems and talked about poetry.[2] Dyer already had a minor reputation as a poet; for Sidney and Greville the fellowship seems to have started their literary careers. Toward the end of its run, it made Greville present for the composition of *Astrophil and Stella*, in which he can be spotted as the caustic friend. He probably saw the sequence's component poems before Penelope Rich ever did. At times we can detect emulous performances on a common topic—the transit of Cupid for instance: "*Love* borne in *Greece*, of late fled from his native place …" (*Astrophil and Stella* 8.1). Sidney's boy god, seeking to get away from "Turkish hardned hart" (2), tries "these North clymes" (5), finds them and then Stella's face too cold and takes refuge in "my close heart" (13), where inadvertently "He burnt unwares his wings, and cannot fly away" (14) and Astrophil is stuck in love. Greville's Cupid has a more sour motive:

---

[1] H. R. Woudhuysen, *Sir Philip Sidney and the Circulation of Manuscripts*, p. 366.
[2] The phrases are Sidney's, from the first of "Two Pastoralls," published in Francis Davison's *A Poetical Rhapsody* (1602); Ringler, p. 260. On the trinity and its works, see Steven W. May, *Elizabethan Courtier Poets*, pp. 69–102.

> *Juno*, that on her head *Loves* liverie carried,
> Scorning to weare the markes of *Io's* pleasure,
> Knew while the Boy in *Æquinoctiall* tarried,
> His heats would rob the heaven of heavenly treasure,
> Beyond the *Tropicks* she the Boy doth banish (*Cælica* 11.1–5)[3]

But this effort of the cuckolded wife of Jupiter to mitigate her own chronic humiliation comes to grief in England, and makes life worse not just for the speaker but for everyone:

> see how that poore Goddesse was deceived,
> For Womens hearts farre colder there than ice,
> When once the fire of lust they have received,
> With two extremes so multiply the vice,
>   As neither partie satisfying other,
>   *Repentance still becomes desires mother.* (9–14)

Sidney and Greville jointly made the mischievous boy Cupid a major player in English love poetry; the former was much more widely read and introduced him to a wider audience, but the latter gave him more of a workout.[4]

We do not know when Greville decided his love poems were being composed for a sequence, but he ended up working at it for the rest of his life. He did not circulate the poems much in manuscript, though three were published by others during his lifetime with musical settings, and one of these, misattributed, was printed with the pirated first edition of *Astrophil and Stella*. There are signs that, influenced by his own experience working on Sidney's literary legacy, Greville did anticipate posthumous publication,[5] as happened five years after his death in a partial collection of his works. A working manuscript survives, containing all but two of the poems, with extensive corrections and revisions, sometimes to the point of illegibility.[6] Both manuscript and printed text identify the poems, despite their metrical variety, as "sonnets" and number them. The final result suggests that Greville had a specific terminus in mind: there are 109 entries, one more than the numbered sonnets in the 1598 text of *Astrophil and Stella*. Greville gave his sequence the title *Cælica*, which itself sounds like a point scored on its predecessor: "If Sidney addressed his love poems to a 'star,' Greville would go him one better by addressing his to a whole galaxy."[7] *Cælica's* unhappy lover is occasionally identified as Philocell, though if the plan ever was to tell the story of Philocell

---

[3] Quotations of Greville's sequence are taken from the first volume of his *Poems and Dramas*, ed. Geoffrey Bullough.
[4] See Richard Waswo, *The Fatal Mirror*, pp. 54–8.
[5] See Gavin Alexander, "Writing and the Hermeneutics of Posthumous Publication."
[6] In addition to Bullough's notes, see W. Hilton Kelliher, "The Warwick Manuscripts of Fulke Greville," and Gavin Alexander, "Final Intentions or Process?"
[7] Waswo, p. 43.

and Cælica, it almost got lost in other business. Cælica is the most frequently named woman, though we also hear of (and from) Myra (in poem 73 she speaks directly to "Myraphill") and Cynthia. Cælica's hair is "aborne" (auburn) in one poem (75.10); she has "blacke haire" in another (58.17) but has been wearing a blonde wig; Cynthia is apparently a natural blonde (56.ii). Myra may have been married (30). Biography is no help in sorting this out.[8] Two or even three of these names can show up, without explanation, in the same poem. It is sensible to take them as referring somehow to the same character, though efforts to rationalize the alternation ("desired, she is Caelica; chaste, she is Cynthia; abrupt, earthly, and confused, she is Myra")[9] do not align as well with the text as one might hope. Individual poems sometimes imply local narrative context; those contexts seldom link up in any clear linear way, though the sequence does have an overarching structure resembling that of *Hekatompathia*. Poem 75, an extended imitation of Sidney's shift to third-person narration in the eighth song, presents a scene in which Cælica gives Philocell what sounds like a definitive dismissal: "*Philocell*, I say, depart, / Blot my love out of thy heart" (173–4). Though the narrator assures us that nothing she does "Can make *Philocell* remove, / But he *Cælica* will love" (217–18), shortly thereafter the poet dismisses Cupid ("*Farewell* sweet Boy"; 84.1) and turns decisively to a higher concept of love. The remaining two dozen poems make good on that break, and we hear no more of the love of women or of "my pretty Boy" (25.1). The decisiveness of the break, however, also heightens the already heterogeneous feel of the collection, punctuated throughout with poems on subjects other than love. All in all, "there are about 57 love-poems" in the usual sense of the term, only a little more than half the total count, and there is justification for seeing Greville's sequence as "not a true love-sequence, but the repository of all those of his shorter pieces that he wished to survive."[10] Yet the thing is, it still reads as something more intense than a miscellany, with a unifying if unevenly developed arc following the speaker's deepening experience of humiliation.

He begins in idealized Petrarchan worship:

> Thou heavenly creature, Judge of earthly merits,
> And glorious prison of mans pure affection,
>   If in my heart all Nymphs else be defaced,
>   Honour the shrine, where you alone are placed. (3.9–12)

---

[8] "There is no indication apart from the poems that Greville ever felt a passionate love for a woman"; R. A. Rebholz, *The Life of Fulke Greville*, p. 53. A friend from court wrote of him after his death that "he lived and dyed a constant Courtier of the Ladies"; Robert Naunton, *Fragmenta Regalia*, p. 32. There were occasional rumors about a potential wife, but he never married. Rebholz sees in some scanty evidence an unmemorable history of relations with women—"Courteous but broken promises of help, mutual teasing, sterile, jocular flirtation, perhaps casual sexual encounters"—and suspects in Greville "a homosexual bias which he controlled or could not admit" (p. 54). A taste of Greville's attitude toward casual copulation between the sexes is provided by a poem of his that did not make it into *Cælica* (no. 69 in Hughey, *Arundel Harington Manuscript* 1: 113–15); see Matthew Steggle, "Greville's Buxton Poem."
[9] Thom Gunn on *Cælica* 74, in Greville, *Selected Poems*, ed. Gunn, p. 101.
[10] Bullough, p. 34.

The tone quickly mutates:

> I sigh, I sorrow, I doe play the foole,
> Mine eyes like Weather-cocks, on her attend:
> Zeale thus on either side she puts to schoole,
> That will needs have inconstancy to friend.
>
> I grudge, she saith, that many should adore her,
> Where love doth suffer, and thinke all things meet,
> She saith, All selfe-nesse must fall downe before her:
> I say, Where is the sauce should make that sweet? (18.5–12)

Adoration becomes acerbic, and grades into edgy conversation, spiced with hints of female promiscuity and male lust. The sweet sauce which the man solicits is not entirely metaphorical.[11] Sexual references can be rudely physical beneath a slight lyric grace. A *blason* of Cynthia's body continues from a relatively conventional treatment of her breasts down to a less commonplace appreciation of her pubic hair:

> Looke where lyes the Milken way,
> Way unto that dainty throne,
> Where while all the Gods would play,
> *Vulcan* thinkes to dwell alone.
> Shaddowing it with curious art,
> Nettes of sullen golden haire,
> Mars am I, and may not part,
> Till that I be taken there. (56.21–4, i–iv)[12]

"Sullen" suggests Cynthia has cultivated a specific visual effect for her nether blondness, a matte finish. It also has a poutiness to it, linked through mythological allusion to the guilty pleasure of being taken (trapped, chained even) in adultery.

One of the most memorable poems bristles with luminous carnality:

> The *nurse-life* Wheat within his greene huske growing,
> Flatters our hope and tickles our desire,

---

[11] In a notorious exchange in Giambattista della Porta's comedy *L'astrologo* (1606) a young woman bantering with her lover relishes the thought of licking up the *salsa* he will create by pounding with his pestle in her mortar; della Porta, *Commedie*, ed. Vincenzo Spampanato, 2: 324. Greville's culinary reference has its immediate source in a poem by Dyer (2.41 in May, *Elizabethan Courtier Poets*, p. 291).

[12] The second half of this quotation is from a passage present in manuscript but missing in the 1633 printed text. Bullough relegates it to his notes, though Kelliher (p. 114) argues that the excision is not a revision but a scribal mistake. The lines were probably removed for reasons of taste but belong in the poem; without them, the reference to "this conceipt" (25) is muddled. On the poem as a deliberately outrageous recrafting of the second song in *Astrophil and Stella*, see Joan Rees, *Fulke Greville*, pp. 94–6.

> Natures true riches in sweet beauties shewing,
> Which set all hearts, with labours love, on fire.
>
> No lesse faire is the Wheat when golden eare
> Showes unto hope the joyes of neare enjoying:
> Faire and sweet is the bud, more sweet and faire
> The Rose, which proves that time is not destroying.
>
> *Caelica*, your youth, the morning of delight,
> Enamel'd o're with beauties white and red,
> All sense and thoughts did to beleefe invite,
> That Love and Glorie there are brought to bed;
>    And your ripe yeeres love-noone (he goes no higher)
>    Turnes all the spirits of Man into desire. (40)

Stopping just before it would taste the melancholy of a *carpe diem* poem, the sonnet gains fierceness from coming two poems after what sounds like a successful seduction, as if the lover has known the giddy satisfaction—usually no more than a fantasy—of enjoying his supposedly virginal beloved at the very peak of her desirabililty:

> *Caelica*, I overnight was finely used,
> Lodg'd in the midst of paradise, your Heart:
> Kind thoughts had charge I might not be refused,
> Of every fruit and flower I had part. (38.1–4)

Yet the reader who senses something ominous in "finely used" (echoing "kyndely ... served" in "They fle from me") would not be wrong:

> But curious Knowledge, blowne with busie flame,
> The sweetest fruits had downe in shadowes hidden,
> And for it found mine eyes had seene the same,
> I from my paradise was straight forbidden.
>
> Where that Curre, Rumor, runnes in every place,
> Barking with Care, begotten out of feare;
> And glassy Honour, tender of Disgrace,
> Stands *Ceraphin* to see I come not there (5–12)

The woman who has yielded to her ardent lover summarily banishes him to fend off rumors that would in fact be true: a version, if you think about it, of where Astrophil and Stella come to in the end (whether Stella actually yields or not), but far more toxic emotionally than anything Sidney writes into his sequence. The toxins get nastier in the concluding couplet: "While that fine soyle, which all these joyes did yeeld, / By broken fence is prov'd a common field" (13–14). The broken fence is the woman's hymen; the lover who is received there thinking he will be the first discovers he is not. Greville fretted with the conjunction in l. 13; it was "Till" and "Yet" before he settled on "While." "Till" suggests that the discovery of the broken fence may not yet have happened; it waits as an unwelcome surprise for the next man, who will find he has been preceded by the speaker. "Yet" and especially "While" imply that the discovery is an ongoing thing, as the speaker learns he is not himself the first in a series of hoodwinked lovers, all of them deceived by Cælica's fuss about virtue. "Bitterness grew with revision!"[13]

And we are barely a third of the way through the sequence. With this bitterness we often seem back in the world of Wyatt's poems, where physical gratification is a possibility but repeatedly comes up against a disheartening truth about desire:

> Alas poore soule, thinke you to master *Love*,
> With constant faith; doe you hope true devotion
> Can stay that God-head, which lives but to move,
> And turne mens hearts, like Vanes, with outward motion. (41.1–4)

Specifically female duplicity and changeableness ("New-fanglenesse," also in "They fle from me," turns up at 36.8) are insistent themes. The cheeriest response Greville can summon is to make them the target of choral male jeering: "*Saylers* and *Satyres*, *Cupids* Knights, and I, / Feare Women that Sweare, *Nay*; and know they lye" (21.13-14). Cupid at one point tries to turn the tables, taunting the lover for having a problem with what is if truth be told an open secret of erotic excitement:

> when I see the poore forsaken sprite,
> Like sicke men, whom the Doctor saith must dye,
> Sometime with rage and strength of passion fight,
> Then languishing enquire what life might buy:
> I smile to see *Desire is never wise*,
> *But warres with Change, which is her Paradise.* (76.9–14)

But if there is a wisdom to that, Greville lacks the light-heartedness to embrace it. Love has in any case already had his answer:

> What shall I doe, Sir? doe me Prentice bind,
> To Knowledge, Honour, Fame or Honestie;
> Let me no longer follow Womenkinde,
> Where change doth use all shapes of tyranny;

---

[13] Bullough, p. 248—a dignified twentieth-century editor moved to an exclamation point.

> And I no more will stirre this earthly dust,
> Wherein I lose my name, to take on lust. (71.13–18)

Sidney had written such a poem—"Leave me ô Love, which reachest but to dust" ("Certain Sonnets" 32.1)—which some readers have wanted to place at the end of *Astrophil and Stella*, though Sidney did not. Greville signs his own sequence with a melodramatically self-denying flourish—"Let no man aske my name, nor what else I should be; / For *Greiv-Ill*, paine, forlorne estate doe best decipher me" (83.98)—and immediately makes what at least in the poetry proves to be his own definitive farewell to Cupid. If Wyatt's unsequenced complaints about the lack of steadfastness in women were ordered somehow, with "Ffarewell, Love, and all thy lawes for ever" (31R/13MT) at the end, we would have a groundplan for the first three-fourths of *Cælica*.

There is a diffuseness to the misogyny of it. The flickering triune mistress is a shadowy object of rage, not directly addressed all that often. The dialogue is usually with Cupid; it is not an exaggeration to say that "Greville is only interested in the relation between love and the lover."[14] That interest is intellectualized and introspective, repeatedly drifting from the love object to the operations of "my darkened minde" (10.8). A mythological fantasia begins as a satire on female slipperiness but grades into something wilder:

> *Pelius*, that loth was *Thetis* to forsake,
> Had counsell from the Gods to hold her fast,
> Fore-warn'd what lothsome likenesse she would take,
> Yet, if he held, come to her selfe at last.
>    He held; the snakes, the serpents and the fire,
>    No monsters prov'd, but travells of desire.
>
> When I beheld how *Cælica's* faire eyes,
> Did shew her heart to some, her wit to me;
> *Change, that doth prove the error is not wise,*
> In her mis-shape made me strange visions see,
>    Desire held fast, till Loves unconstant zone,
>    Like *Gorgon's* head transform'd her heart to stone. (42.1–12)

Recounting those strange visions generates Greville's *canzone delle metamorfosi*, dominated not by the story of Apollo and Daphne but by that of Ixion and Juno:

> From stone she turnes againe into a cloud,
> Where water still had more power than the fire,
> And I poore *Ixion* to my *Juno* vowed,

---

[14] Alexander, "Final Intentions," p. 15.

> With thoughts to clip her, clipt my owne desire:
>   For she was vanisht, I held nothing fast,
>   But woes to come, and joyes already past. (13–18)

Juno was saved from mortal assault by being replaced with a replica made of cloud; Cælica escapes behind her lover's own erotic figurations. Several references in *Cælica* to "embracing clouds" evoke this myth, in one case with explicit citation of its outcome: "*Books be of men, men but in clouds doe see, / Of whose embracements* Centaures *gotten be*" (66.11–12), i.e., sexual congress with fantasms breeds non-existent beings.[15] The lover's own fate is stubborn solitude that he likens to that of Narcissus, whelmed by a fluent but comfortless unreality:

> This Cloud straight makes a stream, in whose smooth face,
> While I the Image of my selfe did glasse,
> Thought Shadowes I, for beautie did embrace,
> Till streame and all except the cold did passe;
>   Yet faith held fast, like foyles where stones be set,
>   To make toyes deare, and fooles more fond to get. (42.19–24)

The lover returns at the end to scorn for Cælica—"Ile hold no more, false *Cælica*, live free" (35)—but his own freedom is more problematic.

A poem shortly after this one is addressed to Absence,[16] the classic scene of Petrarchan love, flattered for four stanzas as the condition in which desire can be most securely nurtured:

> Absence, like dainty Clouds,
> On glorious-bright,
> Natures weake senses shrowds,
> From harming light. ...
> Absence doth nurse the fire,
> Which starves and feeds desire
> With sweet delayes. (45.21–4, 28–30)

The cloudiness of distance shields fulfillment as perpetual promise, unthreatened by reality, where the erotic imagination can have its way:

---

[15] Cf. *Cælica* 102.73–5; *A Treatie of Humane Learning*, st. 4. The story of Ixion and Juno is put to Petrarchan use by Watson, *Hekatompathia* 32, and Barnfield, sonnet 16 (quoted later).

[16] An allegorical figure first met in *Cælica* 13 as an antagonist to Cupid. The poem pairs with *Astrophil and Stella* 17, though Sidney does not mention Absence. At the latter end of his sequence, Sidney plays vigorously with the language of absence and presence, and other Elizabethan sonneteers pick up on it. The motif was probably first worked up in the friendly competitiveness of the Blessed Trinity, though in this case it is likely Greville, with his greater predilection for philosophy and abstraction, who was the originator.

> Presence plagues minde and senses
> With modesties defences,
> Absence is free:
> Thoughts doe in absence venter
> On *Cupids* shadowed center,
> They winke and see. (35–40)

If the poem stopped here, its argument would be that of an anonymous poem called "Absence," which ends in only lightly mocking contentment with a career of sexual fantasy:

> By absence this good means I gaine
> That I can catch her
> Where none can watch her
> In some close corner of my braine:
> There I embrace and there kisse her,
> And so enjoye her, and so misse her.[17]

Greville may indeed be answering this poem, since he uses its argument as a setup. Just as the lover articulates the strategy of winking and seeing, he suddenly finds himself—in the blink of an eye—starkly alone in a bleak landscape:

> But Thoughts be not so brave,
> With absent joy;
> For you with that you have
> Your selfe destroy:
> The absence which you glory,
> Is that which makes you sory,
> And burne in vaine:
> For Thought is not the weapon,
> Wherewith *thoughts-ease* men cheapen,
> *Absence is paine.* (41–50)

A bit later in the sequence, when, in the poem quoted previously, the sight of Cynthia's naked body ("*Cupids* shadowed center") moves the lover to identify himself with Mars, the action heads through a crescendo of mythic self-arousal ("Surely I Apollo am," "I resolve to play my sonne"; 56.xiv, xxi) to an even more desolate climax:

---

[17] The poem was can be found in numerous manuscripts, and was first printed in Davison's *Poetical Rapsody* (1602, with three subsequent editions). It has been attributed to Donne, and Herbert Grierson included it in an appendix of his edition of Donne's *Poetical Works* (pp. 387–8). The poem is now usually attributed to John Hoskyns.

> I gave reynes to this conceipt,
> Hope went on the wheele of lust:
> *Phansies scales are false of weight,*
> *Thoughts take thought that goe of trust,*
> I stept forth to touch the skye,
> I a God by *Cupid* dreames,
> *Cynthia* who did naked lye,
> Runnes away like silver streames;
> Leaving hollow banks behind. (25–34)

Her evaporation leaves him at the place of judgment, and Cynthia's bedroom becomes the gallows at Tyburn:

> There stand I, like *Articke* pole,
> Where *Sol* passeth o're the *line*,
> Mourning my benighted soule,
> Which so loseth light divine.
> There stand I like Men that preach
> From the Execution place,
> At their death content to teach
> All the world with their disgrace. (37–44)

The imagination that saw the nets of Vulcan in Cynthia's pubic hair now experiences something like "the proverbial ejaculation of the hanged man."[18] Greville's most admiring modern reader calls the poem "cold, convinced, and even brutal."[19] It is as if Donne's elegy "Going to Bed" had on some strange assignment been rewritten by a Calvinist.

Which Greville was. No one seriously disputes the label, though there has been debate as to what kind of Calvinist he was, and when. Rebholz identifies Greville's faith with the English covenant theology expounded in works such as Lewis Bayly's *Practice of Piety*, and argues that during the 1610s Greville underwent the kind of conversion experience of which such works spoke: "This conversion assured him that his faith in God's forgiving and justifying grace, formerly so unproductive of moral change as to be suspect, was indeed 'true faith' and a proof of his election."[20] Rebholz admits relying on an autobiographical reading of the last poems in *Cælica* and an unverifiable assumption about their dating; later scholars have shied away from such claims. Brian Cummings identifies Greville with a "lay Calvinism" not defined by the fierce theological disputes about predestination and certainty that came to a head in the Synod of Dort (1619), and also, risking "a contradiction in

---

[18] Roche, *Petrarch and the English Sonnet Sequences*, p. 305.
[19] Winters, *Forms of Discovery*, p. 48.
[20] Rebholz, *Life*, p. 216.

terms," with what he calls "Calvinist scepticism," manifested in Greville's literary style.[21] That distinctive style—"a close, mysterious and sentencious way of writing, without much regard to Elegancy of style, or smoothness of Verse"[22]—is sufficiently undecorative to have been praised in the twentieth century as "plain," but is also often what Greville's own time called "dark," and is still in places impenetrable. Its ungainliness has intrigued critics, as if the challenge to easy understanding had an intellectual and moral urgency to it, though the suspicion remains that it was "simply because Greville knew no other way to write."[23] The religious poems at the end of *Cælica* combine moments of unforgettable clarity—"Life is a Top which whipping Sorrow driveth; / *Wisdome must beare what our flesh cannot banish*" (86.10–11)—with the kind of impacted analysis that weighs down Greville's philosophical poems:

> *Love* is the true or false report of sense,
> Who sent as spies, returning newes of worth,
> With over-wonder breed the hearts offence,
> Not bringing in, but carrying pleasure forth,
>   And child-like must have all things that they see,
>   *So much lesse lovers, than things loved be.* (95.13–18)

That feels like a struggle to say something complex that is resisting being said. In this context there is an acknowledged reason for the sense of struggle, since Protestant spirituality is acutely sensitive to the human talent for contriving subtly idolatrous substitutes for the truth:

> The *Manicheans* did no Idols make,
> Without themselves, nor worship gods of Wood,
> Yet Idolls did in their *Ideas* take,
> And figur'd *Christ* as on the crosse he stood.
>   Thus did they when they earnestly did pray,
>   Till clearer Faith this Idoll tooke away. (89.1–6)

But clearer faith is never a secure achievement, and in the last poems of his sequence Greville pursues distrust of his own comfort as far as he can:

> We seeme more inwardly to know the Sonne,
> And see our owne salvation in his blood;
> When this is said, we thinke the worke is done,

---

[21] Brian Cummings, *The Literary Culture of the Reformation*, pp. 299–300.
[22] Edward Phillips, *Theatrum Poetarum*, p. 247.
[23] Gavin Alexander, *Life after Sidney*, p. 247

> And with the Father hold our portion good:
> > As if true life within these words were laid,
> > For him that in life, never words obey'd.
>
> If this be safe, it is a pleasant way,
> The Crosse of Christ is very easily borne:
> But *sixe dayes labour makes the sabboth day,*
> *The flesh is dead before grace can be borne.*
> > *The heart must first beare witness with the booke,*
> > *The earth must burne, ere we for Christ can looke.* (7–18)

The turn after bidding Cupid farewell in favor of "the Peace, whereto all thoughts doe strive" (85.1) does not itself bring peace. The last poems are if anything more anguished than their predecessors; the furious anatomy of human love is followed by one of human weakness across the board: "though Kings, *Player*-like, act Glories part, / Yet all within them is but Feare and Art" (101.35–6). Some targets are general, even abstract ("O false and treacherous *Probability*"; 103.1), but the most memorable are first-person:

> Wrapt up, O Lord, in mans degeneration;
> The glories of thy truth, thy joyes eternall,
> Reflect upon my soule darke desolation,
> And ugly prospects o're the sprites infernall.
> > Lord, I have sinn'd, and mine iniquity,
> > Deserves this hell; yet Lord deliver me. (98.1–6)

The frustration and abjection of the earthly lover are succeeded by mortification before God. That experience has the sanction of Protestant doctrine: the way to God lies through a ruthless understanding and acknowledgement of one's depravity, pursued past all evasion and what George Herbert calls "articling." Part of the ruthlessness is a scrupulous avoidance of any hint the believer is somehow compelling the grace God might bestow as a result, and Greville is observing that scrupulousness with "yet." Greville repeats those last four words in the second stanza as a refrain, but in the third he changes the refrain as part of a conditional statement making an even more careful distinction:

> If from this depth of sinne, this hellish grave,
> And fatall absence from my Saviours glory,
> I could implore his mercy, who can save,
> And for my sinnes, not paines of sinne, be sorry:
> > Lord, from this horror of iniquity,
> > And hellish grave, thou wouldst deliver me. (13–18)

God would deliver me if I genuinely implored his mercy—if I could do so from sincere regret not for the suffering my sins have caused but for the sins themselves—but I could only do so by an act of grace on God's part. That act, the poem's wording implies, has yet to occur.

What is in doubt is not the speaker's belief in God and His justice, but his trust in his own election as one of the saved. Calvinist theologians argued that such trust would indeed be vouchsafed to the elect, and Rebholz argues that it was so with Greville, but this is a point on which Cummings thinks Greville's Calvinism remained sceptical. Biographically there is no way of telling, though even Rebholz acknowledges that Greville's faith only intensified his pessimism in his last years: "Now he realized that the world was too depraved to be lifted up and he too weak to achieve perfect holiness in it."[24] The final word in *Cælica* is not about the speaker's soul but about humanity and all its efforts and institutions:

> Mans superstition hath thy truths entomb'd,
> His Atheisme againe her pomps defaceth,
> That sensuall unsatiable vaste wombe
> Of thy seene Church, the unseene Church disgraceth;
>   There lives no truth with them that seem thine own,
>   Which makes thee living Lord, a God unknowne. (109.13–18)

This may or may not have been the last poem written; it is the kind of poem a poet might hold back, thinking this is where a still unfinished sequence needed to end. It does give that sequence its bitter shape. The intermittent arc through repeated mortification into the depths of degradation where God's grace might await concludes with a prayer not for that grace but for God's annihilating judgment:

> Yet Lord let *Israels* plagues not be eternall,
> Nor sinne for ever cloud thy sacred Mountaines,
> Nor with false flames spirituall but infernall,
> Dry up thy mercies ever springing fountaines,
>   Rather, sweet *Jesus*, fill up time and come,
>   To yeeld the sinne her everlasting doome. (25–30)

\*

*Cælica* was not released even to a limited public until 1633 (the year John Donne's *Songs and Sonets* were published). By then, a half century after Greville started writing his sequence, a lot had happened in English literature; most of the writers still to be discussed here were dead. Within a couple of years of Sidney's death in 1586, *The Spanish Tragedy* and *Tamburlaine* were played on the London stage. Two months after Zutphen, Greville wrote to Walsingham to block an

---

[24] Rebholz, *Life*, p. 312.

unauthorized printing of what is now known as the *Old Arcadia*, and in collaboration with Matthew Gwynne produced an edition of the incomplete *New Arcadia* in 1590.[25] That year the first three books of *The Faerie Queene* were printed, and a year later there was no blocking an unauthorized printing of *Astrophil and Stella*.[26] Its effect on English poetry almost, for better or worse, defies describing. It did so with a maimed text and some strange packaging. The sonnets (107 of them, unnumbered) are printed separately from the songs (ten of them, numbered), with various individual lines missing and jumbled readings in the ones that were not (sleep, the "baiting place of wit" [39.2], becomes "the bathing place of wits" [p. 16]). There is a bizarre streetfighter introduction ("Put out your rush candles, you Poets and Rimers, and bequeath your crazed quaterzayns to the Chaundlers, for loe, here he commeth that hath broek your legs" [A3ᵛ]) by, of all people, Thomas Nashe, otherwise known as the author of "the only piece of Elizabethan pornography that retained its power to embarrass right-thinking people until well into the twentieth century."[27] In addition there are at the end of the volume "sundry other rare Sonnets of divers Noble men and Gentlemen": thirty-nine poems, twenty-eight of them sonnets, a first payment on Nashe's rowdy promise of astounding things now ready to happen:

> Such is the golden age wherein we live, and so replenisht with golden Asses of all sortes, that if learning had lost it selfe in a grove of Genealogies, wee neede doe no more but sette an olde goose over halfe a dozen pottle pots, (which are as it were the egges of invention) and wee shall have such a breede of bookes within a little while after, as will fill all the world with the wilde fowle of good wits. (A4ᵛ)

One of the additional poems will become *Cælica* 29, though attributed here to "E. O." (the Earl of Oxford?). The sonnets among the sundry—numbered, except for the first, as if they were a sequence, focused on a woman one poem calls "Cynthia"—are signed "S. D." and "Daniell," i.e., Samuel Daniel, not only a correct attribution but a preview of coming attractions. Daniel, 24 years old when Sidney died, had shifting connections to the inner ring of the Sidney circle—he counted at different times both Mary Sidney and Fulke Greville as patrons—and in the late 1580s may have traveled with one of the manuscripts of *Astrophil and Stella* to Italy.[28] He is an obvious candidate for a role in the first publication of the sequence, though he denies it when a year later he publishes a complete sequence of love

---

[25] On Greville's letter to Walsingham, documentation of the kind of behind-the-scenes maneuvering in the Elizabethan literary world that we usually just infer, see Woudhuysen, pp. 416–21; on Gwynne as his collaborator, see Ringler, pp. 532–3.

[26] *Syr P. S. His Astrophel and Stella*. Much about the genesis of this edition is still a mystery. For what is known, see Ringler, pp. 447–57; Woudhuysen, pp. 356–84.

[27] Roger Kuin, *Chamber Music*, p. 180.

[28] The manuscript ended up in Scotland, apparently handed by George Dymoke to William Fowler, who gave it in turn to William Drummond (Woudhuysen, pp. 357–9).

poems named after the woman now called Delia (though "Cynthia" remains in sonnet 40).[29] There are fifty numbered sonnets, including all but four of those from 1591, capped with a four-stanza "Ode." Over the next decade *Delia* becomes a public work in progress, with sonnets dropped, added, and rearranged, and individual lines rewritten. A fifty-four-sonnet version is printed later in 1592, and fifty-five-sonnet versions appear in 1594, 1595, and 1598; with Daniel's 1601 *Works*, reissued in 1602 and, posthumously, in 1623, a fifty-seven-sonnet version, with a a new poem ("A Pastorall") at the end following the "Ode," becomes standard. The first 1592 edition also follows *Delia* with *The Complaint of Rosamond*, a 742-line poem in rhyme royal explicitly linked to the sonnet sequence.[30] The male complaints of the sonnets are reflected in those of Rosamond Clifford, a king's mistress forced into suicide; her ghost links her poem to what came before in a direct address to the poet:

> *Delia* may happe to deygne to read our story,
> And offer up her sigh among the rest,
> Whose merit would suffice for both our glorie,
> Whereby thou might'st be grac'd, and I be blest. (43–6)

Perhaps the poet's personation of a woman's suffering as well as his own may soften Delia's stony heart, and "thereby thou maist joy, and I might rest" (56).[31] The *Complaint* is also an announcement that Daniel's poetic debut with a sonnet sequence is only the starting point for a literary enterprise reaching into other genres (historical epic, verse letters, verse and prose discussions of poetry, verse drama, prose history, miscellaneous short poems—not as self-consciously diversified an *oeuvre* as Spenser's but similar in intent). The *Complaint* was printed with *Delia* in every Renaissance edition, though when Daniel issued his collected works in 1601 and 1602 it preceded rather than followed the sonnet sequence, with *Delia* separately paginated at the end. That is a confused ordering in some ways, but also, if inadvertently, a statement: Daniel's sonnet sequence is the alpha and the omega of his career.

The rationale of some revisions is clear.[32] "Cynthia" belatedly becomes "Delia" in 1594. Daniel has a way of writing pentameters that come up a syllable short, though with enough grace that you do not necessarily notice them: "My spotles

---

[29] Except as noted, I quote Daniel from *Poems and a Defence of Ryme*, ed. Arthur Colby Sprague. For *Delia* Sprague gives the fifty-sonnet edition, the numbering of which has become standard and is the one I use here for references. The other editions are collated in Sprague's textual apparatus, which includes texts of sixteen sonnets that are part of the sequence at some point but not in the fifty-sonnet version. There is no single version of the sequence to consider standard.

[30] On the place of this poem in its own tradition, see John Kerrigan, *Motives of Woe*, especially p. 164.

[31] A "business arrangement" that Roche, putting his own adjective in quotation marks, calls "shady" (p. 347).

[32] See Edward Haviland Miller, "Samuel Daniel's Revisions in *Delia*."

love hoovers with white wings" (12.1). The lilt there might indeed look like a deliberate effect, but it gets hunted down and fixed in 1594: "My spotlesse love hoovers with purest wings" (1594). One sonnet in 1591 has a unified octave (ABBA ABBA), and is the only sonnet in the sequence conforming to the distinctive rhyme pattern of *Astrophil and Stella*; that may or may not be the reason Daniel removes it before his sequence becomes *Delia*, but the effect in any case is of general adherence to Surrey's 4-4-4-2 English rhyme scheme (though a handful of sonnets added from 1594 onward use the scheme of linked quatrains best known from Spenser's *Amoretti*). On the other hand, Daniel does seem to have taken note of Sidney's aversion to feminine rhymes in sonnets, though he does not put Sidney's name to it; in his *Defence of Ryme* (1603) he thanks "my kinde friend and countriman Maister *Hugh Samford*" for the tip, asserts "feminine Rymes to be fittest for Ditties," and writes of his own effort to keep them out of his more serious work.[33] They start systematically disappearing from *Delia* from 1594 onward, though not completely; one sonnet (17) has a feminine ending for every line, and keeps that state through all editions. Numerous changes have no formal motivation, and can even look like a mistake. "Yet let her say that she hath doone me wrong, / To use me thus and knowe I lov'd so long" (19.13–14) becomes in 1601 "Yet sure she cannot but must thinke a part, / She doth me wrong, to grieve so true a hart." The second version hobbles its first line with some clumsy syntax and never quite recovers its confidence, though the point may indeed be that loss of confidence: the prospect of what Delia might say has faded into a fantasy of what she might think. Other revisions mark or anticipate the saddening passage of time. When Delia's "amber locks" (14.1) become "snary locks" in 1594, they may not actually lose their color, but that color is no longer what her lover sees when he thinks of them. They are "golden" in 30.2 and 33.14/34.1 (the last two, though not the first, changed to "sable" in 1601), yet with the prospect of becoming silver. The lover's own state is charted in a downward arc from 1591—"dearest blood my fierie passions sealeth"—through 1592—"my best blood my younge desiers sealeth" (20.4)—to 1594 and beyond: "age upon my wasted body steales."[34] Even when the sense is not substantially changed, some of the blood drains from it: "Waile all my life, my griefes do touch so neerely" (16.13) becomes, in 1601, "This is my state, my griefes do touch so neerly."

There are only wisps of implied narrative. "If Beautie thus be clouded with a frowne …" (19.1): "thus" seems to say that something has just happened, but "if" suspends that possibility as possible conjecture. Did Delia actually frown, or at least change her expression for the worse? Her obsessed lover half-realizes he could be imagining it. Astrophil has similar worries, but puts them to the test in

---

[33] Sprague, pp. 156–7. "Hugh Samford" is Hugh Sanford, secretary to Mary Sidney's husband and tutor to her son.

[34] Miller thinks the change shows "the mellowness of Daniel's middle age … transforming agonized frustration into sober acceptance" (p. 62); it sounds wearier to me than that.

a way we never see Delia's lover doing. Events presented in narrative form defy disentangling from the conceits by which they are delivered:

> Whilst by her eyes pursu'd, my poore hart flew it,
> Into the sacred bosome of my deerest:
> She there in that sweet sanctuary slew it,
> Where it presum'd his safetie to be neerest. (26.1–4)

For those who missed it, a headnote added in 1594 sets it out: "Alluding to the Sparrow pursued by a Hawke, that flew into the bosome of Zenocrates." (The reference is to Diogenes Laertius 4.2.10, which is worth looking up.) Some fatal encounter from which the rest of the sequence might be seen to follow is intimated early on:

> her no sooner had my view bewrayd,
> But with disdaine to see me in that place:
> With fairest hand, the sweet unkindest maide,
> Castes water-cold disdaine upon my face. (5.5–8)

But whatever may have happened is inaccessibly encrypted within an allusion to Petrarch's *canzone delle metamorfosi*, climaxing in the myth of Actaeon (*Canz.* 23.141–60). A standard interpretation of that myth is at the forefront of Daniel's mind, the conceit which encompasses the entire sonnet:

> Which turn'd my sport into a Harts dispaire,
> Which still is chac'd, whilst I have any breath,
> By mine owne thoughts: set on me by my faire,
> My thoughts like houndes, pursue me to my death. (9–12)

The biographical tradition invented an unlikely scene in which Petrarch came upon Laura bathing nude in the waters of the Vaucluse (which are formidably cold); any reconstruction of the encounter between Delia and her lover is no more reliable.[35] The only overt biographical indicators are two poems (44 in the original sequence, with another added in 1594) about the lover's foreign travels, but they do nothing meaningful to give the sequence narrative shape. Some linear direction is provided by concatenated sonnets where the last line of one informs the first line of the next; most of these come in pairs, though there is one chain of five. But there is no obvious thread of development across the whole, and, aside from getting longer, the successive versions read much the same, minor adjustments

---

[35] Svensson, *Silent Art*, pp. 68–91. A graduate student once confidently told me that the primal scene in the sequence was a reception at which Delia threw her drink into her would-be lover's face, with the whole love story meant to be seen as a farce. For all the poem tells us, we are free to imagine it that way.

of the same material. You can in fact get a reasonably good idea of *Delia* from the incomplete, unauthorized sequence tacked on to the first printing of *Astrophil and Stella*.

The one exception is a group of four sonnets introduced halfway through (one reintroduced, having been in the 1591 volume) in the second edition of 1592, where the emotion seems to acquire a new extremity: "Still in the trace of my tormented thought, / My ceaselesse cares must martch on to my death."[36] This poem, the first of the four, stays in the sequence, though in 1601 the wording softens: "Still in the trace of one perplexed thought, / My ceasles cares continually run on." The third, addressed "To M. P." (Mary Pembroke?), is the most aggressive, with an arresting metaphor for the speaker's revulsion at his state:

> Like as the spotlesse *Ermelin* distrest,
> Circumpass'd round with filth and lothsome mud:
> Pines in her griefe, imprisoned in her nest,
> And cannot issue forth to seeke her good.
> So I invirond with a hatefull want ...

Daniel encountered the conceit in doing his his translation of Paolo Giovio's dialogue on *imprese* (1555), where, under the motto *Malo mori quam foedari* (I prefer to die rather than be defiled), he found an account of how the female ermine, "compassed about with a bancke of dung," chooses "rather to perish by hunger and thirst, then by escaping through the mire to defile her self, and spot the polished white of her precious skin."[37] Nobody knows what to make of this. The Petrarchan lover (as far as we know he is still the one speaking) appears to present his frustrated solitude as an attempt, even at the cost of his own life, to preserve his chastity (he calls his own love "spotles" at 12.1) in a depraved environment. The ermine is a symbol of female sexual purity, so adopting it this way involves an interesting cross-gender identification (which Daniel emphasizes with his gendered pronouns), and seems to imply that his lady is part of the depravity. This may be working too hard to fit the conceit into a Petrarchan armature. Delia is not mentioned in the poem, so the "filth and lothsome mud," despite the sound of it, may indeed not be sexual and the occasion of the speaker's distress not erotic—though if so he is demonstrating, against convention, that there are things that have notably more power over him than love.[38] Or Daniel may simply have been fascinated by the conceit in Giovio but found that when he tried to work it into his

---

[36] For the texts, see Sprague, pp. 180–1. Joan Rees discusses them in *Samuel Daniel*, pp. 14–21.
[37] *The Worthy Tract of Paulus Jovius*, sig. Cv$^r$. See Joseph Kau, "Daniel's *Delia* and the *Imprese* of Bishop Paolo Giovio."
[38] Rees (*Samuel Daniel*, p. 16) thinks that "M. P." is the "M. P." mentioned in the preface of Daniel's translation from Giovio, and proposes "Master Parker," i.e., Robert Parker, a possible friend of Daniel's from Oxford who suffered and eventually emigrated for his Puritan allegiances and might have been particularly sympathetic to Daniel's own angry sense of alienation.

sequence it proved unmanageable. For whatever reason, it disappears from *Delia* in the next edition, taking with it an enigmatic intensity which briefly fluttered the main agenda of the sequence.

Which would be to write a canonical Petrarchan sonnet sequence in English. *Astrophil and Stella*, in its brilliance, is not that; Greville cannot really be said to try. *Delia*, precisely in its attenuated narrative, approaches a kind of lyric purity in which, over and over, nothing happens. The man loves a woman who does not love him in return; she never changes her mind, and he writes poems about that. Individual sonnets enact the emotions and rationalizations with which he confronts his situation. In doing so, Daniel, perhaps the most cosmopolitan of the Elizabethan sonneteers, sought nurture in an impressive exploitation of continental models. No other English poet is as systematic and artful about it.[39] Watson is amateurish and obvious in comparison. Time abroad seems to have made a big impression.[40] Daniel wrote to Walsingham in 1586 about his excitement at being in "Paris, the Theater of *Europe*"; in Italy he claimed to have discussed the current state of English poetry with Guarini, and may have showed him a manuscript of *Astrophil and Stella*.[41] The name of Daniel's poetic mistress alludes to the most intellectualized of the continental sequences, Maurice Scève's *Délie* (an anagram for *l'idée*, as "Delia" is an anagram for "ideal"). The iconic conclusion of *Canzoniere* 140 (*"ché bel fin fa chi ben amando more"*), which both Wyatt and Surrey had translated, provides the last line of the "Ode"—and hence, until 1601, the last line of the sequence: "well he'ends for love who dies." There is a lapidary quotation from *Canzoniere* 35 in the final sonnet. At least a dozen sonnets in the 50-sonnet version of *Delia* are translations or close imitations of identifiable French or Italian poems; four more are added in later editions. Most of the originals are sonnets, though there are also madrigals, such as Guarini's *"Deh dimmi Amor se gli occhi di Camilla"*; that becomes one of the poems Daniel added in the second edition of 1592, "Oft doe I muse, whether my *Delias* eyes." *Delia* 31 reworks two stanzas from Tasso's *Gerusalemme liberata* (16.14–15)—stanzas already englished by Spenser in the *Faerie Queene* (2.12.74–5), one of several cases in which the trail leads back to more than one text that we can be confident Daniel knew. The previous sonnet in *Delia*, one of the sequence's better-known poems—"I once may see when yeeres shall wrecke my wronge"—looks like fairly close translation of a sonnet by Philippe Desportes—*"Je verray par les ans vangeurs de mon martyre"* (*Cléonice* 62)—which in turn looks like fairly close translation of a sonnet by Tasso: *"Vedrò de gli anni in mia vendetta ancora"* (*Rime amorose* 56). Scholars have fussed in such cases over which is Daniel's official source, and the effort can be illuminating

---

[39] The most comprehensive account of the Italian and French sources of *Delia* is Pierre Spriet, *Samuel Daniel*, pp. 208–34. Svensson's poem-by-poem *esposizioni* of the fifty-seven-poem sequence trace out an even more detailed network of Renaissance intertextuality.
[40] See Mark Eccles, "Samuel Daniel in France and Italy."
[41] Woudhuysen, p. 359.

about details and sometimes even reach a conclusion (in this case Desportes, who with Daniel imagines his beloved's hair turning silver where Tasso thinks it will be white). But the stemma often turns out to be a complicated root system. *Delia* 15 ("If that a loyall hart and faith unfained") derives simultaneously from a sonnet by Desportes (*"Si la foy plus certaine en une âme non feinte"* [*Diane* 1.8]) and from Desportes's source, Petrarch's *Canzoniere* 224 ("*S'una fede amorosa, un cor non finto*"), which as it happens Wyatt had also translated ("Yf amours faith, an hert unfayned" [13R/12MT]).[42] Daniel does seem to have had a special affinity with Desportes (still alive when *Delia* was written), but the translations and imitations in Daniel's sequence pay homage not so much to particular continental poets as to the ramifying, imitative culture of international Petrarchism, hitherto represented in English literature most memorably through Astrophil's self-serving sarcasm about it. The unconcealed imitativeness is now comfortably part of the English poet's playbook.

To this Daniel brings his own sensibility, with a mimosa-like instinct for pulling back that in his *Musophilus* the interlocutor (apparently Fulke Greville, once more the caustic friend) presents as a debility rooted in his commitment to poetry:

> This sweet inchaunting knowledge turnes you cleene
> Out from the fields of naturall delight,
> And makes you hide unwilling to be seene
> In th'open concourse of a publike sight:
> This skill wherewith you have so cunning beene,
> Unsinewes all your powres, unmans you quite. (494–9)

In *A Defence of Ryme* Daniel cites the impulse to avoid the fray as a flaw in his own make-up: "irresolution and a selfe distrust be the most apparent faults of my nature, and ... the least checke of reprehension, if it savour of reason, will as easily shake my resolution as any mans living."[43] He says this in some surprise at his willingness to enter into public dispute with Thomas Campion's combative *Observations in the Art of English Poesie* (1602) in favor of a new English prosody grounded in classical quantitative principles. Daniel acquits himself well in the debate, and many think he has the best of the argument, but when he comes to his *peroratio*, where the rhetorician's confidence is conventionally at its most stirring, Daniel's timidity manifests itself in eerily transfigured form. The main argument is that poets should not try to contest the verdict of custom, but commonsensicalness becomes in the last paragraph a trap door into a dizzyingly nihilistic conclusion:

> we always bewray our selves to be both unkinde, and unnaturall to our owne native language, in disguising or forging strange or unusuall wordes, as if it were

---

[42] See Patricia Thomson, "Sonnet 15 of Samuel Daniel's Delia."
[43] Sprague, p. 130.

to make our owne verse seeme an other kind of speach out of the course of our usuall practice ... when our owne accustomed phrase, set in the due place, would expresse us more familiarly and to better delight, than all this idle affectation of antiquitie, or noveltie can ever doe.... But this is but a Character of that perpetuall revolution which wee see to be in all things that never remaine the same, and we must heerein be content to submit our selves to the law of time, which in a few yeeres wil make al that, for which we now contend, *Nothing*.[44]

Two years earlier, Daniel decided for the collected edition of his works to give his sequence a strangely similar ending:

> Let's love, the sun doth set, and rise againe,
> But when as our short light
> Comes once to set, it makes eternall night.[45]

Fade to black. Again the fade-out comes after some uncharacteristic combativeness, in this case a lyric celebration of a golden time of what used to be called free love, imagined to be "th'use of th'auncient happie ages" back before the arrival of "That Idle name of winde: / That Idoll of deceit, that emptie sound / Call'd HONOR," back when the only rule for human love was "*That's lawfull which doth please.*" Were such a regime to return, it would abolish Petrarchan love, which centers on the virtuous woman's refusal. Daniel raises the possibility of that abolition, and then disappears with it into the void.

The poem itself is a translation from the Italian: Tasso's "O bella età de l'oro," from the end of the first act of *Aminta* (1573). Notorious enough on its own, it has more outrageous descendents in seventeenth-century England, notably Thomas Carew's "A Rapture." The conclusion of the Italian poem is in turn a translation, from one of classical literature's best known love poems: "*soles occidere et redire possunt; / nobis, cum semel occidit brevis lux, / nox est perpetua una dormienda*" (Catullus, *Carmina* 5.4–6; suns can set and return; with us, when once the brief light sets, it is an endless single night to be slept out). With this conclusion, Tasso's poem goes from being a polemic against sexual denial to being a poem about human mortality. The absence of any reference to an afterlife looks like part of Tasso's imagining of "th'use of th'auncient happie ages" ("*l'uso de l'antiche genti*"): a specifically pagan sensuality, and more urgent (and thrilling) for it. A line of Renaissance *carpe diem* poems in the seventeenth century descends from Catullus, to different effects depending on how the components of his argument are deployed. Tasso, and with him Daniel, use only the first six lines of Catullus's poem, which then goes on in the seventh to his manic catalogue of kisses ("*da mi basia*

---

[44] Sprague, p. 158.
[45] Not in Sprague; I quote from Svensson, pp. 378–80.

*mille, deinde centum ...*"; give me a thousand kisses, then a hundred ...), energized precisely by confronting the prospect of endless night. The definitive equivalent in English is Marvell's "To his Coy Mistress," where a famously brash encounter with mortality—"Worms shall try / That long preserv'd Virginity" (27–8)—sparks a climactic burst of erotic heroism:

> Now let us sport us while we may;
> And now, like am'rous birds of prey,
> Rather at once our time devour,
> Than languish in his slow-chapt pow'r. (37–40)

The alternative, where the contemplation of death is postponed until after the call for present pleasure, is a dying fall given classic form in Herrick's "Corinna's *going a Maying*":

> So when or you or I are made
> A fable, song, or fleeting shade;
> All love, all liking, all delight
> Lies drown'd with us in endlesse night.
> Then while time serves, and we are but decaying;
> Come, my *Corinna*, come, let's goe a Maying. (65–70)

The love enjoined in the curtain line is already infected with its own decay. For the final conclusion of his sequence, Daniel finds in Tasso's poem a version of *carpe diem* closer to Herrick's than to Marvell's.

Even before Daniel adds that ending, *carpe diem* poems have appeared in *Delia*. The topic does not figure in Petrarch's *Canzoniere*, where female chastity is never challenged as an ideal and a Christian afterlife is always anticipated; appeals to seize the day in Petrarchist poetry represent a change, in part driven or enabled by classical pagan precedent. The argument enters *Delia* in the sonnet based on the stanzas in Tasso's epic, themselves going back to a poem in elegiac couplets in the *Appendix Vergiliana*, the concluding couplet of which leaves its trace over an impressive spread of Renaissance poetry: "*collige, virgo, rosas dum flos novus et nova pubes, / et memor esto aevum sic properare tuum*" (*De rosis nascentibus* 49–50; gather roses, virgin, while your flower and youth are fresh, and remember that your age hurries on).[46] Unlike Tasso and an array of other Renaissance poets,[47] Daniel does not take over the famous tagline, but the argument is the same:

---

[46] The poem is now considered late classical. My translation of *pubes* is, for lack of a usable English equivalent, delicate; the word can also specify, as in modern anatomical language, the genital area, and is so used by Vergil (*Aeneid* 3.427).

[47] A sampling: "*cogli la rosa, o ninfa, or ch'è 'l bel tempo*" (Lorenzo de' Medici, *Corinto* 193); "*cogliàn la bella rosa del giardino*" (Angelo Poliziano, *Canzoni a ballo* 3.26); "*Cueillez dés aujourd'huy les roses de la vie*" (Ronsard, *Sonnets pour Helene* 2.24.14); "*dum fata sinunt et nigra Sororum / stamina, verque*

> No Aprill can revive thy withred flowers,
> Whose blooming grace adornes thy glorie now:
> Swift speedy Time, feathred with flying howers,
> Dissolves the beautie of the fairest brow.
> O let not then such riches waste in vaine;
> But love whilst that thou maist be lov'd againe. (31.9.14)

That last line becomes the first line of the next sonnet, which continues the same argument: "But love whilst that thou maist be lov'd againe, / Now whilst thy May hath fill'd thy lappe with flowers ..." (32.1–2). With the continuation, though, the focus shifts from the call for present love to the decay that awaits, and from her lover's present ardor to the way it will be: "Men doe not weigh the stalke for that it was, / When once they finde her flowre, her glory passe" (32.13–14). This ending becomes the starting point for what follows:

> When men shall finde thy flowre, thy glory passe,
> And thou with carefull brow sitting alone:
> Received hast this message from thy glasse,
> That tells thee trueth, and saies that all is gone. (33.1–4)

We are here into the five-sonnet *catena* that is the best-defined subunit in the sequence, creating a brief sense of directional purpose against some general milling about in an unchanging situation. That direction is away from the prospect of Delia's yielding, or even from imagining it. What her lover reaches for now is different:

> I that have lov'd thee thus before thou fadest,
> My faith shall waxe, when thou art in thy wayning.
> The world shall finde this miracle in mee,
> That fire can burne, when all the matter's spent:
> Then what my faith hath beene thy selfe shalt see,
> And that thou wast unkinde thou maiest repent.
> Thou maiest repent, that thou hast scorn'd my teares,
> When Winter snowes uppon thy golden heares. (33.7–14)

He has moved back into more orthodox Petrarchan territory (*Canz.* 12), and moves even deeper in the two remaining sonnets in the chain. Though Delia may, no, will lose her beauty, the poems he writes about her will preserve it in lasting form:

*viret nobile, carpe rosas*" (Janus Secundus, *Elegies* 1.5.45–6); "*Cogliam la rosa in su 'l mattino adorno*" (Tasso, *Gerusalemme liberata* 16.15.5); "Gather the Rose of love, whilest yet is time" (Spenser, *Faerie Queene* 2.12.75.8); "Gather ye Rose-buds while ye may" (Herrick, "To the Virgins, to make much of Time" 1).

> This may remaine thy lasting monument,
> Which happily posteritie may cherish:
> These collours with thy fading are not spent;
> These may remaine, when thou and I shall perish.
> If they remaine, then thou shalt live thereby;
> They will remaine, and so thou canst not dye. (34.9–14)

This is the opening to make the pedigree he hopes for explicit:

> Thou canst not dye whilst any zeale abounde
> In feeling harts, that can conceive these lines:
> Though thou a *Laura* hast no *Petrarch* founde,
> In base attire, yet cleerely Beautie shines.
> And I, though borne in a colder clime,
> Doe feele mine inward heate as great, I knowe it:
> He never had more faith, although more rime,
> I love as well, though he could better shew it. (35.1–8)[48]

The passing bravery of *carpe diem* grades into the compensatory affirmation of poetry's immortalizing powers.

This is not exactly surprising. The *catena* uncoils in the shadow of the poem preceding it, a confident assertion of those powers, imitated as it happens from Tasso:

> Goe you my verse, goe tell her what she was;
> For what she was she best will finde in you.
> Your firie heate lets not her glorie passe,
> But Phenix-like shall make her live anew. (30.11–14)

Daniel is indeed the person who makes this motif such a prominent one in English sonneteering; Wyatt showed no interest in it, and you will not find it in *Astrophil and Stella* or for that matter *Cælica*. It enters *Delia* early, in a sonnet that begins as if it were a complaint: "Faire is my love, and cruell as sh'is faire" (6.1). The conjunction is significant; another poet might have written "but" (and did: "Fayre ye be sure, but cruell and unkind" [Spenser, *Amoretti* 56.1]). As Daniel's catalogue of Delia's paradoxicality progresses, it stops sounding like any kind of criticism—"A modest maide, deckt with a blush of honour, / Whose feete doe treade greene pathes of youth and love" (5–6)—and by the third quatrain the seeming contradictions unequivocally belong together—"Chastitie and Beautie, which were deadly foes, / Live reconciled friends within her brow" (9–10)—and the sonnet ends recognizing what the poet himself has to show for loving such a woman:

---

[48] The metrical anomaly in line five is fixed in the second edition of 1592: "And I, though borne within a colder clime."

> had she pittie to conjoine with those,
> Then who had heard the plaints I utter now.
> O had she not beene faire, and thus unkinde,
> My Muse had slept, and none had knowne my minde. (11–14)

The unattainable Laura is becoming the attainable laurel. This paradigm eventually inspires some of his grandest and most memorable verse:

> These are the Arkes the Tropheis I erect,
> That fortifie thy name against old age,
> And these thy sacred vertues must protect,
> Against the Darke and times consuming rage. (46.9–12)

Distinguishing the poetry he is writing from more expansive kinds of poetry he might be expected to produce ("Let others sing of Knight and Palladines" [46.1]), Daniel is laying proud claim to his own territory in a landscape that is both literary and, in a surprisingly specific reference, literal:

> None other fame myne unambitious Muse,
> Affected ever but t'eternize thee:
> All other honours doe my hopes refuse,
> Which meaner priz'd and momentarie bee. …
> No no my verse respects nor Thames nor Theaters,
> Nor seekes it to be knowne unto the Great:
> But *Avon* rich in fame, though poore in waters,
> Shall have my song, where *Delia* hath her seate.
> *Avon* shall be my Thames, and she my Song;
> Ile sound her name the Ryver all along. (48.1–4, 9–14)

"Unambitious" is tactical. If there is a plot to Daniel's plotless sequence, it is the almost triumphant acceptance of the poetic calling made possible by his hopeless love.

Almost. Even here Daniel pulls back; the fanfares of sonnets 46 and 48 only partly offset a "diminuendo effect"[49] in the poems flanking them. The first is another of Daniel's best-known sonnets: "Care-charmer sleepe, sonne of the Sable night, / Brother to death, in silent darknes borne" (45.1–2). The allure of sleep is its relief from an overwhelming sense of failure and shame, felt from the start ("Looke on the deere expences of my youth" [1.9]) and never really dissipated:

> let the day be time enough to morne,
> The shipwrack of my ill-adventred youth:

---
[49] Svensson, p. 334.

> Let waking eyes suffice to wayle theyr scorne,
> Without the torment of the nights untruth. (5–8)

Sleep is a familiar destination in Petrarchan poetry, a place to find the fulfillment denied in waking reality. Daniel hopes for an even more extreme retreat:

> Cease dreames, th'ymagery of our day desires,
> To modell foorth the passions of the morrow:
> Never let rysing Sunne approve you lyers,
> To adde more griefe to aggravat my sorrow. (9–12)

A sleep beyond dreams. The couplet, glancing at the fable of Ixion, takes some of that back, but the final hope is still never to revisit the daylight world: "let me sleepe, imbracing clowdes in vaine; / And never wake, to feele the dayes disdayne" (13–14). The poet longs for a state as close as possible to death without ceasing to exist. The last two sonnets curtail the imagined audience for his poetry:

> sith she scornes her owne, this rests for me,
> Ile mone my selfe, and hide the wrong I have:
> And so content me that her frownes should be
> To my' infant stile the cradle, and the grave.
> What though my selfe no honor get thereby,
> Each byrd sings t'herselfe, and so will I. (49.9–14)

In the end he folds his wings:

> I thus doe live cast downe from myrth,
> Pensive alone, none but despayre about mee;
> My joyes abortive, perisht at their byrth,
> My cares long liv'de, and will not dye without mee.
> This is my state, and *Delias* hart is such;
> I say no more, I feare I saide too much. (50.9–14)

*Solo et pensoso* (*Canz.* 35.1): Daniel's is the purest sequence of Petrarchan love that English has to offer.

\*

The year of the first authorized editions of *Delia* also saw the publication of *Diana. The praises of his mistres, in certaine sweete sonnets. By H. C.* "H. C." is Henry Constable, who had been a courtier of modest rank in Elizabeth's court but in 1591 entered the service of Henri IV in France; he would return to England to serve James I. The volume contains twenty-three sonnets, twenty of them in a sequence numbered in Italian. Constable follows Sidney's formal precedent more carefully than Daniel: all of the sonnets are in one of the rhyme schemes in *Astrophil and Stella*, and there are no feminine rhymes.[50] A connection with Sidney is also discreetly signalled by an unnumbered sonnet headed "A calculation upon the birth of an honourable Ladies daughter, borne in the yeare, 1588. & on a Friday"—information that identifies the lady as Penelope Rich, the overt subject of several other poems by Constable. The poet's beloved at one point takes ill (*Sonnetto sesto*, as in *Astrophil and Stella* 101) and a friend tries to talk him out of it'all (*Sonnetto settimo*, as in *Astrophil and Stella* 14 and 21), but (more in Daniel's vein) the implied narrative is static, and the volume begins and ends with the prospect of making the beloved famous: "by the winde which from my sighes doo come, / your praises round about the world is blowne" (*Ultimo sonnetto*). With Daniel and Constable, the Elizabethan sonnet sequence finds its traction in the public arena.

In 1593 four more are printed: *Licia*, anonymous but known to be by the elder Giles Fletcher; *Phillis*, by Thomas Lodge; *The Tears of Fancie*, attributed to a "T. W." who may be Thomas Watson, returning to the *genre* after a dozen years for a try at the canonical fourteen-line form; and *Parthenophil and Parthenophe*, by Barnabe Barnes, an ambitious collection of verse forms dominated by 105 numbered sonnets. In 1594 appear *Ideas Mirrour* by Michael Drayton, *Coelia* by William Percy, the anonymous *Zepheria*, and expanded versions of *Delia* and *Diana*; in 1595, a sequence of *Certaine Sonnets* in Richard Barnfield's *Cynthia*, the *Alcilia* of "J. C.," the *Emaricdulfe* of "E . C.," Spenser's *Amoretti*, and a fourth edition of *Delia*; in 1596, *Fidessa* by Bartholomew Griffin, *Diella* by "R. L." (Richard Lynche), *Chloris* by William Smith. In the mid-90s Philip Sidney's younger brother Robert was working on a sequence he never published. Sir John Davies is probably the author of a serious ten-sonnet sequence about "Philomel," and definitely the author of a satiric 9-poem sequence of "Gullinge Sonnets"; both circulated in manuscript at about this time. *Laura* by "R. T." (Robert Tofte), printed in 1597, is the last of the great burst, though the *genre* stays in the public eye with what becomes the standard text of *Astrophil and Stella* (finally) in 1598 (with reissues in 1599 [in Edinburgh], 1605, 1613, 1621), the mutation of Drayton's sequence into *Idea* in 1599, and further incarnations of *Delia* (1598, 1601, 1602), *Idea* (1600, 1602, 1608, 1610, 1613, 1616, 1619), and *Alcilia* (1613, 1619). A smaller burst of new activity follows the accession of James, when Scots poets become interested. William Alexander's *Aurora* is printed in 1604, Alexander Craig's *Amarose Songes, Sonets, and Elegies* in 1606,[51] David Murray's *Caelia* in 1611. William Fowler's

---

[50] The sonnets in the 1592 volume are culled from a larger collection that has survived in a manuscript that forms the basis of the modern critical text—*The Poems of Henry Constable*, ed. Joan Grundy—where the Italian titles are consigned to the textual apparatus. For the sonnets cited here, see pp. 136, 157, 163, 134, 135.

[51] More an anthology than a sequence; the sonnets are not numbered, and eight beloveds are addressed in rotation. These include one with the name of a famous Greek prostitute, Lais, and another

*The Tarantula of Love*, probably composed sometime in the mid-1580s, remains unpublished until the twentieth century.[52] The Anglo-Irish Richard Nugent publishes his own *Cynthia* in 1604,[53] and new sequences from English writers continue to appear: John Davies of Hereford's *Wittes Pilgrimage* in 1605, and of course *Shake-speares Sonnets* in 1609. English sonneteering has by this point lost its novelty but not its resourcefulness; some of the most memorable sonnets in *Idea*, including one of the touchstone poems of the tradition—"Since ther's no helpe, Come let us kisse and part"—do not appear until the last revision in 1619. This episode in English poetry only concludes in 1621 when Sidney's niece Mary Wroth publishes *Pamphilia to Amphilanthus* with her *Urania*, a prose romance in which the two lovers in her sonnets are major characters. She is continuing a family tradition set by her uncle and her father. Two dozen years later, when Milton publishes a sonnet sequence (including five sonnets and a *canzone* in Italian), he is performing a more deliberate and difficult act of literary retrieval.

What did this regiment of sonneteers think they were doing? Laureate ambition is frequently in evidence, though disowning it is for a while part of the convention. The author of *Zepheria* makes the boldest statement in a poem to his fellow sonneteers, "*Alli veri figlioli delle Muse*" (to the true children of the Muses), where both the aspiration and the pedigree are explicit:

> Ye moderne Lawreats famousd for your writ,
> Who for your pregnance may in *Delos* dwell,
> On your sweete lines eternitie doth sit,
> Their browes enobling with applause and lawrell. ...
> From forth dead sleepe of everlasting darke,
> Fame with her trumps shrill summon hath awakt
> The Romayne *Naso* and the *Tuskan Petrarch*,

inventively named after what sounds like a medical condition: Lithocardia, Lady Hardening-of-the-Heart.

[52] For recent scholarship on the date, see Sebastiaan Verweij, "The Manuscripts of William Fowler," pp. 10–12. As mentioned previously, Fowler came into possession of one of the few manuscripts of *Astrophil and Stella*, probably in 1591–92, but the dates seem wrong for that to have prompted his own sequence; the genealogy of *Tarantula* is probably through Petrarch and the poetry of the sixteenth-century Scots court rather than through English practice. (The language of the sequence is a form of Middle Scots—a sample is given below—rather than the lightly inflected Modern English of the later Scots Petrarchists.) Fowler was certainly working directly from Petrarch; he translated the *Trionfi* and the influence of the *Canzoniere* on *Tarantula* is overt. See R. D. S. Jack, "William Fowler and Italian Literature," pp. 486–7. Fowler's title, possibly added later (no spiders or for that matter dancers appear in the poems themselves), may have been suggested by Castiglione's *Cortegiano*, where early in the first book Cesare Gonzaga compares the effects of love to those of the tarantula's venom; it could also have come from Sidney's revised *Arcadia* (1.9; fol. 38ᵛ). Fowler's Calvinism makes *Tarantula* something of a pair with *Cælica*; see Sarah Dunnigan, *Eros and Poetry at the Courts of Mary Queen of Scots and James VI*, pp. 149–63, and Elizabeth Elliott, "*Eros* and Self-Government."

[53] Nugent's sequence has long escaped notice; Roche lists it (p. 520) but has nothing to say about it. There is now a scholarly edition by Angelina Lynch, with a substantial introduction by Anne Fogarty. The author's name is firmly attested, but there were two contemporary Richard Nugents in the Old English community who might be meant (Fogarty, pp. 11–19).

> Your spirit-ravishing lines to wonder at.
> Oh theame befitting high mus'd *Astrophil* ...

The bravado of this is shaded by the anonymity of the poet, unusual among these sonneteers (a few others hide, with varying success, behind initials). The effect resembles the overlay of bragging and self-effacement at the end of *Delia*. With time boasting gets easier; a sonnet in *Idea* professes humble service to the beloved's celebrity—"Whilst thus my Pen strives to eternize thee"—but ends cheerfully dropping the pretense: "My Name shall mount upon Eternitie" (44.1, 14 in 1619; a poem first published in 1599). Daniel and Drayton are the two poets to capitalize most successfully on the promise of sonneteering as the gateway to a diversified career as a poet, in fulfillment of what both of them later assert as a deeply rooted ambition. "This is the thing that I was borne to do, / This is my Scene, this part must I fulfill," says Daniel's Musophilus to his sceptical interlocutor (*Musophilus* 577–8). Drayton claims in 1627 to have been devoted to poetry "From my cradle," and to have pestered his tutor at the age of ten about his career plans: "cannot you, quoth I, / Make me a Poet? doe it if you can, / And you shall see Ile quickly be a man."[54] The two most monumentally self-conscious poetic careers of the English Renaissance do not make their debut with a sonnet sequence in quite the same way, but they pointedly include one. Spenser's *Amoretti* appears between the two big installments of the *Faerie Queene*, as if he were belatedly satisfying a professional expectation. Milton prints the first ten of what eventually becomes a twenty-three-poem sequence in his 1645 *Poems*, but not at the front of the volume. When it comes, though, sonnet 23 (23 being Petrarch's number of initiation, his age when he first saw Laura and the ordinal of the *canzone delle metamorfosi*) acquires an uncanny valedictory significance as in effect "the last sonnet of the British Renaissance": "O as to embrace me she enclin'd, / I wak'd, she fled, and day brought back my night."[55]

Instructions for writing individual sonnets had been available in English since Gascoigne's *Certayne Notes*, but there is essentially no public guidance for the writing of sonnet sequences. The writers had no particular name for them; the designation "sonnet sequence" is visible in embryo in Gascoigne's "Sonets in sequence," but the term itself only comes later. Italian commentaries on Petrarch venture structural analyses of his *Canzoniere* using a template from classical rhetoric, as if it were an oration; Lars-Håkan Svensson formulates this as a tripartite plan of *proemio-narratione-uscita*, though he applies it only to *Delia*.[56] Thomas Roche presents far tighter numerological analyses of a wide range of English

---

[54] Spingarn, *Critical Essays of the Seventeenth Century* 1: 134–5.
[55] Spiller, *Development of the Sonnet*, pp. 196–7.
[56] Svensson, pp. 26–9, with reference to Bernard Weinberg, "The *Sposizione* of Petrarch in the Early Cinquecento."

sequences, as well as the *Canzoniere* itself.[57] Carol Thomas Neely's less ambitious model is easier to credit: "composition and revision of individual sonnets over a period of time, followed (or accompanied) by selection, arrangement, and rearrangement"[58] into a two-part structure similar to the one given formal definition in the final autograph manuscript of Petrarch's sequence. There, almost two-thirds of the way through the sequence, blank pages and a decorative capital letter signal a new start, after which Laura's death is announced; the two parts acquire the labels *In vita* and *In morte*. Until Milton makes additions to his own sequence in 1673, no beloved in the English sonnet sequences dies,[59] but several notable sequences manifest something like Petrarch's "division into two unequal parts": "The first part sets forth the static relationship of the adoring/lamenting poet-lover to an immovable beloved .... In the second, shorter part there is alteration—in the beloved, the poet, the relationship."[60] In *Astrophil and Stella* the change is the irruption of Astrophil's lust into the open, a move which provokes its definitive frustration; a formal break after sonnet 71 ("But ah, Desire still cries, give me some food") might properly dramatize the shift, though Neely locates it somewhat earlier, "in the vicinity" of sonnet 63.[61] In other sequences things play out to a variety of conclusions: "abrupt stops which freeze lover and beloved in their impasse, formal detachment which diffuses the conflicts into other poetic modes, or, occasionally, a denouement which resolves the plot."[62] In a few instances there is, well before the end, a flat rejection of love, so that the second part of the sequence almost amounts to a changing of the subject. The case that makes Neely's model especially interesting is Shakespeare's, where the sequence is on the face of it two sequences, the first much longer than the second, involving two different beloveds, with some narrative overlap but presented one after the other. Seen within the paradigm of the two-part structure, this switch is still drastic but also intentional, not some accident of editorial history. Neely's structure is not universal in English sequences, but it is sufficiently widespread, and well-marked in some of the more memorable sequences, to be worth having in mind while reading any of them.

Titles like *The Tears of Fancie* and *Wittes Pilgrimage* suggest the agenda is displaying the ingenuity of their authors. The fashionability of the *genre* fuels some grandly reckless writing, with a competitiveness happy to gallop straight off the cliff:

---

[57] Roche, pp. 32–69, 259–71, 281–94, 356–68, 415–24, 453–61, 534–80—taking inspiration from Alastair Fowler's similar analysis of *Astrophil and Stella* in *Triumphal Forms*, pp. 174–80.
[58] Carol Thomas Neely, "The Structure of English Renaissance Sonnet Sequences," p. 361.
[59] In the English sequence that Charles d'Orléans composes in the early fifteenth century the lady does die, only to be replaced by another lady who looks almost exactly like her. "The reader has to conclude that in this collection, one lady is pretty much like another"; A. E. B. Coldiron, *Canon, Period, and the Poetry of Charles of Orléans*, p. 180.
[60] Neely, p. 368.
[61] Neely, p. 371.
[62] Neely, p. 360.

> Poore worme, poore silly worme, (alas poore beast)
> Feare makes thee hide thy head within the ground,
> Because of creeping things thou art the least,
> Yet every foote gives thee thy mortall wound.
> But I thy fellow worme am in worse state ...
> (Griffin, *Fidessa* 27.1–5)

It is hard at this distance to say when cleverness grades into parody, intentional or otherwise. The primary readership, despite the fiction of the poems, would have been in many cases cadres of ambitious young men, preternaturally watchful for something to make fun of; *Fidessa* comes with a preface "To the Gentlemen of the Innes of Court," and several other sequences contain something similar. Occasionally the mockery happened in public. That was Barnes's unhappy fate when in his sixty-third sonnet he invoked the *canzone delle metamorfosi*—"Jove for Europaes love tooke shape of Bull ..."—and proceded to speculate about self-transformations in which he might even outdo the king of the gods: "Would I were chang'd but to my mistresse gloves ... Or else that cheane of pearle ... Or her to compasse like a belt of golde ..."[63] Fetishes like these have Petrarchist precedent (honored by Romeo: "O that I were a glove upon that hand" [*Romeo and Juliet* 2.2.24]), but piling things up like this is Barnes's contribution, from which he springs aloft into vatic dementia:

> Or that sweet wine, which downe her throate doth trickle,
> To kisse her lippes, and lye next at her hart,
> Runne through her vaynes, and passe by pleasures part.

Jean-Antoine de Baïf had imagined being transformed into his mistress's wine, but not with this outcome. A speaker in one of Nashe's satires expressed concern for Barnes's safety: "the next time his Mistres made water, he was in danger to be cast out of her favour."[64] John Marston and Thomas Campion followed up with similar jokes in print. The sonnet has a reputation as the *ne plus ultra* of grotesque sonneteering wit, though such judgments are probably made in ignorance of sonnet 29 of *Wittes Pilgrimage*:

> Some say the Weezel-masculine doth gender
> With the Shee-Weezel only at the Eare
> And she her Burden at hir Mouth doth render;
> The like (sweet Love) doth in our love appeare:
> For I (as Masculine) beget in Thee

---

[63] I quote Barnes's sequence from the edition of Victor A. Doyno. For the background and reception of this poem, see pp. 162–5.
[64] Thomas Nashe, *Have with You to Saffron-Walden*, sig. Q2ᵛ.

> Love, at the Eare, which thou bearst at the Mouth
> And though It came from Hart, and Reynes of me
> From the Teeth outward It in thee hath growth.
> My Mouth, thine Eares, doth ever chastly use
> With putting in hot Seed of active Love;
> Which, streight thine Ear conveyeth (like a Sluce)
> Into thy Mouth; and, there but Aire doth prove:
> Yet Aire is active; but, not like the fire
> Then ô how should the Sonne be like the Sire?[65]

An unforgettable first quatrain loses some drive in subsequent lines, but the zoö-anatomical conceit ("reynes" are kidneys, seen as a seat of passion) stays on track. The weaselly man speaks sweet but fiery nothings into the woman's ear, and in transit through her body they lose their fire and change into a different element, air; "hot seed of active Love" impregnates her with cool disdain, active in a negative way, to which she gives birth at her mouth by saying No. The speaker still has trouble accepting this outcome, and wonders if there is a way to reverse it. Perhaps the words of this poem in his beloved's ear will help, though of course (Nashe was out of commission by this point, but some acolyte might make the observation) she may have trouble hearing them because of the weasel still mounted up there.

Conceits like these are limiting cases of a wittiness usually kept under better control, and can help us appreciate what better poets achieved with it, both before and after the craze. But extremity itself can observe weird proprieties, as when Parthenophil passes as close to "pleasures part" as possible without actually reaching it: getting to know Parthenophe from the inside by way of her urinary tract, he still does not, technically (a close call), terminate the virginity which her name honors. Davies's lover similarly inseminates his lady's body without officially seducing her—the intercourse in question is entirely conceptual, as is the resulting pregnancy—and something similar can be said about Griffin's "poore silly worme," who hides his head within the ground and even so is doing better than his author. The Petrarchan premise of unfulfilled desire continues to dominate even as Petrarchist poets vigorously explore the ways in which that desire can indulge itself. Sonneteers repeatedly test that limit without breaching it, though in a very few cases they do. Barnes is, as it happens, the most outrageous example, building his sequence to an unparalleled triple sestina in which Parthenophe, drugged by

---

[65] "Sluce" in l. 11 may sound odd to modern ears, but Lynche, writing of "my over-watched eyes," has "the sluce of their uncessant flowing" (*Diella* 33.1–2), and Barnes applies the term to the hydraulics of his beloved's beauty: "with loves purest sanguine Cupid writes / The prayse of bewtie through the vaynes which blew bee, / Conducted through loves sluice to thy face rosie" (Elegy 1.16–18). For weasel sex, see Edward Topsell, *The Historie of Foure-Footed Beastes*, pp. 728–9. The legend that weasels give birth at the mouth informs Ovid's myth of Galanthis (*Metamorphoses* 9.306–22); George Sandys, from his observation of opossums in Virginia, expresses scepticism (*Ovid's Metamorphosis Englished, Mythologized, and Represented in Figures*, ed. Karl K. Hulley and Stanley T. Vandersall, p. 441).

witchcraft and riding a goat, is brought in a daze to a maddened Parthenophil to submit to the act which she has evermore denied:

> Dye magicke bowes, now dye, which late were kindled:
> Here is mine heaven: loves droppe in steede of teares.
> It joynes, it joynes, ah both embracing bare:
> Let *Nettles* bring forth *Roses* in each woode,
> Last ever verdant woodes: hence former furies:
> Oh dye, live, joye: what? last continuall night. (97–102)

Blips of derangement in the phrasing place the poem in a mostly covert line of Renaissance poems enacting sexual intercourse in something like real time.[66] The conclusion of the sestina is the conclusion of the sequence, following immediately on Parthenophil's orgasm with grim finality:

> Tis now acquitted: cease your former teares,
> For as she once with rage my bodie kindled,
> So in hers am I buried this night. (109–11)

End of story, with no tenderness accompanying the man's satisfaction. In a different direction, two sequences resolve the man's frustration in the sanctioned way, through marriage. Spenser's *Amoretti* is the more significant, accepting the challenge of showing how we get from the one-sided Petrarchan stalemate to the happy ending of mutuality. Alexander's *Aurora* is much more abrupt, and if you are not paying attention you may miss what happens in the last few poems (see Appendix B). A possible third is Tofte's *Laura*, which ends with even greater abruptness, unclear what if anything is supposed to have happened.[67] Aside from this handful (and the always special case of Shakespeare), Petrarchan sequences in the British Isles end with male desire unsatisfied and often affronted.

It is more because of this than in spite of it that these sequences secure the reputation that Sidney in his *Defence of Poesie* hoped to ward off, that, "larded with passionate Sonnets," poetry "abuseth mens wit, trayning it to wanton sinfulnes and

---

[66] One of Aretino's *sonnetti lussuriosi* transcribes a dialogue between a man and a woman copulating, their separate voices becoming indistinguishable as they reach climax: "*Adesso, adesso faccio signor mio, / Adesso ho fatto, e io, Ahime, o Dio*" (I'm coming, I'm coming my lord I've come, and I, o my, o God). An English poem in seventeenth-century manuscripts gives the monologue of a woman having fully clothed, not entirely welcome sex ("You mare my ruffs") which we come upon *in medias res*: "Naye, phewe nay pishe? nay faythe and will ye, fye." (Afterwards she invites the gentleman, as she calls him, to stay for supper.) See Bette Talvacchia, *Taking Positions*, pp. 218–19; Arthur F. Marotti, *Manuscript, Print, and the English Renaissance Lyric*, pp. 77–8. Both these examples imagine the woman taking at least some pleasure in the encounter; Barnes and Parthenophil show no interest in that part of it.

[67] "So, if my parting bitter was and sad, / Sweete's my returne to thee, and passing glad" (*Laura* 3.40.1–2). Notes to the reader suggest that the publication was unauthorized and there was textual confusion at the ending.

lustfull love."⁶⁸ Conceits of ultimately chaste entry into the beloved's digestive system or aural canal are just fantastical versions of the more literal action in poems like the second song in *Astrophil and Stella* or *Cælica* 56, where actual rape is a prospect from which the poem veers off at the last moment. Tantalization heightens allure and rouses the imagination, and Petrarchism by the sixteenth century is more voluptuous than Petrarch ever is. Dreams of Laura in the *Canzoniere*, most of which come after her death, are dreams of loss and moral instruction, offered "*in quel suo atto dolce onesto*" (341.4 [with that sweet chaste bearing of hers]). Dream women for Petrarch's followers come with a different carriage and the dreams trend towards fantasies of the forbidden bliss—even for a Scots Calvinist:

> is this the breist quhair chastetie is schrynde?
> ar these the hands proud rebells to desyre?
> now in my armes I hald my hoped hyre,
> now in my armes I glaspe my gratious dame:
> contenewe, love, my conqueist I requyre.
> so in my sleip and dreames these words I frayme.
> (Fowler, *The Tarantula of Love* 23.7–12)⁶⁹

Such poems end with the dreamer awaking to disappointment, but while the dream lasts the fantasy flourishes. Two lavish instances precede Parthenophil's rape of Parthenophe, one with her ("bounde / With her enfolded thighes in mine entangled, / And both in one selfe soule plac'de, / Made an Hermaphrodite, with pleasure ravish't" [Madrigall 13.9–11]), and for good measure one with a previous love, Laya ("At length he doth possess her whoale, / Her lippes, and all he would desier" [Ode 8.41–2]). Fletcher, wondering "Why dy'd I not when as I last did sleepe?" (*Licia* 29.1), recalls exploring an erotic landscape that Ovid explores in the waking daze of noon:

> in that darke there shone a Princely light:
> Two milke-white hilles, both full of Nectar sweete:
> Her Ebon thighes, the wonder of my sight,
> Where all my senses with their objectes meete:
> I passe those sportes, in secret that are best,
> Wherein my thoughtes did seeme alive to be;
> We both did strive, and wearie both did rest:
> I kist her still, and still she kissed me. (5–12)

The last two lines remember *Amores* 1.5.25, both in Latin ("*cetera quis nescit? lassi requievimus ambo*") and in Marlowe's translation ("Judge you the rest: being tirde

---

⁶⁸ Gregory Smith, *Elizabethan Critical Essays* 1: 186.
⁶⁹ Text from vol. 1 of *The Works of William Fowler*, ed. Henry W. Meikle.

she bad me kisse"), the climax of Ovid's most straightforward poem about satisfied lust. The pre-coital lingering over the woman's breasts and thighs is also there in Ovid's poem; Fletcher's unexpected reference to the latter as "Ebon" rhymes with references to Licia's "Ebon hands" (39.7) and "pearles inclosed in an Ebon pale" (52.6), and is probably less interesting than it seems, reflecting a latinate confusion of *ebenus*, ebony, with *eburneus*, ivory (arousal addles the poet's philology). The repeated "still" in the last line signals that the kissing does not, as Marlowe perhaps unintentionally implies, begin only after the climax of the lovemaking but has been constant and (again in contrast with Marlowe) mutual from the start.

Not everything that can happen in dreams can happen in real life, though a surprising amount apparently can:

> It is not life which we for life approve,
> But that is life when on hir woul-soft pappes,
> I seale sweet kisses, which do batten love:
> And doubling them do treble my good happes.
> (Lodge, *Phillis* 6.5–8)

The only kisses in the *Canzoniere* are the ceremonious ones that an unidentified dignitary bestows on Laura's eyes and forehead (238.12–14); in English Petrarchism, they become commonplace. As Sidney demonstrated, the lover may have to take some trouble and risk to secure the privilege, but the narrative attenuation of most sequences obscures that effort, leaving just the sensual harvest:

> Thy corall coloured lips how should I pourtray
> Unto the unmatchable patterne of their sweet?
> A draught of blessednesse I stole away
> From them when last I kist, I tast it yet:
> So did that sugrie touch my lips en-sucket. (*Zepheria* 23.1–5)

(The kiss this lover can still taste may have been stolen, but it was not the first kiss, only the most recent.) The body of Petrarch's Laura, mostly diffracted into metaphors of gold, snow, pearls, etc., has at best a flickering presence in the *Canzoniere*, and as far as breasts are concerned there are only a half dozen or so decorous references to her "*bel giovenil petto*" (37.102 [lovely youthful breast]) or "*angelico seno*" (126.9; angelic breast), always in the singular: referring to her breast ("*torre d'alto intelletto*"; 37.103 [tower of high intellect]) rather than her breasts (which would require a word like *mamelle*) makes a difference.[70] Astrophil, urging would-be poets to get past "poore *Petrarch's* long deceased woes" (15.7), entices them with something much more ample: "if (both for your love and skill)

---

[70] Peter Hainsworth, *Petrarch the Poet*, p. 121.

your name / You seeke to nurse at fullest breasts of Fame, / *Stella* behold, and then begin to endite" (12–14).⁷¹ Fame's nourishing breasts are metaphorical, but it is looking at Stella that is going to make a man imagine them. The sonneteers Sidney inspires keep that faith: "The Mouth of true Love sucks true Pleasures Brests" (*Wittes Pilgrimage* 20.7). Lodge contemplates his lady snuggling Love "twixt her teates":

> The lad that felt the soft and sweet so nye,
> Drownd in delights, disdaines his liberty.
> And sayd, let *Venus* seeke another sonne,
> For heare my onely matchlesse Mother is:
> From whose fayre orient Orbes the drinke doth ronne,
> That deifies my state with greater blis:
> Thys sayd, he suckt, my Mistresse blushing smyld,
> Since Love was both her prisoner and her child.
> (*Phillis* 39.15, 17–24)

Part of what makes the *Amoretti* work is Spenser's incorporation of such lushness into his scrupulously legitimate courtship of a future wife. The kiss finally granted immediately blossoms into a sensuality that starts with floral sweetness—"Comming to kisse her lyps, (such grace I found) / Me seemd I smelt a gardin of sweet flowres" (64.1–2)—and refuses to stop:

> Her goodly bosome lyke a Strawberry bed,
> her neck lyke to a bounch of Cullambynes:
> her brest lyke lillyes, ere theyr leaves be shed,
> her nipples lyke yong blossomd Jessemynes. (9–12)

Kisses, breasts, flowers, sweet odors everywhere. Lovers also get excited at the sight of dimples.⁷²

What is arguably the most luscious physicality in English Petrarchism comes, interestingly, in an openly homoerotic sequence, Barnfield's run of twenty sonnets about the hopeless longing of Daphnis for Ganymede:

---

⁷¹ As it happens, the two 1591 quartos (followed by the often-anomalous Houghton manuscript) read "brest," one of their characteristic slips.
⁷² "The Graces sport in her cheekes dimpled pits" (*Emaricdulfe* 5.6); "When sweetly hath appear'd in cheeke the dimple / (Their love enthron'd swayes powrefull Monarchy)" (*Zepheria* 28.3–4); "the Clift / Of this faire Cliffe (thine Alablaster chinne)" (*Wittes Pilgrimage* 2.1–2); "The daintie pot that's in thy chin, / Makes many a heart for to fall in" (Alexander, *Aurora*, Song 8.49–50). The dimples that appear when Shakespeare's Adonis smiles at Venus "as in disdaine" (*Venus and Adonis* 241–2) have an electrifying effect on the goddess of love: "These lovely caves, these round inchanting pits, / Opend their mouthes to swallow Venus liking: / Being mad before, how doth she now for wits?" (247–9).

> Sweet Corrall lips, where Nature's treasure lies,
> The balme of blisse, the soveraigne salve of sorrow,
> The secret touch of loves heart-burning arrow,
> Come quench my thirst or els poor *Daphnis* dies. (6.1–4)[73]

The only narrative event in the sequence is Daphnis's coy revelation of his desire in sonnet 11; there is no sign it alters anything. The shift in gender leaves the *genre* undisturbed:

> Sometimes, when I imagine that I see him,
> (As love is full of foolish fantasies)
> Weening to kisse his lips, as my loves fee's,
> I feele but Aire: nothing but Aire to bee him.
> Thus with *Ixion*, kisse I clouds in vaine:
> Thus with *Ixion*, feele I endles paine. (16.9–14)

Embracing nothingness is inseparable from being aware that it is all about the body:

> Cherry-lipt *Adonis* in his snowie shape,
> Might not compare with his pure Ivorie white ...
> His lips ripe strawberries in Nectar wet,
> His mouth a Hive, his tongue a hony-combe,
> Where Muses (like Bees) make their mansion.
> His teeth pure Pearle in blushing Correll set.
> Oh how can such a body sinne-procuring,
> Be slow to love, and quicke to hate, enduring? (17.1–2, 9–14)

Were we in any uncertainty as to what Daphnis has in mind, "sinne-procuring" dispenses with it. He is no better off than a heterosexual Petrarchist, aroused and frustrated by a damnable temptation taunting him at every opportunity. An

---

[73] I quote from Richard Barnfield, *The Complete Poems*, ed. George Klawitter. Daphnis's desire for Ganymede was already set out, luxuriantly, in two lengthy laments in *The Affectionate Shepheard*, which Barnfield had published anonymously in 1594 (with a dedication to Penelope Rich). There, Daphnis, eventually presented as an older man, despairs of winning Ganymede away from "faire *Guendolena* Queene of Beautie." A prefatory note in *Cynthia* "To the curteous Gentlemen Readers" indicates that writing about "the love of a Shepheard to a boy" had caused some kind of scandal, and Barnfield defends himself by citing Vergil's second eclogue. The question of whether Barnfield's work represents a serious moral or conceptual challenge to prevailing morality is discussed by Kenneth Borris, "'Ile hang a bag and a bottle at thy back'"; he thinks it does, but the argument takes work. Sam See is more confident in "Richard Barnfield and the Limits of Homoerotic Literary History." Barnfield acquires a modest reputation as a poet; one of the Ganymede sonnets (15) appeared, with attribution, in *Englands Helicon* in 1600. He disappears from view in the seventeenth century; it used to be thought he died in 1627, leaving a son and thus presumably having been married, but the evidence for that is a will now thought to be his father's.

exemplary moment in Tofte's *Laura* makes clear that you do not actually need to see the beloved's sin-procuring body to be reduced to helpless lust:

> (taking on me pittie) graciously
> My Mistres hem of garment trailing downe
> Toucht mee, and mee revived suddenly:
> Then if such vertue be within her gowne,
> Imagin what doth stay her corps within,
> Which who seeth, through sweetnes needs-must sin. (1.38.5–10)

\*

The sequence with which Mary Wroth concludes the great vogue that her uncle did not know he was starting strikes a different chord:

> burning you will love the smart,
> When you shall feele the waight of true desire,
> So pleasing, as you would not wish your part
> Of burthen should be missing from that fire.
> But faithfull and unfained heate aspire
> Which sinne abollisheth, and doth impart
> Salves to all feare, with vertues which inspire
> Soules with divine love; which shewes his chaste Art.
> (*Pamphilia to Amphilanthus* P81.1–8)[74]

This concerning a beloved with less physical presence in this sequence than Laura in Petrarch's. Only once is there any indicator that the beloved is male (P47.10–14).[75] There are passing references to his breast (P3.5, P30.3, M96.5) and his lips (P5, P91.17; "love-begetting lips" at M113.10). What we hear most of are his eyes, which are unforgettable and commanding:

> Deare eyes how well indeed, you doe adorne
> That blessed Sphere, which gazing soules hold deare?
> The loved place of sought for triumphs, neere
> The Court of Glory, where Loves force was borne. (P2.1–4)

This dominance is the main thing we know about them. In *Urania* we finally learn, in passing, what color those eyes are—"best Gray inclining, ore indeed

---

[74] Quotations and references for Wroth's sequence are from Ilona Bell's edition (done with Steven W. May). This edition gives texts of both the printed version of 1621 and a manuscript which differs from it in many specifics; I designate these P and M respectively, with reference to the sequential numbering Bell and May provide (which differs from Wroth's own).

[75] Clare R. Kinney, "Mary Wroth's Guilty 'secrett art,'" p. 69; Roger Kuin, "More I Still Undoe," p. 443.

blewish"[76]—but that information does not make it into Pamphilia's poems. Like headlights in the night, his gaze effectively blinds his lover and her readers to the rest of the visual field ("The Sunne most pleasing, blindes the strongest eye" [P5.5]). The faculty of seeing is, for her, a power of abstraction:

> When last I saw thee, I did not thee see,
>   It was thine Image which in my thoughts lay
>   So lively figur'd, as no times delay
>   Could suffer me in heart to parted be. (P24.1–4)

This elision of the corporeal into the imagined is, in the neo-Platonic version of Petrarchan love, the beginning of wisdom:

> to escape the torment of this absence and to enjoy beauty without suffering, the Courtier, aided by reason, must turn his desire entirely away from the body and to beauty alone, contemplate it in its simple and pure self ... and in his imagination give it a shape distinct from all matter ... remembering always that the body is something very different from beauty, and not only does not increase beauty but lessens its perfections.[77]

There are times when *Pamphilia to Amphilanthus* looks as if it might be providing English Petrarchism, in a break with what had become the main drift of things, with its first serious neo-Platonic sonnet sequence answerable to continental expectations, in which erotic passion is turned to wholly noble account:

> When chaste thoughts guide us, then our minds are bent
>   To take that good which ills from us remove:
>   Light of true love brings fruite which none repent;
>   But constant Lovers seeke and wish to prove.
> Love is the shining Starre of blessings light,
>   The fervent fire of zeale, the root of peace,
>   The lasting Lampe, fed with the oyle of right,
>   Image of Faith, and wombe for joyes increase. (P78.5–12)

The sequence has indeed been so read.[78]

Wroth seemed bred for some such destiny. She was born a year after Philip Sidney's death into a family that, as the extent of Philip's achievement as a writer

---

[76] *The Second Part of the Countesse of Montgomery's Urania* (= *Urania* II), ed. Josephine A. Roberts, Suzanne Gossett, and Janel Mueller, p. 206.

[77] Baldassare Castiglione, *The Book of the Courtier*, trans. Charles S. Singleton, p. 351.

[78] Elaine V. Beilin, *Redeeming Eve*, pp. 232–43; Barbara Kiefer Lewalski, *Writing Women in Jacobean England*, pp. 251–63.

became clear, increasingly saw itself as England's premier literary family, possibly a dynasty. Others saw it that way too; Ben Jonson said so in authoritative style.[79] After Philip's death, Mary completed his translation of the Psalms, translated Petrarch's *Triumphus Mortis* on her own, and published unanonymously two significant translations of contemporary French works and an original verse pastoral. She became known for a time as the genius of a social and literary circle which Nicholas Breton (Gascoigne's stepson) called "a kind of little Court" and compared to the legendary court of Urbino described by Castiglione.[80] Robert Sidney made his own try at writing a sonnet sequence while serving in Philip's old office of Governor of Flushing. Philip's only child, his daughter Elizabeth, also wrote poetry; none of it has survived, but Jonson told William Drummond she "was nothing inferior to her Father *Sir P.* Sidney in Poesie,"[81] and hailed her as Nature's defiance of the gendered rules of inheritance:

> the *destinies* decreed
> (Save that most masculine issue of his braine)
> No male unto him: who could so exceed
> *Nature*, they thought, in all, that he would faine.
> At which, shee happily displease'd, made you:
> On whom, if he were living now, to looke,
> He should those rare, and absolute numbers view,
> As he would burne, or better farre his booke. (*Epigrammes* 79.5–12)

Were your father alive today, he would recognize his daughter as the better poet, and probably become a better poet himself because of it. Elizabeth died in 1612, but Robert's daughter Mary (who married Sir Robert Wroth in 1604) was in place to fill her role. In 1621 her double homage to her uncle's two major works was printed in one substantial 600-page volume, under her own name and with her Sidney pedigree detailed on the title-page. Jonson, who "cursed Petrarch for redacting Verses to Sonnets,"[82] surmounted his annoyance to compose a sonnet praising her for improving his own craft as Elizabeth might have improved her father's:

> I that have beene a lover, and could shew it,
> Though not in these, in rithmes not wholly dumbe,

---

[79] See Michael G. Brennan, "'A SYDNEY, though un-named.'"
[80] Nicholas Breton, *Wits Trenchmour*, sig. F2ᵛ; *The Pilgrimage to Paradise*, sig. ¶2ʳ.
[81] Jonson, *Informations to William Drummond of Hawthornden*, section 12 (Sibbald transcription). Quotations from Jonson are taken from the old-spelling text, ed. David Gants, in *The Cambridge Edition of the Works of Ben Jonson Online*.
[82] *Informations*, section 4.

> Since I exscribe your Sonnets, am become
> A better lover, and much better Poët. (*Under-wood* 30.1–4)

The dynasty had been secured into the second generation, and without the need for a male line.

That was of course wishful thinking; the 1621 publication was not a triumph but a scandal, the target of something more serious than Nashe's mockery of Barnes.[83] Early in 1622 Edward Denny, Baron of Waltham, circulated an abusive poem calling Wroth "Hermophradite in show, in deed a monster," and continuing in that vein for twenty-six lines denouncing her and her "Idell book." Wroth wrote directly to Denny with flashing sarcasm ("This day came to my handes some verses under the name of the Lord Denny's but such vile, rayling and scandalous thinges, as I could not beleeve they proceeded from any but some drunken poett") and composed her own twenty-six-line poem using the same rhymes: "Hirmophradite in sense in Art a monster." The epistolary exchange continued through three more letters, with no backing down on either side. Denny was specifically affronted by what he took to be an unflattering portrait of himself and his son in a brief inset story in *Urania*; the shoe does fit, though Wroth righteously denied having any such thing in mind. Others agreed that she had written a *roman à clef* and pushed the envelope—John Chamberlain, writing to a friend overseas, told him the word at St. Paul's was that she "takes great libertie or rather licence to traduce whom she please"[84]—but Denny went farther than that. He ended objecting to female literary careers, at least this kind: "leve idle bookes alone / For wise and worthyer women have writte none." In one of his letters, he told Wroth to stop writing "lascivious tales and amorous toyes" and tried to shame her with the memory of Mary Sidney, who had died the previous year: "followe the rare, and pious example of your vertuous and learned Aunt, who translated so many godly books and especially the holly psalmes of David." He hinted at worse things he could say:

> common oysters such as thine gape wide
>    And take in pearles or worse at every tide ....
> How easy wer't to pay thee with thine owne
>    Returning that which thou thy self hast throwne
> And write a thousand lies of thee at least
>    And by thy lines describe a drunken beast[85]

We do not know how intimidated Wroth was by this. She did write to the Duke of Buckingham that she was withdrawing her book from the market, but the letter

---

[83] The relevant texts are given by Josephine A. Roberts in *The Poems of Lady Mary Wroth*, pp. 32–5, 236–41.
[84] *The Letters of John Chamberlain*, ed. Norman Egbert McClure, 2: 427.
[85] On the surprisingly complex oyster insult, see Mary Ellen Lamb, *Gender and Authorship in the Sidney Circle*, pp. 157–9.

predates the exchange with Denny and there is no record of an actual recall. She does not seem to have abandoned lascivious tales and toys: a substantial continuation of *Urania* survives in manuscript.

Much depends on how concerned she was about what Denny might actually know, and we can guess what that might be. Two years after writing about *Urania* Chamberlain reported from his usual sources: "Here is a whispering [a favorite word of Chamberlain's] of a Lady that hath ben a widow above seven yeares, though she had lately two children at a birth. I must not name her though she be saide to be learned and in print."[86] This has to be Wroth. Widowed since 1614, she had by 1624 given birth to two illegitimate children, their existence kept quiet but not invisible and now well attested. The liaison that produced them may well have begun earlier, perhaps much earlier, since it was with someone Wroth had known all her life: her first cousin William Herbert, son of Mary Sidney, as of 1601 himself Earl of Pembroke—and, on a small scale, yet another literary Sidney, whose poems were published posthumously in 1660.[87] The attraction that brought them together would have had powerful doses of social and literary glamor in the mix; whatever else it may have been, it was also the Sidney family's love affair with itself, though that would not necessarily have made it welcome to the family that nurtured it. Marriage between first cousins was technically incestuous in Catholic countries, but not in England; marriage between Mary and William would not have been out of the question, though it would have meant passing up the opportunities presented by exogamy. The two cousins did each marry someone else in the fall of 1604, Mary going first by a little over a month. When her husband died ten years later, William's wife was still alive (and indeed outlived him), so the connection that resulted in their two children could only be illicit.

We may be getting a little closer to how things played out in a pair of poems by the two lovers that may voice a pointed exchange between them at a critical moment. Both eventually appeared in print, but they also survive in manuscript versions whose readings sharpen their relevance to how things were between Herbert and, as she was about to become, Wroth.[88] "Why with unkindest Swiftnes doest thou turne" is a man's aggrieved address to a woman who had surrendered her virginity to him on a lovingly remembered night in "thy pleasant garden and that Leavy mount" (8), and pledged that "from the time thou gav'st the spoiles to me / thou wouldst maintetaine a spotles chastity / and unprophain'd by any second hande" (17–19). Yet within three days, "thou new love, did'st in thy hart

---

[86] Chamberlain 2: 575.
[87] On this ineptly assembled volume, see Gary Waller, *The Sidney Family Romance*, pp. 159–88. Herbert has been one of the prime candidates for the young man in Shakespeare's sonnets; I am letting that pass, but the topic is still alive. See Penny McCarthy, "Autumn 1604"; Mary Ellen Lamb, "'Love is not love.'"
[88] The case has been made by Garth Bond, "Amphilanthus to Pamphilia," and Bell, *Pamphilia to Amphilanthus*, pp. 38–44 and 267–73. Bond provides transcriptions of the manuscript texts, which Bell reprints. See also Mary Ellen Lamb, "'Can you suspect a change in me?'"

devise / and gav'st the reliques of thy virgin head / upon the easiest prayers as could be said" (27–30). He ends spitefully dismissing her as damaged goods, sounding like Greville to Cælica:

> Thus doe I leave thee to the multitudes
> that on my leavings hastily intrudes
> Injoy thou many or rejoice in one
> I was before them, and before me none (73–6)

By the time the poem appeared in the 1660 edition of Herbert's poems, it was shorn of lines making the whole situation even more fraught: "the powers of the night may oft have seene us, / and heard the contracts, that have binn betweene us" (11–12). This is the language of spousals, private verbal commitments (the witnesses in this case poetically licensed) which could have legally enforceable consequences.[89] In "Sweete solitarines joy to those hartes," an aggrieved woman protests her unjustified rejection by a lover who has condemned her to a nightmare of lost happiness: "Forgetting pleasures late embracd with love / Linckt with a fayth the world cold nev'r move / Chaind in Affection I hopt shold nott change" (53–5). Part of her pain is receiving his rejection "in thys very Place / Of Earths best blessings" (23–4), which she is compelled to remember is the place where they had made love: "You tell mee that I first did her [here] knowe love / And mayden Passions in thys roome did move" (27–8). Before Wroth revised the poem for a male character in her romance to compose,[90] it bore the title "Penshurst Mount," one of the special places on the Sidney family estate, where a tree had been planted at Philip's birth.[91] Jonson gives it mythic elaboration in "To Penshurst" (10–18). This would also be the "Leavy mount" in Herbert's poem, and Ilona Bell has vigorously argued for connecting these and other dots to outline a cruelly intense sequence of events in 1604: after consummating her love for her cousin, Mary succumbed to family pressure to agree to a marriage with Robert Wroth, moving William to denounce her faithlessness and her in turn to reaffirm her devotion to him by refusing to consummate her marriage. (Except for the last part, this scenario closely resembles a fictional one imagined in the early seventeenth century for Philip Sidney and Penelope Rich; see Appendix A.) Bell makes some serious imaginative leaps assembling her theory, but it has an arresting consistency with what we do know—including the fact that the Wroths were childless until shortly before Robert's death ten years later.[92]

---

[89] See David Cressy, *Birth, Marriage, and Death*, pp. 267–81.

[90] *The First Part of the Countess of Montgomery's Urania* (= *Urania* I), ed. Josephine A. Roberts, pp. 133–4.

[91] See Marion Wynne-Davies, "'So Much Worth,'" pp. 86–91.

[92] Wroth may have suffered miscarriages before the birth of her son James in 1614; see Margaret P. Hannay, *Mary Sidney, Lady Wroth*, p. 146. On Wroth's involvement with Herbert in 1604, see pp. 98–109. Hannay's conclusions are guarded and do not include a scene as dramatic as what Bell proposes,

Part of the allure of Bell's proposal is the horribly realistic messiness of the situation it reveals and the emotions in play, with everyone seemingly doing what they feel they must (*tout le monde a ses raisons*). It seems appropriate that Wroth would be the one to round off what her uncle started with a sequence whose biographical reality compares with the one behind *Astrophil and Stella*; that itself turned out to be part of the family tradition. She had evidently studied and shared her uncle's exacting interest in poetic form. With one exception she observed his rule of excluding feminine rhymes from the sonnets in the published version of her sequence (like him, she employs them liberally in her "songs"); and she made more (and more telling) use than any other English sonneteer of the French rhyme scheme that intrigued her uncle, where the couplet comes in ll. 9–10, at the head of the sestet.[93] And as with him, this formal attentiveness confronted a tumultuous emotional experience about which we would like to know more but which we can still document more convincingly and compellingly than we can the real-life origins of other English sonnet sequences. In Wroth's case, the same experience informed *Urania*, where it is, along with that of many of the lives around her, refracted through an endlessly unfolding landscape of unevenly, often confusingly told stories; the result is irresistible and absorbing to anyone familiar with Wroth and her world, but hard to keep track of and not very readable over the long haul, without the narrative assurance of her uncle's *Arcadia*. It is different with *Pamphilia to Amphilanthus*.

The woman's name—"all loving" in Greek—conflates the names of the heroines of *Arcadia*, Pamela and Philoclea. The man's name, a character in *Urania* tells us, means "lover of two,"[94] and that has become the usual gloss. The Greek looks like a conflation of *amphi* and *philanthrôpos*, something like "fond of people in both directions," a euphemistic label for the aspect of his character most relevant to the love story: the unending indecisiveness of his devotion to Pamphilia, or for that matter to anyone. The action in *Urania* shows him by turns oblivious to her love for him, pledging his love for her once he learns of her feelings, falling for someone else, yet again declaring his love for Pamphilia, yet again straying,

---

but they are not inconsistent with it; she assumes Mary's feelings for William were already in play, and does not rule out their having been consummated with some presumption of marriage. See also p. 189 for more extreme speculation, which Hannay neither endorses nor dismisses, that Mary's involvement with William remained continuous up to the birth of their known children, and that her apparent son by Robert Wroth was William's as well, perhaps with her impotent or infertile husband's consent. This would have been unlikely and highly risky but, as Hannay points out, "lovers sometimes do take risks."

[93] The only feminine rhymes in the printed version of *Pamphilia and Amphilanthus* are at P10.9, 12 ("tarry" and "marry"). The manuscript version has a sonnet, M116, where all the rhymes are feminine, alternations of only two words ("anguish" and "languish"); the eccentricity of this itself signals serious self-consciousness about form. There are twenty sonnets with the French rhyme scheme in *Astrophil and Stella*, 40 in the printed *Pamphilia to Amphilanthus* (disallowing three ambiguous cases); on the latter, see Clare R. Kinney, "Turn and Counterturn." Robert Sidney is aware of the French rhyme scheme, but uses it only twice in his thirty-five sonnets.

[94] *Urania* I, p. 300.

in ways that become harder and harder to understand or predict. Things escalate in the unpublished continuation when he and Pamphilia go through a form of *verba de praesenti* marriage (this one with human witnesses) followed quickly, on a false report of Pamphilia's betrothal to the king of Tartary, by his marriage to the princess of Slavonia—a marriage which he then declines to consummate, though he subsequently responds to a summons from his new inlaws to repeat the ceremony and finish the business at hand. Whether he finally fulfills his conjugal obligations the narrator does not bother to tell us. Before the manuscript ends, an impressive young man known as Faire Designe turns up and is apparently Amphilanthus's son, though with no indication by whom. Pamphilia's devotion to Amphilanthus is by contrast steady, though often kept to herself or confided to friends and overt only when it intermittently seems to be welcome. His chronic faithlessness and her obdurate loyalty become topics of conversation within the narrative, and twice prompt interventions from concerned parties: Amphilanthus promises with combative assurance that he will change, has changed ("I fear onely that I shall sett you all such a patterne of Constancy, as the wourke will bee soe hard noe woeman can learne itt, pick itt out"); Pamphilia states emphatically that she never will change ("To leave him for being false, would shew my love was not for his sake, but mine owne, that because he loved me, I therefore loved him, but when hee leaves I can doe so to").[95] Eventually Wroth's narrative control or perhaps interest begins to fray. After Amphilanthus's marriage, Pamphilia does indeed marry the king of Tartary and gives birth to his son, but there is also another reconciliation with Amphilanthus, this one almost comically encumbered with a leg injury she has suffered while hunting; the reconciliation is apparently still in effect when the manuscript breaks off. Before it does so we are told that she has been widowed (and her son, like Wroth's son by Robert Wroth, has also died), though the husband subsequently appears to be still alive, sailing with her and Amphilanthus to Cyprus. Wroth seems undecided where she wants things to go. When a friend attempts to reassure Pamphilia of her lover's successful reformation—"when hee shall see you againe, bee assured hee will bee (nay, hee can bee noe other then) as truly ore att least as passionately loving you as ever"—the response is short and sharp: "What care I for passion? Lett mee have truthe." The friend backs off into

---

[95] *Urania* II, p. 28; I, p. 470. The heroism of female constancy in love runs through numerous storylines in *Urania*; see Lamb, *Gender and Authorship*, pp. 163–76. A few pages after Amphilanthus's startling claim to male superiority on this score, it shows up again in a poem known to be by Herbert ("Had I loved butt att that rate"), here identified as a poem by Amphilanthus about his love for another woman, and sung in his presence by Pamphilia (*Urania* II, pp. 30–1); see Lamb, "'Can you suspect,'" pp. 60–4. We may be getting a glimpse of lovers' quarrels in which Herbert insisted that Wroth's suspicions about his constancy constituted destructive inconstancy on her part. Men can of course get competitive in other directions as well; Wroth at one point has Pamphilia pick up a book whose subject comes uncomfortably close to home: "the subject was Love, and the story she then was reading, the affection of a Lady to a brave Gentleman, who equally loved, but being a man, it was necessary for him to exceede a woman in all things, so much as inconstancie was found fit for him to excell her in, hee left her for a new" (*Urania* I, p. 317). She throws the book down.

cynicism: "Amphilanthus is a man. Why, did you ever knowe any man, especially any brave man, continue constant to the end?"[96] Here and elsewhere, Clare Kinney argues, both character and author, "weary of those unending rehearsals of loss and reconciliation," confess, "flickeringly," a deepening disillusion with the interminable saga they have been sharing: "there may be another story here, one in which the 'truth' of the complaining, aging, lamed body insists on not being disturbed yet once more by the exigencies of passion."[97]

Little if any of the narrative incident that keeps the romance busy for 600,000 words is visible in the sonnet sequence. Wroth is unique in presenting her sequence in conjunction with a detailed third-person narrative containing the lovers in the poems. In his *Vita nuova* Dante embeds love poems in a first-person narrative that explains the circumstances in which the poems were composed, but what Wroth does is different. There are poems in *Urania* composed or recited or read by characters in the story, and twelve of them may be found in the manuscript version of the sequence, but none of the poems in the published sequence are in the romance. Wroth clearly worked on the poems and the narrative as part of the same project, but at some point made a distinction in her own mind between them; for the poems remaining in the sequence, none bear obvious signs that we are meant to place them somehow at particular moments in the story.[98] That story is itself more fantastical than the narratives implied by other Petrarchan sequences; its world is something like that of *Orlando furioso*, a fanciful, expansive version of seventeenth-century geopolitics (about halfway through the published part Amphilanthus is elected Holy Roman Emperor, and he later leads a successful military expedition against Persia) dotted with magical, semi-allegorical locales in which numerous characters periodically find themselves detained. We would have no way of deducing such a context from the sonnet sequence, and it makes less sense to think of the prose narrative as the objective reality around the sequence's lyric utterances than as the running confabulation or dreamwork of the speaker of those lyrics. Within the sequence, reality is almost exclusively the world of the speaker's intense feelings about a man she never names. We catch glimpses of a vaguely courtly-pastoral environment like that of *Astrophil and Stella*, but we do not get to see much of it; it is a world from which Pamphilia (like Astrophil in sonnet 30) is withdrawn even as she is part of it:

> When every one to pleasing pastime hies,
>    Some hunt, some hauke, some play while some delight
>    In sweet discourse, and musicke shewes joyes might:
> Yet I my thoughts doe farre above these prize. (P26.1–4)

---

[96] *Urania* II, p. 110.
[97] Clare R. Kinney, "'Beleeve this butt a fiction,'" p. 248.
[98] Lewalski, p. 252, does suggest that the poems of Pamphilia's that Amphilanthus reads at one point (*Urania* I, p. 320) are the fifty-five-poem first version of the sequence.

The setting usually implied is Petrarchan solitude, where society consists, as she puts it in one poem, of Night, Silence, and Grief: "from you three I know I cannot move, / Then let us live companions without strife" (P43.13–14). The most salient narrative event is the *innamoramento* presented metaphorically in the first poem:

> In sleepe, a Chariot drawne by wing'd Desire,
>   I saw; where sate bright *Venus* Queene of Love,
>   And at her feete her Sonne, still adding Fire
>   To burning hearts, which she did hold above,
> But one heart flaming more then all the rest,
>   The Goddesse held, and put it to my breast,
>   Deare Sonne now shut, said she, thus must we winne. (P1.5–11)

This action remembers the first sonnet in Dante's *Vita nuova* and Petrarch's memory of it in his *canzone delle metamorfosi* (*Canz.* 23.67–74), though here the speaker is the recipient rather than the donor of the alien heart. The initiation is decisive; in the manuscript there are brief memories of what life was like before (M63, M113), but they vanish in the printed text.

The overwhelming emotion for Pamphilia since then, the subject of most of the poems, is the torment of being in love, primarily "paines which absence makes me now indure" (P23.12). As she gives voice to those pains many of the expressive resources of Petrarchism slip into place: "In coldest hopes I freeze, yet burne, ay me" (P14.5). But we can also sense that the context is a complementary opposite to that of the classic male Petrarchan lover: its anguish is not that of unsuccessful courtship, but of infidelity and desertion. That is the case with Gaspara Stampa, the most important female Petrarchist of sixteenth-century Italy; her sequence sets out a classically female story of seduction and abandonment as she composes sonnet after sonnet to the upper-class lover who has left and, she gradually understands, will never be heard from again. There is no reason to think that Wroth would have known Stampa's poems, but the place they both find in the tradition is already waiting: what would it be like if the ardent male lover were finally to have his way? The behavior not only of the fictional Amphilanthus but also of the historical William Herbert provides similar answers. About the time that he became Earl of Pembroke in 1601 (Wroth was fourteen), Herbert impregnated and refused to marry Mary Fitton, a young woman at court, and was briefly imprisoned. We have less detail on subsequent affairs (aside from the one with his cousin), but they garnered him a posthumous reputation as "immoderately given up" to women (to whom "he sacrificed himself, his precious time, and much of his fortune").[99] The last of these connections would have been with Christian Cavendish, the widowed Countess of Devonshire, who was with him when he died and effectively became

---

[99] Edward Hyde, Earl of Clarendon, *The History of the Rebellion and Civil Wars in England* 1: 45–6.

his literary executor—a role which under other circumstances might have been Wroth's.[100] Pamphilia's sonnet sequence is even more elusive than most examples of the *genre* about narrative specifics, but a broad consistency with what happens in her romance and her life is still evident. A rival may make a fleeting appearance in one poem (P56). The closest we come to an encounter with Amphilanthus is a pained expectation of his departure:

> Pray doe not use these wordes, I must be gone;
> Alasse doe not foretell mine ills to come:
> Let not my care be to my joyes a Tombe;
> But rather finde my losse with losse alone. (P71.1–4)

These are the only words the man speaks in the sequence, and we have them only in the woman's anticipation of what he is about to say. The tense and weary tone suggests that she speaks from experience, remembering what he has said before, possibly more than once, and what it has meant.

A poem about three-quarters of the way through the manuscript version of the sequence is clearly an *aubade*—"The birds doe sing, day doth apeere / arise, arise my only deere" (M77.1–2)—an indication that Pamphilia and Amphilanthus have spent the night together:

> Then with those eyes inrich thy love
> from whose deere beams my joye doth move
> shine with delight on my sad hart,
> and grace the prize wun by theyr dart. (13–16)

That is how it was in real life, though we cannot be sure of the timing; *Urania* is evasive.[101] The *aubade* is not in the printed version of the sequence; Bell argues that its removal, along with other less drastic changes, is deliberate bowdlerization on Wroth's part, meant to obscure any suggestion of sexual intimacy between the lovers and turn the manuscript text "into a work suitable for public consumption."[102] The manuscript version, in other words, is not a work in progress but the "unexpurgated" text, and hence the one to read. The contrast between the two versions is not I think as great as Bell makes it sound, and not enough to dislodge the printed version's authority as the author's last known intentions. The exclusion of the *aubade* does not remove the consummation from the story, only from the present tense of the sequence's timeline; references throughout look back to a state

---

[100] Hannay, *Mary Sidney*, pp. 260–2.
[101] The obvious time for Pamphilia and Amphilanthus to consummate their love would be after their spousal ceremony in the manuscript continuation. There are two missing pages at that point; see *Urania* II, pp. xxv–xxvii, 60.
[102] Bell, *Pamphilia to Amphilanthus*, p. 10. The publication caused scandal anyway, though not as far as we know because of the sonnet sequence.

of happiness and fulfillment the speaker wants to recapture or hold onto, at least in memory. The first comes very early:

> when as a memory to good
> Molested me, which still as witnes stood,
> Of those best dayes, in former time I knew:
> Late gone as wonders past (P4.9–12)

This from the one poem that Wroth added to the sequence in the printed version. Sometimes the memory is hopeful—"stay thy swiftnes cruell Time, / And let me once more blessed clime / to joy, that I may praise thee" (P35.19–21)—but more often not: "hope is past to win you back againe, / That treasure which being lost breeds all your paine" (P54.2–3).[103] In the end Pamphilia's only comfort is eloquent sorrow:

> I that of all most crost,
> Having, and that had have lost,
> May with reason thus complaine,
> Since love breeds love, and Loves paine. (59.1–4)

This is her kinship with Stampa within the gender options of Petrarchism and the life of privilege in early modern Europe: "her desire ... is not crying out for the food it never had ... but speaks to a hunger once satisfied and now unassuaged."[104]

Where does Pamphilia end up? The first fifty-five poems constitute a likely first version of the sequence.[105] The unit has a strict formal structure: runs of six sonnets followed by a song, a module repeated seven times. The last module lacks a concluding song; instead, both manuscript and print have the signature "Pamphilia," and the manuscript has a blank page. M4 is replaced by an entirely new sonnet in print (quoted previously), and a handful of sonnets from later in the manuscript displace others in earlier positions, but otherwise differences between the manuscript and the printed text are minor. Poem 55 in both versions offers what could stand as a conclusion, a fiery resolution to go on loving at any cost:

> Mine eyes can scarce sustaine the flames, my heart
> Doth trust in them my passions to impart,
> And languishingly strive to shew my love.

---

[103] The second-person pronouns bleed into each other without actually being confusing; "you" in l. 2 would be Amphilanthus and in l. 3 Pamphilia. Her surge of hope runs the two identities together. The poem in l. 1 officially addresses "mine eyes."

[104] Kinney, "Mary Wroth's Guilty 'secrett art,'" p. 72.

[105] On partitioning the sequence and the various climaxes that result, see Gavin Alexander, "Constant Works"; Heather Dubrow, "'And Thus Leave Off,'"; Margaret P. Hannay, "The 'Ending End' of Lady Wroth's Manuscript of Poems."

> My breath not able is to breath least part
>   Of that increasing fuell of my smart;
> Yet love I will, till I but ashes prove. (P55.9–14)

A pun in the last line (already used in M4) announces, to those in the know, the name of the poet's real-life love. At the end of the less clearly structured second half of the sequence, the manuscript also concludes with fire, but not as sacrificial self-immolation:

> My state I see, and you your ends have gain'd
>   I'me lost, since you have mee obtain'd,
> Yett though I can nott please your first desire
>   I yett may joye in scorners fire;
> As Salimanders in the fire doe live
>   soe shall love flames my living give,
> And though against your minde I bee, and move
>   forsaken creatures feede on love;
> Doe you proceed, you one day may confess
>   you wrong'd my care, when I care less. (M117.25–34)

Pamphilia's burning love will not destroy her but strengthen her, possibly preserve her for a time when her lover will feel more pain than she does. The salamander, sturdier in its relation to fire than the more spectacular phoenix, is a figure to which Stampa was drawn (*Rime* 206.2), though Wroth likely came across it in Petrarch (*Canz.* 207.41; also Lodge, *Phillis* 38.12). Stampa avails herself of the metaphor as she moves on to an equally passionate new love. This never seems an option for either Pamphilia or Wroth, but M117 does bring a new pleasure, a hint of vindictiveness that is rare but obviously gratifying. Wroth keeps the poem, but not in the sequence; in *Urania* a woman whom Amphilanthus has left in order to return to Pamphilia inscribes it in a tree (with "minde" in l. 31 changed to "will") and experiences "great spleene against him, and affection to her selfe for her bravenesse" as she rereads it.[106] To conclude the print sequence Wroth uses a sonnet already in the manuscript sequence (M110), where it is followed by the same "Pamphilia" signature as M55. The poem could already have been envisioned as a possible ending. All seven poems after it in the manuscript are eliminated or moved to *Urania* in the 1621 publication. Pamphilia's sole address to her Muse, it sounds like a valedictory poem—"My Muse now happy lay thy selfe to rest" (P103.1)—and ends things on an unexpectedly quiet note:

> Leave the discourse of *Venus*, and her sonne
>   To young beginners, and their braines inspire

---

[106] *Urania* I, pp. 326–7.

172  PETRARCHAN LOVE AND THE ENGLISH RENAISSANCE

> With storyes of great Love, and from that fire,
> Get heat to write the fortunes they have wonne.
> And thus leave off; what's past shewes you can love,
> Now let your Constancy your Honor prove. (9–14)

The fire now burning—both to love and to write of love—is for others, not her.[107] This might seem an arbitrary curtailment of the turbulence we have been reading, except that the final line settles on what had been one of the major themes all along.

The approach to this conclusion runs through the "Crowne of Sonnets dedicated to *Love*," a 14-sonnet *corona* (linked poems where the last line of the last is the first line of the first) placed roughly where Daniel's *catena* comes in *Delia*, a bit before the end. It is preceded by two songs dismissively mocking Cupid for reasons which the sequence has made quite clear:

> Feathers are as firme in staying,
> Wolves no fiercer in their praying.
> As a childe then leave him crying,
> Nor seeke him so giv'n to flying. (P74.17–20)

Then comes an abrupt palinode—

> O pardon *Cupid*, I confesse my fault,
> Then mercy grant me in so just a kinde:
> For treason never lodged in my minde
> Against thy might, so much as in a thought. (P76.1–4)

—and the offer of a propitiatory gift:

> a Crowne unto thy endlesse praise,
> Which shall thy glory and thy greatnesse raise,
> More than these poore things could thy honor spight. (12–14)

The *corona* follows, beginning in bewilderment and a fusillade of anxious choices:

> In this strange Labyrinth how shall I turne,
> Wayes are on all sides, while the way I misse:
> If to the right hand, there in love I burne,
> Let mee goe forward, therein danger is.

---

[107] "It is hard to imagine a much more emphatic conclusion, especially since Pamphilia *does* stop writing: the second part of *Urania* includes no poems attributed to her"; Hannay, "The 'Ending End,'" p. 16.

> If to the left, suspition hinders blisse:
> Let mee turne back, shame cryes I ought returne ... (P77.1–6)

Various potential narratives are intimated, though the reader must fill in the details ad lib. The conclusion is not even to try to choose—Theseus did not find the way through his labyrinth by his own cleverness—but to trust to the dictates of a greater power: "that which most my troubled sense doth move, / Is to leave all and take the threed of Love" (13–14).

The poems that follow accordingly offer Wroth's *summa* of love's authority and power.[108] Here she makes the approach to neo-Platonic theory quoted earlier:

> When chaste thoughts guide us, then our minds are bent
> To take that good which ills from us remove:
> Light of true love brings fruite which none repent;
> But constant Lovers seeke and wish to prove. (P78.5–8)

This the first appearance of "chaste" in the print version of the sequence. The shepherdess in a pastoral dialogue in the manuscript had said, "none unto so chaste a minde / should ever bee unjust" (M65.27–8), but Wroth moved that poem to *Urania*. In the *corona* the word is suddenly important, linked with a term that is already key, "constant." Pamphilia insisted on the latter virtue from the start: the flames in her breast "burne in truest smart, / Exciling thoughts, that touch Inconstancy, / Or those which waste not in the constant Art" (P3.6–8). In the *corona* constancy remains central, but the praise of love acquires something new, a longing for a more intense conviction of purity:

> Please him, and serve him, glory in his might
> And firme hee'le be, as Innocency white,
> Cleere as th'ayre, warme as Sun's beames, as day light
> Just as Truth, constant as Fate, joyd to requite. (P79.9–12)

The unspecified "you" being addressed—indifferently the reader, the poet, and her beloved—is enjoined to a strenuous effort of transcendence in this direction:

> faithfull and unfaigned heate aspire
> Which sinne abollisheth, and doth impart
> Salves to all feare, with vertues which inspire
> Soules with divine love; which shewes his chast Art. (P81.5–8)

---

[108] What follows is richly indebted to Kinney's discussions in "Mary Wroth's Guilty 'secrett art,'" pp. 76–81; "Turn and Counterturn," pp. 94–8; and "Escaping the Void," pp. 30–4.

This union of constancy and chastity unfolds a vision of blessed, transformative mutuality which is one of Wroth's most remarkable passages:

> To joyne two hearts as in one frame to moove
> Two bodies, but one soule to rule the minde
> Eyes which must care to one deare Object binde,
> Eares to each others speach as if above
> All else, they sweete, and learned were; this kind
> Content of Lovers witnesseth true love.
> It doth inrich the wits, and make you see
> That in your selfe which you knew not before,
> Forcesing you to admire such gifts should be
> Hid from your knowledge, yet in you the store. (P82.3–12)

If this is neo-Platonism, it is neo-Platonism like that of Donne's "Extasie," including rather than transcending the beloved, embracing rather than rejecting the body. Such love is chaste not in its asceticism but in its unforced constancy, a fidelity on both sides on which there is no need to insist. When we have learned Love's lesson, we watch not one another out of fear.

The formal integrity of the *corona* is so strong that some treat it as a separate composition, apart from *Pamphilia to Amphilanthus*. Placed as it has come down to us, it is the sequence's *scène à faire*, the one decisive thing that *happens* in this largely static or cyclical situation. It sets out Pamphilia's vision of, not the love which is hers, but the love to which she aspires, and enacts her attempt to achieve it. In the course of the *corona* that attempt dissipates before our eyes. The failure is predicted formally. A fourteen-sonnet sequence is what Kinney calls a "hypersonnet," with a *volta* expected after the eighth sonnet; in that sonnet dangers begin to be named even as the poet continues to affirm her vision:

> Made of Vertue, joyn'd by Truth, blowne by Desires,
> Strengthned by Worth, renew'd by carefulnesse,
> Flaming in never-changing thoughts: bryers
> Of Jealousie shall here misse welcomnesse. (P84.5–8)

The word "jealousy"—watching one another out of fear—changes the poem's weather: "the very act of banishing the emotion threatens to reinscribe it."[109] Jealousy has been a sinister presence from early on:

---

[109] "Turn and Counterturn," p. 95. Kuin calls the attention to jealousy in Wroth's sequence "perhaps its most original feature" ("More I Still Undoe," p. 155); Kinney's exploration of it is the most searching so far.

> In night when darknesse doth forbid all light;
> Yet see I griefe apparant to the show,
> Follow'd by jealousie, whose fond tricks flow,
> And on unconstant waves of doubt alight. (P20.5–8)

The word's reference is abstract and vague—"untethered" is Bell's term[110]—and at times actively confusing. Indeed, as Kinney points out, some of Wroth's "most subversive and significant syntactic ambiguity ... is to be found at the very moments when the lyric speaker vigorously attempts to purge the insinuations of jealousy from her poetry."[111] It is a touchy subject, prompting evasion. Sometimes it sounds as if Pamphilia might mean her lover's suspicions about her own fidelity or the invidious curiosity of third parties. The reference is most candid in a mythological conceit that in the printed version of the sequence Wroth places shortly after the *corona*, when "*Juno* still jealous of her husband *Jove*" comes down to earth to track him and his latest paramour. She meets Pamphilia, who gives her a restrained but tart reply: "I saw him not (said I) although heere are / Many, in whose hearts, Love hath made like warre" (P97.1, 13–14).

Amphilanthus's infidelity is nowhere specifically indicated, but the next sonnet names its source, a menacing force that can dress up as love: "If Lust be counted Love, 'tis falsely nam'd, / By wickednesse, a fairer glosse to set / Upon that Vice, which else makes men asham'd" (P85.9–11). In some eccentric mythography, Pamphilia declares that her service in love is not to Venus, whose lasciviousness is all too well known, but to her son, "where sinne / Never did dwell, or rest one minutes space" (5–6). Cupid has here fully evolved from the more familiar "wanton Childe" (P64.5) of English Renaissance love poetry into "an honored and powerful King ruling a court of noble Love"[112]—but because of his parentage he can still be corrupted by the sensual pleasures that allured many male sonneteers: "What faults he hath in her did still beginne, / And from her breast he suck'd his fleeting pace" (P85.7–8). The silent logic here is that the ideal Pamphilia wishes to worship (not too strong a term; gods are involved) is male, but one she is forced to acknowledge is susceptible to female contamination. That is as close as she can come to soiling her image of her lover, but dark clouds keep gathering over the effort that until the eighth sonnet had seemed so assured: "wantonnesse, and all those errors shun, / Which wrongers be, Impostures, and alone / Maintainers of all follies ill begunne" (P86.10–12). Against these perversions she summons her resolve to pledge devotion to the true god of love; doing so involves returning to the first-person singular for the first time since the opening sonnet of the *corona*,

---

[110] Bell, "'A too curious secrecie,'" p. 40.
[111] "Mary Wroth's Guilty 'secrett art,'" p. 73.
[112] Lewalski, p. 260.

only to come up against the limits of its power and authority.[113] What she most wants to offer has all along not been hers to pledge:

> To thee then, Lord commander of all hearts,
>   Ruler of our affections, kinde, and just,
>   Great King of Love, my soule from faigned smarts,
>   Or thought of change, I offer to your trust,
> This Crowne, my selfe, and all that I have more,
> Except my heart, which you bestow'd before. (P89.9–14)

Kinney compares this to the punchline of *Astrophil and Stella* 71 ("But ah, Desire still cries, give me some food.").[114] If this means that the Great King of Love already possessed her heart, the exception would be of no consequence, but Pamphilia says he took it from her only to give it to someone else. Even that might pass for commonplace love-talk if it were not for what cannot quite be said: Amphilanthus does not embody the ideal she needs him to.[115] But that is so, and the vision of the *corona* slips away: her heart is not in it. She keeps trying, but threats crowd in:

> The tribute which my heart doth truely pay,
>   Is faith untouch'd, pure thoughts discharge the score
>   Of debts for me, where Constancy beares sway,
>   And rules as Lord, unharmd by Envies sore.
> Yet other mischeifes faile not to attend,
>   As enemies to you, my foes must be.
>   Curst Jealousie doth all her forces bend
>   To my undoing, thus my harmes I see.
> So though in Love I fervently doe burne,
> In this strange Labyrinth how shall I turne? (P90.5–14)

Pamphilia is literally back where she was at the beginning, at a loss for what choice to make in the labyrinth she has been unable to transcend. As a poet Wroth would of course have seen that from the start: the form she chose requires it.

Kinney tellingly contrasts the *corona* with "Lindamira's Complaint," a mini-sequence in the voice of a character we never meet. Pamphilia gives her history in *Urania*, "faigning it to be written in a French story," and follows it with seven sonnets which Pamphilia has herself composed from the imaginary prose original, "because I lik'd it, or rather found her estate so neere agree with mine"; the person

---

[113] A subtly announced moment first noted, I think, by Kim Walker, *Women Writers of the English Renaissance*, p. 188.

[114] "Mary Wroth's Guilty 'secrett art,'" p. 81.

[115] As a character in *Urania*, Pamphilia is more forthright: "rather then my lips shall give the least way to discover any fault in him, I will conceale all though they breake my heart" (I, p. 462). In the sonnet sequence, the self-censorship is internal as well as external.

with whom Pamphilia shares it finds it "some thing more exactly related than a fixion" but is too discreet to inquire further.[116] The married Lindamira has been abandoned by her lover after fourteen years: "I onely for twise seaven yeares love shall gaine / Change, worse then absence, or death's cruelst paine" (2.12–13). Her verse response is compact and fierce, "a complaint with attitude."[117] The sonnets run through the parallels with Pamphilia's case with efficiency and anger more clear-eyed both about her lover's failings and her own capacity for denial than anything Pamphilia writes on her own behalf:

> Yet Hope tis true, thy faults did faire appeare
>   And therefore loth to thinke thou counseldst me
>   Or wilfully thy errors would not see
>   But catch at Sunne moates which I held most deare
> Till now alas with true felt losse I know,
>   Thy selfe a Bubble each faire face can blow. (5.9–14)

(You are nothing, lover, until the next pretty face tells you you are everything.) "Re-reading these sonnets after encountering *Pamphilia to Amphilanthus*, one finds a clarification before the fact, a proleptic demystificatory gloss, of the longer sequence's troubled poems."[118] The ventriloquized Lindamira ends with an astonishing, defiant embrace of the emotion that in the *corona* Pamphilia most fears and wishes to banish: "If this be jealousie, then doe I yeeld, / And doe confesse I thus goe arm'd to field, / For by such Jealousie my love is led" (7.1–14). This would be one of the affirmative choices not made at the beginning of the *corona*, a possible if destructive route out of the labyrinth, with serious damage to the masonry. Within the expansive landscape of *Urania* Pamphilia can imagine such a path and even imagine taking it. The inner world of her own sonnet sequence, however, has its own laws, and her *corona* ends with a diminished thing, not Lindamira's militant jealousy but the emotionally depleted constancy affirmed in Pamphilia's last poem, saluting the promise of "young beginners" but offering her no inspiration or ambition for further love or even poetry.

---

[116] *Urania* I, pp. 499, 502, 505; the sonnets themselves are on pp. 502–5.
[117] "Turn and Counterturn," p. 100.
[118] "Turn and Counterturn," p. 98.

# 5
# Courtiers

The literary ancestry of Madonna Laura, as she is often called in the Renaissance, runs back to the lady of the troubadours. One of their favored names for her, *midons*, enfolds an androgynous symbolic transaction, applying a term of unambiguously masculine power and prestige (*dons* = *dominus* rather than *domina*) to an unambiguously female object. The simplest English translation, "my lord," elides the gender paradox, which would remain visible in the Latin *mea dominus*.[1] The lover takes for granted that his relation to his lady is one of vassal to master. That metaphorical transfer, from the political and social reality of the twelfth- and thirteenth-century courts of southern France to the secretive arena of love poetry, is one of the great innovations that Occitan poetry brings to European literature—heterosexual desire in classical antiquity never has this kind of prestige—and long outlives its abstraction from that context in the hyperbolic subservience, even abasement, of a man before a lordly woman. Troubadour lyrics sometimes imply or are said to imply narratives in which the woman's power has its literal dimension within the world of the court—she is the potentially adulterous wife of the lover's lord, with her own patronage to bestow or withhold—but scholars now distrust such narratives, which are less common than they have been made to sound. In later poetry, where the poets themselves become less exclusively aristocratic, the transferred sense of the woman's power becomes more and more prominent, and her political and social authority fades. Petrarch's Laura may or may not have been the wife of a count; the only glimpse we get of her public standing is when she is ceremonially kissed by that visiting dignitary in *Canzoniere* 238.

Still, the political potential in *midons* remains, coming into play when opportunity presents itself. In the late 1460s, the young Lorenzo de' Medici, seeking to enhance his never quite official authority as Florence's *signore*, began the spectacular cultural program that has become part of the legend of the Renaissance as a period, a nexus of art, poetry, and public festival celebrating the city's new status as the center of Italian, indeed European culture. Lorenzo himself wrote Petrarchan sonnets; two colorful public *giostre*, in 1469 and 1475, were won respectively by Lorenzo and his brother Giuliano; both occasions were commemorated in poems which mythologized them as expressions of love by the two young men for two

---

[1] See Glynnis M. Cropp, *Le Vocabulaire courtois des troubadours*, pp. 29–37. *Mea dux* occurs in the *Carmina burana*; see Peter Dronke, *Medieval Latin and the Rise of the European Love-Lyric*, 2nd ed., pp. 304–6.

young Florentine women. Botticelli's *Primavera* is part of this; the figure of Flora in that painting probably depicts Giuliano's beloved.[2] The poets writing on the two jousts, Luigi Pulci and Angelo Poliziano, both address Lorenzo as the master of these ceremonies, and both poeticize his name into Lauro. The great pun at the heart of Petrarch's *Canzoniere*, in other words, presides; the name of the lord of Florence differs in a single vowel from that of Petrarch's beloved. With apocopation, even that difference evaporates:

> Et tu, ben nato Laur, sotto il cui velo
> Fiorenza lieta in pace si riposa,
> né teme i venti o 'l minacciar del celo
> o Giove irato in vista piú crucciosa,
> accogli all'ombra del tuo santo stelo
> la voce umil, tremante e paurosa;
> o causa, o fin di tutte le mie voglie,
> che sol vivon d'odor delle tuo foglie.
>
> (Poliziano, *Stanze per la giostra de Giuliano de' Medici* 1.4)

And you, well-born Laurel, under whose shelter happy Florence rests in peace, fearing neither winds nor threats of heaven, nor irate Jove in his angriest countenance: receive my humble voice, trembling and fearful, under the shade of your sacred trunk; o cause, o goal of all my desires, which draw life only from the fragrance of your leaves.[3]

Worldly authority with its blessings is now an aesthetic authority, nurtured by the fame of Petrarch's beautifully articulated love for Laura. In Lorenzo's Florence, that allure is cultivated, at least for a time, as political power.[4]

When Pulci hails Lorenzo as "*il Läur mio, sempre costante*" (*La giostra di Lorenzo de' Medici* 11.1 [my Laurel, ever constant]), he inadvertently, uncannily anticipates the period's most dramatic superimposition of Petrarchan love and worldly politics, when a strong-willed, unmarried, and ultimately unattainable woman ascends the throne of England to rule for over 40 years, and takes as a defiantly ungirlish motto a Latin equivalent of the phrase Pulci uses of Lorenzo: *semper eadem*, always the same. Elizabeth's successful reign is the unpredictable event which gives English Petrarchism its special claim to eminence. Nowhere else is a woman invested with this kind of regal power over a court of contentious men maneuvering for her favor, and she rose to the occasion with a strategic system of

---

[2] See Charles Dempsey, *The Portrayal of Love*.
[3] Text and translation are from *The Stanze of Angelo Poliziano*, trans. David Quint.
[4] Lorenzo had been breathing this air since he was a boy. At the age of eleven, riding a white horse, he led a company of young aristocrats as part of a public procession modeled on the Triumph of Love in Petrarch's *Trionfi*; see Konrad Eisenbichler, "Political Posturing in Some 'Triumphs of Love,'" pp. 370–4.

flirtation which was a major feature of her reign; it is impossible to write its history without including somehow the endlessly shifting choreography of her relations to a series of male favorites. This may have been a sideshow to the real politics of what was unfolding—that may have been the point—but it nevertheless (or accordingly) consumed an immense amount of energy and attention. Francis Bacon included it, with admiration, in his eulogy of Elizabeth as one of her *arcana imperii*—"she suffered her self to be courted and wooed, and refused not to be seen upon the scene of Love, even beyond the condition of her Age"—adding that "this, if it be gently construed, wanted not also a share in admiration .... But if it be severely scanned, then greater is the wonder."[5] Literary critics since the 1980s have been intensely interested in the result, a tiltyard of political erotics where "young, ambitious, and thwarted courtiers acted out a fantasy of political demand, rebellion, and submission."[6] This environment was the immediate or proximate context of much of what becomes known as Elizabethan literature, and there has been a sustained and sophisticated reinterpretation of that literature with this in mind. In some places the reinterpretation is straightforward:

> When we find such terms as "fortune," "suitor," "hope," "envy," "favor," "despair" and "love" in both letters of clientage and in the poetry coined for the queen as well as that circulated among members of a court coterie, then, it can be nothing else but a language for negotiating with a patron for the client's position. Neither allegorical nor secretly encoded, this is quite simply a political language.[7]

There are Elizabethan poems for which to say this is simply to identify their manifest content. Leonard Tennenhouse, whom I am quoting, immediately gestures at taking things further: "It is from such a political perspective, I would argue, that we should understand Shakespeare's sonnets." The most notable recipient of such understanding has actually been *Astrophil and Stella*; Sidney identified Stella as Penelope Rich, but the sequence has proved responsive to readings by which its real audience is the Queen: "That it was not addressed to the queen, in the midst of a prevailing fashion for courtly compliment of her, may have been its most pointed aggression against her central authority. [Sidney] would not play politics by her rules but would turn her Petrarchan forms to his own purposes."[8] Such arguments lean heavily on "may have been," but there is indeed good evidence that for most of his adult life Sidney's Queen was very much on his mind, enough to give credibility to political readings of his sequence.

The roster of poems openly about or addressed to Queen Elizabeth is not itself an impressive one. An anecdote preserved by her antic godson John Harington

---

[5] Bacon, *The Felicity of Queen Elizabeth*, p. 39.
[6] Louis Adrian Montrose, "Shaping Fantasies," p. 84.
[7] Leonard Tennenhouse, *Power on Display*, p. 33.
[8] Maureen Quilligan, "Sidney and His Queen," p. 188.

offers a possible glimpse of the genesis of one of them. At a dinner in 1594 where the Queen "tastede my wifes comfits, and did moche praise her cunninge in the makinge," she "stoode up and bade me reache forthe my arme to reste her thereon," and Harington quickly made a note to himself: "Oh, what swete burden to my nexte songe.—Petrarcke shall eke out good matter for this businesse."[9] We have no reason to think or wish the poem was ever actually written (it might still turn up), but the anecdote catches the literary atmosphere at court at the height of the sonnet craze, when it did not take much to produce a Petrarchan sonnet, or at least the idea for one. Writing before the craze, Dyer and the Earl of Oxford produced poems in other forms in which they struck dramatic Petrarchan postures, and scholars know or suspect some of them to concern Elizabeth. One by Dyer was publicly performed before her as part of the entertainment at Woodstock in 1575:

> I am most sure that I shall not attaine
> The onely good wherein my joy doth lye.
> I have no power my passions to refraine,
> But wayle the want which nought else may supply.
> 
> (Dyer 1.13–16)[10]

The voice came from an oaktree. In the printed text ten years later, the speaker's name is not given but implied to be common knowledge: "assuredlie I see greate invention therein, and yet no more then the just fame of the deviser doth both deserve and carrie."[11] A personal appeal concerning Dyer's eroded standing at court may well be involved.[12] Several of the *Vannetyes and Toyes* that Arthur Gorges collected, probably from the 1580s, are adaptations of French sonnets by DuBellay and Desportes for English courtly occasions, three of them explicitly praising the Queen in regal but witty terms. "To the greate Macedon my fayre Queene I compare / whose manly harte by valure so Conquerd nations" begins one, to end with a Petrarchan twist:

> But gryefe alas to tell amydste this Pompe and pryme;
> Quaylde were his Conquestes throughe mortall Destenye
> As hir bewtyfull lymmes triumphant over tyme
> Are banyshte sweete delights throughe Devyne chastytie
> 
> (Gorges 61.1–2, 13–16)[13]

---

[9] Harington, *Nugae Antiquae* 2: 210–11. It is possible that the tasting of the comfits and the taking of the arm occurred on separate occasions, but their documentation has come down to us together.
[10] May, *Elizabethan Courtier Poets*, p. 289.
[11] *The Queenes Majesties Entertainement at Woodstock*, sig. C2ᵛ.
[12] See Ralph M. Sargent, *The Life and Lyrics of Sir Edward Dyer*, pp. 30–4; Duncan-Jones, *Sir Philip Sidney*, pp. 101–2.
[13] Quotations and references for Gorges are from *The Poems of Sir Arthur Gorges*, ed. Helen Estabrook Sandison. Other French adaptations identified as being about the Queen are 47 and 49;

A fourth imitation from the French may also concern the Queen, and if so is notably more intimate in occasion and tone than the others: "To my unspotted fayth I may compare / the daynty gartyer which yow gave to mee" (82.1–2). It was not unusual for Elizabeth to award small tokens of this sort to her favorites, and the "eglantynes and lyllyes" (7) on the garter are in her style.[14] The ground for making such calls, though, is treacherous. A sonnet of Constable's begins as if it might also be addressed to the Queen with a conceit similar to one Gorges develops:

> Sweete Soveraigne sith so many mynds remayne
> Obedient subjects at thy beautyes call
> So many thoughts bound in thy hayre as thrall
> So many hearts dye with one lookes disdayne

But the destination of its argument is not divine chastity:

> To fight thow needst no weapons but thyne eyes
> Thy hayre hath gold enough to pay thy men
> And for theyre foode thy beautie will suffice
> For men and armoure (Ladie) care have none
> For one will soonest yeeld unto thee then
> When he shall meet thee naked and alone[15]

The misdirection may be intentional, and the joke on us.

The first of Elizabeth's favorites, the Earl of Leicester, wrote as far as we know no poems to her.[16] For his successors, however, the confluence of personal and political yielded poetry of some substance and urgency. The tempestuous career of the last and most dangerous of them, Robert Devereux, the second Earl of Essex (Penelope Rich's brother, remember, and also the husband of Philip Sidney's widow), sparked from him about a dozen poems of unusual single-mindedness: "functional, autobiographical, and directed primarily to the Queen,"[17] all obviously moves in that career, some of them datable to specific moments of crisis. Their manner, as Steven May says, "was well adapted to his utilitarian purpose. Whatever the degree of his reading in and admiration for the finest poetry of his age,

---

see also 109, "Verses sung to Queene *Elizabeth* by a Mairmead as shee past upon the Thames to Sir Arthur Gorges house at Chelsey."

[14] May, *Elizabethan Courtier Poets*, pp. 112–13.

[15] A sonnet added in the 1594 edition (Grundy, *Poems of Henry Constable*, p. 126).

[16] Leicester did (probably) anticipate his successors in composing poetry while imprisoned in the Tower, though this would have been ca. 1554; see no. 290 (a translation of Psalm 94) in Hughey 1: 340–1. The poem has nothing in particular to do with Elizabeth, but as it happens she was also a prisoner during some of his time there.

[17] May, "The Poems of Edward DeVere ... and of Robert Devereux," p. 21; quotations that follow are on the same page. I cite Essex's poems from this edition, the text of which is also available in *Elizabethan Courtier Poets*, pp. 250–69.

scarcely a trickle of the new style [of poets such as Sidney and Spenser] filtered into his own writing." Essex's three sonnets might be describable in a very general sense as poems of Petrarchan praise—

> Never did Atlas such a burthen beare
> As shee, in holding up the world opprest,
> Supplying with her vertue every where
> Weaknes of friends, errors of Servants best. (3.5–8)

—and complaint:

> I loved her whom all the world admird,
> I was refused of her that can love none;
> And my vaine hopes which far to hie aspird
> Are dead and buried, and for ever gone. (5.5–8)

But any engagement with the tradition is slight. The one poem clearly by Essex to attain a measure of fame outside the narrow court circles within which and of which he wrote is his last and longest, a 384-line poem of anxious repentance for a wide range of sins before "the Judge.... At whose sterne lookes all creatures are afraide" (11.77–8):

> O could mine eies send trickling teares amaine,
> Never to cease till my eternall night,
> Till this eye-flood his mercy might obtaine,
> Whome my defaults have banisht from his sight;
> Then could I blesse my happy time of crying,
> But ah, too soone my barren springs are drying. (85–90)

Elizabeth is never referred to, though there is a feint early on—"thou faire Queene of mercy and of pittye" (25)—which immediately takes an unexpected turn: "Whose wombe did once the World's Creator carry" (26). Doing so gives the poem a distant affinity with *Vergine bella*, the concluding poem in Petrarch's *Canzoniere*, where the Virgin Mary replaces Laura in the poet's worship, but there is no need to think that this precedent was anywhere on Essex's mind. His poem was fully motivated and shaped by the occasion; it would have been written in the Tower during the last days before his beheading for treason in February 1601, after his defiance had collapsed and he was naming names (including his sister) to representatives of the Crown. The poem was published, anonymously, later that year as "The Passion of a Discontented Minde"; it was for a time attributed to Nicholas Breton, but

Essex's authorship is now secure. The poetic tradition he joined was one specific to Renaissance England, of versified last words written in prison shortly before execution by the state.

*

For all its desperate sincerity, Essex's poem is not the most memorable example of that *genre*. That distinction goes to his predecessor, Walter Ralegh, Essex's sometime ally but more often bitter rival. Ralegh indeed wrote more than one unforgettable poem in that line—but then he had more than one occasion to write one. Also, even though many of his court poems were exercises in what May calls "utilitarian poetics," Ralegh had an interest in poetry in its own right. His debut in print was a poem commending Gascoigne for *The Steele Glas* (1576); he discussed *The Faerie Queene* with Spenser and graced its first installment with a celebratory sonnet (1590). His interest in his own poems was not enough for him to keep track of them (he was a busy man), and what we have of his poetry are scattered remains; but readers of these remains have over the centuries responded to what Michael Rudick calls "a felt need" for "the confection of a poetic career large enough, diverse enough, and dedicated enough to seem answerable to the achievements in other departments of Ralegh's life."[18] Ralegh had a reputation as a poet by 1589, when Puttenham placed him among the current "crew of Courtly makers Noble men and Gentlemen of her Majesties owne servauntes, who have written excellently well" (Essex does not make the list), singles him out for his "vayne [i.e., vein] most loftie, insolent, and passionate," and even quotes one of his poems to Elizabeth.[19] Agnes Latham, assembling an edition of Ralegh's poetry in the mid-twentieth century, endorses Puttenham's judgment (with emphasis on "insolent") and expresses disappointment at only being able to come up with forty-one canonical poems and twelve *dubia*: "it is strange that the work of a poet who ranked so highly among his contemporaries, and whose name acquired a romantic fascination for posterity, could have been lost almost completely."[20] She thinks there was once much more. We cannot assume that, but enough of what we have has a distinctiveness that makes it reasonable to speak of his body of work, his *oeuvre*.

Part of it is a settled bleakness, a negativity accepted without protest or consolation. That should be no surprise; it is what Ralegh's legendary self-presentation— "a tall, handsome, and bold man ... damnable proud"[21]—looks like on the back side of the tapestry. His best-known poem is a straight-up argument against youthful

---

[18] Michael Rudick, ed., *The Poems of Sir Walter Ralegh*, p. xvii.
[19] Puttenham, *Arte*, pp. 61, 63 (1.31), and 198 (3.19). On "insolent," not exactly meant as a compliment but registering the forcefulness of Ralegh's poetic voice, see Anna Beer, *Patriot or Traitor*, p. 135.
[20] Agnes Latham, ed., *The Poems of Sir Walter Ralegh*, p. xxiv.
[21] Aubrey, *Brief Lives* 2: 182.

joy and pleasure in the reply of an unimpressed nymph to Marlowe's "Come live with me and be my love"; the two poems were printed together in *The Passionate Pilgrim* (1599) and *Englands Helicon* (1600) and later by Izaak Walton (1653) as a matched set. The exchange is more mordant than some readers quite realize. Marlowe precisely does *not* use the classical *carpe diem* argument that is standard in English Renaissance seduction poems and that Ralegh himself employs elsewhere.[22] Marlowe's shepherd leaves it to the nymph to bring up *invida aetas* as a reason *not* to seize the day. Her mind is already in the desert landscape that awaits, and she welcomes no distraction. There would be moral and religious arguments to be made about the sinfulness of illicit sexual pleasure and the urgency of turning one's attention to heavenly pleasures, but those arguments are not being made here. The nymph's conclusion is not Stella's—"Tyran honour doth thus use thee, / *Stella's* selfe might not refuse thee" (viii.95–6)—but something more pallid and certainly less gratifying to her eager young man:

> But could youth last, and love stil breed,
> Had joyes no date, nor age no need;
> Then those delights my mind might move
> To live with thee, and be thy love. (45B.45–8)

The transience of youthful pleasure and desire makes them not precious but worthless.

Such a disposition might seem to have little use for Petrarchism's decorativeness, though that is still in Ralegh's repertoire:

> Nature that washt her hands in milke
>   and had forgott to dry them,
> In stead of earth tooke snow and silke
>   at Loves request to trye them,
> If she a mistresse could compose
> To please loves fancy out of those:
>
> Her eyes he would should be of light,
>   A violett breath, and Lipps of Jelly,
> her haire not blacke, nor over bright,
>   and of the softest downe her Belly.
> As for her inside hee'ld have it
> only of wantonnesse and witt. (43B.1–12)

---

[22] In "Now Serena, bee not coy," an expansive imitation of Catullus 5 and 7 (poem 44 in Rudick's edition, from which I cite Ralegh's poetry). Serena may be Bess Throckmorton; the name is linked by Spenser with that of Timias, a character shadowing Ralegh, in the sixth book of the *Fairie Queene*.

Filling the woman with "wantonnesse and witt" curves things in an un-Petrarchan direction.[23] In one state of the text (43A) Ralegh leaves it there, but in another he reverses course back to something more conventional:

> At Loves entreaty, such a one
>    nature made, but with her beauty
> she hath framed a heart of stone,
>    so as Love by ill destinie
> must dye for her whom nature gave him
> because her darling would not save him. (43B.13–18)

The poem's real reversal, however, is about to happen:

> But Time which nature doth despise,
>    and rudely gives her love the lie,
> makes hope a foole, and sorrow wise,
>    his hands doe neither wash, nor dry,
> But being made of steele and rust,
> turnes snow, and silke, and milke, to dust:
>
> The Light, the Belly, lipps and breath,
>    he dimms, discovers, and destroyes.
> with those he feedes, but fills not death,
>    which sometimes were the foode of Joyes;
> yea time doth dull each lively witt,
> and dryes all wantonnes with it. (19–30)

The poem delivers a point-by-point demolition of its own *blason* of the woman's attractiveness, not forgetting wantonness and wit but reserving them for the end, as if their extinction ("into ashes all my Lust") were the final outrage.

The poem about the woman's loss of beauty as she ages is an established *genre* in Petrarchism, beginning with Petrarch himself (*Canz.* 12). The argument can go in several directions, sometimes more than one in a single poem. Ronsard's "*Quand vous serez bien vielle*" (*Sonnets pour Helene* 2.24) shifts three times before deciding to end as a *carpe diem* poem. Ralegh's poem makes no injunction to present pleasure; indeed, without the stanza about the woman's stony heart, the reference to wantonness and wit might suggest that she and the speaker have already taken such pleasure. But there is no expression in the poem of the speaker's desire for the woman; the first-person singular is nowhere present, and the gratification of being

---

[23] But not without parallel. In the 1594 edition of *Diana*, Constable adds a sonnet ("Of an Athenian youngman have I red") which affirms, hopefully, "the wittiest women are to sport inclind," adding "honor is pride, and pride is naught but paine" (Grundy, pp. 193–4).

loved by her is nowhere in sight or mind. Nor is there anything about immortality through poetry. The relentlessness of the woman's demolition hints at something like revenge, an aspiration occasionally explicit in the tradition ("These Lines that now thou scorn'st, which should delight thee, / Then would I make thee read, but to despight thee"),[24] but even that motive evaporates when the woman vanishes into an all-inclusive first-person plural:

> O cruell Time which takes in trust
>     our youth, our Joyes and all we have,
> and payes us but with age and dust,
>     who in the darke and silent grave
> When we have wandred all our wayes
> shutts up the story of our dayes. (31–6)

Ralegh's poem finds its way to a nihilistic purity that seemed attractive decades later on the eve of his execution in 1618, when he repurposed the last stanza as a poem on its own and left a copy at the Gatehouse in Westminster where he had been kept prisoner. Not quite willing to leave it at that, he added a couplet introducing a note of religious consolation, though one that takes back even as it offers: "And from which earth and grave and dust / the Lord shall raise me up I trust" (35A.7–8). Repeating the rhyme of "trust" and "dust," the affirmation falls short of the "sure and certaine hope of resurrection to eternal life" of the Anglican service for the dead, and also adds a prosodic anomaly: the familiar sixain stanza is now an octave ending in two couplets, looking something like rhyme royal but not quite. A hurried bit of plastering incompletely obscures the evidence of where the poem used to stop. Ralegh had thirteen years in the Tower under sentence of death to refine his attention on that outcome. The main project of that unplanned leisure, his *History of the World*, which in almost 800 pages makes it up to 168 BC, abruptly terminates with an almost blasphemous peroration on Death as the greatest power in human history: "It is he that puts into man all the wisdome of the world, without speaking a word; which GOD with all the words of his Law, promises, or threats, doth not infuse. ... It is therfore Death alone that can suddenly make man to know himselfe."[25] Both the curtailment of the project and the peroration were likely prompted by the death in 1612 of Prince Henry, Ralegh's patron and his only reasonable prospect for a pardon. Writing out "O cruell Time" six years later was a kind of capstone to this monumental concentration of Ralegh's thought.

Our knowledge of the context of "O cruell Time" as a stand-alone poem depends on notations in the surviving texts; one of these was in print not long after Ralegh's

---

[24] Drayton, *Idea* 8.13–14; first printed in 1619.
[25] Ralegh, *The History of the World*, p. 776.

execution, and their cumulative testimony is generally accepted. Internal evidence identifies another poem as being on the same subject. It is much more overtly religious, and begins cheerfully meditative:

> Give me my Scallop shell of quiet,
> My staffe of Faith to walke upon,
> My Scrip of Joy, Immortall diet,
> My bottle of salvation:
> My Gowne of Glory, hopes true gage,
> And thus Ile take my pilgrimage. (54A.1–6)

The tone shifts, becoming satirical as the pilgrim looks back toward the world:

> From thence to heavens Bribeles hall
> Where no corrupted voyces brall,
> No Conscience molten into gold,
> Nor forg'd accusers bought and sold,
> No cause deferd, nor vaine spent Jorney,
> For there Christ is the Kings Atturney:
> Who pleades for all without degrees,
> And he hath Angells, but no fees. (35–42)

But none of this gets us ready for what is coming:

> And this is my eternall plea,
> To him that made Heaven, Earth and Sea,
> Seeing my flesh must die so soone,
> And want a head to dine next noone,
> Just at the stroke when my vaines start and spred
> Set on my soule an everlasting head.
> Then am I readie like a palmer fit,
> To tread those blest paths which before I writ. (51–8)

A commonplace about mortality (any death is too soon for someone who wants to go on living) slides without warning into the specificity of not being around for lunch the next day, and then into the even greater specificity of the speaker's arterial spray as the headsman's ax makes lunch indeed an impossibility. The soul's genial pilgrimage to heaven suddenly has to accommodate imagery from a modern horror movie, and the "everlasting head" that descends to replace the one just excised is not much less cartoonish. The poem's consolatory agenda is not complete without a disorienting plunge into black comedy. Some manuscript sources assign this poem also to Ralegh's last night, but the text in fact appeared (anonymously) in print in 1604, fourteen years earlier. If it is indeed by Ralegh (there are no other serious candidates), it would be the product of his earlier imprisonment under sentence of death in 1603, when he received notice of the new King's reprieve only on the morning of his scheduled decapitation.

This was not Ralegh's first experience of such confinement. In 1580 he served time in both the Fleet and the Marshalsea, and in 1592 came his first imprisonment in the Tower. He was not there on a capital charge (probably—we are not in fact sure what the charges were), but any commitment to the Tower sent a grim message. ("I doe not like the tower of any place"; *Richard III* 3.1.68.) Once they started coming, Ralegh's life accumulated such messages, in increments of seriousness that can be felt in the bass line of much of his poetry. Yet another of his most unforgettable poems is assigned in one manuscript to a real or expected last night before execution. The testimony here is isolated and weak, possibly more the manuscript owner's response to the coldness of the poem itself than to any real information about its origins. But the coldness is powerful enough to prompt such imaginings, and the poem is one of the touchstones of English Renaissance poetry:

> What is our Life the play of passion
> our mirth the Musick of Division
> our Mothers wombes the Tyreing houses be
> where we are drest for lives shorte comedie
> the Earth the stage Heaven the Spectator is
> who sitts and veiwes whosoere doth Acte amiss
> the graves which hydes us from the scorching Sunn
> are like drawn Curtaines till the play is done
> thus playeing post wee to our latest rest
> and then we die in earnest not in Jest (29C)[26]

This development of a familiar trope is matched only by Macbeth facing his final desolation:

> Life's but a walking Shadow, a poore Player,
> That struts and frets his houre upon the Stage,
> And then is heard no more. It is a Tale
> Told by an Ideot, full of sound and fury
> Signifying nothing. (*Macbeth* 5.5.24–8)

Stephen Greenblatt draws a sharp contrast between the record of Thomas More's time in the Tower and Ralegh's:

---

[26] Rudick prints three versions of the poem from the six sources that attribute it to Ralegh. It circulated in some sixty manuscripts, whose textual interrelationship Rudick despairs of reconstructing; 29A and 29B end with l. 8.

Instead of More's rich humanity and deep faith in God, instead of the love and forgiveness that radiated from him at the close of his life, there is Ralegh's cold brilliance, a heroism more pagan than Christian, the subtle last stab at his enemies. More, like Ralegh, was a consummate actor, a man who knew how ... to "make a part of his own." But strip away More's role and you are left with his unshakable faith in Christ; strip away Ralegh's role and you look into the abyss.[27]

That abyss also turns out to be the landscape for an epic love story unlike anything else in Renaissance literature.

\*

Renaissance literature holds open the space for such a love story, like a slot in some periodic table. If Elizabeth's court was the miraculous venue in which the fusion of the erotic and the political in the word *midons* might finally be acted out in full epic reality, Ralegh during his period in the sun was the favorite who might have had the bravado and talent, if he had had the time, to give it literary expression. His *disiecta membra* include poems definitely about or addressed to the Queen, and the possibility that others could be added to that list if we just knew where to look has at times energized literary scholars. In 1960 Walter Oakeshott assembled from Latham's edition and new possible attributions a sequence of twenty-nine poems which he presented as the intimate poetic record of Ralegh's relations with Elizabeth from 1581 to 1592.[28] Things begin in an ambitious deference full of expectation—"happy state is none without delay. / Then must I needes advaunce my self by skyll, / And lyve, and serve, in hope of your goodwyll" (7.11–12)—but quickly reach a Petrarchan deadlock that sounds both regal and lethal:

> A secret murder hath bene done of late,
> Unkindnes founde, to be the bloudie knife,
> And shee that did the deede a dame of state,
> Faire, gracious, wise, as any beareth life.
> ...
> You kill unkinde, I die, and yet am true,
> For at your sight, my wound doth bleede anew.[29]

Oakeshott's reconstruction entails a frequently vulnerable network of speculation. He is himself skeptical about four poems; a dozen do not make it into Rudick's austerely "historical" edition. Much is made of a "Ralegh group" in *The Phoenix Nest*[30] and of verbal and stylistic similarities between anonymous poems and poems we

---

[27] Stephen Greenblatt, *Sir Walter Ralegh*, p. 16. In *Renaissance Self-Fashioning*, Greenblatt deconstructs More's vision as something more paradoxical and conflicted ("at once utterly clear and utterly elusive" [p. 57]), but the contrast with Ralegh still stands.
[28] Walter Oakeshott, *The Queen and the Poet*, pp. 129–209.
[29] *Phoenix Nest*, pp. 70–1.
[30] See Rudick, "The 'Ralegh Group' in *The Phoenix Nest*."

know or think we know to be Ralegh's. Oakeshott also does not hesitate much in taking references to a sonnet lady in regal terms—"O haires of right that weares a roial crowne, / O hands that conquer more than Cæsars force"[31]—as literal references to the Queen; the sonnet of Constable's quoted previously shows the riskiness of this. Oakeshott acknowledges that within the conventions of the time the lines might be "an allegory addressed by any poet to any mistress," but then just says, less tentatively than Latham, they are not.[32] His sequencing of "The Poems to Cynthia" has not won general acceptance.

Still, two important items, involving seven poems, easily survive scrutiny as poems by Ralegh to and about the Queen at inflamed moments in their relationship. The first, part of an exchange of poems with her on the question of her fidelity, is extremely interesting. The second is astonishing.

The exchange of poems was available to Oakeshott only in fragmentary, unrecognizable form. In 1589 Puttenham actually printed passages from both Ralegh's poem and Elizabeth's reply, with attribution but without any indication that they were part of a dialogue.[33] Full texts of the matching poems only became available with the discovery of a transcript in the Wiltshire Record Office from the 1620s.[34] Ralegh's poem is a protest at being deserted:

> Fortune hath taken thee away my Love
> my loves Joy and my sowles heaven above
> Fortune hath taken thee away my princes
> my worldes delight and my true fancies mistris (15D.1–4)

There is no serious doubt that "my princes" is the Queen, or that the emotional hyperbole is generated by the commonplace though dangerous dynamics of court favor; the best guess relates this to the rise of Essex in 1587, threatening to displace Ralegh, who occupied the place earlier held by Leicester. It seems tactful for Ralegh to ascribe Elizabeth's change of affection to the impersonal power of Fortune, though he is not averse to some personal aggrandizement in the process:

> Then will I leave my Love in fortunes hands
> then will I leave my love in worthlesse bands
> And onlie love the sorrowe Due to me
> Sorrowe hencefourth that shall my princes bee (13–16)

---

[31] *Phoenix Nest*, pp. 68–9.
[32] Oakeshott, p. 151.
[33] Puttenham, pp. 198, 236 (3.19).
[34] The texts are printed by May, *Elizabethan Courtier Poets*, pp. 318–19, and by Rudick as 15D.

192   PETRARCHAN LOVE AND THE ENGLISH RENAISSANCE

That last line aligns Ralegh with the exiled Ovid in his *Tristia* (1.3.86)[35] and supplies momentum for affirming his own moral superiority. I will, he continues,

> onlie Joy that fortune conqueringe kinges
> Fortune that rules on earth and earthlie thinges
> Hath tane my Love in spite of vertues might
> so blind a goddesse did never vertue right
>
> With wisedomes eyes had but blind fortune sin [seen]
> then had my love my love for ever bin
> But Love farewell though fortune conquer thee
> no fortune base shall ever alter me. (17–24)

Consciously or not, Ralegh adapts Machiavelli's contrast between *fortuna* and *virtù* and aligns himself with a moralized version of the latter. He, at least, remains faithful in his affections, unlike the purportedly powerful woman who has submitted, as rulers do, to the dictates of Fortune ("You kill unkinde, I die, and yet am true"). Ralegh has called her bluff on her own boast: *semper eadem*.

Queen to play:

> Ah silly pugg wert thou so sore a frayd
> mourne not my wat nor be thou so dismaid
> It passeth fickle fortunes powre and skil
> to force my harte to thinke thee any ill (25–8)

Elizabeth was fond of less than dignified nicknames for her suppliants (her French suitor Alençon was, no kidding, her "frog"), and she immediately drops the tone of things by using two pet terms for Ralegh, Pug and Wat (the latter evoking the Devonshire accent that Ralegh never tried to lose). The shift in key is part of the message: Calm down, you are being silly, I have not changed. In 1587 Elizabeth was certainly not replacing Ralegh with Essex, though she did apparently insist he learn to share; some interesting documentation shows her working to reassure both courtiers and curtail their impulse to snipe at each other.[36] But her poem to Ralegh is not merely reassuring. If blaming Fortune was meant to head off any sense that he was criticizing her, that strategy failed; she swiftly makes it clear that she feels insulted:

> no fortune base thou saist shall alter thee
> And may so blind a wretch then conquer me

---

[35] See my discussion in "Translating the Rest of Ovid," pp. 48–50.
[36] See May, *Elizabethan Courtier Poets*, pp. 121–3.

> no no my pug though fortune weare not blind
> assure thie selfe she could not rule my mind.
> ...
> Fortune I grant somtimes doth conquer kinges
> And rules and raignes on earth and earthlie thinges
> but never thinke that fortune can beare sway
> if vertue watche and will not her obay. (29–32, 37–40)

He has lazily assumed she is just like any other ruler, an all-too-predictable cliché, with the further innuendo that her fickleness owes something to the fact that she and Fortune are both female. Elizabeth turns the argumentative tables on her aggrieved lover by staking her claim on that watchful and independent *virtù* capable of prevailing over *fortuna*, and uses his own metaphor against him—it had seemed so clever at the time—by calling him "sowre sorrowes servant" (35) because of his craven, hasty, undignified surrender to that new princess of his. He is the one who is being unfaithful (and womanish). Elizabeth concludes that all may yet be well if he just stops whingeing, but not without reminding him of the august moral wisdom that he has evidently forgotten (he could have found it in a famous text of Boethius that she partly translated), and also adding a friendly warning:

> Dead to all Joyes and living unto woe
> slayne quite by her that never gave wiseman blow
> revive againe and live without all dread
> the Lesse afrayde the better shalt thou spead. (45–8)

Continuing displays of timorous oversensitivity could adversely impact his professional advancement. *Verbum sapienti*.

If it were not for Puttenham, we would assume that the poems circulated very narrowly. The rather quick appearance of lines from both poems in print suggests otherwise. Rudick thinks Ralegh and the Queen distributed copies to serve their separate purposes, and were addressing others as well as (possibly even more than) each other: "Ralegh would 'publish' his in the court circle as a means of challenging his antagonist obliquely and rallying his friends. The Queen would publish hers as a means of announcing policy."[37] The lines printed by Puttenham would not in themselves have served either agenda, but he may have culled them for his own purposes from copies that had become at least semi-public. At the same time, the careful formal equivalence of the two poems, and also the way Elizabeth's adroitly reworks the argumentative challenge with which Ralegh's presents her, have a reciprocating intimacy which suggests teamwork, as in a *pas de deux*

---

[37] Rudick, ed., *Poems*, p. xl.

where the wariness or animosity of the paired dancers is reworked as we watch into choreography. It is not beyond imagining that Ralegh consciously acts as a kind of straight man, supplying the Queen with material he knows she can artfully reconfigure, in expectation of a mutual aesthetic satisfaction—the satisfaction of the *tenso* (*tenzone*), cultivated in European poetry since the troubadours—that simultaneously alleviates even as it draws its energies from the dangerous reality of their situation. It may be the closest glimpse the poetry allows us of what the actual intimacy between the two of them might, at its best, have been like.

\*

The next look we get, intimacy is at best a cursed memory:

> My boddy in the walls captived
> feels not the wounds of spighfull envy.
> butt my thralde mind, of liberty deprived,
> fast fettered in her auntient memory,
> douth nought beholde butt sorrowes diinge face,
> such prison earst was so delightfull
> as it desirde no other dwellinge place,
> Butt tymes effects, and destines dispightfull,
> have changed both my keeper and my fare,
> loves fire and bewtys light I then had store,
> butt now closs keipt, as captives wounted are
> that food, that heat, that light I finde no more,
>    Dyspaire bolts up my dores, and I alone
>    speake to dead walls, butt thos heare not my mone. (25)

Literal imprisonment could be borne, even shrugged off, and metaphorical imprisonment in love has been in its time a joy from which the speaker had no wish to be freed—but things have changed, disastrously, and both imprisonments are now mutually reinforcing torments of solitary confinement. Ralegh is unquestionably the author; the poem is one of four, surviving in a single copy in his handwriting. The manuscript was discovered in 1870 among the Cecil papers at Hatfield House, where it presumably came into the possession of Ralegh's problematic friend and eventual nemesis Robert Cecil (Burghley's son). The sonnet is preceded by a brief, cryptic poem that seems, though with mysterious intent, to remember "They fle from me": "If Synthia be a Queene, a princes, and supreame, / keipe thes amonge the rest, or say it was a dreame" (24.1–2).[38] The sonnet then stands as an introduction to two lengthy fragments (a total of 544 lines, not including cancellations) identified as being from the last two books of a larger work called "the Ocean to

---

[38] Oakeshott, pp. 174–5, makes the bravest try at decoding this poem, but without much confidence.

Scinthia" or "the Oceans love to Scinthia."[39] If the rest of that poem ever existed, it might have been one of the defining works of Renaissance literature, Petrarchan love blossoming into an epic of imperial conquest. Spenser makes references in the first installment of the *Faerie Queene* (1590) and then again in *Colin Clouts Come Home Againe* (1595) to having read or heard from some such work in progress, though the character of the work changed in the interval from "faire Cinthias praises" (as in the dedicatory sonnet to Ralegh in 1590) to "a lamentable lay, / Of great unkindnesse, and of usage hard, / Of *Cynthia*" (*Colin Clout* 164–6). The earlier references may be to parts of the poem now lost.[40] But it is also believable that Ralegh was just talking a good game to his neighbor in Ireland, and in composing the Hatfield manuscript summarily conjured the previous books into imagined existence.[41] Writers do that. The Hatfield manuscript as it stands makes powerful reading. The raggedness of the longer poems—"half-rhymes, unfinished sentences, stanzas of three, five or six lines among the quatrains, the movement in a sort of broken spiral from beginning to end"[42]—just enhances the effect; in Lewis's judgment, "what is unfinished is more impressive, certainly more exciting, than what is finished."[43] Critics have become less restrained; for Louis Montrose, the truncated epic is "Ralegh's plaintive masterpiece."[44]

Some references in the Hatfield manuscript ("If to the livinge weare my muse adressed ..." [26.5], and so on) have been taken to imply that Elizabeth was dead by the time Ralegh was writing, so that the imprisonment in question would be Ralegh's second stay in the Tower after 1603.[45] But as the poem proceeds what

---

[39] The heading of the first fragment in the manuscript is "The 21th: and last booke of the Ocean to Scinthia." Latham and others have taken the number there to be "11," which would make the second fragment the 12th book and round the project off with the number of books of the *Aeneid*, but see Stacy M. Clanton, "The 'Number' of Sir Walter Ralegh's *Booke of the Ocean to Scinthia*."

[40] Squaring the record on this assumption works better by postulating revisions in the text of *Colin Clout*; see Kathrine Koller, "Spenser and Ralegh." If, as the Hatfield manuscript already suggests, what Ralegh had in mind was a cycle of poems in a variety of forms rather than a canonical succession of narrative books, a thirty-two-line lyric in praise of Cynthia may be our one taste of the earlier part. It survives in Ralegh's autograph, though not in the same manuscript as what we take to be the Tower poems. The third stanza resonates in an epic context: "She as the valley of perue / whose summer ever lastethe / tyme conquringe all she mastreth / by beinge allwaye new" (23.9–12). A suggestion of the Song of Solomon arcs breathlessly into the sixteenth century: the silver mines at Potosí had already made Peru known as the most opulent source of treasure in the New World, and the overtone in "conquringe" and "mastreth" is imperial.

[41] He may also have been thinking of the poem's reception: "if Queen Elizabeth were alive when Ralegh was preparing this manuscript, he would know that the number he chose to give the poem could help impress her when and if she read it" (Clanton, p. 201), and the higher the count the better. Clanton also suggests 22 may have some undiscovered numerological significance.

[42] Joyce Horner, "The Large Landscape," p. 206. I share her impression "that Ralegh is feeling for a form he never found, that he is not even sure what kind of poem he is trying to write" (p. 207). Catherine Bates impressively relates the poem's conspicuous signs of disorder to the dynamics of melancholia and abjection: *Masculinity, Gender and Identity in the English Renaissance Lyric*, pp. 136–73.

[43] Lewis, *English Literature in the Sixteenth Century*, p. 520.

[44] Montrose, "Of Gentlemen and Shepherds," p. 441. Greenblatt also uses the term "masterpiece" (*Sir Walter Ralegh*, p. 12).

[45] See Duncan-Jones, "The Date of Raleigh's '21th: And Last Booke of the Ocean to Scinthia,'" though she argues the case with hesitation. Some aspects of the poems do, as she shows, read very differently

is meant by "death" is shifty and metaphorical—the death of love, also the poet's own state as he writes—and consensus now relates the manuscript to Ralegh's first time in the Tower a decade earlier, after the most important rupture with Elizabeth. Subsequently he was restored to favor but never again at the same level. The provocation, obliquely intimated by Ralegh himself ("when first my fancy erred ..." [3]),[46] was unambiguously his, a straightforward and even ordinary act of infidelity: he impregnated and secretly married Elizabeth (Bess) Throckmorton, since 1584 a Gentlewoman of the Privy Chamber, i.e., one of the Queen's intimate companions. Ralegh was sufficiently aware of how the Queen would take this to lie baldly about it for several months—"something he invariably did under pressure"[47]—even though there was no way to keep the truth from coming out, certainly not after the birth of a son in March 1592. In August both Walter and Bess (as it is convenient to call her, to distinguish her from other Elizabeths), having been detained and questioned, were sent to the Tower. The evidence suggests their romance was the genuine thing—Ralegh risked as much with his marriage as John Donne later did with his—and lasted; later correspondence shows mutual devotion during his imprisonment under King James. The Queen's wrath is comprehensible as entirely practical and justifiable distress at finding the politics of favoritism gaining access into what she liked to think was her private demesne, but there could also be genuine hurt and anger at the revelation that Ralegh's neo-Petrarchan passion for her was, well, a poetic fiction. Even if she somehow knew that was the case (probably everybody did), the demonstration of it could cut deep; emotions in fiction are very real emotions. There is, however, no documentation of the Queen's feelings. On Ralegh's side the estrangement brought forth a lover's vehemence that did make it into the record. In the heat of the moment he wrote to Cecil of how news that the Queen was leaving London while he was being confined at Durham House sent him into hyperbolic despair:

> My hart was never broken till this day that I here the Queen goes away so far off whom I have followed so many yeares with so great love and desire, in so many jurneys, and am now left behinde her and in a darke prison all alone. While shee was yet nire att hand, that I might here of her once in to or three dayes my sorrows weare the less, but yeven now my hart is cast into the deapth of all misery .... she is gonn in whom I trusted, and of mee hath not on thought of mercy nor any respect of that that was. Do with mee now, therfore what you list. I am more wery

---

with the later dating. Alexander M. Buchan, in "Ralegh's *Cynthia*—Facts or Legend," connects the poem to Ralegh's dust-up with Essex in 1589.

[46] Later (26.338) Ralegh refers to his "error," the enigmatic term Ovid uses for the mistake that led to his exile (*Tristia* 2.207).

[47] Anna Beer, *My Just Desire*, p. xiv.

of life then they are desirus I should perishe, which if it had bynn for her, as it is by her, I had bynn to happelye borne.[48]

In his own letter to Cecil, Ralegh's kinsman Arthur Gorges described the explosive result when Ralegh actually glimpsed the royal barge out on the Thames:

> as a mann transported with passion; he sware to Sir George Carew that he wolde disguyse hymeselfe; and gett into a payer of Oares to Ease hys mynde butt with a syght of the Queene; or els he protested his harte wolde breake. But the trusty Jaylor ... flatly refused to permitt hyme. But in conclusion uppon this dissputte they fell flatt owt to colloryq outragius wordes; with stryving and struggling att the doores. ... and in the fury of the conflyct, the Jaylor he had hys newe perwygg torne of hys crowne. / And yet heare the battle ended not, for att laste they had gotten owte theyr daggers. ... I feare Sir W. Rawly; wyll shortely growe to be Orlando furioso; If the bryght Angelyca persever agaynst hyme a lyttle longer.[49]

The literary allusion (to a poem the Queen's godson had just finished translating) is on target: a lyric scene from *Astrophil and Stella* ("O happie Tems, that didst my Stella beare" [103.1]) is flushed with epic fury passing into madness. Ralegh would have expected and wanted the scene to be reported back to the Her Majesty.[50]

What Ralegh's new wife may have made of all this is beyond deciphering.[51] She might have been pragmatic enough to think nothing needed explaining or even

---

[48] *The Letters of Sir Walter Ralegh*, ed. Agnes Latham and Joyce Youings, p. 70; the letter is dated July 1592.

[49] Helen Estabrook Sandison, "Arthur Gorges, Spenser's Alcyon and Ralegh's Friend," pp. 657–8; dated July 26, 1592.

[50] On these letters, see Marion Campbell, "Inscribing Imperfection," pp. 233–7.

[51] One reason Duncan-Jones favors a later date is that locating Ralegh's extravagant declarations of emotional dependence on one Elizabeth in the immediate context of his marriage to another gives the Cynthia poems what seems to her an "unsatisfactory and even repulsive character" ("Date," p. 152): he spent what he had of a honeymoon writing pages and pages about how much he loved another woman. Beer, accepting the earlier dating, sets herself against the traditional treatment of Bess by her husband's biographers as "his sexual victim and his political nemesis," and intuits significant agency in her behavior, even "involvement at the highest levels in a challenge to the power, authority, and future of the Queen herself" (*My Just Desire*, pp. xv–xvi). If Bess knew about the poem, she might have accepted it as an attempt, however desperate or bizarre, to regain the Queen's favor. We have a letter that Bess wrote from the Tower to Sir Moyle Finch and his wife Elizabeth Heneage, requesting advice and help in securing her own release (including the possibility of forwarding a letter to the Queen), while also expressing concern for her husband and showing her familiarity with the delicacy and self-control needed in such maneuvering. "I asur you truely I never desiaried nor never wolde desiar my lebbarti with out the good likeking ne advising of Sur WR," she says, and urges restraint "if hit shuld doo him harme to speke of my delivery" (*Report on the Manuscripts of Allan George Finch* 1: 34; see Raleigh Trevelyan, *Sir Walter Raleigh*, pp. 182–3). Further letters from 1594 to 1618, most to Robert Cecil, one to King James, all of them in one way or another on her husband's behalf, are printed by Edward Edwards, *The Life of Sir Walter Ralegh* 2: 397–414. There is no mention of Bess in any of Walter's letters until 1594, and his first surviving letter to her dates from 1603; on what their correspondence shows about their married life, see Latham and Youings, pp. lv–lvi, and, more astringently, Beer, *My Just Desire*, pp. 87–91. Carew Ralegh was conceived in 1604, during Walter's second imprisonment; Beer discusses but does not endorse the possibility that Walter was not the father (pp. 166–8). During his

198  PETRARCHAN LOVE AND THE ENGLISH RENAISSANCE

excusing; she knew from several years' experience what force the Queen's person and authority could have at close range, and also had her own cards to play in the social and political game of which her pregnancy and marriage were inescapably a part. The marriage did, at least in the long run, survive Ralegh's immersion in a self-styled epic poem about his seemingly total emotional dependence on the Elizabeth he was not married to. The two fragments supposedly from that epic are about nothing but that dependence, obsessively reaffirmed after any support from her has been withdrawn:

> The minde and vertue never have begotten
> a firmer love, since love on yearth had poure [power]
> a love obscurde, but cannot be forgotten
> to great and stronge for tymes Jawes to devour,
> contayninge such a fayth as ages wound not
> ...
> though of the same now buried bee the joy
> the hope, the cumfort, and the sweetness ended,
> but that the thoughts, and memores of thees
> worke a relapps of passion, and remayne
> of my sadd harte the sorrow suckinge bees
> the wrongs recevde, the scornes perswade in vayne
> ...
> But in my minde so is her love inclosde
> and is therof not only the best parte
> but into it the essence is disposde ...
> Oh love/the more my wo/to it thow art
> yeven as the moysture in each plant that growes
> yeven as the soonn unto the frosen ground
> yeven as the sweetness, to th'incarnate rose
> yeven as the Center in each perfait rounde,
> as water to the fyshe, to men as ayre
> as heat to fier, as light unto the soonn
> Oh love it is but vayne, to say thow weare
> ages, and tymes, cannot thy poure outrunn. ... (26.380–4, 411–16, 426–37)

dire last 15 years there is no evidence of a rift between him and Bess; his letters contain some powerful expressions of gratitude for her efforts on his behalf:

> I send you all the thankes which my heart can conceive or my words can express for your many travailes and care taken for mee, which, though they have not taken effect as you wished, yett my debt to you is not the less, but pay itt I never shall in this world (*Letters*, p. 263 [1603]).

This letter acquired some fame, and was printed after his death as *Sir Walter Rawleighs Farewell to his Lady*.

The two poems are the monologue of this voice, cycling repetitively within a narrowing range of moods. In places it gestures toward happier times, when Elizabeth seemed to inhabit the version of herself, chaste but nurturing, that Spenser put into the *Faerie Queene* as Belphoebe; the gesture, however, is borne on a sense of loss:

> Thos streames seeme standinge puddells which before,
> Wee saw our bewties in, so weare they cleere
> Belphebes course is now observde no more
> that faire resemblance weareth out of date
> our Ocean seas are but tempestius waves
> and all things bass that blessed wear of late (269–74)

We catch glimpses of what the earlier books of the poem, if they ever existed, might have been like. Their central conceit can be found in compact form in a Petrarchan sonnet by Charles Best: "Looke how the pale *Queene* of the silent night, / Doth cause the *Ocean* to attend upon her."[52] Ralegh makes "the Oceans love to Scinthia" into an epic celebration of the mythic and erotic teamwork through which England began the acquisition of its overseas empire: Sir "Water" Ralegh, whom Spenser (in a poem using the same verse form as Ralegh's long fragment) called "the shepheard of the Ocean" (*Colin Clout* 66), serving at a distance the moon goddess who controls the tides. That could have been a bravura poetic performance: love at a distance makes great things happen—makes history. But by the time we get that glimpse, what is given is already being taken back:

> Shee gave, she tooke, shee wounded, she appeased.
> The honor of her love, love still devisinge
> woundinge my mind with contrarye consayte
> transferde it sealf sumetyme to her aspiringe
> sumetyme the trumpett of her thoughts retrayt
> To seeke new worlds, for golde, for praise, for glory,
> to try desire, to try love severed farr
> when I was gonn shee sent her memory
> more stronge then weare tenthowsand shipps of warr
> to call me back, to leve great honors thought
> to leve my frinds, my fortune, my attempte
> to leve the purpose I so longe had sought
> and holde both cares, and cumforts in contempt (56–68)

Behind those last lines may be Ralegh's aggrieved memory of being recalled by the Queen earlier in the year from personal command of a fleet that had set

---

[52] Davison, *A Poetical Rhapsody*, ed. Hyder E. Rollins, 1: 56.

out for Panama on the track of Spanish treasure. In the poem, Cynthia turns his epic striving into paralyzed self-contradiction: "Such heat in Ize, such fier in frost remaynde / such trust in doubt, such cumforts in dispaire" (69–70). Here the Petrarchan legacy is paradox that makes nothing happen, nothing beyond the speaker's seemingly endless contemplation and articulation of his fallen state.

Ralegh does not settle for the familiar icy fire; part of what gives his poem its feel of endlessness is his pursuit of just the right metaphor for his state. He slides immediately into something unexpectedly domestic and quiet—"mich like the gentell Lamm, though lately wayned / playes with the dug though finds no cumfort ther" (71–2)—and then, beginning a sentence that will run for thirty-one lines, into something shockingly brutal—

> But as a boddy violently slayne
> retayneath warmth although the spirrit be gonn,
> and by a poure in nature moves agayne
> till it be layd below the fatall stone (73–6)

—and then into an appeal to the ordinary course of nature—

> Or as the yearth yeven in cold winter dayes
> left for a tyme by her life gevinge soonn,
> douth by the poure remayninge of his rayes
> produce sume green, though not as it hath dunn (77–80)

—and then yet further, as the rigorously sustained syntax grapples with a near-chaos of exfoliating comparisons.[53] Other metaphors from outside the usual run of Elizabethan poetizing keep turning up later in the poem:

> all is desolvde, our labors cume to nought
> nor any marke therof ther douth indure
> no more then when small dropps of rayne do fall
> uppon the parched grounde by heat up dried
> no coolinge moysture is percevde att all
> nor any shew or signe of weet douth byde (235–40)

Driving these tropes is a feeling that the speaker's state makes no sense, is something irrational, unnatural, though the right metaphor might somehow bring it closer to intelligibility.

The presiding metaphor, given powerful expression early on and reappearing at intervals, is of the speaker as the dazed inhabitant of a ruined pastoral landscape:

---

[53] On the "exceptionally subtle and masterful use of syntax" in this sentence, see Donald Davie, "A Reading of 'The Ocean's Love to Cynthia,'" pp. 85–8.

> Lost in the mudd of thos hygh flowinge streames
> which through more fayrer feilds ther courses bend,
> slayne with sealf thoughts, amased in fearfull dreames,
> woes without date, discumforts without end,
> from frutfull trees I gather withred leves
> and glean the broken eares with misers hands,
> who sumetyme did injoy the waighty sheves
> I seeke faire floures amidd the brinish sand (17–24)

When Ariosto's Orlando discovers the *locus amoenus* where the woman he had pursued through so many adventures had given herself to another man, he attacks that landscape with all the terrifying violence of which he is capable, reduces it to rubble, and collapses into a catatonia that lasts for three days (*Orlando furioso* 23.129–32); Gorges in his literary reference anticipates the collapse as well as the violence. We may also be put in mind of the quieter scene in Dürer's *Melencolia I*, where a dejected angel, usually seen as female, sits surrounded by instruments of knowledge and craft—a compass, an hourglass, balance scales, a saw, pincers, a planer, hammer and nails—which we sense she knows how to use and used to care about. They are now so much clutter. In Ralegh's poem the knowledge and craft are those of poetry, with which he had transformed his vision of Cynthia into the epic of their love:

> Oh, princely forme, my fancies adamande
> Devine consayte, my paynes acceptance,
> Oh, all in onn, oh heaven on yearth transparant
> the seat of joyes, and loves abundance
> Out of that mass of mirakells, my Muse,
> gathered thos floures, to her pure sences pleasinge
> out of her eyes (the store of joyes) did chuse
> equall delights, my sorrowes counterpoysinge (41–8)

The debris of that effort now surrounds him, with no will left to have it otherwise. The poem, as Robert Stillman puts it, "emerges ... from the absence created by the now exhausted order of symbols with which Ralegh had once surrounded the Queen," and enacts, in Greenblatt's phrase, "the tragedy of the imagination."[54] The aftermath is a living death which the poet struggles to describe:

> sume sweeter wordes, sume more becumming vers,
> should wittness my myshapp in hygher kynd.
> but my loves wounds, my fancy in the hearse,

---

[54] Robert E. Stillman, "'Words cannot knytt,'" p. 37; Greenblatt, *Sir Walter Ralegh*, p. 94.

> the Idea but restinge, of a wasted minde,
> the blossumes fallen, the sapp gon from the tree.
> the broken monuments of my great desires,
> from thes so lost what may th'affections bee,
> what heat in Cynders of extinguisht fiers? (9–16)[55]

In the next-to-last district of the last circle of hell Dante finds men whose sin of treachery has already frozen their souls into the ice of eternal damnation even though they are not yet dead and their bodies, as one of them puts it, still live and eat and drink and sleep and put on clothes (*Inferno* 33.91–157). As they continue to work through the contingencies of everyday existence, the ultimate fate of their souls has not only been decided but has already begun. Ralegh's epic breaks its own mood with a tantalizing reference to the clock time of ordinary life, but having done so it traces an arc from what was then ambitiously undertaken into a cursed eternal present:

> Twelve yeares intire I wasted in this warr
> twelve yeares of my most happy younger dayes,
> butt I in them, and they now wasted ar
> of all which past the sorrow only stayes (120–3)[56]

"So wrate I once and my mishapp fortolde," he goes on (124), having just quoted verbatim the refrain from an earlier poem of his (17)—though he had made the same forecast, and more emphatically, in his poem to the Queen: "Sorrowe hencefourth that shall my princes bee" (15D.16). She had turned his plaint into a taunt by calling him "sowre sorrowes servant" (15D.35), intending to snap him out of it, but in the Cynthia poems Sorrow's monarchy seems absolute and unending. That endlessness is the baffling endlessness of the poem itself. Its author tries to cut it off:

---

[55] On the tropes of living death, see Bates, *Masculinity*, pp. 153–6.

[56] There is no need to take the time span of twelve years too literally, but 1580 makes a suitable starting point. Ralegh had styled himself *de curia*, "of the court," since at least 1577, but Mathew Lyons argues that a "defining realignment ... earning him access to the highest circles at court" came in 1580, when he was involved in the slaughter of disarmed Spanish and Italian troops at Smerwick in western Ireland. Europe was appalled but Elizabeth was apparently delighted; Ralegh was entrusted by Lord Grey with carrying back to Whitehall a cache of confidential and sensitive documents found among the dead. Ralegh was in England by the end of the year, and Lyons finds the scene worth dramatizing: "This time as he entered the presence chamber, its high gilt ceiling inscribed with the dates of great English battles, and made his way through the press of people gathered there, the rush-strewn floor swallowing the sound of his steps, he must have known he had been gifted a moment to remake himself.... Not many English captains returned to court from Ireland with their reputation enhanced and the swagger of a clearly defined victory in their gait" (*The Favourite*, pp. 174, 176; see also, more soberly, May, *Sir Walter Ralegh*, p. 4). If the reality was anything like this, Ralegh would remember the moment. *Incipit vita nova.*

> Butt stay my thoughts, make end, geve fortune way
> harshe is the voice of woe and sorrows sounde
> cumplaynts cure not, and teares do butt allay
> greifs for a tyme, which after more abounde (26.474–7)

If he is not in fact in hell, there is in fact a way out—"Do then by diinge, what life cannot doo" (496)—an exhortation that brings back the gentler possibilities of the pastoral landscape as a place where grief can be assuaged by letting go:

> Unfolde thy flockes, and leve them to the feilds
> to feed onn hylls, or dales, wher likes them best
> of what the summer, or the springetyme yeildes
> for love, and tyme, hath geven thee leve to rest (497–500)

The prospect of making an end of it this way recalls *Astrophil and Stella*: "Go my flocke, go get you hence, / Seeke a better place of feeding …" (ix.1–2). Ralegh also remembers Colin Clout's hanging up of his pipe at the end of *The Shepheardes Calender* and looks to even more decisive action:

> My pipe, which loves own hand, gave my desire
> to singe her prayses, and my wo upon
> Dispaire hath often threatned to the fier
> as vayne to keipe now all the rest ar gonn. (505–8)

And, not without a backward look, his thoughts turn to heaven:

> my steapps ar backwarde, gasinge onn my loss,
> my minds affection, and sowles sole love,
> not mixte with fanceys chafe, or fortunes dross,
> to god I leve it, who first gave it me,
> and I her gave, and she returnd agayne,
> as it was herrs, so lett his mercies bee,
> of my last cumforts, the essentiall meane (514–20)

Which is where things may well have been intended to end. Yet, at the last moment, the fragment stops not with an ending but with a reaffirmation of the endlessness from which the speaker had been trying to escape: "But be it so, or not, th'effects, ar past, / her love hath end. my woe must ever last" (521–2).

Indeed, there is more. A second fragment follows, much shorter, in a different verse form (and with less irregularity), unambiguously unfinished; it bears the somewhat enigmatic heading "The end of the boockes, of the Oceans love to Scinthia, and the beginninge of the 22 boock, entreatinge of Sorrow."

The beginning that follows the end is a muted continuation of the sorrow that came before:

> My dayes delights, my springetyme joies fordunn,
> which in the dawne, and risinge soonn of youth
> had their creation, and weare first begunn,
> do in the yeveninge, and the winter sadd
> present my minde, which takes my tymes accompt
> the greif remayninge of the joy it had. (27.1–6)

Cynthia has moved on, making the rupture decisive in showing her favor elsewhere, though reminding her lover as she does so of what he worshipped in her:

> my tymes that then rann or'e them sealves in thes
> and now runn out in others happiness
> bringe unto thos new joyes, and new borne dayes,
> so could shee not, if shee weare not the soonn,
> which sees the birth, and buriall, of all elce,
> and holds that poure, with which shee first begunn (7–12)

But the wake she leaves is still one of diminished things and convictions of what might be or might have been:

> levinge each withered boddy to be torne
> by fortune, and by tymes tempestius,
> which by her vertu, once faire frute have borne,
> knowinge shee cann renew, and cann create
> green from the grounde, and floures, yeven out of stonn,
> by vertu lastinge over tyme and date (13–18)

With something of a jolt, the once proud first-person singular becomes a collective plural receiving a somber, shadowy benediction that trails off mid-sentence, with a comma:

> levinge us only woe, which like the moss,
> havinge cumpassion of unburied bones,
> cleaves to mischance, and unrepayred loss,
> for tender stalkes, (19–22)

In the manuscript that final half-line, hinting at a springlike revival that may or may not be happening, and may or may not include the speaker, stands alone on the verso, the rest of the page blank. A less ambiguous comfort is that of the moss that shows compassion. In the diminution that governs the second fragment, the gently spreading cover brings the wasted landscape a minimalist blessing from its lowest form of life. Moss has no roots, no proper stems or leaves; it produces no flowers or fruit or seeds, has no shape or structure aside from those of whatever it grows upon, and plays little if any apparent role in the food chain. And it grows, quietly, endlessly, almost anywhere. For a mind at the end of its tether, hoping to be done with desire and predilection, this could be the speaker's solace, a consoling image of what he has come to, maybe even an ideal of sorts. He might indeed decide to stop here.

If we are right about the dating, though, the composition of the poem was in real life interrupted by the news that, after a maddening lack of success, the privateering fleet which Elizabeth would not let Ralegh command in person had captured a fabulously stocked Spanish treasure galleon, the *Madre de Dios*, and brought it to harbor in Dartmouth, where its cargo threatened to disappear into a chaos of looting. Ralegh was the man with the savvy and style to take control of the situation, and he was provisionally released in September 1592 to do so. By his own accounting he salvaged some £80,000 for the Crown as a kind of ransom, and by the end of the year he and his wife were free again. During the next spring they conceived another child, who was christened with his father's name in November. By the end of the year after that, Ralegh was sailing to the New World at the head of his own expedition, and this time he would get there. The high drama with the Queen was over, but his life and career were on course again, and the next shipwreck would not come until after a change in monarchs. The relevance of and inspiration for the Cynthia poems, probably just abandoned in the Tower, were things of the past. There is no evidence that Robert Cecil or anyone else read the poems or paid them any mind (they would have made very strange reading, as they still do) until the nineteenth century. That their author had not completely forgotten them is indicated by the recurrence, along with some other wording, of the odd conceit of the moss in two of three surviving versions of a verse petition to Queen Anne during his final two confinements between 1603 and 1618 (32.22–4, 33.10–12). It is missing in the version (34) that was probably finally sent.[57]

---

[57] On these three poems and their dating, see May, *Sir Walter Ralegh*, pp. 115–23. Mary Wroth comes independently to the moss trope in *Pamphilia to Amphilanthus*: "Nor can I as those pleasant wits injoy / My owne fram'd wordes which I account the drosse / Of purer thoughts, or reckon them as mosse" (P45.5–7). Comparing her own poetry to moss has some similarity to Ralegh's metaphor, but any hint of vitalism is blocked by the rhyme with "dross."

# 6
# William Shakespeare

The asymmetrical bell curve of sonneteering in English peaks in 1594–95, with a decline more gradual than its rise, and never complete. It is something of a commonplace of English literary history that by the seventeenth century sonnets have become unfashionable, but that is only by the frenetic standard of a craze no one would need or want to repeat. ("They darkened the air; they emerged by their thousands.")[1] The longterm legacy of that craze is the permanent naturalization of this exotic form as an option in English poetry; it still holds its place in the popular imagination as the canonical form for love poetry. The semi-autobiographical sonnet sequence periodically surfaces in the work of major poets. During his last decade Robert Lowell writes almost exclusively in a fourteen-line unrhymed form, and shapes just under a hundred such poems into *The Dolphin* (1973), a narrative of the erotic upheaval in his own life at the time.[2] The 115 poems that John Berryman publishes in 1967 as *Berryman's Sonnets* (a title mirroring the 1609 *Shake-speares Sonnets*) are a sequence about an adulterous affair of his own, ending with a haunting reenactment in (literally) modern dress of a resonant moment in its now distant literary past:

> The weather's changing. This morning was cold,
> as I made for the grove, without expectation,
> some hundred Sonnets in my pocket, old,
> to read her if she came. Presently the sun
> yellowed the pines & my lady came not
> in blue jeans & a sweater. I sat down & wrote.[3]

She was not there among the pinetrees, and here is what she was wearing. Petrarch's encounters with Laura take a similar course:

---

[1] Patrick Cruttwell, *The Shakespearean Moment*, p. 16.
[2] Robert Lowell, *The Dolphin*, ed. Saskia Hamilton. This edition and Hamilton's simultaneous edition of *The Dolphin Letters* fill out the compositional history of the sequence and its biographical context. The poems give the narrative obliquely and elliptically, but it is clear that Lowell thought of it as a narrative and expected his readers to follow it. *Letters* complements the poems with what is in effect an epistolary novel in which the voice of Elizabeth Hardwick, the discarded wife, dominates to powerful effect.
[3] John Berryman, *Berryman's Sonnets*, intro. April Bernard, p. 115.

>     Ove porge ombra un pino alto od un colle
> talor m'arresto, et pur nel primo sasso
> disegno co la mente il suo bel viso. ...
>     et quanto in più selvaggio
> loco mi trovo e 'n più deserto lido,
> tanto più bella il mio pensier l'adombra.
> Poi quando il vero sgombra
> quel dolce error, pur lì medesmo assido
> me freddo, pietra morta in pietra viva,
> in guisa d'uom che pensi et pianga et scriva.
> (*Canz.* 129.27–9, 46–52)

Where a tall pine or a hillside extends shade, there I sometimes stop, and in the first stone I see I portray her lovely face with my mind. ... and in whatever wildest place and most deserted shore I find myself, so much the more beautiful does my thought shadow her forth. Then, when the truth dispels that sweet deception, right there in the same place I sit down, cold, a dead stone on the living rock, like a man who thinks and weeps and writes.

The Elizabethan sonnet sequences themselves, however, have not had an afterlife commensurate with their collective import. Professionals continue to study them and apportion honors and scorn, *Astrophil and Stella* remains a fascination and delight for anyone taking the trouble to get to know it, but no complete sequences and very few individual sonnets have made their way into the higher echelons of remembered poems in English. The great exception is of course Shakespeare. At least eight of his sonnets are among the best-known poems in the language, recognized and even memorized by many who do not think of themselves as having any great affinity for poetry, and the entire sequence continues to be printed and presumably bought in uncountable editions in sometimes luxurious formats. As I write this, during the covid-19 pandemic, the actor Patrick Stewart has been doing a daily live reading of Shakespeare's sonnets one by one on Instagram, as a comfort in bad times. The charisma of Shakespeare's name has a lot to do with this, since without it the sequence would probably now be one of the least read rather than the most famous. It once seemed as if that might become its fate. The sonnets are not treated editorially as part of Shakespeare's *oeuvre* until the eighteenth century, and then with some colorful reluctance. George Steevens, annotating one of the first editions, makes clear his dislike of sonneteering in general—"quaintness, obscurity, and tautology, are to be regarded as the constituent parts of this exotick species of composition .... I profess I am one of those who should have wished it to have expired in the country where it was born"—and makes no exception for Shakespeare:

Such laboured perplexities of language, and such studied deformities of style, prevail throughout these Sonnets, that the reader (after our best endeavours at explanation) will frequently find reason to exclaim with Imogen:

> "I see before me, neither here, nor here,
> "Nor what ensues; but have a fog in them
> "That I cannot look through."[4]

In another edition thirteen years later he refuses to include them.[5] History has not been kind to Steevens, but he put his finger on something. Beyond the usual anthology pieces (sometimes even there), the arguments of a surprising number of the individual sonnets remain difficult and fatiguing to follow, tricky and discouraging even for specialists. Helen Vendler, one of their most skillful, resourceful, and admiring readers, admits that "some still elude me."[6] Stewart, coming to sonnet 59 ("If their bee nothing new, but that which is, / Hath beene before"), declined to read it, saying he did not know how to recite a poem he found baffling. After my own enforced first trek through the sequence as an undergraduate, I presented my professor with the text of sonnet 155, a Shakespearean *cento* of lines from fourteen different sonnets, which I insisted made as much sense as some of the stuff he had just made us read. (I forget his response.)

Even just as further information about Shakespeare, the sonnets are frustrating. It has proved difficult to fit them into our other knowledge about his life and career. The plays mention sonneteering as a familiar feature of contemporary life (extended backward so that the Dauphin and the Duke of Orleans—the latter a poet in real life though not a sonneteer—can banter about it on the eve of Agincourt [*Henry V* 3.7.39ff]). There is a reference in print to Shakespeare's own "sugred *Sonnets* among his private friends" from 1598.[7] Two of them (128 and 144) had been written by 1599 when they were printed in a volume called *The*

---

[4] *Supplement to the Edition of Shakspeare's Plays ... by Samuel Johnson and George Steevens*, 1: 682 and 606; the quotation is from *Cymbeline* 3.2.78–80.

[5] "We have not reprinted the Sonnets, &c. of Shakspeare, because the strongest act of Parliament that could be framed, would fail to compel readers into their service"; *The Plays of William Shakspeare*, ed. Samuel Johnson and George Steevens, 1: vii. Edmund Malone, who actually edited the sonnets for the *Supplement*, was not much more enthusiastic: "I do not feel any great propensity to stand forth as the champion of these compositions" (1: 684). George Eliot, the sonnets much on her mind while she was at work on *Middlemarch*, put it on record that no more than twenty-four of them seemed to her worth reading; see Jane Kingsley-Smith, *The Afterlife of Shakespeare's Sonnets*, pp. 178–84.

[6] Helen Vendler, *The Art of Shakespeare's Sonnets*, p. xiv.

[7] Francis Meres, *Palladis Tamia*; Gregory Smith, *Elizabethan Critical Essays* 2: 317. Of the reception of the 1609 quarto we know nothing certain except that the actor Edward Alleyn (not a member of Shakespeare's company) bought a copy for 5d (5 pense). Individual sonnets appear in seventeenth-century manuscripts: see Gary Taylor, "Some Manuscripts of Shakespeare's Sonnets"; Katherine Duncan-Jones, ed., *Shakespeare's Sonnets*, 2nd ed., pp. 453–66; Arthur F. Marotti, "Shakespeare's Sonnets and the Manuscript Circulation of Texts in Early Modern England." There is evidence of circulation within the elite Herbert-Sidney circle, including (Marotti, pp. 197–8) the splicing of a version of

*Passionate Pilgrim*, and all of them had been written by 1609. One refers to the passage of three years from the time when "first I saw you fresh which yet are greene" (104.8). It is a reasonable guess that Shakespeare, like the rest of the Elizabethan poetry guild, wrote most of his sonnets during the 1590s, though allusions have been plausibly detected in sonnet 107 that would place it (and maybe subsequent sonnets as well) after Elizabeth's death in 1603. Around such meager evidence arguments for dating the poems have paced undecisively, probing for connection with other questions about the situation within which Shakespeare's sequence was written and made public. Consensus has proved subject to dispersal by the next investigator looking at the file, and it is hard to speak of progress. We do not know if the 1609 volume, with its cryptic dedication, was authorized or pirated. If it was authorized, the ragged state of the text suggests the author was not available or even interested when it was being set (the mere presence of 145, 153, and 154 looks on the face of it like some kind of printshop mix-up). We have no direct testimony as to why the sonnets were not in the First Folio, an omission not corrected for more than a century; it has often been thought that they were considered scandalous, though there are different theories as to what the scandal was.

The most maddeningly self-renewing debates have of course been over the identity of the figures traditionally called (as they will be here) the young man, the dark lady, and the rival poet. Identifications suggested by the 1940s fill almost 200 pages in Hyder Rollins's Variorum edition.[8] Later discussions have generally relitigated proposals already on offer, though Elaine Scarry has recently made a detailed argument in favor of, astonishingly, two entirely new candidates for the young man and the rival poet: the sonneteer Henry Constable and, held back for effect until late in the book, King James VI of Scotland. Scarry's presentation is unfailingly attentive and perceptive, and her identifications make Constable a much more interesting figure than he has been before and also open up some brilliant and moving analyses of individual poems of his and Shakespeare's (which she thinks are at times in direct dialogue with each other). Those readings are impressive enough to disarm or at least distract readers uneasy with the kind of cryptological work which has a shady history in Shakespearean scholarship (Scarry begins by searching out individual Shakespearean lines which contain, or almost contain, the letters needed to spell out "Henry Constable"), or with casting the role of the young man with someone Shakespeare's age, if not a year or two older. Outside the spell of Scarry's way with individual poems the case is no more firmly grounded, no less reliant on coincidence and leaps of faith, than the best of its predecessors. Stepping sensibly aside into the third person, she says of her thesis, "its author only *believes* it to be

---

sonnet 106 with a poem of William Herbert to make a single thirty-two-line poem; see Kingsley-Smith, pp. 43–54, 64–6.
[8] *A New Variorum Edition of Shakespeare: The Sonnets* 2:177–294.

true; she does not *know* it to be true."[9] As far as prying into Shakespeare's sequence is concerned, biography makes a rubbery fulcrum.

Bracketting biography out of the discussion, however, does not dispose of the implied narrative of the poems themselves: in general a narrative of successive emotional states, behind which certain events are momentarily visible or partly visible.[10] That there is such a narrative, spotty and uneven, has been sensed by many readers. A few poems offer general statements or affirmations, but most present themselves as speech acts within some situation that a reader will, consciously or otherwise, sketch in while reading just to understand the poem. Some clusters of poems link to one another, bringing a continuity of action into view. The roughness of that continuity over longer stretches is paradoxically one of the stronger arguments in favor of the sequence's biographical roots: "if Shakespeare had set out to make an objective sequence with a fictional story, he would surely have done a better job of it."[11] We can be confident, art being art, that what happens in the poems is not exactly what happened in real life, but the art is what we have in front of us and is also the main reason we still care about the poems. Fifty years on from my first bumpy encounter with Shakespeare's sonnets, I have come to think that they reveal their full and considerable power only in the context of their implied narrative, which is not all that obscure but requires time and patience to take in. That narrative is worth setting out with more confidence than has lately been the case.[12]

\*

Scholars have brought severe scepticism to bear on that narrative, and much of that scepticism is on its own terms unanswerable. The conventional understanding, stated as fact by Steevens and Edmund Malone in 1780,[13] has been that sonnets 1–126 concern the speaker's love for a young man, and 127–54 his love for a dark-haired, apparently dark-complexioned woman. These are the "Two loves ... of comfort and dispaire" contrasted in one of the poems: "a man right faire" and "a woman collour'd il" (144.1, 3, 4). The key textual evidence is the distribution of gender references (fewer than they would be in some romance language). In the first group the beloved is sometimes clearly identified as male and never clearly identified as female; in the second the situation is reversed. This does not necessarily mean any of the poems without such indication of gender

---

[9] Scarry, *Naming Thy Name*, p. 6.
[10] Vendler, uncompromisingly scornful of biographical readings, is sharply attuned to this aspect of things: "Shakespeare is especially concerned ... to punctuate his sequence with moments of visible drama. It is on these dramatic 'turns' that all putative reconstructions of the 'narratives' behind the sequence have been based" (p. 88).
[11] Cruttwell, p. 4.
[12] Obviously I do not agree that respect for the received order of the sequence is "misguided and destructive" (Kingsley-Smith, p. 250). I do not see how it forecloses comparable respect for the other things that have been made of the sequence's constituent poems unless you just decline to be interested in them.
[13] *Supplement* 1: 579, 682.

have to concern the same category of beloved as their immediate neighbors, and Margreta de Grazia has accurately noted how much leeway the sequence as we have it leaves in this matter: "what Malone's clear-cut division has obscured is the astonishing number of sonnets that do not make the gender of the addressee explicit. Shakespeare is exceptional among the English sonneteers ... in leaving the beloved's gender unspecified in so many of the sonnets: about five-sixths of them in the first 126 and just less than that in the collection entire."[14] Sonnets usually thought to concern a man may well have concerned a woman, and *vice versa* (or more than one man or more than one woman). "This is not," de Grazia nevertheless goes on, "to say that Malone got it wrong," and for her own purposes proceeds to accept Malone's version of things. Two years later Heather Dubrow sets out "to interrogate the conventional wisdom about the sonnets' addressees more radically than de Grazia and others have done," and lays down some rapid-fire hypotheticals: "what if we were to admit the possibility that one of the highly erotic poems after 126 refers to the Friend?" etc. Having done so, though, Dubrow is mostly noncommittal about her answers, which hover in the realm of "admit the possibility," and she indeed affirms that "my aim is neither to advocate any of these alternative readings nor to dismiss more familiar ones out of hand ... but to suggest that the sequence permits a reader to construct any number of narratives."[15] The sequence has of course always permitted that, and, beginning with John Benson's edition of 1640, readers, professional and otherwise, have indeed done it. Efforts with literary flair, such as Oscar Wilde's "The Portrait of Mr. W. H." (1889), still have a claim on our attention, but most have faded.[16] Dubrow's more serious agenda is a suspicion of narrativity itself and "a more general impulse towards linearity and even teleology" which in interpretations of Shakespeare's sequence she sees having misogynist consequences or even intent:

> Critics' unacknowledged anxieties about the possible homoerotic undertones in this text may have led them to replicate one of the most common narratives our culture scripts: the regendering of guilt. That is, by imposing on the Sonnets the

---

[14] Margreta de Grazia, "The Scandal of Shakespeare's Sonnets," p. 97.
[15] Heather Dubrow, "'Incertainties now crown themselves assur'd,'" pp. 115, 116, 127–8.
[16] Rollins gives a *catalogue raisonné* of suggested reconfigurations of the sonnet order in his *Variorum* 2: 74–116. The most ambitious effort since then is the attempt of Brents Stirling to develop a more or less scientific methodology in *The Shakespeare Sonnet Order: Poems and Groups*. The collection as Stirling rearranges it "remains a miscellany" (p. 42); it also does not disturb Malone's divison between 1–126 and 127–54. The most dramatic response to Dubrow's invitation has been Ilona Bell's proposal ("Rethinking Shakespeare's Dark Lady") that some of the angriest of the dark lady sonnets are addressed to the young man as part of a previously undetected narrative in which the supposedly promiscuous woman has actually rejected the speaker's advances, prompting him to write poems slandering her, only to discover to his horror that she had been an innocent virgin seduced by the young man's deceitful promise of marriage ("thy bed-vow broake" [152.4]).

plot I have outlined, Shakespeareans can deflect onto the Dark Lady's corruption anxieties about homoerotic corruption and betrayal.[17]

Still, this is not an argument for (or against) some particular ordering or reading of the sonnets; it is a reminder to critics to keep their eyes open to what they may be doing unawares. On a practical level, the absence of specific evidence gendering the beloved as female in any poem before 126 or as male in any poem after that does place the burden of proof on those who would disallow Malone's partition of the sequence, and that proof has not been forthcoming.

The sequence begins slowly and repetitiously, but also, once you start to notice, with a sense of advancing continuity that gives the first twenty sonnets a pretty firm narrative coherence.[18] A male reader (who would have only himself to blame; I do not see the misdirection as intentional) might briefly be able to convince himself that he was reading, as would be expected in a sonnet sequence, a man's courtship of a coy mistress:

> From fairest creatures we desire increase,
> That thereby beauties *Rose* might never die,
> But as the riper should by time decease,
> His tender heire might beare his memory:
> But thou contracted to thine owne bright eyes,
> Feed'st thy lights flame with selfe substantiall fewell,
> Making a famine where aboundance lies,
> Thy selfe thy foe, to thy sweet selfe too cruell. (1.1–8)

The speaker might be trying to persuade a woman to become his wife and bear his children. This amounts to a shift in the usual *carpe diem* arguments from "persuasions to enjoy" (the common seventeenth-century term) to what Joseph Pequigney calls "persuasions to breed,"[19] and the shift brings with it a patriarchal perspective that might not in practical terms be the most seductive way to go: I want a child by you so I can have a proper heir. The second quatrain, however, returns to form by deploying a trope established in sonneteering by Petrarch himself (*Canz.* 45–6). Refusal of the speaker's request could only be because of the sin of Narcissus, whose cry of frustration in Ovid is translated in l. 7: "*inopem me copia fecit*" (*Metamorphoses* 3.466; plenty has made me poor). The argument continues in subsequent poems, developing the trope as a canny Petrarchan seducer would.[20] If the speaker here challenges his addressee's narcissism, that is not in order to

---

[17] Dubrow, "'Incertainties,'" pp. 129–30.
[18] Joseph Pequigney, *Such Is My Love*, pp. 18–29, is good on the back-and-forth of this. See also Robert Crosman, "Making Love Out of Nothing at All," though he takes things only up to sonnet 17.
[19] Pequigney, p. 10.
[20] Sonnet 2 was indeed reconfigured in manuscript for Caroline readers as a seduction poem addressed to a young woman; see Kingsley-Smith, pp. 59–62.

crush it but rather to gratify it in another and more rewarding way, one that leads not into isolation but into the full cycle of life. Your child can be your mirror, as you were for your own mother:

> Thou art thy mothers glasse and she in thee
> Calls backe the lovely Aprill of her prime,
> So thou through windowes of thine age shalt see,
> Dispight of wrinkles this thy goulden time. (3.9–12)

This quatrain is perhaps the best bit of poetry in the sequence so far. Larry McMurtry uses it as the epigraph for his novel *Terms of Endearment* (1975), where it indeed applies, beautifully and movingly, to a mother and a daughter pregnant with her first child. Sonnet 3, however, has already made clear for the first time in the sequence that the addressee is male, being urged to have a child and heir by some as yet undesignated woman:

> Looke in thy glasse and tell the face thou vewest,
> Now is the time that face should forme an other,
> Whose fresh repaire if now thou not renewest,
> Thou doo'st beguile the world, unblesse some mother.
> For where is she so faire whose un-eard wombe
> Disdaines the tillage of thy husbandry? (1–6)

The encouragement of the vanity of the young man, as we now know him to be, intensifies; he is being sent back to his mirror to savor the beauty that procreation has a chance of preserving and the most desirable of women are bound to find irresistible. The speaker bestowing this flattery is not overtly asking anything for himself, and we may wonder what he is doing here. He has said nothing so far to indicate his standing in this situation; he has not even called the young man "friend" (and will not until 30.13). There is no positive evidence to support the theory that the speaker is someone brought in, possibly in his capacity as poet, to lure the spoiled heir of a noble house into accepting his responsibility for continuing the line, but that would be consistent with the peculiar configuration here implied. However it came about, it is set to change before our eyes.

After a run of sonnets saying more or less the same thing, the temperature changes:

> For shame deny that thou bear'st love to any
> Who for thy selfe art so unprovident.
> Grant if thou wilt, thou art belov'd of many,
> But that thou none lov'st is most evident (10.1–4)

The reproach against the young man has become more aggrieved; he is not just "to thy sweet selfe too cruell," but is causing pain to others, on whose behalf the poet takes it upon himself to speak. Sonnet 10 moves on to Shakespeare's clearest hint that these victims are the poet's wealthy employers—

> For thou art so posssest with murdrous hate,
> That gainst thy selfe thou stickst not to conspire,
> Seeking that beautious roofe to ruinate
> Which to repaire should be thy chiefe desire (5–8)

—but suddenly makes it personal:

> O change thy thought, that I may change my minde,
> Shall hate be fairer log'd then gentle love?
> Be as thy presence is gracious and kind,
> Or to thy selfe at least kind harted prove,
>   Make thee an other selfe for love of me,
>   That beauty still may live in thine or thee. (9–14)

Vendler catches the force of this: "Sonnet 10 is the first poem to use the first-person singular, *I* and *me*. Such a moment in lyric is the equivalent of the entry of a new *dramatis persona* on the stage: its effect cannot be overestimated."[21] It is bold of the speaker to presume that his opinion should *matter* this much to the young man. Apparently during the course of what many readers register as one of the less interesting stretches of the sequence something has been stirring to give the poet the confidence and sense of urgency to take the risk. After he has laid open claim to the young man's love, things are not going to be the same.

To what extent the young man honors his poet's claim is something that, by the very nature of the sonnet sequence, we do not get to see. The young man does apparently allow his poet to keep talking. As that talking continues, the first-person singular becomes more frequent and active, now capable of getting a poem started—"When I doe count the clock that tels the time, / And see the brave day sunck in hidious night ..." (12.1–2)—and the language of affection becomes startlingly personal:

> Who lets so faire a house fall to decay,
> Which husbandry in honour might uphold,
> Against the stormy gusts of winters day
> And barren rage of deaths eternall cold?

---

[21] Vendler, p. 88.

> O none but unthrifts, deare my love you know,
> You had a Father, let your Son say so. (13.9–14)

The argument is still that the young man should marry and have a child, though halfway through the second decade of sonnets another possibility works its way in: "all in war with Time for love of you / As he takes from you, I ingraft you new" (15.13–14). The reference is to the poems that we are now reading. In his role as poet the speaker ventures to move from persuading the young man to marry and start a family to himself performing a service analogous to what the still unselected wife might perform: giving the young man's beauty a way to survive the ravages of time. In the air is a metaphor going back to Plato: the highest mystery of human love is the way in which the love between older and younger men gives birth not to children but to achievements of moral, artistic, and intellectual beauty (*Symposium* 207c-9e). Shakespeare does not quite say as much; he might have read Plato's dialogue in Latin or French, though it is not especially likely. The procreation sonnets nevertheless hover on the verge of a ravishing affirmation of what the speaker's bond with the young man could be or possibly already is: "Refusing to beget copies of himself within some happy maiden womb, the young man instead inspires, inseminates, the poet to write sonnets that celebrate and thus preserve the friend's beauty."[22] The speaker pulls back, as if he were about to go too far:

> But wherefore do not you a mightier waie
> Make warre uppon this bloudie tirant time?
> And fortifie your selfe in your decay
> With meanes more blessed then my barren rime? (16.1–4)

We return to procreation, though something of the argument for literary immortality bleeds through: "you must live drawne by your owne sweet skill" (14). In the next poem the project of immortalizing the young man's beauty in verse is reaffirmed, but also seen as insufficient without that other project:

> If I could write the beauty of your eyes,
> And in fresh numbers number all your graces,
> The age to come would say this Poet lies,
> Such heavenly touches nere toucht earthly faces. ...
>     But were some childe of yours alive that time,
>     You should live twise, in it and in my rime. (17.5–8, 13–14)

Yet something extraordinary is about to happen. Those prospective children disappear from the sequence, never to be heard of again. And the next poem is,

---

[22] James Schiffer, ed. *Shakespeare's Sonnets*, p. 49.

without warning, the first of the hyperbolically famous sonnets: "Shall I compare thee to a Summers day?" (18.1). There it is all about poetry:

> But thy eternall Sommer shall not fade,
> Nor loose possession of that faire thou ow'st,
> Nor shall death brag thou wandr'st in his shade,
> When in eternall lines to time thou grow'st,
>   So long as men can breath or eyes can see,
>   So long lives this, and this gives life to thee. (9–14)

The grand effect may be partly an accident of literary history—if sonnet 18 were not so well known, it might not sweep the scene with quite such a burst of light and warmth and gratitude—but even taken down a notch, the effect is still there. The poem carries no indicator of the gender of its addressee, and it is one of the young man sonnets Dubrow suggests could more challengingly be reassigned to the dark lady.[23] I think, though, its dramatic impact is stronger where it is for catching the sense of erotic release as the speaker's desire for the young man has finally worked its way into the open air from its muffled beginnings. The seeming lapse in the plotline is actually something that *happens* in the plot. It is often said that one of the main "un-Petrarchan" features of Shakespeare's sequence is the absence of any poems of courtship, but that is not the case; the opening run of sonnets dramatizes a flirtation of which the suitor, as can happen in real life, comes only by stages to an awareness that that is what it is.

That awareness is clinched with what was long the most indigestible poem in the sequence:

> A womans face with natures owne hand painted,
> Haste thou the Master Mistris of my passion,
> A womans gentle hart but not acquainted
> With shifting change as is false womens fashion.
> An eye more bright then theirs, lesse false in rowling:
> Gilding the object where-upon it gazeth,
> A man in hew all *Hews* in his controwling,
> Which steales mens eyes and womens soules amaseth.
> And for a woman wert thou first created,
> Till nature as she wrought thee fell a dotinge,
> And by addition me of thee defeated,
> By adding one thing to my purpose nothing.
>   But since she prickt thee out for womens pleasure,
>   Mine be thy love and thy loves use their treasure. (20)

---

[23] Dubrow, "'Incertainties,'" p. 124.

In one of the few secure advances in the critical tradition, a tectonic shift in attitudes toward homosexuality has in the twenty-first century finally dislodged a serious clog from discussions of the young man, and especially of this poem. Steevens does not temporize on sonnet 20: "It is impossible to read this fulsome panegyrick, addressed to a male object, without an equal mixture of disgust and indignation."[24] It is impossible not to think that this disgust and indignation partially fuels his criticism elsewhere of Shakespeare's craftsmanship as a sonneteer. Serious appreciation of the sequence was for two centuries distracted by the need or at least hope somehow to deny or avoid or ignore the imputation that its dominant topic is male homoerotic passion, but with the air cleared the odd conceit of sonnet 20 says just that. Shakespeare is less florid about it than Barnfield, but, even as he is making a joke, more serious. The feelings roused in the speaker by the young man are the feelings roused in him by a beautiful woman, and they are both emotional and physical: within fourteen lines they lead his thoughts to the design of the human genitals. Arguments otherwise are happily now wasted motion, of interest only as part of the past history of Shakespearean criticism. The bold display in sonnet 20 of the nature of the poet's love immediately follows the first full-throated fanfare of "high conquistadorial rhetoric"[25] about the power of poetry: "doe thy worst ould Time, dispight thy wrong, / My love shall in my verse ever live young" (19.13–14). The speaker of these poems, lifted with his now acknowledged desire and a conviction of his own powers, comes to a point of high exhilaration.

\*

Then what? When the conceit fully unfolds, the speaker in sonnet 20 feels stymied in his now clearly sexual "purpose": after all that ravishing feminization, Nature gave the young man a penis rather than a vagina. One could see the speaker's arch frustration as a playful joke among those in the know ("Well, nobody's perfect"); attempts have been made to parse the couplet as a more open anticipation of carnal satisfaction between the two men.[26] Joseph Pequigney, though, in the first unembarrassed and still the most thoroughgoing discussion of the young man sonnets as the story of a gay male love affair in a recognizably modern sense, does accept the more obvious reading of the "practical program for dealing with the situation at hand": "The end of the discourse is to solicit for the poet the undivided and exclusive love of the youth, and love is disassociated from sexual activity, which the second proposal concedes to women in the plural, to no one of them in particular."[27] (Any children those women might produce are no longer of interest.)

---

[24] *Supplement* 1: 596.
[25] Neil L. Rudenstine, *Ideas of Order*, p. 28.
[26] See Stephen Orgel, *Impersonations*, p. 57. Scarry, writing in 2016 and casually taking physical intimacy between Shakespeare and Constable almost for granted, suggests (p. 10) that it begins between sonnets 17 and 18.
[27] Pequigney, p. 35.

But Pequigney also thinks this resolution only lasts perhaps a dozen sonnets, and the speaker and the young man soon become lovers in the physical sense. For one thing, he detects across the ensuing sonnets language indicating an ongoing sexual relationship. Some of this is simply an insistence, with which there is no disagreeing, that the speaker's terms of endearment have the intensity we associate with sexual passion. Pequigney, though, looking through lenses ground by Eric Partridge and others, also makes out specific physical business coded into lines like "Kissing with golden face the meddowes greene; / Guilding pale streames with heavenly alcumy" (33.3–4). With a glance back at *Venus and Adonis* (229–40), Pequigney sees "meddowes greene" as referring "to the lower parts of the body and probably to 'the pubes'", while "the 'pale streams' ... suggest seminal fluid," so that "the line may be paraphrased 'enriching an orgasm with delectable magic.'"[28] The coding is, to be sure, not rigorously one-to-one:

> The verb *to ride (on)* is a fascinating signifier in the Sonnets, where it occurs three times, and with the idea of penial insertion common to the signifieds. Nevertheless, the acts performed differ in each instance. In Sonnet 33, the cloud-man "rides on" the "face" of the sun-youth, to suggest fellatio. At 137.6, the mistress is the whorish "bay where all men ride," coitally .... And at 89.10 to "ride upon" the youth's "deep" refers to anal intercourse.[29]

Anyone who has taught or taken a college English course in the last half century knows the enjoyment of doing this sort of thing, and there is no reason that enjoyment should not include, as indeed it now does, homosexual and well as heterosexual *double entendres*. (Pequigney passes up the opportunity offered by two references to a viscous "salve" [34.7, 120.12] that my students did not miss.) But literary criticism in our time also shows that, with ingenuity and patience, you can do this with almost any text. Pequigney's argument needs steadier evidence to establish that he has uncovered a sixteenth-century cipher for referring to forbidden acts instead of simply finding what a late twentieth-century interpreter expects or wants to find. His briefer but more important argument is that the "compromise" reached with "the Master Mistris of my passion" *has* to be unsustainable: "The speaker of sonnet 20 presents himself in an unstable plight. ... His passion has been evoked but wants an acceptable mode of expression. ... Something will give; either the passion will subside, or the friends will engage in physical enjoyment of each other." This conviction authorizes the close reading for sexual innuendo in the poems that follow. Pequigney is conscious of what he is disallowing—"Sonneteers are, I am aware, notoriously capable of sustaining themselves in a worshipful state

---

[28] Pequigney, p. 108.
[29] Pequigney, pp. 120–1.

of ungratified desire"—but takes this to be a defining tenet of Shakespearean exceptionalism: "this sonneteer ... is hardly a conformist to Petrarchan conventions."[30] Maybe; but, for all the ostentatious unconventionality of Shakespeare's sequence, there is an argument to be made against that exceptionalism.[31] Especially within a sixteenth-century context, Pequigney is hasty dismissing the possibility that "a worshipful state of ungratified desire" would be able to sustain itself here as it does elsewhere.

Lust, an ingenious and resourceful power despite its reputation for stupidity, can intensify as well as disrupt idealization. An example is to hand in the closest Renaissance analogue to the young man sonnets, Michelangelo's poems on Tommaso de' Cavalieri, and one in particular:

> Non è sempre di colpa aspra e mortale
> d'una immensa bellezza un fero ardore,
> se poi sì lascia liquefatto il core,
> che 'n breve il penetri un divino strale.
>     Amore isveglia e desta e 'mpenna l'ale,
> né l'alto vol preschive al van furore;
> qual primo grado c'al suo creatore,
> di quel non sazia, l'alma ascende e sale. (260.1–8)[32]

Savage ardor for immense beauty is not always a harsh and mortal sin if it leaves the heart so melted that an arrow from heaven can quickly pierce it. Love rouses and awakens and gives wing, and does not restrict empty fury from higher flight; from that first step, which does not satisfy it, the soul ascends and climbs.

The octave gestures toward some fusion of carnal and divine love, something affirmed in several poems of Donne's, but that turns out not to be the goal. *Fero ardore* passes instead through a kind of vanishing point into a different realm altogether; in making this clear, the sestet manifests another, uncanny parallel with Shakespeare's sequence:

> L'amor di quel ch'i' parlo in alto aspira;
> donna è dissimil troppo; e mal conviensi
> arder di quella al cor saggio e verile.
>     L'un tira al cielo, e l'altro in terra tira;
> nell'alma l'un, l'altr'abita ne' sensi,
> e l'arco tira a cose basse e vile. (9–14)

---

[30] Pequigney, p. 41.
[31] In addition to what follows, see my "Shakespeare's Petrarchism."
[32] I quote the text of Enzo Girardi, reprinted in Michelangelo, *Rime*, intro. Giovanni Testori.

The love of which I speak aspires to the heights. Woman is too different; it is unfitting for a wise and manly heart to burn for her. The one draws to heaven, and the other draws to earth; the one lives in the soul, the other in the senses, and draws its bow at things base and vile.

The contrast between noble and debased love is a contrast between the soul and the body, and also a gender contrast, anticipating the contrast between the young man and the dark lady. Michelangelo is responding to the Florentine Neoplatonism of Marsilio Ficino, but Plato's *Symposium* is more nuanced than this. Its final word on love is not Diotima's speech, building to the abstraction of desire from all physicality, but the drunken satyr play that follows, with its vivid picture (217e–19d) of an aroused Alcibiades, used to getting what he wants, spending the night snuggled under a cloak with Socrates and trying more aggressively than ever to "gratify" (*charizesthai*) the "truly godlike and wonderful" old man, beautiful in all his ugliness. Socrates will not allow it, and Alcibiades finds his feelings of attraction and admiration stronger than ever; the speech on love he contributes to the evening ends up being an encomium of the man he wants to have sex with and cannot. We are given to understand (222b) that it is like that as well between Socrates and the other young men present. As Plato frames things, and especially in this dialogue, his theory of an idealized love is rooted in the erotically fraught and elegantly contentious life of this exclusive all-male circle, where, even when all has been said about love's transcendent divinity, petty but intense jealousies about things like seating arrangements are still in play (222e–23a). As the theory becomes famous, and especially during its revival in the Renaissance, this frame tends to get slighted or suppressed and "platonic" love moves toward its pallid modern meaning. Its impassioned origins continue to tell, however, especially in courtly circles that have, by their very nature, significant affinities with the Socratic coterie, and provide a plausible template for the young man sonnets. From the speaker's point of view, at any rate—but it is exactly there that the drama of Shakespeare's sequence takes place.

What has often seemed one of Shakespeare's most difficult sonnets becomes relatively straightforward in this context:

> They that have powre to hurt, and will doe none,
> That doe not do the thing, they most do showe,
> Who moving others, are themselves as stone,
> Unmooved, could, and to temptation slow:
> They rightly do inherrit heavens graces,
> And husband natures ritches from expence,
> They are the Lords and owners of their faces,
> Others, but stewards of their excellence:
> The sommers flowre is to the sommer sweet,

> Though to it selfe, it onely live and die,
> But if that flowre with base infection meete,
> The basest weed out-braves his dignity:
> > For sweetest things turne sowrest by their deedes,
> > Lillies that fester, smell far worse then weeds. (94)

This is one of the few poems in the sequence without an addressee. It almost has no speaker; its pronouns are all third-person, mostly plural, and its affirmations are all general. Despite that, it is informed by a strong emotional force, with an *incipit* that is one of the most arresting in the entire sequence. The sonnet's impersonality gives it a stand-alone look, and it has been read as having no particular connection with the young man. Locating it in the sequence where it is, though, enriches it, so that the same impersonality gains in emotional impact, registering anger and hurt so fierce that they can only be handled by stepping back from the fiction of direct address. The couplet, done up as proverbial folk-wisdom, resolves these emotions into what the speaker at least hopes will be a healing contempt. The problem has long been with ll. 2–4, sometimes through uncertainty as to what the unnamed (unnameable?) "thing" is, more seriously because of what looks like a mixture of qualities where "ironies are almost inordinate, an ebb and flow between approval and disapproval ambiguating the text."[33] The common assumption is that the first quatrain is a conflicted picture of the young man, "a desperate search for terms of praise with which to describe someone who has caused only pain," part of a strategy that "skirts around the unutterable: that the friend's deeds are unbearably at odds with his face."[34] A believable place to end up, but the route there is I think skewed from the somewhat simpler path that the poem's argument actually takes. The first quatrain, aside from the first six words, is not a description of the young man but of what he should be; it sets out, with touches of sarcasm but no irony, a coherent ideal for someone of his beauty and attractiveness. His failure or perhaps just disinterest in living up to that ideal is his corruption. Michael Schoenfeldt, in an important if somewhat lonely article, argues that critics' discomfort with the virtue of being "as stone, / Unmooved, could," is a failure of historical imagination:

> The poem's urgent endorsement of cool stability can only be understood against the unstable, overheated self, susceptible to the insanities of insubordinate desire,

---

[33] John Kerrigan, ed., *The Sonnets and A Lover's Complaint*, p. 290. The confusions the sonnet generates in critics are most densely displayed in William Empson's famous essay (1935), which opens with the calculation that the poem suggests "4096 possibilities of thought, with other possibilities"; I find the essay harder to follow than the poem: "*lilies* are separated from the *flower* by a colon and an intervening generalisation, whereas the flower is only separated from the cold people (not all of whom need be lilies) by a colon; certainly the flower as well as the lily is in danger, but this does not make them identical and equal to W. H."; "They That Have Power," pp. 89, 99.
[34] Colin Burrow, ed., *Complete Sonnets and Poems*, p. 568.

that is depicted in the other sonnets and is a product of the period's medical, theological, and philosophical inheritance. Under this dispensation, modes of constraint we construe as unhealthy repression are coveted as acts of self-government necessary for the protection of self and other. ... The difficulty we have in reading this poem without ironizing its endorsement of self-discipline measures some of the distance separating the modern fetish of desire from the Renaissance fetish of control.[35]

There are ironies in the poem, but the contemporary impulse is to read them in the wrong direction. "By describing the ideal of constancy in terms of lifeless stone, Shakespeare knowingly deploys conventional anti-Stoic terminology," but he "invokes such denigrating terminology not to render the poem's larger claims for self-control ironic but rather to reclaim this vocabulary from the critics of stoical demeanor, and to remind us of the costs and difficulties of sustaining the ethical stability the poem demands."[36]

The not quite mentionable "thing" the young man most does show would be acting on his extraordinary beauty and attractiveness to selfish and heartless ends. He could have, perhaps already has had quite a successful career as seducer. He certainly has the potential to be archetypally good at it, as the previous sonnet had affirmed: "How like *Eaves* apple doth thy beauty grow, / If thy sweet vertue answere not thy show" (93.13–14). Abstention from that predatory career would not be the "duplicity" often mentioned in critical discussions but principled self-restraint. Those who possess the young man's kind of allure are widely recognized as having the power to hurt. In love poetry, especially Petrarchan love poetry, the hurt is usually the sadistic or indifferent rejection of a would-be lover, but the twist in sonnet 94 is that the speaker is tormented by, in effect, the young man's failure to be an unattainable Petrarchan lady to his admirers—or at least to his other admirers. If the love between the speaker and his beloved is indeed "platonic" in the foundational sense of the term—homoerotically intense and physically unconsummated—then the discovery or even suspicion that the young man has elsewhere been acting on the temptation from which he and the speaker abstain would come as an even sharper blow, the sting of guilty envy being added to the horror of watching an icon connive in its own desecration. The young man was supposed to have behaved like Socrates, exercising the wisdom and self-control that made the Socratic circle work, but has turned out—likely to the surprise of no one but his idealistic lover—to be Alcibiades. But then those we love most intensely have a way of turning hostile or indifferent to the image of them which we cherish and carry with us. Indeed, they may be only dimly aware of it, or not at all.

[35] Michael Schoenfeldt, "The Matter of Inwardness," pp. 312, 320.
[36] Schoenfeldt, p. 316.

The credibility of this picture of what is going on is strengthened by one of the few other rigorously impersonal sonnets, the one about lust:

> Th'expence of Spirit in a waste of shame
> Is lust in action, and till action, lust
> Is perjurd, murdrous, blouddy full of blame,
> Savage, extreame, rude, cruell, not to trust,
> Injoyd no sooner but dispised straight,
> Past reason hunted, and no sooner had
> Past reason hated as a swollowed bayt,
> On purpose layd to make the taker mad.
> Mad in pursut and in possession so,
> Had, having, and in quest to have, extreame,
> A blisse in proofe and provd a very wo,
> Before a joy proposd behind a dreame,
>    All this the world well knowes yet none knowes well,
>    To shun the heaven that leads men to this hell. (129)[37]

This is sufficiently strong stuff that one early seventeenth-century reader crossed the poem out in a surviving copy of the quarto.[38] It comes just inside the dark lady subsequence. It is usually connected to the speaker's unambiguously sexual affair with her, and indeed sets the tone for what follows. There is, however, aside from "swollowed bayt," no overt reference to the object of desire, let alone to its gender. The focus is entirely on the desiring subject, and primarily on the male orgasmic experience, where stretches of derangement and emptiness are hinged on a spasm of intense pleasure. It is an experience toward which the speaker has come to feel helpless revulsion, and the way it is put here could refer to sex with men as well as with women. Modern resistance to attributing such revulsion to Shakespeare may bear comparison with older resistance to attributing homosexual feeling to him, but it was an emotion to which his place and time gave voice—"Doing, a filthy pleasure is, and short" (Ben Jonson, translating from Petronius, *Underwood* 90.1)—and as a playwright Shakespeare understood it as something the noblest of his characters might feel:

> Nay but to live
> In the ranck sweat of an inseemed bed
> Stewed in corruption, honying, and making love
> Over the nasty stie. (*Hamlet* 3.4.91–4; Hamlet to his mother)

---

[37] I accept emendations that have been almost universal since Malone. In l. 9 the quarto has "Made In pursut" and in l. 11 "A blisse in proofe and proud and very wo." The breathlessness of the latter has something to be said for it, though the before-after rhetoric of the third quatrain makes a strong case for "proud" = "prov'd," i.e., having been experienced. Normalizing "u/v" to bring this out, however, does obscure the relevance of the adjective "proud" to sexual arousal at its height (pride that goes before its fall).

[38] Duncan-Jones, *Shakespeare's Sonnets*, p. 17.

An "inseemed bed" is one where the sheets have been treated with grease (usually pork fat); the lines suggest a nightmarish mix of organic secretions, an environment where even honey is vile. One of the most acute observations resulting from J. B. Leishman's patient canvass of Shakespeare's sonnets against the repertoire of classical and Petrarchan conventions available to him is the discreet but consistent avoidance of the *carpe diem* argument, even where it might seem called for:

> We do not find Shakespeare reminding his friend that he will only be young once, that the time will come when those Maids of Honour will no longer be casting such melting glances upon him as they are doing today, and that he will regret that he did not 'gather the Rose of love whilst yet was time'. In fact, nowhere in Shakespeare's sonnets is there anything approaching an invitation to pleasure.[39]

The closest Shakespeare comes are his persuasions to breed, but those are distinguishable from persuasions to enjoy, and the distinction takes on more meaning the more you think about it. The absence of *carpe diem* is a feature with which Shakespearean sonneteering distinguishes itself from the general run of Renaissance Petrarchism—though not, as Leishman also notes, from Petrarch himself, who in his *Canzoniere* feels acutely the pressure of time and bodily decay but never employs that as a seducer's argument. Here and elsewhere, Shakespere's showy deviation from the norms of contemporary Petrarchism is on another level a return to origins.

*

No laurels are mentioned in Shakespeare's sequence, but the Petrarchan ambition for poetic immortality that germinates in the procreation sonnets and reaches full height in sonnet 19 is sustained throughout the young man subsequence:

> Not marble, nor the guilded monuments
> Of Princes shall out-live this powrefull rime,
> But you shall shine more bright in these contents
> Then unswept stone, besmeer'd with sluttish time. (55.1–4)

The boast traces to Horace ("*Exegi monumentum aere perennius / regalique situ pyramidum altius*"; *Odes* 3.30.1–2, I have built a monument more enduring than brass, loftier than the royal ruins of the pyramids), though centering it on the beauty of the loved one shows Petrarch's mark. The unexpected note is "sluttish time," but Leishman's argument makes the insult of a piece with Shakespeare's attitude toward seizing the day: "In their poetry on the topics *carpe diem* and *carpe florem* the ancient poets and their imitators are ... recommending a co-operation with Time, submission to the conditions it imposes; urging those they address to seize Time, to make the best use of Time. ... Shakespeare ... will have none of this

---

[39] J. B. Leishman, *Themes and Variations in Shakespeare's Sonnets*, 2nd ed., p. 100.

collaboration with the enemy."⁴⁰ The most direct defiance (again remembering Horace) is one of the last of the young man poems:

> No! Time, thou shalt not bost that I doe change,
> Thy pyramyds buylt up with newer might
> To me are nothing novell, nothing strange,
> They are but dressings of a former sight (123.1–4)

The constancy of which the speaker boasts is not just a constancy of thought and action—the areas in which this Stoic virtue is most naturally asserted—but also a constancy of affection, where human beings are notoriously volatile. The boast asserts the power of mind over feeling, and some of the happiest sonnets in Shakespeare's sequence use "think" and "thought" in ways so casual they may escape notice:

> When to the Sessions of sweet silent thought,
> I sommon up remembrance of things past,
> I sigh the lacke of many a thing I sought,
> And with old woes new waile my deare times waste ....
>    But if the while I thinke on thee (deare friend)
>    All losses are restord, and sorrowes end. (30.1–4, 13–14)

The setting is solitude, which the mind has no trouble populating; the convening of these sessions sounds like a habitual thing. Most of the poem is given over to memories of loss and disappointment, which until the couplet seem endless but then are wholly redeemed by the mere thought of the "deare friend." The simplicity of that message is a major source of its fame—though if the poem were being written in the present day, we would probably assume that what is being affirmed is the richness and depth of the speaker's relationship with that friend, the effectiveness with which they understand and support each other emotionally. But Shakespeare's friend is not actually present and indeed does not have to do anything in order to have the effect he does; his lover "does not dare to claim any active participation by the young man in the restoration of happiness."⁴¹ The speaker, alone, simply summons him up as a thought. It is, in this important sense, a Petrarchan love poem, standing beautifully on its own but also giving the sequence one of its most blissful and peaceful moments.

There are deeper journeys into solitude:

> When most I winke then doe mine eyes best see,
> For all the day they view things unrespected,

---
⁴⁰ Leishman, p. 100.
⁴¹ Vendler, p. 168.

> But when I sleepe, in dreames they looke on thee,
> And darkely bright, are bright in darke directed. ...
> All dayes are nights to see till I see thee,
> And nights bright daies when dreams do shew thee me.
> (43.1–4, 13–14)

The lover longs for dreams of his beloved—presumably because the young man is absent, though the poem never quite tells us that. In context l. 13 suggests not a wish that the young man should hurry back but an eagerness to dream again. The language implies that dreams are a superior reality, better than what the daylight world has to offer; "winke" (as in *Cælica* 45.40) is shy and unpretentious, but the notion that eyes see best when closed is consistent with a Platonic stance toward ordinary reality and aligns Shakespeare's sonnet with attempts to translate Petrarchan love poetry into Neoplatonic terms, not to mention Helena's often-quoted discourse on love in *Midsummer Night's Dream*: "Love lookes not with the eyes, but with the minde: / And therefore is wingd *Cupid* painted blinde" (1.1.234–5).[42] Near the end of the young man subsequence is a bolder advocacy for a waking dream state, a walking hallucination:

> Since I left you, mine eye is in my minde,
> And that which governes me to goe about,
> Doth part his function, and is partly blind,
> Seemes seeing, but effectually is out:
> For it no forme delivers to the heart
> Of bird, of flowre, or shape which it doth latch,
> Of his quick objects hath the minde no part,
> Nor his owne vision houlds what it doth catch:
> For if it see the rud'st or gentlest sight,
> The most sweet-favor or deformedst creature,
> The mountaine, or the sea, the day, or night:
> The Croe, or Dove, it shapes them to your feature.
>    Incapable of more, repleat with you,
>    My most true minde thus makes mine eye untrue. (113)[43]

---

[42] Not to mention the Beach Boys: "Close my eyes, she's somehow closer now / Softly smiles, I know she must be kind" ("Good Vibrations").

[43] The 1609 quarto reads "maketh mine untrue" in the last line. Malone (*Supplement* 1: 673) keeps this reading, arguing that "untrue" is a substantive, and adduces a parallel in Milton ("Prevenient Grace descending had remov'd / The stonie from thir hearts"; *Paradise Lost* 11.3–4), though he also suggests that we could insert "eye" between "mine" and "untrue." Robert Cartwright conjectures "maketh m'eye (or m'eyne) untrue"; *The Sonnets of William Shakspeare*, p. 35. Editors continue to vary among these and a few other possibilities. There is no uncertainty about what is meant, and in the absence of a stronger analogy for "untrue" as a substantive I follow what seems to me the path of least resistance.

I only have eyes for you. To be in love this way is always to see what you want to see; the experience is not just of blessedness but also of power. This poem makes it even clearer than sonnet 43 that the visions the lover sees are active contradictions of objective truth, transformations of what he still recognizes as common reality into his private reality, a willed delusion not compromised (at least for the duration of fourteen lines) by the continuing realization that it is just that. In putting it this way, Shakespeare, whether he knew it or not, evokes some of the most quietly extreme moments in Petrarch—"*se l'error durasse, altro non cheggio*" (*Canz.* 129.39 [if the deception should last, I ask for no more])—and indeed comes the closest he ever does to offering his equivalent to a particular sonnet of Petrarch's:

> Pien de quella ineffabile dolcezza
> che del bel viso trassen gli occhi miei
> nel dì che volentier chiusi gli avrei
> per non mirar giamai minor bellezza,
>
> lassai quel chi' i' più bramo ....
>
> In una valle chiusa d'ogn' intorno,
> ch' è refrigerio de' sospir miei lassi,
> giunsi sol con Amor, pensoso et tardo;
>
> ivi non donne ma fontane et sassi
> et l'imagine trovo di quel giorno
> che 'l pensier mio figura ovunque io sguardo. (116.1–5, 9–14)

Full of that ineffable sweetness which my eyes drew from her lovely face on that day when I would gladly have closed them so as never to look on any lesser beauties, I departed from what I most desire. ... In a valley closed on all sides, which cools my weary sighs, I arrived alone with Love, full of care, and late; there I find not ladies but fountains and rocks and the image of that day which my thoughts image forth wherever I may glance.

Of English sonneteers of consequence, Daniel is the only one to go as far as Shakespeare in this direction.

Shakespeare, however, never stays there. Sonnet 113 is linked to 114, where the speaker turns back on himself: "Or whether doth my minde being crown'd with you / Drinke up the monarks plague this flattery?" (1–2). The unsatisfactory reality whose presence is never denied is always there to press its claims, at times with what seems like conclusive force. "Farewell thou art too deare for my possessing," one poem begins (87.1), initiating a densely legalistic argument in which "too deare" indeed turns out to mean, "you cost too much, I cannot afford you." Back in the real world, dreams have to be paid for. When you cannot do that you have to wake up: "Thus have I had thee as a dreame doth flatter, / In sleepe a King, but waking no such matter" (13–14). (That word "flattery" again.) This poem comes about two-thirds of the way through the young man poems. Narrative coherence might seem to need it moved to the end, or perhaps to have it signal the exit of one young man from the story and the arrival of another, though either of those actions would denature what is in front of us. That a love story could come to a moment of seemingly decisive rupture and in the next poem resume as if nothing had changed or even happened is actually one of the "realistic" features of Shakespeare's implied narrative. We hear one end of a tense conversation and do what we can to intuit the rest; discontinuities in that monologue give us that chance, while an idealistic lover given to Petrarchan self-absorption must repeatedly get it together again after an encounter with unwelcome reality. By sonnet 33 something has, off-stage, happened or been thought to happen, something acutely experienced as a betrayal, and the lover's response sets a pattern whereby some version of the same thing apparently keeps happening. It can be painful, and baffling, to watch.

Sonnet 33 begins poetically, though there is that word again:

> Full many a glorious morning have I seene,
> Flatter the mountaine tops with soveraine eie,
> Kissing with golden face the meddowes greene;
> Guilding pale streames with heavenly alcumy (1–4)

The rising sun is a loving monarch blessing his kingdom with a look that, like the young man's eye ("Gilding the object where-upon it gazeth"), adds a greater beauty to what is already there in the landscape. But the conceit generates its own *volta*:

> Anon permit the basest cloudes to ride,
> With ougly rack on his celestiall face,
> And from the for-lorne world his visage hide
> Stealing unseene to west with this disgrace (5–8)

Atmospheric conditions interfere with the light and bring a kind of ugliness and, as the day progresses toward sunset, shame. The darkening language prepares the formal comparison:

> Even so my Sunne one early morne did shine,
> With all triumphant splendor on my brow,
> But out alack, he was but one houre mine,
> The region cloude hath mask'd him from me now. (9–12)

The specific nature of the offense—the tenor of those metaphorical clouds—remains unstated. It could be sexual or social or (probably) some mixture of both, a de facto desertion of the speaker for some privacy from which the speaker is excluded; "region cloude" seems continuous with the plural "cloudes" and more than just a third party may be involved. We sense the poem has one more turn to make, and an obvious one seems built into the ruling conceit: these clouds will blow past and I will see my sun again. What we get is stranger than that: "Yet him for this, my love no whit disdaineth, / Suns of the world may staine, when heavens sun staineth" (13–14). The sun is not just temporarily concealed but permanently disfigured, yet that disfigurement only dramatizes the speaker's continued devotion, no matter what. The triumphant logic of the conceit ends up being: this shameful episode is yet one more way in which my love is like the sun!

As a consolation that might even be a joke, though a joke with possibly very deep pain to it. Figuring how far the sarcasm slices into the affirmative conclusion is not easy and may be the most important uncertainty in the sequence as a whole. The speaker does this sort of thing a lot. Two poems later:

> No more bee greev'd at that which thou hast done,
> Roses have thornes, and silver fountaines mud,
> Cloudes and eclipses staine both Moone and Sunne,
> And loathsome canker lives in sweetest bud. (35.1–4)

At the end of sonnet 34 the speaker had been caught off guard when the young man was suddenly weeping—"Ah but those teares are pearle which thy love sheeds" (34.13)—and his lover hurries to reassure him by using the trick that he had used before to reassure himself: the stain on your character is just another way in which you are like a rose, a silver fountain, the moon and the sun. Then a more anodyne generalization—"All men make faults"—becomes unexpectedly reflexive:

> and even I in this,
> Authorizing thy trespas with compare,
> My selfe corrupting salving thy amisse,
> Excusing thy sins more then thy sins are (5–8)[44]

The deictic "this" in Shakespeare's sonnets usually means "the poem you are reading now," though here it is more pointed: the lover's way of "excusing" the young man's behavior with strategically chosen metaphors—"excusing" a term Puttenham groups with "flattery" in his morphology of courtly verse.[45] The speaker,

---

[44] For l. 8 the 1609 quarto has "Excusing their sins more then their sins are." Malone emends "their ... their" to "thy ... thy" and with most editors I follow his lead, though Duncan-Jones has "these ... these" and Vendler "thy ... their."

[45] Puttenham, *Arte*, pp. 184–5 (3.16), defining "the figure *Paradiastole*, which ... we call the *Curryfavell*, as when we make the best of a bad thing."

himself a poet, is doing exactly one of the things that poets do. That action is also acknowledged as an act of self-corruption equal to if not greater than whatever the young man has done, and an aural pun intensifies the judgment on their joint "sins":

> For to thy sensuall fault I bring in sence,
> Thy adverse party is thy Advocate,
> And gainst my selfe a lawfull plea commence,
> Such civill war is in my love and hate,
>   That I an accessary needs must be,
>   To that sweete theefe which sourely robs from me. (9–14)

To his thought-crime of sense, the speaker adds judicial malpractice: an attorney is sabotaging his own case in court. But we understand that he is defending himself against a far more important charge, which may or may not have been made to his face. How can you say I do not love you?

This is hardly the last episode of such abasement in Shakespeare's sequence. A little before the midpoint of the young man subsequence is a particularly breathtaking example:

> Being your slave what should I doe but tend,
> Upon the houres, and times of your desire?
> I have no precious time at al to spend;
> Nor services to doe til you require.
> Nor dare I chide the world without end houre,
> Whilst I (my souveraine) watch the clock for you,
> Nor thinke the bitternesse of absence sowre,
> When you have bid your servant once adieue. (57.1–8)

The lover has spoken of his "vassalage" before (26.1), but this is the first occurrence of the word "slave" (to be repeated before the sonnet is done). The metaphor of political subservience that has been around since the troubadours and receives new energy in Elizabeth's court here appears in an extreme form, applied in a pitiless way to the intimate sorrow spawned by the beloved's absence. The speaker knows he has no rights at all in that absence, which he must accept without question or complaint. Even as he does so he cannot not think of the company his love is now keeping, and why; but he knows that when he does so his charge is to find a way in which this is all somehow to the credit of the young man. As indeed he does:

> Nor dare I question with my jeallous thought,
> Where you may be, or your affaires suppose,

>     But like a sad slave stay and thinke of nought
>     Save where you are, how happy you make those. (9–12)

The young man who is not here is imagined bringing light and joy to those for whom he has deserted his lover—being yet again like the sun, which ever moves on to rise elsewhere. The speaker's overriding need is to hold on to his admiration of the one he loves, no matter what it takes, as if that were a form of heroism: "So true a foole is love, that in your Will, / (Though you doe any thing) he thinkes no ill" (13–14). Writing poems like this (with, in this instance, an encrypted signature) helps him do it.

The impulse to neutralize this strain in the sonnets as "mock sincerity," "weighted with sarcasm,"[46] or some such, is almost irresistible. There is a lot of it; the cumulative effect can be quite uncomfortable. For Winters it is a major factor in his generally low opinion of the sequence: "there is in a large number of the poems an attitude of servile weakness on the part of the poet in the face of the person addressed; this attitude is commonly so marked as to render a sympathetic approach to the subject all but impossible."[47] Dubrow, calling the lover's behavior "passive-aggressive," sees more agency here, though with a hint of pathology to it.[48] If, as most critics have done,[49] we imagine the young man as his lover's social superior—probably by a fair amount—then a reading of the speaker's repeated self-abasement as merely cynical and pragmatic (he has learned what people like this need to hear) is possible, and would at least preserve our sense of his mental stability, however dishonest. Short of that, it is very tempting to register the subservience as ironic, a coded protest that the young man will recognize as easily as the reader. Vendler on this point, though, makes a telling protest of her own that "irony ... does not always improve a poem," and indeed, "if present, it would vitiate any poem dealing with capitulatory love."[50] As far as I know, "capitulatory love" is

---

[46] Bruce R. Smith, *Homosexual Desire in Shakespeare's England*, p. 260; Pequigney, p. 61.

[47] Winters, *Forms of Discovery*, pp. 52–3. He continues, "It will not do to reply that this is a convention of the courtly style and should not be taken seriously. If it is a convention of the courtly style, then it is a weakness in that style." Some allowance is still worth making for the cultural context; it is part of the lore of the time that outrageously comic self-abasement really could work. A story made the rounds in Shakespeare's day about Francesco Dandolo's strategy for getting Clement V to revoke the collective excommunication of Venice: "that worthy Ambassadour ... having effectually tried all other possible meanes of persuading, and seeing now no other hope in the world of prævayling, cast himself prostrate at the feete of the prynce, and crept under his Table lyke A Dogg: lying there in most base and abject manner, untill atlast with fountaines of teares and all dutyes of extreme humility, he bredd compassion in A heart of flynte, & wunne the inexorable Tyrant to his purpose" (*Gabriel Harvey's Marginalia*, p. 97; "heart of flynte" is directly from the idiom of Petrarchism). Leah Whittington has an interesting discussion of subservient supplication in the present day at the end of *Renaissance Supplicants*, pp. 196–200.

[48] Dubrow, *Captive Victors*, p. 253; she is uneasy about the clinical sound of the term, and does not use it in her main discussion of excuse-making in the sequence, pp. 206–13.

[49] Pequigney is an exception, at least as far as noble rank is concerned, though his dissent comes in asides (pp. 12, 88, 233–4). Roche rejects wholesale the idea that the young man was of "high station" and attributes the theory to "unshakable snobbery" (*Petrarch and the English Sonnet Sequences*, p. 382).

[50] Vendler, p. 327 (on sonnet 71).

a nonce formulation on her part, but it is a good one.[51] She feels the need for a term outside the usual critical categories, because what she is talking about presents a challenge to modern critics' usual way of doing business:

> The hyperboles of love say something to us about passion itself; and critics' uneasiness with (overmastering) passion means an uneasiness with Shakespeare's *Sonnets* themselves. It is true that there is irony in the *Sonnets* .... But there are also, I believe, sonnets of hapless love—intended as such by the author, expressed as such by the speaker. Shakespeare does not encourage us, in such cases, to second-guess the speaker.[52]

Vendler writes on behalf of "the reader's sympathy with the speaker, not an adverse or ironic judgment on him," though the response called for by the speaker's persistence in excusing the young man while simultaneously knowing and showing how insupportable that persistence is ("All men make faults, and even I in this") may be something more somber and difficult than sympathy. This is behavior verging on what we would now call addiction. The term Shakespeare himself might choose would be madness—and in one of its dimensions that could be where this story is headed:

> Past cure I am, now Reason is past care,
> And frantick madde with ever-more unrest,
> My thoughts and my discourse as mad mens are.
> At randon from the truth vainely exprest. (147.9–12)

The excusing is one manifestation of a pattern found in many of Shakespeare's sonnets: "The language is designed to persuade us ... that an assertion may be true which we know to be contrary to fact."[53] The art of it is finding an argument that will turn a manifest failing or defect to advantage, and Shakespeare becomes quite resourceful at that. Sometimes, of course, the magic works, and sometimes it does not. The trickery may pass notice because it is often so fully assimilated to the occasion; it is the pattern underlying some of his most poised and admirable poems, ones that have stood successfully on their own outside of the sequence:

> That time of yeare thou maist in me behold,
> When yellow leaves, or none, or few doe hange
> Upon those boughes which shake against the could,
> Bare ru'ind quiers, where late the sweet birds sang. (73.1–4)

---

[51] Leishman (p. 229) suggests the term "possessionless love," translating Rilke's *die besitzlose Liebe*, a kind of self-abnegation the German poet thought possible only for women (prominent on his list is Gaspara Stampa).
[52] Vendler, p. 327.
[53] Anne Ferry, *All in War with Time*, p. 5.

Lines like these have won the poem an entirely justified immortality; two more quatrains on the speaker's autumnal decay, neither forgetting the seasons that are past nor ignoring the one that is to come, develop the theme brilliantly. But there is a turn waiting in the couplet, and its move is to exploit the sense of loss in the first twelve lines as a source of strength: "This thou percev'st, which makes thy love more strong, / To love that well, which thou must leave ere long" (13–14). *Because* I am, slowly but visibly and inexorably, aging and (of course) dying, *therefore* your love for me is stronger. Perception of human mortality makes the present more dear: a version of the classic *carpe diem* argument, though not as a seducer's ploy but as an affirmation of what is already there. Or to move onto somewhat different terrain: what might make me less desirable is actually making me more attractive. However you put it, the quatrains pose a problem that the couplet solves. In lucky instances, such solutions give individual sonnets the aesthetic triumph that has earned them an independent life all of their own, but their success is always and sometimes very quickly vulnerable to what is going on in the implied plot. There are more examples to come. Set this poem into the context of the sequence, and something ominous quickly becomes visible: the speaker is not reporting what the young man feels, but telling him. The poem's conceit looks like the lover's way of preempting and denying a felt threat that his beloved is pulling away; once you notice that, the use of "leave" in the last line where you might expect (or think you remember) "lose" strengthens the sense of threat.

With things like this in mind, Vendler has an eye for places where the speaker asserts a reciprocity in his relationship with the young man. The most interesting thing about them is that he generally does so, she argues, "without any real reciprocity being present."[54] It is part of the formal premise of a sonnet sequence that, unless the poet makes special provision, we never hear directly from the beloved, so that the reader is even more handicapped than the lover in deciding what the young man's feelings actually are. He is not exactly silenced, since presumably he gets to have his say to his lover; we just do not get to hear what that is. What we do get to hear makes it worse; Eve Kosofsky Sedgwick highlights one of the key problems with the way in which the story is presented: "The youth's changes, disloyalties, qualms, self-divisions, *arrières-pensées*, are so comprehensively anticipated and personified by his admirer—in order to preserve the image of the beloved as simple and single-hearted to a degree that, the speaker knows, no one *can* be—that the image of the youth himself is flattened and all but effaced."[55] Critics filling in the blank have often not been kind: Northrop Frye characterizes the young man as "an unresponsive oaf as stupid as a doorknob and as selfish as

---

[54] Vendler, p. 171.
[55] Sedgwick, *Between Men*, pp. 43–4. Sedgwick's influential discussion ends inconclusively with her admitted disappointment that the sequence is not a novel, but she is right that things can be seen and learned by treating it as if it might be.

a weasel."[56] The young man's tears at the end of sonnet 34 tell against this picture, though comparable evidence of his responsiveness elsewhere is hard to come by. There are some affirmations that the speaker is loved in return—"happy I that love and am beloved" (25.13)—but those are just that, a lover's affirmations of what he very much wants to be true. The belief that the young man returns the speaker's love in something like equal measure is a part of the image to which the speaker is fiercely devoted, and can be found nestled in some of his most abject conceits. Perhaps the most notorious of these, his plea, ostensibly out of consideration for the young man's own reputation, to be consigned to complete oblivion—"Noe Longer mourne for me when I am dead" (71.1)—presumes, at least rhetorically, that without this intervention the young man *will* mourn; as an address to the young man in the here and now, the poem makes most sense as an attempt to deliver an emotional shock, even a kind of bullying, in hopes of seeing once more those tears like pearls that in the past brought comfort. Mutual love comes to seem over the course of the sequence more and more like a fantasy, yet the speaker's determination to hold on to the fantasy persists:

> So shall I live, supposing thou art true,
> Like a deceived husband, so loves face,
> May still seeme love to me, though alter'd new:
> Thy lookes with me, thy heart in other place. (93.1–4)

"So true a foole is love" from two decades earlier no longer fits; it is too much of a boast. The bleakness toward which the lover is moving is something Petrarch knew about, dark terrain most of his imitators never explored:

> Quel ch' i' fo veggio, et non m'inganna il vero
> mal conosciuto, anzi mi sforza Amore
> che la strada d'onore
> mai nol lassa seguir chi troppo il crede. (*Canz.* 264.91–4)

I see what I am doing, and I am not deceived by an imperfect knowledge of the truth; rather Love forces me, who never lets anyone who too much believes him follow the path of honor.

Petrarch's Christian conscience tells him he is courting damnation while trying to dicker with his own mortality: "*non m'assolve / un piacer per usanza in me sì forte / ch' a patteggiar n'ardisce co la Morte*" (124–6; I am not freed from a pleasure so strong in me by habit that it dares to bargain with Death). Shakespeare thinks of

---

[56] Northrop Frye, "How True a Twain," p. 96.

the irresistible disobedience that brought death into the world: "How like *Eaves* apple doth thy beauty grow" (93.13).

The narrative rhythm of most of the young man subsequence is of recurrent if shadowy episodes when the young man's real or suspected unfaithfulness cannot be ignored. Between these the speaker's agitation subsides and affirmative if sometimes strangely complicated declarations of affection become possible. Vendler, however, senses a shift around the century mark: after sonnet 99, "Shakespeare writes a narrative of self-blame rather than blame of the beloved."[57] The excusing comes to be directed not at the young man but at the speaker: "My love is strengthned though more weake in seeming, / I love noe lesse, though lesse the show appeare" (102.1–2). The spark for this would be either a feeling on the speaker's part or a complaint on the young man's that their love, as manifested in the poems we have been reading, has gone somehow stale—though that may be no more than a decline in the poet's productivity. In response that poet dips into classical mythology, an opulent resource of which Shakespeare makes much use elsewhere but little in his sonnets:

> Our love was new, and then but in the spring,
> When I was wont to greet it with my laies,
> As *Philomell* in summers front doth singe,
> And stops hir pipe in growth of riper daies (5–8)

I am just being like the nightingale, whose song tapers off as the seasons move on—but do not draw the wrong conclusion. In fact, *these* are the good old days:

> Not that the summer is lesse pleasant now
> Then when her mournefull himns did hush the night,
> But that wild musick burthens every bow,
> And sweets growne common loose their deare delight. (9–12)

Yet again what may seem a weakness is actually a sign of strength, or at least depth of feeling: "Therefore like her, I some-time hold my tongue: / Because I would not dull you with my songe" (13–14). In this refulgent summer, I am merely being considerate. The superior authenticity of eloquent silence to copious speech is a well-established Petrarchist topic and Shakespeare has used it before in the sequence: "others, for the breath of words respect, / Me for my dombe thoughts, speaking in effect" (85.13–14). Here it feels curtailed, shyer and less assertive than

---

[57] Vendler, p. 424. Coincidentally or not, sonnet 99 ("The forward violet thus did I chide") draws attention itself as an anomalous rfifteen-line sonnet, thanks to a fifth line added to the first quatrain. It is also a, for Shakespeare, uniquely close imitation of another Elizabethan sonnet, one by Constable ("The violet of purple coloure came"; Grundy, *Poems of Henry Constable*, p. 130) and integral to Scarry's theory about the identity of the young man; her account of the dialogue between the two poems (pp. 33–6) stands on its own without the theory.

usual ("some-time"), tailored to the occasion of making an apology and hoping it will be accepted.

Such occasions become more urgent and difficult. Immediately after the famous, much quoted and recited poem that asserts love's transcendent constancy—"Let me not to the marriage of true mindes / Admit impediments, love is not love / Which alters when it alteration findes" (116.1-2)[58]—the young man poems enter their last decade with a harrowing run of confessed faithlessness:

> Accuse me thus, that I have scanted all,
> Wherein I should your great deserts repay,
> Forgot upon your dearest love to call,
> Whereto al bonds do tie me day by day,
> That I have frequent binne with unknown mindes,
> And given to time your owne deare purchas'd right,
> That I have hoysted saile to al the windes
> Which should transport me farthest from your sight. (117.1-8)

The way this is phrased, the lover's offense could be easily trivialized (I know you have not been seeing that much of me lately), though we simultaneously see that, the way things are between these two men, making oneself scarce is not a trivial offense; the last two lines amount to a guilty admission that active avoidance (seeking room to breathe, as if on the high seas) has been on the lover's mind. The sonnet ends acknowledging guilt but also appealing for forgiveness with one of the speaker's most desperate and aggressive excuses:

> Bring me within the level of your frowne,
> But shoote not at me in your waken'd hate:
>   Since my appeale saies I did strive to proove
>   The constancy and virtue of your love. (11-14)

If sonnet 116, as its language implies, bestows upon the speaker's love for the young man something like the sanction of a marriage ceremony, the immediate consequence looks like a rough wedding night, with some painful stocktaking. Things get worse:

---

[58] "Sonnet 116 is the most universally admired of Shakespeare's sonnets. Its virtues, however, are more than usually susceptible to dehydration in critical comment. The more one thinks about this grand, noble, absolute, convincing, and moving gesture, the less there seems to be to it"; Stephen Booth, ed., *Shakespeare's Sonnets*, p. 387. Adopting language from the marriage ceremony in the *Book of Common Prayer*, the poem tries to fuse mutuality with single-minded devotion, though the paradox of this is in view by the end of the first quatrain. A seventeenth-century rewriting of Shakespeare's sonnet for a musical setting by Henry Lawes easily excises the language from the marriage ceremony (Duncan-Jones, *Shakespeare's Sonnets*, p. 465).

> Like as to make our appetites more keene
> With eager compounds we our pallat urge,
> As to prevent our malladies unseene,
> We sicken to shun sicknesse when we purge.
> Even so being full of your nere cloying sweetnesse,
> To bitter sawces did I frame my feeding;
> And sicke of wel-fare found a kind of meetnesse,
> To be diseas'd ere that there was true needing. (118.1–8)

The guilt and queasiness become more physical; lines may have been crossed that previously had been respected. Things may have come to a moment of truth, which the speaker in his instinctive fashion tries to turn to account:

> O benefit of ill, now I finde true
> That better is, by evil still made better.
> And ruin'd love when it is built anew
> Growes fairer then at first, more strong, far greater.
>   So I returne rebukt to my content,
>   And gaine by ills thrise more then I have spent. (119.9–14)

Conjuring a happy ending out of a moment of misery is by now a familiar move, but even so the sestet has a new gravity to it, a sense that things previously held back are now out in the open. If the young man poems indeed have a happy ending, it is in the next sonnet:

> That you were once unkind be-friends mee now,
> And for that sorrow, which I then didde feele,
> Needes must I under my transgression bow,
> Unlesse my Nerves were brasse or hammer'd steele.
> For if you were by my unkindnesse shaken
> As I by yours, y'have past a hell of Time,
> And I a tyrant have no leasure taken
> To waigh how once I suffer'd in your crime.
> O that our night of wo might have remembred
> My deepest sence, how hard true sorrow hits,
> And soone to you, as you to me then tendred
> The humble salve, which wounded bosomes fits!
>   But that your trespasse now becomes a fee,
>   Mine ransoms yours, and yours must ransome mee. (120)

In this new and possibly healing honesty about mutual betrayal, the speaker finds a powerful sense of reciprocal feeling that has long eluded him.

The remaining six poems are not clear on where this leaves things. The defiant address to Time in sonnet 123 sounds like a ringing reaffirmation of sonnet 116—"This I doe vow and this shall ever be, / I will be true dispight thy syeth and thee" (123.13–14)—but it does so without making any specific reference to the young man or for that matter to love. The young man is directly addressed in sonnet 126 in unusually tender terms ("O thou my lovely Boy" [126.1]), but with a valedictory sense that his eternal youthfulness is still only temporary:

> If Nature (soveraine misteres over wrack)
> As thou goest onwards still will plucke thee backe,
> She keepes thee to this purpose, that her skill,
> May time disgrace, and wretched mynuits kill.
> Yet feare her O thou minnion of her pleasure,
> She may detaine, but not still keepe her tresure!
> Her *Audite* (though delayd) answer'd must be,
> And her *Quietus* is to render thee. (5–12)

In sonnet 20 Nature fell a-doting on him at his creation, and has kept him as her own Ganymede ("thou minnion of her pleasure") for as long as possible, but her rival Time will inevitably foreclose and take possession. Vendler suggests that the speaker's "final solution" in these last poems to the problem of "maintaining love for an unpredictably unfaithful beloved" is "to separate completely the act of love from its object, and to make it absolute in its own grandeur, without respect to the worth of the beloved." This is, she adds, "a drastic but sublime (and also tragic) solution."[59] The most affirmative narrative of the poet and the young man is Scarry's:

> Though their love for each other almost certainly began in the mid to late 1580s, it is not unreasonable to believe they remained true to one another over the next two decades. ... Four centuries—not two decades—have substantiated [Shakespeare's] vow that his beloved will be kept alive by the breath of future readers. That he kept his love alive for one brief human lifetime should not be doubted.[60]

She says this, of course, in the conviction that she is talking directly about Shakespeare and Constable. Pequigney, careful to insist he is not talking about biography, finds in the young man poems a picture of an intense, sometimes tumultuous, but loving, satisfying, and fully sexual love affair. He also, though, finds from sonnet 100 onwards a "waning of love for the Master Mistress ... a convoluted process that may be interrupted and resisted but appears to proceed

---

[59] Vendler, p. 189.
[60] Scarry, p. 94.

irreversibly,"[61] at the end of which the speaker may well be ready to move on. The diminuendo is certainly there, and other critics have sensed its like in the general arc of the young man sonnets.[62] It is, however, not so pronounced or clear-cut that what is in front of us could not also be a story of endurance rather than of fading away. The speaker's compulsive excuse-making, which can seem in the moment pitiful or delusional, could ultimately just be part of how emotional business manages to get done within this fraught and potentially impossible relationship. (Stranger things have happened.) We do not get to see the other parts (we are free to guess), but during the time of the sequence they more or less work together to keep things going, and the three years reported in sonnet 104 may open onto more.

It would of course be easier to feel that way about it if the sequence as a whole actually ended here. Which brings us to the dark lady.

\*

The young man's partners in infidelity seem to be multiple and for the most part shadowy. If I were trying to coax a novel or film out of the sequence, those partners would in general be male, and from the intimidating social circle in which the young man usually moves (he is himself "a place where the elite meet").[63] One partner certainly is male, the so-called rival poet of sonnets 78–86, an episode leading to the decisive though (apparently) temporary break in sonnet 87. Whether the offenses are sexual is similarly ambiguous; I would guess some are, though receiving love poems from another poet is so specific a mimicry of the young man's relationship with the speaker as to make the distinction almost meaningless. The most dramatic episode, though, is clearly sexual, and involves a woman, and not just any woman. The usual reading of the evidence is that she and the speaker are already sexually involved, and at some point she takes the young man to bed as well.[64] The story mostly unfolds in the second subsequence, but sonnets 40–2, addressed to the young man, seem part of it as well ("That thou hast her it is not all my griefe" [42.1]). One implication of the way this is laid out is that sonnets 127–52 concern a short but intense episode that disrupts the longer-running story at a relatively early point. The violation of chronology has not proved all that much of a problem for readers, and revisiting the searing experience with the dark lady after things with the young man have run their course has its own logic, both thematic and psychological.

---

[61] Pequigney, p. 189.
[62] E.g., Ferry, *All in War*, pp. 49–63.
[63] Sedgwick, p. 40.
[64] Pequigney argues that, with one exception, the speaker's jealous suspicions in the sequence are unfounded. That exception is the episode behind sonnets 33–5, which results from the young man's sexual relations with a third party, though not with the dark lady. In general, "the youth was innocent of the sensual looseness with which he was forever being taxed" (p. 142), including anything involving the speaker's mistress.

Her darkness is there from the start.[65] It is beneficiary of one of the sequence's most ingenious acts of excusing:

> In the ould age blacke was not counted faire,
> Or if it weare it bore not beauties name:
> But now is blacke beauties successive heire,
> And Beautie slanderd with a bastard shame (127.1–4)

"Fair" has long been a synonym for "beautiful," but things have changed. Generations of women had become obsessed with cosmetics and hair dye:

> For since each hand hath put on Natures power,
> Fairing the foule with Arts faulse borrow'd face,
> Sweet beauty hath no name no holy boure,
> But is prophan'd, if not lives in disgrace. (5–8)

This is Hamlet, speaking to Ophelia: "I have heard of your paintings too well enough, God hath given you one face, and you make your selfes another" (*Hamlet* 3.1.142–4). Here, though, this is said by way of praising a rare woman who is otherwise:

> Therefore my Mistresse eyes are Raven blacke,
> Her eyes so suted, and they mourners seeme,
> At such who not borne faire no beauty lack,
> Slandring Creation with a false esteeme (9–12)

That she does not color her hair is admirable enough, but her lover attributes this abstention to something more admirable, a disapproving sorrow at what other women insist on doing to their bodies. That testimony to her moral integrity achieves precisely the result which their cosmetics were aiming for: "Yet so they mourne becomming of their woe, / That every toung saies beauty should looke so" (13–14). She has changed the rules.

Shakespeare's speaker never has occasion to excuse the young man's physical appearance. As with Amphilanthus in Pamphilia's poems, we learn nothing about

---

[65] On a physical level, the woman's blackness is a matter of hair color (like Wyatt's "Brunet"), with some reference to skin color ("her brests are dun" [130.3], "a woman collour'd il" [144.4]). G. B. Harrison proposed that she was a well-known black prostitute of the time, one "*Lucy Negro* Abbess de Clerkenwell" (*Shakespeare at Work*, pp. 64, 310–11). That proposal went nowhere, but the sense of some kind of racial (and racist) subtext has been explored over the last few decades, with de Grazia (pp. 101–7) arguing that miscegenation rather than homosexuality is the true "scandal" of the sequence. Discussion has been sometimes with reference to historical black women in Shakespeare's England, but mostly through the "language of blackness" and "semiotics of color." See especially Kim F. Hall, "'These bastard signs of fair'"; Marvin Hunt, "Be Dark but Not Too Dark"; and, for an overview, Kingsley-Smith, pp. 229–42.

it aside from its dazzling effect on his lover. The dark lady's corporeal presence, on the other hand, is famously catalogued:

> My Mistres eyes are nothing like the Sunne,
> Currall is farre more red, then her lips red,
> If snow be white, why then her brests are dun:
> If haires be wiers, black wiers grow on her head (130.1–4)

Readers who come at this through sonnet 127 will already sense what is going on, though they could pick up on it from other cues, including the poem immediately after the one in which the speaker's love for the young man comes fully into the open:

> So is it not with me as with that Muse,
> Stird by a painted beauty to his verse,
> Who heaven it selfe for ornament doth use,
> And every faire with his faire doth reherse ....
> O let me true in love but truly write,
> And then beleeve me, my love is as faire,
> As any mothers childe, though not so bright
> As those gould candells fixt in heavens ayer (21.1–4, 9–12)

The mockery is aimed not at the loved one but at the fake glamour from which the loved one offers such a blessed escape. The seemingly perverse *blason* of the dark lady admits enough in the way of uninflated statements of affection to enable us to recognize its final, literal return to earth:

> I love to heare her speake, yet well I know,
> That Musicke hath a farre more pleasing sound:
> I graunt I never saw a goddesse goe,
> My Mistres when shee walkes treads on the ground. (130.9–12)

A down-to-earth woman has much, perhaps everything, to recommend her in competition (if that is even the right word) with a goddess. The sonnet is a gleeful dismissal of Petrarchist conventions—so effective that it is all many modern readers will even know of those conventions—and that last line implies what other sonnets confirm: not the least convention being dismissed, apparently from the very start, is unassailable chastity. This woman enjoys sexual love, and welcomes it. Those paying attention will not be surprised by the final turn: "And yet by heaven I thinke my love as rare, / As any she beli'd with false compare" (13–14). "I thinke" quietly reasserts a Petrarchan frame of reference at a deeper level ("But if the while I thinke on thee"), one where it can welcome rather than exclude erotic excitement and pleasure. The satire has been at the expense not of "a muddy complexion, bad breath and a clumsy walk"[66] but of the mendacities of "false compare" to which it seems this woman is happily immune.

The happiness matches that of sonnet 127 and its immediate successor, which celebrates the speaker's arousal as his mistress plays a virginal and he envies the keys as she strikes them: "Give them thy fingers, me thy lips to kisse" (128.14). Collectively the three poems initiate the second subsequence with a burst of eager sexual excitement. By the time we get to 130, though, that promise has received the rude shock of 129: "The expence of Spirit in a waste of shame / Is lust in action." The poem discloses no overt connection to the sequence around it, but by 131 its toxins show up in the ground water as the speaker continues to praise her unfashionable beauty: "Thou art as tiranous, so as thou art, / As those whose beauties proudly make them cruell" (131.1–2). Tyrannical cruelty is a *cliché* about Petrarchan ladies, but what conventionally gives them the power to exercise it is their beauty. The understated but sharp-edged "so as thou art" assumes in this case that does not apply. Nevertheless, the power is still hers: "For well thou know'st to my deare doting hart / Thou art the fairest and most precious Jewell" (3–4). As a wittily backhanded compliment, this follows tracks already laid down, but the tone is ominously new. The speaker expands on the eccentricity

---

[66] Duncan-Jones, *Shakespeare's Sonnets*, p. 47. Duncan-Jones herself takes the supposedly insulting description to be indeed insulting, and the whole subsequence to be an extended misogynist joke. It is certainly possible to imagine sonnet 130 getting raucous laughs from the boys at the Middle Temple, and the couplet, delivered with the right timing, bringing down the house. (A roomful of boys can laugh at anything.) For readers in other contexts, much hinges on the reference to the woman's breath: "in some perfumes is there more delight, / Then in the breath that from my Mistres reekes" (7–8). Booth's note on the force of "reekes" summarizes the state of the linguistic question: "A modern reader must be cautioned against hearing this word as the simple insult it would be if a modern writer had written the line; the primary energy of 'to reek' and 'a reek' was still in communicating the ideas of emitting vapor and of vapor emitted; the narrow modern senses, 'to stink' and 'a stench' ... do not emerge until the late seventeenth century. However, commentators often over-caution modern readers: both the verb and the noun were already well on their way toward their modern meanings in Shakespeare's time" (p. 454). Usage elsewhere in Shakespeare indeed keeps close company with abuse: "your reeking villany" (*Timon of Athens* 3.6.93), etc. On the other hand, whatever level of disgust "reekes" brings to sonnet 130 breaks the profile of the poem's *blason*; otherwise the lady merely falls short of some hyperbolic and implicitly comic expectations, without any sign of revulsion at what she actually is. There are of course perfectly pleasant gradations of red less red than coral, and in historical context the "black wiers" of the woman's hair merely suggest black threads, not some grotesquerie from "a world of industrial wiring and wire fences" (Booth, p. 454). The catalogue's climax, "My Mistres when shee walkes treads on the ground," is a kind of tautology, applying to any woman with the use of her legs. Also, "reekes" is the last word in l. 8, the traditional site of the *volta* in an Italianate sonnet, and l. 9 immediately sounds the poem's first open declaration of delight—"I love to hear her speak"—and sets an upward course toward the affirmation in the couplet: "And yet by heaven I thinke my love as rare ...." See Richard Strier, *The Unrepentant Renaissance*, pp. 76–8 ("the point is that sonnet 130 is a love poem"). In 1899, Samuel A. Beadle, a formerly enslaved African American, publishes a deft imitation that is definitely a love song, building through a somewhat abashed start ("She is not yellow, white nor gray, and so / Must be something else") to an enraptured climax that amplifies what Shakespeare mutes: "'Her voice?' A chord escaped from paradise" (Kingsley-Smith, p. 241). Seeing that literary transaction as agonistic rather than collaborative seems to me a choice on the interpreter's part.

of his response, unpacking what in the previous poem had been benignly confined to the word "thinke":

> Yet in good faith some say that thee behold,
> Thy face hath not the power to make love grone;
> To say they erre, I dare not be so bold,
> Although I sweare it to my selfe alone.
> And to be sure that is not false I sweare
> A thousand grones but thinking on thy face,
> One on anothers necke do witnesse beare
> Thy blacke is fairest in my judgements place. (5–12)

The sonnet has been working its way back to the conceit of sonnet 127. There it had been confidently asserted that the world had come around to the speaker's opinion about blackness, but things have changed—or perhaps he has just stepped into the trap that his own conceit has set. The couplet springs it: "In nothing art thou blacke save in thy deeds, / And thence this slaunder as I thinke proceeds" (13–14). We have heard the last of anything resembling joy connected with sexual love.

The narrative implication is that sonnet 129 registers the speaker's knowledge of the woman's infidelity, which (with a one-sonnet delay that is itself not unrealistic) hits with unexpected force. That the black deeds in question involve the young man is quickly confirmed, though (as with Wroth's judgment of Cupid and Venus) the blame falls solidly on the woman:

> Beshrew that heart that makes my heart to groane
> For that deepe wound it gives my friend and me;
> I'st not ynough to torture me alone,
> But slave to slavery my sweet'st friend must be. (133.1–4)

In the first subsequence, the young man is at times directly reproached—"Aye me, but yet thou mightst my seate forbeare" (41.9)—but the accusations are softened by the speaker's uncontrollable impulse to excuse him:

> Those pretty wrongs that liberty commits,
> When I am some-time absent from thy heart,
> Thy beautie, and thy yeares full well befits,
> For still temptation followes where thou art. (41.1–4)

In the dark lady poems, the power and agency are remorselessly hers:

> So now I have confest that he is thine,
> And I my selfe am morgag'd to thy will,

> My selfe Ile forfeit, so that other mine,
> Thou wilt restore to be my comfort still:
> But thou wilt not, nor he will not be free,
> For thou art covetous, and he is kinde (134.1–6)

The contrast will end in the stark opposition of the "two spirits" who "do sugiest me still, / The better angell is a man right faire: / The worser spirit a woman collour'd il" (144.2–4). Yet even as the drama gets simplified into white and black, the poet's desire to use his way with words to put a good face on what is happening asserts itself at a new level of edginess:

> Who ever hath her wish, thou hast thy *Will*,
> And *Will* too boote, and *Will* in over-plus....
> The sea all water, yet receives raine still,
> And in aboundance addeth to his store,
> So thou beeing rich in *Will* adde to thy *Will*,
> One will of mine to make thy large *Will* more. (135.1–2, 9–12)

The frantic punning on "Will" as a proper name has been seized on as a biographical clue. We happen to know the author was called Will, and if the young man and, say, the woman's husband went by the same name, that would certainly fit. Punning the names of her sexual partners on a rude slang term for the male genitals, slang we can on the evidence of this poem extend to the female genitals as well, gathers everything up into some spectacularly obscene trash-talking whose argument is that the woman's promiscuity is fine and dandy as long as she keeps the speaker on her team. The more, the merrier; with all these Wills, all is well.

The "cutely boyish"[67] voice here is a brittle confection (he is no longer a boy) and is barely sustained through one more sonnet. What replaces it is stranger and often harder to figure. One of the best-known sonnets—one of only two to appear in print before the 1609 edition—offers a look at an uneasy relationship sustained by some interlocking accommodations:

> When my love sweares that she is made of truth,
> I do beleeve her though I know she lyes,
> That she might thinke me some untuterd youth,
> Unlearned in the worlds false subtilties. (138.1–4)

---

[67] Sedgwick's term, p. 37. She does more justice than anyone to the giddy outrageousness of the poem's conceit: "it is funny, even as it is very insulting, to court someone on the basis simply that she will not know you are there. (It is insulting even aside from the attribution of promiscuity, insulting through an image that some women might also find appealing: female sexuality as a great sociable melting-pot, accommodating without fuss the creatures it has admitted through sheer inattention.)"

The woman is unfaithful and lies about it, but things continue as before between them because her lover decides to believe her (he does not just say he pretends to believe her) while still knowing the truth. The reason he gives is not just that he does not want to make waves; he *wants* to seem naive *so that* she will think him inexperienced and (therefore) young. As the conceit is further elaborated it becomes clear that reciprocal deceits that do not deceive are involved:

> Thus vainely thinking that she thinkes me young,
> Although she knowes my dayes are past the best,
> Simply I credit her false speaking tongue,
> On both sides thus is simple truth supprest (5–8)

He believes what he knows to be untrue as part of an unspoken deal that she will do him the same favor: she will think of him as young even when she knows perfectly well he is not. The poem's author was in fact no older than 35, and to make sense of this we have to recognize the euphemism in play: her infidelity has, as would only be expected, made him doubt his ability to satisfy her sexually. It has to be obvious to both of them that he no longer has the libido of an eighteen-year-old (a high standard), but for him even to hold on to what he has it is important that she not actually say that. What is sketched is a horribly plausible picture of an almost domestic relationship (are they living together?) held in place by a silently negotiated agreement on what not to bring up. That tacit agreement is their deepest intimacy. The third quatrain calls this mutual consideration:

> But wherefore sayes she not she is unjust?
> And wherefore say not I that I am old?
> O loves best habit is in seeming trust,
> And age in love, loves not to have yeares told. (9–12)

But the sharper formulation in the couplet, where the mutuality is certified by the first-person plural, involves a bitter pun: "Therefore I lye with her, and she with me, / And in our faults by lyes we flattered be" (13–14). It is as though sexual love itself were in some inescapable way a lie—or, in a final use of the term that has accrued a very personal animus in the course of the sequence, flattery.

The poem has come across as one of "throwaway world-weary acceptance," though it has also been called "perhaps the most terrible poem of the whole sequence ... and also the nakedest."[68] At least so far; the arrangement it sets out does not in any case endure. No one would expect it to. The notion that the man's attempt to act naive would somehow translate into sexual satisfaction for the woman is some kind of joke, and his fear that she will think him old bears no comparison with her fear, if there even is any, that he will call her unfaithful. What

---

[68] Burrow, p. 134; Cruttwell, p. 13.

he has on her is nothing like what she has on him; the symmetry of their stand-off is illusory. In the next sonnet he is already trying to renegotiate:

> O call not me to justifie the wrong,
> That thy unkindnesse layes upon my heart,
> Wound me not with thine eye but with thy toung,
> Use power with power, and slay me not by Art (139.1–4)

That opening has something of the feel of a threat—do not push me too far—though the only threat the man can think of is to come up with some justification of the woman's behavior. We have already seen that as the speaker's reflex action in moments of emotional crisis. He is actually thinking of what that justification will be in the rest of the quatrain; it turns out to involve a change in the arrangement in the previous sonnet:

> Tell me thou lov'st else-where; but in my sight,
> Deare heart forbeare to glance thine eye aside,
> What needst thou wound with cunning when thy might
> Is more then my ore-prest defence can bide? (5–8)

Earlier he had striven to keep her silent about her infidelity. Now he asks her to be honest about it when they are alone, but when they are together in company not to flirt openly with other men. The public image of the two of them as a couple is sufficiently important to him to be worth preserving, regardless of what the public might actually think. Even as he asks for this, though, he presents his excuse (his term) for what she has been doing. Momentarily feeling spry, he seizes on the *cliché* of the lady's lethal eye-beams, already something of a plaything for poets ("The huge massacres which her her eyes do make" [*Amoretti* 10.6]), and turns it inside out:

> Let me excuse thee, ah my love well knowes,
> Her prettie lookes have beene mine enemies,
> And therefore from my face she turnes my foes,
> That they else-where might dart their injuries (9–12)

He has only to say this to know it does not work: "Yet do not so, but since I am neere slaine, / Kill me out-right with lookes, and rid my paine" (13–14). By the next poem honesty does not work either:

> If I might teach thee witte better it weare,
> Though not to love, yet love to tell me so,
> As testie sick-men when their deaths be neere,
> No newes but health from their Phisitions know. (140.5–8)

Now he is asking her not just to go along with the pretense but actively to lie to him. To motivate her he sounds as if he is going to appeal to her pity—"For if I should dispaire I should grow madde" (9)—but that is only on the way to professed concern for her own reputation:

> And in my madnesse might speake ill of thee,
> Now this ill wresting world is growne so bad,
> Madde slanderers by madde eares beeleeved be.
>   That I may not be so, nor thou belyde,
>   Beare thine eyes straight, though thy proud heart goe wide.
>   (10–14)

Lie to me or I might do something crazy, like (pause for effect) criticize you. The narrative in sonnets 138–40 is a spiral of increasingly dishonest and embarrassing deals which the speaker proposes to the dark lady and which, point by point, she either rejects or simply ignores.

Here we get to witness the speaker's instincts as a lover coming into more intimate contact with another will than anywhere else in the sequence. The intimacy is between sexual partners, conflict at unforgivingly close quarters; the absence of anything quite like this in the first subsequence is one reason for thinking that the love there is indeed not sexually enacted. The woman's contrary will is felt in a series of implied but abrupt refusals to go along, and in the process the character of the dark lady escapes some of the flattening that the young man suffers from the speaker's habitual preempting of his actions and reactions. Even through the noise of her lover's anger and loathing, her steadfast disinterest in any of the degrading accommodations he proposes displays an integrity that he is rapidly shedding. As he does so, he descends into the hell of the last dozen or so sonnets, no longer articling with the dark lady but swept up into his own derangement:

> My love is as a feaver longing still,
> For that which longer nurseth the disease,
> Feeding on that which doth preserve the ill,
> Th'uncertaine sicklie appetite to please (147.1–4)

Hoping to steady himself, he recurs to the initial conceit of the subsequence and its bitter twist in sonnet 131—

> Past cure I am, now Reason is past care,
> And frantick madde with ever-more unrest,
> My thoughts and my discourse as mad mens are,
> At randon from the truth vainely exprest.
>   For I have sworne thee faire, and thought thee bright,
>   Who art as black as hell, as darke as night. (9–14)

—and to the conviction that it all comes down to his cursed gift for looking not with the eye but with the mind:

> O me! what eyes hath love put in my head,
> Which have no correspondence with true sight,
> Or if they have, where is my judgment fled,
> That censures falsely what they see aright? (148.1–4)

With the young man that gift of love and imagination has room to breathe. We do not get the full story, but the crises have a rhythm to them, and reconciliation, even if it is the reconciliation of silence, follows the pain. With the dark lady things progressively narrow to a severe accounting. The critic most attentive to this configuration of the sequence as a whole has been Joel Fineman, tracing the course of a "poetry of praise" contorting itself to come to terms with an unworthy object: "much of what the young man sonnets do implicitly is preparation for what the dark lady sonnets subsequently say explicitly."[69] His specific argument, together with the sense that the second subsequence is "the core of the whole work," is directly contested by Colin Burrow, citing stylometric and other evidence that it "includes the earliest poems to be written" and his own judgment that it reads "more like a starting-point than a conclusion."[70] But this is to refuse what, unanswerable questions of dating and intention aside, the received order of the poems (Patrick Cruttwell thinks "Shakespeare's theatrical cunning had something to do with it")[71] most powerfully has to offer. The dark lady sonnets make a retrospective statement, as if a survivor were sorting through the emotional carnage of it all, on what the whole experience comes to. Vendler is articulate on the dramatic force of the ending as it stands, especially from sonnet 147 on: "Each of these poems gains sinister strength from its fellows in the cluster. A psychological dynamic larger than what can be represented in fourteen lines binds the poems. The final clear-sighted and dry-eyed embrace of complete, voluntary perjury would lack full effect if it had not been preceded by self-deception, displacements of agency, and tears."[72] The *dénouement* comes in sonnet 152, a poem with "something heroic" to it "as the speaker abandons all defenses" and for the first time "blames himself more than the woman, both for his moral fault and for his betrayal of discourse itself"[73]:

---

[69] Joel Fineman, *Shakespeare's Perjured Eye: The Invention of Poetic Subjectivity in the Sonnets*, p. 160. Other takeaways from Fineman's ambitiously theorized work are less sturdy, especially his attempt to make good on his subtitle: "The dark lady sonnets ... directly identify the poet not only with the cross-coupling, copulating copula between male and female, but also with what lies between the poet's showing and hiding, between his fair and unfair, between his presence and his absence, between his whole and hole, between his one and none" (pp. 293–4).
[70] Burrow, pp. 133–4.
[71] Cruttwell, p. 11.
[72] Vendler, p. 625.
[73] Vendler, pp. 625, 641.

> But why of two othes breach doe I accuse thee,
> When I breake twenty: I am perjur'd most,
> For all my vowes are othes but to misuse thee:
> And all my honest faith in thee is lost.
> For I have sworne deepe othes of thy deepe kindnesse:
> Othes of thy love, thy truth, thy constancie,
> And to inlighten thee gave eyes to blindnesse,
> Or made them swere against the thing they see.
>   For I have sworne thee faire: more perjurde eye,
>   To swere against the truth so foule a lie. (152.5–14)

The abandonment of defenses is however not complete; confessing this way recovers some sense of righteousness. The most brutal and candid humiliation comes three poems earlier: "Canst thou O cruell, say I love thee not, / When I against my selfe with thee pertake?" (149.1-2). This opening seems headed toward the argument that the speaker will indeed make in the next poem: "If thy unworthinesse raisd love in me, / More worthy I to be belov'd of thee" (150.13–14). For the moment, though, he keeps to the role of his adversary's attorney, mercilessly cataloguing the way he knows, and probably has always known, his behavior comes across to others:

> Doe I not thinke on thee when I forgot
> Am of my selfe, all tirant for thy sake?
> Who hateth thee that I doe call my friend,
> On whom froun'st thou that I doe faune upon,
> Nay if thou lowrst on me doe I not spend
> Revenge upon my selfe with present mone?
> What merrit do I in my selfe respect,
> That is so proude thy service to dispise,
> When all my best doth worship thy defect,
> Commanded by the motion of thine eyes. (149.3–12)

Lines 5–6 offer a brief but painful glimpse, from farther outside the speaker's self-involvement than we usually get, at the social context within which this is all playing out. And the turn in the couplet abruptly makes the reckoning through another's eyes even harsher: "But love hate on for now I know thy minde, / Those that can see thou lov'st, and I am blind" (149.13–14). For a shocking moment he even admires her. When her eye and her mind look upon the world they both see the same thing, and she has all too accurately taken his measure.

# Afterword

Placing the dark lady poems where they are delivers the speaker at the end of Shakespeare's sequence into what Yeats in one of his own sonnets calls "the desolation of reality." It is arguably the coldest conclusion of any of the Renaissance Petrarchist sequences, though also, arguably, one that was waiting to happen.

Throughout the *Canzoniere* the prospect that Laura will be a redemptive force in her lover's life—*the* redemptive force, his Beatrice—flows as a promise or at least a possibility until in the last few poems he feels his carefully counted time running out:

> Tennemi Amor anni ventuno ardendo
> lieto nel foco et nel duol pien di speme;
> poi che Madonna e 'l mio cor seco inseme
> saliro al Ciel, dieci altri anni piangendo. (364.1–4)

Love held me twenty-one years gladly burning in the fire and full of hope amid sorrow; since my lady, and my heart with her, rose to Heaven, ten more years of weeping.

And then it is all too clear that it has all been a shameful and dangerous mistake: "*Omai son stanco, et mia vita reprendo / di tanto error che di vertute il seme / à quasi spento*" (5–6; now I am weary and I reproach my life for so much error, which has almost extinguished the seed of virtue). The last sonnet emphatically renounces "*i miei mali indegni et empi*" (365.5; my unworthy and wicked sufferings), which wasted those years on the wrong kind of love: "*I'vo piangendo i miei passati tempi / i quai posi in amar cosa mortale*" (1–2; I go weeping for my past time, which I spent in loving a mortal thing). The renunciation of Laura is, however, no sooner voiced than elided into appeals to more secure sources of comfort: "*Re del Cielo, invisibile, immortale, / soccorri a l'alma disviata et frale*" (365.6–7; invisible, immortal King of Heaven, help my strayed frail soul)—and then in the *canzone* that concludes the sequence:

> Invoco lei che ben sempre rispose
> chi la chiamò con fede.
> Vergine, s' a mercede
> miseria estrema de l'umane cose
> giamai ti volse, al mio prego t'inchina,

> soccorri a la mia guerra
> ben ch' i' sia terra et tu del Ciel regina. (366.7-13)

I invoke her who has always replied to whoever called on her with faith. Virgin, if extreme misery of human things ever turned you to mercy, bend to my prayer; give succor to my war, though I am earth and you are queen of Heaven.

From Laura, now just "*poca mortal terra caduca*" (121; a bit of deciduous mortal dust), he turns to another figure of female glory, "*di sol vestita, / coronata di stelle*" (1–2; clothed with the sun and crowned with stars). It is only a prayer at this point, but prayer was as close as Petrarch ever came to Laura. Mary steps into her place, and he is not alone.

What slips past in the process, and keeps many readers from quite registering that the sequence ends with Petrarch's *rejection* of Laura and all that she has meant to him, is the moment where he *is* suddenly alone, after 31 years—a moment like the one of frightened nakedness in the presence of his folly that he does dramatize earlier, in the *canzone* that immediately precedes the news of Laura's death:

> Canzon, qui sono ed ò 'l cor via più freddo
> de la paura che gelata neve,
> sentendomi perir senz' alcun dubbio ...
> che co la Morte a lato
> cieco del viver mio novo consiglio,
> et veggio 'l meglio et al peggior m'appiglio. (264.127–29, 134–36)

Song, here I am, and my heart is much colder with fear than frozen snow, since I feel myself perishing beyond all doubt ... for with Death at my side I seek new counsel for my life, and I see the better but I lay hold on the worse.

That last line translates famous words from a speech of Medea's in Ovid's *Metamorphoses* (7.20–21: "*video meliora proboque, / deteriora sequor*"), which subsequently take their own place in the afterlife of the *Canzoniere*.[1] They inform the dire wisdom Shakespeare states early in the dark lady sonnets as a truth about the entire human race: "All this the world well knowes yet none knowes well, / To shun the heaven that leads men to this hell" (129.13–14). Shakespeare's speaker subsequently finds no one to pray to—if pray is even the word—but his own soul, "the center of my sinfull earth," which he calls upon to nourish itself on the decay of his body: "So shalt thou feed on death, that feeds on men, / And death once dead, ther's no more dying then" (146.1, 13–14). That is the only touch of religious comfort

---

[1] I give a catalogue in "Shakespeare's Petrarchism," pp. 177–78, 181—to which add Gambattista Marino, *L'Adone* 12.219.7–8.

on offer, and it scarcely alleviates the fearsomeness of what both poets face. The dispersal of richly cultivated illusions, the *desengaño* that always shadows erotic enchantment, brings not just sorrow and regret, certainly not relief, but a kind of terror, the taste of a damnation to which the lover is self-condemned.

The dark lady poems mark not just the terminus of Shakespeare's sequence but a defining limit of Petrarchan love in its full scope. Few Petrarchan poets touch that limit, most never approach it, but it is always there, if only on the horizon. Wyatt's ravishing lonely affirmation—"It was no dreme: I lay brode waking"—is heroic defiance at a distance. Greville, alternatively, is the most furious in his iconoclastic drive to divest himself, and his self, of all illusions, going beyond human love to the soul's solitude before God, though he is not quite the poet he needs to be to bring it off.[2] Others variously avoid, ignore, exploit, enrich, deepen, or trifle with the possibility that the ambitious, highly wrought love of which they so copiously write is all stuff and nonsense or worse; their multiple, unpredictable, occasionally sublime strategies for doing so energize one of the great centuries of English love poetry. Within this tradition, Shakespeare's sequence as we have it converges on a uniquely stark, humiliating dead end, which may—you never know—have been personal as well as conceptual. Whenever he wrote those poems, of course, he did still have some plays to write.

---

[2] The much quieter George Herbert is, without reference to profane love, better at it: "Now I am here, what thou wilt do with me / None of my books will show: / I reade, and sigh, and wish I were a tree" ("Affliction" [I], 55–57). That last line may put us in mind of Ralegh's moss.

APPENDIX A

# Astrophil and Stella: *Utrum Copularentur*

The Latin phrase in the title [whether they copulated] was coined by H. I. Marrou to designate the frequently debated question of whether or not we should understand troubadour lyric to refer to sexually consummated desire.[1] I use it here to highlight a lesser puzzle that has never to my knowledge been worked through as fully as it deserves. In *Astrophil and Stella*, what are we meant to assume happens between the two characters after the end of the fourth song? Are we meant to assume anything? What difference would it make one way or another?

In the 1598 edition, the fourth song comes at the climax of Astrophil's increasingly open, aggressive, and confident attempt to secure Stella's sexual compliance. They are together at night, close enough for him to touch her, with nobody else (according to Astrophil) likely to interfere ("Your faire mother is a bed" [iv.37]).[2] Stella has presumably consented to this meeting, and it has been a while since there was anything secret about what Astrophil wants. They could, here and now, without further ado, copulate. The song is immediately followed by a sonnet and another song that signal a major change in relations between the two ("Alas, whence came this change of lookes" [86.1]), with no clear indication of how they got from where things were to where they are now. We have to fill that in on our own. Russell M. Brown, the only critic I have found to pose the question directly, treats it in a short note as a question about the fourth song.[3] That poem has a quickly grasped formal set-up: in nine six-line stanzas of tetrameter couplets, Astrophil makes his case to Stella for five lines, and in the sixth line she repeatedly gives the same reply: "No, no, no, no, my Deare, let be." That refrain is the second direct quotation (the first was in sonnet 63) and the first complete sentence attributed to Stella in the sequence, and in it she makes the reply that we may assume she had determined to make when she agreed to the meeting. But Astrophil is a wily tactician and Sidney a clever poet, and a reader familiar with his ways will expect a twist in which either Stella changes her reply (she does not) or the meaning of her reply changes as the words stay the same (a well-known song technique). Indeed, Astrophil switches in the last stanza to blaming Stella's refusal for his imminent death, maybe suicide ("Soone with my death I will please thee" [iv.53]), so that her words this time mean she does not want that either. In this highly charged encounter, things have taken a sharp turn. That turn is the point of the poem, its *aliquid salis*. Brown sees the extrapolation as obvious: "faced with the choice between yielding or having her lover kill himself, Stella asks that he not do the latter—and by implication yields"; surrendering her chastity changes everything for the worse, and with it "comes the 'change of looks' and the consequent degeneration of the love affair."

---

[1] Henri Davenson (= H. I. Marrou), *Les Troubadours*, p. 149. The phrase is taken up by William D. Paden, Jr., "*Utrum Copularentur*: Of *Cors*."
[2] Ringler, oddly, thinks Astrophil is outside Stella's window, as in the ninth song (p. xlv); Richard McCoy, paying closer attention, places him in her bedroom (*Sir Philip Sidney*, p. 100). I imagine some gallery or courtyard of the sort where Gascoigne's F. J. first has his way with Dame Elinor.
[3] Russell M. Brown, "Sidney's *Astrophil and Stella*, Fourth Song."

Brown's note does get cited, and, aside from a brief remark by Heather Dubrow, I have seen no direct attempt to refute its argument. It is, however, unusual to find someone explicitly accepting his conclusion, and nobody is quite as emphatic about it as he is. Richard McCoy affirms that "Stella's denial finally turns into assent," Clark Hulse that the end of the fourth song provides "as clear a statement of consummation as we can expect from a diplomatic poet."[4] (As it happens, both McCoy and Hulse emphasize the biographical content of the sequence; Hulse argues that Penelope Rich is specifically intended as the prime reader of the poems.) More commonly we meet with remarks, usually in passing, that take the non-consummation of the affair as a given, needing no further conversation: "Stella is ... the quintessential Petrarchan lady in her ... leading [Astrophil] on and yet never allowing him fulfillment"[5]; "Sidney comes closer than most writers in the tradition to depicting a successful seduction, but Astrophil, like his fellows, is finally stopped short."[6] This remains, I think, the common wisdom. Occasionally critics, using one of modern criticism's foundational terms, characterize the fourth song as "ambiguous" in its outcome: "an ambiguous assignation and a moment of uncertain intimacy."[7] The least evasive path, seldom taken, is to formulate the possibilities—"Astrophil either got what he wanted only to lose it, or was finally told off decisively for crossing too many boundaries"—and then to make an honest interpreter's choice: "the former seems more likely to me."[8] Usually discussions do not raise the question at all, even where they might be expected to do so.[9]

That readers would be called upon to fill in narrative silence here is no surprise. It has been and to a considerable degree remains conventional, in all but the most graphic literature, to rely on the audience's knowingness about human sexual behavior, that sense of what we are supposed to know without having to be told, to fill in certain gaps. Such knowingness is uniquely skittish; there are few topics on which human beings are less candid, or more anxious about how their knowingness will be assessed by others. It also changes over time, and the effort, difficult enough in the world we know firsthand, "to disentangle boasts, confessions, overtones, undertones, jokes, the unthinkable, the taken-for-granted, the unmentionable-but-often-done-anyway, etc.,"[10] faces possibly insuperable difficulties across a distance of four centuries. Dealing with the narrative lacuna after the fourth song calls for a tricky act of informed historical imagination. As it happens, oblique but I think relevant evidence of how *Astrophil and Stella* may have come across to near contemporaries can be found in an exchange of fictional verse letters between Sidney and Penelope, preserved in a manuscript dated 1623.[11] The text of neither letter is complete, but enough is there to show the writer recrafting the narratives of both *Astrophil and Stella* and the known facts of Sidney's life. This fictional Sidney is surprised and enraged at Penelope over her marriage, which he did not know about, and which was directly commanded by Queen Elizabeth (in real life, he did and it was not). Penelope in her reply is explicit about how far things with Sidney have already gone:

---

[4] McCoy, p. 99; Clark Hulse, "Stella's Wit," p. 283.
[5] Gary F. Waller, "The Rewriting of Petrarch," p. 72.
[6] Ann Rosalind Jones and Peter Stallybrass, "The Politics of *Astrophil and Stella*," p. 62.
[7] Ronald Levao, *Renaissance Minds and Their Fictions*, pp. 173–4.
[8] Elizabeth M. Hull, "All My Deed But Copying Is," p. 188.
[9] Fienberg, in her article arguing for Stella's increasingly visible agency over the course of the sequence, is only more conspicuous than most in moving directly from the fourth song to the eighth song without saying or implying anything about what exactly Stella does at the end of the former; see "The Emergence of Stella," pp. 13–14.
[10] Sedgwick, *Between Men*, p. 35.
[11] Josephine A. Roberts, "The Imaginary Epistles of Sir Philip Sidney and Lady Penelope Rich."

> god knowes how much I blush to tell the trueth
> thou hadst the crop and Conquest of my youth
> how can thy hart then yeelde against loves nature
> to play the Tyrant on a Ravisht creature
> ravisht, twice ravisht, by thy merc'lesse power
> first of my hart next of my mayden dower (55-60)

Despite the sound of reproach, Penelope actually concedes that her lover is the wronged party, and hints at making amends:

> But say that I am maried as I am
> Can that forbid mee to bee still the same.
> I love thee as I did nay better, better
> and will though I give still still bee thy debter (69-72)

This Stella (whose lover indicates in his own epistle [78-9] that he has already decided to call her that) is unchaste before her marriage (and not with her future husband) and thinking of adultery almost immediately after.

This fictional Penelope would not be out of place in the Elizabethan court or its successor.[12] The licentiousness of sexual behavior in such environments is possibly a transhistorical constant; and with all due allowance for gossip and misogynist confabulation, we have good evidence that, even under a watchful virgin queen, sexual activity outside of marriage was a regular option in Sidney's vicinity not just for men but also for women.[13] A notable instance is Penelope Rich herself after Sidney's death. Sometime around 1590 she became the mistress of Sir Charles Blount, who had served with Sidney at Zutphen. That year, with Penelope looking on, he wore Sidney's colors at the Accession Day tilt, a coded declaration to those in the know that he was Stella's new champion, promptly reported to the public with a heavy-handed reference to the still unpublished sonnet sequence:

> Comes Sir *Charles Blunt* in *Or* and *Azure* dight,
> Rich in his colours, richer in his thoughts,
> Rich in his Fortune, Honor, Armes and Arte.[14]

Added to these colors were "his eyes great, blacke, and lovely,"[15] which lodged in the memory of many who knew him—the color of Laura's eyes, and of both Penelope's and Stella's. Penelope went on bear Charles five children, meeting him it seems regularly at Essex House and elsewhere while continuing her life as Lady Rich. In 1605, though, she was divorced by Rich *a mensa et thoro* (from bed and board) on her own admission of adultery. She did not officially say with whom; her husband had a list of dates and places. The next month she married her lover, by that point Earl of Devonshire. Other examples are not far to seek;

---

[12] See Johanna Rickman, *Love, Lust, and License in Early Modern England*.

[13] On Elizabeth's reign, see Rickman, pp. 27-68. Elizabeth was indeed sensitive about sexual misbehavior among her female attendants and the male courtiers closest to her, though that did not keep it from happening; punishment could include banishment from the court and imprisonment. Outside that circle, discipline was largely left up in the traditional way to "families, friends, and kin" (p. 67), with varying results.

[14] George Peele, *Polyhymnia*, sig. B1$^r$. On the tournament, see Sally Varlow, *Lady Penelope*, pp. 122-4.

[15] Fynes Moryson, *An Itinerary*, p. $^2$45.

256  APPENDIX A

Grace Ioppolo groups Penelope, admiringly, with her mother Lettice Knollys, her sister Dorothy, and her sister-in-law Frances Walsingham (Sidney's widow, married to Penelope's brother) under the rude twentieth-century rubric "those Essex girls," all of them enmeshed in complicated networks of sexual and political scandal connected in one way or another to the earldom of Essex.[16] A few critics have drawn attention to the actualities of upper-class sexual behavior in talking about *Astrophil and Stella*,[17] but most discussion has continued to defer to the restrictive code of female behavior set out in contemporary religious and humanist writings, as if that were for better or worse the only one in play. The alternative was obviously never codified, but developed and maintained in the behavior of its participants. Even they probably could not have said exactly what the rules were. There were certainly rules whose violation could have dire consequences, but their operation was unpredictable, dense with imperfectly transparent hypocrisy and subject to opportunistic improvisation and, always, political and dynastic calculation. Aristocratic and erotic self-assurance would have played a big role.[18] Penelope's brother said of her shortly before his execution, "she must be looked to for she had a proud spryt [spirit]"[19]; she was detained and examined in connection with his rebellion but, unlike a dozen male co-conspirators (four of whom were executed), never charged. For almost two decades her adultery, neither flaunted nor hidden, seems to have had little effect on her social standing or that of her lover. In 1595 they stood as godparents at the christening of Robert Sidney's son Robert (Philip Sidney's posthumous nephew). Under the new king of England after Elizabeth's death in 1603, Penelope became a lady of the new queen's drawing chamber and Charles a member of the Privy Council. Disgrace did not come until the two married, violating the terms of a divorce that was technically a legal separation, the rules on which had recently been tightened under the new regime, with bigamy now a felony.[20] It was then that James denounced her, to her new husband's face, as "a fair woman with a black soul."[21] In legal squabbling over Charles's will after his death in 1606, Penelope found herself called in court documents "an Harlott Adultresse Concubyne & Whore."[22] She died, reportedly penitent, the next year.

Such real-life narratives were not typical, but they were certainly possible, and having them in mind as a context for Sidney's fictional Stella, as many of the sequence's first readers likely would, confirms that what happens in the silence at the end of the fourth song after she is tricked into changing her tune could indeed be the consummation of their affair. That is something that a woman of her character and station might indeed be expected to do. But that does not settle things. The problem is that, as Dubrow puts it, "it is hard to believe that

---

[16] Grace Ioppolo, "Those Essex Girls," p. 77. To be fair, Walsingham, the shadowiest of this group, is in it not for sexual scandalousness but for her second and third marriages: to the Earl of Essex, executed for treason, and to the Catholic Earl of Clanricarde, for whom she herself converted to Catholicism and left the court.

[17] Hull, "All My Deed," pp. 177–80; Sanchez, "'In My Selfe,'" pp. 10–11.

[18] Penelope's presence at her divorce hearing had an interesting effect on the archbishop of Canterbury (John Whitgift), who presided. The senior primate of the Church of England made what struck one observer as pointedly friendly remarks about Penelope, who was in the eyes of the law and the church without question the guilty party, and pointedly hostile remarks about her supposedly wronged husband; see Rickman, p. 128.

[19] Reported in a letter to Charles Blount from the Earl of Nottingham, a commissioner at Essex's trial; *The Tanner Letters*, p. 37.

[20] The divorce proceedings, the question of remarriage, and the testamentary litigation that eventually resulted are detailed at some length by Rickman, pp. 127–38.

[21] Reported by Sir William Sanderson in his *Aulicus Coquinariae* (a defense of James against a satirical attack on his reign), p. 112.

[22] Rickman, p. 136; the merciless assault on Penelope during this litigation is set out vividly by Sylvia Freedman (herself a lawyer) in *Poor Penelope*, pp. 175–89.

in a sequence as carefully written as this one, other signs of that event would not be manifest in some form, however coded, in adjoining poems."[23] Brown finds those signs in the hurriedly evoked "degeneration of the love affair" in the rest of the sequence; this follows from his evident assumption that Stella's quick and decisive reaction to sex with Astrophil (which would not be her first sexual experience) would be disgust. The big problem with that reading is the eighth song, where the tone of Stella's speech is simply not one of revulsion. More acutely than that, nothing in that speech suggests that they are already lovers, and a key stanza strongly implies some important line has not yet been crossed:

> Therefore, Deere, this no more move,
> Least, though I leave not thy love,
> Which too deep in me is framed,
> I should blush when thou art named. (viii.97–100)

Stella's previous compromising blush, immediately before sonnet 66 (which *probably* nobody else noticed), was prompted by Astrophil's presence. She is on the point of forbidding that presence in the future; what she imagines now is hearing him mentioned when he is not there, and she feels that if she resists his current appeal she could be safe on that score. That is not the only way to read these lines, but it is the most straightforward, and consistent with her bitter decision not to endanger her standing as a baron's wife.

One proposal would remove the incongruity by reordering the sequence. Ann Romayne Howe, calling the placement of the fourth song "the grossest error in editing" in the 1598 text, argues that sonnet 63, the notorious "Grammer rules" poem about double negatives, is obviously a reply to the fourth song, and therefore the fourth song should be moved to that position in the sequence.[24] Doing so would locate the song at an earlier, less fraught moment in the story, and also give it a flippant closure that would disperse the sense that anything momentous is about to happen. To this there are two ready objections, one pedantic—sonnet 63 is a response to Stella's saying "no, no," while the fourth song has her saying "No, no, no, no," quadruple rather than double negatives—and one less so: making the sonnet the answer to the song ignores the change of direction that is the central conceit of the song. If the double negative rule is applied, then Astrophil is celebrating the revelation that Stella *does* want him to die. The burden of proof is in any case on the argument for changing the received order of the sequence, and no editor has acted on Howe's suggestion.

Margaret Simon's observation of the ways in which the eighth song recapitulates with a difference events from the fourth song opens the door to a more sophisticated way of dissolving the problem. She inclines to accepting Brown's argument about the fourth song, decides that it has a "finally undecidable outcome," but proposes that whatever happened was unpleasant enough that Astrophil wants to fictionalize it into something better: "The eighth song can be seen as a rewriting, by Astrophil himself, of the (always undecidable) status of their relationship," a replacement narrative that he can offer up to Stella (and himself) in the spirit of sonnet 45 ("I am not I, pitie the tale of me" [45.14]). "One of the most complete narrative moments in the poem," then, "can be seen as not contributing at all to any narrative movement in the sequence"; the eighth song is "a fiction-within-a-fiction."[25] This would be consistent with a certain tranced mood to the whole scene reported in the poem, but Simon is careful not to push her claim beyond "can be seen as." Hulse, confidently

---

[23] Heather Dubrow, *Echoes of Desire*, p. 116.
[24] Howe, p. 166.
[25] Simon, pp. 96–8.

accepting Stella's surrender to Astrophil at the end of the fourth song, does what he must to accept the narrative authority of the eighth song as well and spells out the consequences for what he had been presenting as "a poetry of enjoyment." Stella sets an example for Astrophil in willfully speaking as if the lovemaking had never taken place (she is the mistress in "They fle from me" insisting that it *was* a dream), and this "socially necessary denial of the evidence of the Fourth Song ... demolishes the grounds for Stella's refusal even as it advances them," in deference to "a mere social pretense, of no more weight than a king's covenant."

> To be told in this context that only "Tyran honour" refuses Astrophil, not Stella's self, is to adopt the language of libertine pastoral ... in order to assert the repressive values of the court. ... Astrophil has attempted to rebel against that power, and briefly won Stella to join him, but the subversive moment is by its nature brief, unstable, offering only a glimpse of the desired end.[26]

Of course, the hegemonic discourse prevails, and in just about the same terms, if Stella does not surrender sexually to Astrophil, since the distinction between "Tyran honour" and "*Stella's* selfe" acknowledges the same desire in either case; in either case, her decision not to act on that desire is made in what she recognizes as emotionally dishonest conformity to her marriage vows. In the moment, it would certainly have mattered a great deal to the characters whether they had sex, but such urgency has a famous capacity for not lasting, and both ways the story comes to the same end. Critics affirming that the narrative of the sequence is ambiguous on *utrum copularentur* tend to sound as if the ambiguity is deliberate and meaningful, but such claims would make more sense if more were obviously at stake in the choice between the two alternatives. Things are perhaps a bit more interesting if Astrophil and Stella do have sex, since then his expressions of continuing love and desire in the eighth song would mean that her new status as a fallen woman makes no difference to him, at least not yet.[27] There are contexts in which that might be surprising, but here it is not a point of emphasis, not much more than a nuance. The critical maneuvering simplifies if we are willing to accept that the sequence is not as carefully written as it might have been, that Sidney introduced a narrative uncertainty on this point inadvertently while following through, as a practicing poet would, on the structure of the fourth song on its own terms: the refrain will repeat until its import changes. Poems can have their own mind. (The song was later published as a stand-alone poem entitled "The Sheepheard to his chosen Nimph."[28]) My own gloss, consistent with the eighth song, is that at the end of the fourth song Stella, even as she realizes she has been manipulated into saying what she does, also realizes for perhaps the first time the full scope of her feelings for Astrophil and the consequent danger to her situation. It is that unnerving realization that makes her pull back, and produces her "change of lookes."

---

[26] Hulse, pp. 283-4.

[27] Astrophil in this case would resemble Pyrocles after his seduction of Philoclea in the first version of the *Arcadia*; neither seducer would illustrate the stern principle enunciated toward the end of *The Four Foster Children of Desire*, in which Sidney participated: "when BEAWTIE yeeldeth once to desire, then can she never vaunt to bee desired againe"; Henry Goldwel, *A briefe declaration*, sig. Bvi^v. A poem addressed to Anne Vavasour advances the same standard: "For this be sure, the crop being once obtain'd, / Farewell the rest, the soil will be disdain'd" (anonymous in manuscript, ascribed to Walter Ralegh in a 1660 publication; Rudick 18.17–18). A rougher formulation "to a Lady residing at the Court" is attributed to the third Earl of Pembroke, Mary Wroth's lover: "if with one, with thousands thou'lt turn Whore; / Break Ice in one place, and it cracks in more"; *Poems written by the right honorable William Earl of Pembroke*, p. 115.

[28] *Englands Helicon*, sig. B1.

I leave that as my understanding of the literary work. Despite the usefulness and even inevitability of, with due care, reading biography into the sequence, I have no confidence in reading the sequence back into the biography, and certainly not on this particular point. Still, neither Sidney's nor Penelope's most recent biographers have much use for the notion that the two had a full-fledged affair. Duncan-Jones suspects the reality was relatively playful: "all along ... Sidney may have been writing these explosively passionate love poems because Penelope Devereux ... had asked him to do so, even as his sister had 'desired' him to write the *Arcadia*," resulting in "a kind of literary charade, in which both real-life participants knew exactly what was going on."[29] The poems themselves are no grounds for denying that. What we do know is that after things in real life ran their course, whatever that was, Penelope's marriage was indeed an unhappy one. When she found herself encountering an interested young man, with beautiful black eyes, who knew Sidney and bore with him some of the glory that Sidney had gone on to acquire at his death, she was effectively granted for a second time a choice she had, consciously or not, made before. This time she chose differently, though with no poet to tell the story.

---

[29] Duncan-Jones, *Sir Philip Sidney*, p. 246; see also, at greater length, her "Sidney, Stella and Lady Rich," pp. 182–90. Varlow in her biography of Penelope spends little time on the question: "If Philip and Penelope *were* an item, they covered their tracks remarkably well" (p. 83). The evidentiary case for a consummated love affair requires crediting an account, from a single source, of Sidney's conscience-striken regret on his deathbed for "a Vanitie wherein I had taken delight" related to "my Ladie Rich" (Jean Robertson, "Sir Philip Sidney and Lady Penelope Rich"), and further interpreting this statement as "an admission of adultery" (as does Freedman, p. 60). On the slenderness of this reed, see Duncan-Jones, "Sidney, Stella and Lady Rich," pp. 172–4.

APPENDIX B

# The Afterlife of Petrarch, *Canzoniere* 23

"*Nel dolce tempo*," *Canzoniere* 23, the first *canzone* and longest poem in Petrarch's sequence, is his most comprehensive and complex exposition of his laureate career, an ostensibly autobiographical account, beginning in the past tense and shifting at the end into the present, of how the speaker came to the condition in which most of the other, more conventionally lyric poems take place. Together with "*I'vo pensando*" (*Canz*. 264), which opens the second of the sequence's two divisions, it provides a kind of map within which the other, shorter poems—mostly sonnets—may be placed. If there is a single poem in the sequence to read, this is the one. Yet it is also one of the least imitated poems of the sequence. Petrarch's longer forms generally are not the ones that his avatars translate and adapt; crafting a sonnet was enough work for most of them, and the demands of forms like the *canzone* and the *sestina* were more forbidding. When English poets do translate one of Petrarch's *canzoni*, they simplify it formally. Wyatt puts "*Quel antiquo mio dolce empio signore*" (*Canz*. 360) into Chaucerian rhyme royal (73R/8MT), "*Se è debile il filo a cui s'attene*" (37) into poulter's measure (76R/98MT), and begins a translation of "*Di pensier in pensier, di monte in monte*" (129) into the same meter (153R/MT102); Spenser's *The Visions of Petrarch* turns "*Standomi un giorno solo a la fenestra*" (323) into a sequence of seven sonnets. The thematic complexity of "*Nel dolce tempo*," rising at times to a surreal turbulence, is a further problem for its assimilation, and is probably sufficient to explain the faintness of its presence in the work of poets otherwise involved in creating an English Petrarchism.

In Chapter 3, I cite its presence (to my knowledge previously unnoted) in a passage from the *Arcadia* precisely because of its comparative rarity, and even it looks less like purposed allusion than evidence of Sidney's casual reliance on what a generalized Petrarchism had come to be, an authoritative source on how things play out between men and women in this kind of love. More direct address in English to Petrarch's especially challenging poem is hard to find. A translation of the second stanza into iambic hexameter couplets is printed in *The Courtiers Academie* (1598), itself a translation of Annibale Romei's *Discorsi cavallereschi*; two lines from the first stanza are quoted in Robert Tofte's translation of Benedetto Varchi's *The Blazon of Jealousie* (1615).[1] Signs of more than passing interest from Gascoigne were discussed previously in Chapter 2. The most eye-catching influence of "*Nel dolce tempo*" on English Renaissance poetry involves its mythography, by which the emotional career of the lover becomes a sequence of stories from Ovid's *Metamorphoses* in what Thomas Greene describes as Petrarch's "*lyricization* of epic materials."[2] Things begin straightforwardly, with Laura as Daphne and the speaker implicitly as Apollo, but receive a disorienting twist when the speaker himself is transformed into the laurel tree. That myth is the first in a confusing sequence as the lover successively suffers the fates of Phaethon, Cygnus, Battus, Byblis, Echo, and Actaeon, each fate seemingly terminal (as they are in Ovid) but then followed by another; a telling identification with Narcissus is suggested without ever being made overt. This intricate conceit gets simplified in sonnets by imitators where the lover is imagining the transformations he might undergo in trying to get his lady into bed. Ronsard published

---

[1] See Boswell and Braden, *Petrarch's English Laurels*, pp. 168, 275, 280.
[2] Thomas M. Greene, *The Light in Troy*, p. 115.

in 1552 an influential sonnet on the topic ("*Je vouldroy bien richement jaunissant*" [*Les Amours* 20]), which begins with the myth of Danaë and ends with an explicit invocation of Narcissus. Two English imitations of it appear in print in 1593, a sonnet by Thomas Lodge ("I would in rich and golden coloured raine") and a poem in sixains in *The Phoenix Nest* ("Would I were chaung'd into that golden showre").[3] That same year Barnabe Barnes includes his own fantasia on the theme in *Parthenophil and Parthenophe*, which ends with his widely ridiculed version of Jove's golden shower (see Chapter 4). Ben Jonson tactfully omits that part when his Volpone tries to lure Celia "in changed shapes [to] act OVIDS tales":

> Thou, like EUROPA now, and I like JOVE,
> Then I like MARS, and thou like ERYCINE,
> So, of the rest, till we have quite run through
> And weary'd all the fables of the gods. (*Volpone* 3.7.220–4)

Ovid's stories become scenarios for bedroom gymnastics, Aretino's postures in mythic dress-up.

These are familiar passages, though seldom if ever seen in connection with "*Nel dolce tempo*." Cases where a practicing poet in English is verifiably thinking of Petrarch's *canzone* as a whole are rare. For one example in Greville's *Cælica*, see Chapter 4. Two others, tracking the Petrarchan original more closely, have received little attention. Neither is as good or interesting a poem as Petrarch's, but both are genuine responses to its challenge, and have their reasons for what they do.

The first is in Tottel's *Songes and Sonettes*, an anonymous 304-line poem in tetrameter quatrains (ABAB) that has Petrarch's *canzone* as a foundational text (185R/154M). A streamlined imitation attributed to "F. G." appears in a later anthology.[4] None of the Petrarchan source texts in Tottel are identified; the first recorded recognition of this one was by George Nott in the early 19th century.[5] The poem's unambitious diction—C. S. Lewis praises it as a first-rate example of the drab style[6]—would not readily set you looking for a Petrarchan source, and a researcher into the fortunes of the *canzone delle metamorfosi* would be put off by the excision of all the classical mythology. A good deal is added to the source text, including almost everything after about line 160. What we do have is the speaker's generally Petrarchan story of having lived in "libertie," then losing that liberty by falling in love with a seemingly unattainable woman and suffering in that state for some time. With the mythology, though, has also disappeared the remorselessly cyclical character of that suffering. At about the midpoint, the un-Petrachan thing happens to break the cycle: the woman unexpectedly says Yes, and the speaker is blissfully happy: "for eche greefe, I felt afore, / I had a blisse in recompence" (191–2). But it turns out there is more: "O blinde joye, who may thee trust? / For no estate thou canst assure?" (217–18). The woman dies, and the speaker is inconsolable. The same thing happens to Laura about two-thirds of the way through the *Canzoniere*, so that in a sense the English poem is a digest not just of "*Nel dolce tempo*" but of the whole of Petrarch's sequence. But it does not feel that way. Ramie

---

[3] Lodge, *Phillis* 34; *Phoenix Nest*, pp. 73–4. Both English versions equivocate at the conclusion, obscuring Ronsard's more straightforward wish, imitated from *Canzoniere* 22.31–3, for an unending night with his beloved.
[4] *The Paradyse of Daynty Devises* (1576), pp. 22–3; Rollins edition, pp. 30–1.
[5] In an unpublished edition of Tottel; see Rollins's edition, 2: 268. The first announcement in print appears to have been by Emil Koeppel, "Studien zur Geschichte des englischen Petrachismus im sechzehnten Jahrhundert," pp. 88–9.
[6] Lewis, *English Literature in the Sixteenth Century*, p. 238.

Targoff, in the only real addition to the poem's critical tradition since Lewis, takes note of it because it does not end with any anticipation of the reunion of the lovers in the afterlife; there are not even the spectral or visionary visitations from beyond the grave found in the last century of the *Canzoniere*.[7] The ending is despair: "Lo, thus I seke myne own decaye, / And will, till that I may it finde" (303–4).

Lewis's description of what has happened is that the English poet "sees his original through the eyes of Chaucer and produces ... an abridged version of the mourner's narrative in the *Boke of the Duchesse*."[8] I think it is more drastic than that: the tightly coiled, enigmatic intensity of "*Nel dolce tempo*" unspools into a linear narrative: lyricized epic reverse engineered as fairly simple storytelling. The most complex features of the original are cut or rearranged out of existence. The contrast is so extreme as to make the connection between the two poems sound trivial or even an annotator's fantasy—but it is neither of those. Except for the word "libertie" I have not yet quoted the specific verbal evidence that the English poet had Petrarch's poem in mind and quite possibly in front of him. His opening tracks five lines of the Italian in expanded pararphrase:

> perché cantando il duol si disacerba,
> canterò com' io vissi in libertade
> mentre Amor nel mio albergo a sdegno s'ebbe;
>   poi seguirò sì come a lui ne 'ncrebbe
> troppo altamente e che di ciò m'avenne. (4–8)

because, singing, pain becomes less bitter, I shall sing how then I lived in liberty while Love was scorned in my abode; then I shall pursue how that chagrined him too deeply, and what happened to me for that.

> Sythe singyng gladdeth oft the hartes
> Of them that fele the panges of love:
> And for the while doth ease their smartes:
> My self I shall the same way prove.
>   And though that love hath smit the stroke,
> Wherby is lost my libertie:
> Which by no meanes I may revoke:
> Yet shall I sing, how pleasantly.
>   Ny twenty yeres of youth I past:
> Which all in libertie I spent:
> And so from fyrst unto the last,
> Ere aught I knew, what loving ment.
>   And after shall I syng the wo,
> The payne, the greefe, the deadly smart:
> When love this lyfe did overthrowe,
> That hydden lyes within my hart. (1–16)

The English poet skips the famous *incipit* of the original—"*Nel dolce tempo de la prima etade*," a "poetic" touch for which he does not have much use—to get to the business of

---

[7] Ramie Targoff, *Posthumous Love*, p. 226.
[8] Lewis, p. 238.

telling what he is going to tell us, and why. The why, a classical *sententia* from Horace,[9] goes at the very front. I will tell my story because doing so is therapeutic; it eases the pain.

As he gets into his story, he leaves the details of Petrarch's poem behind—none of that bizarre mythology—but just before the midpoint, in seemingly total despair, he begins quoting Petrarch again:

> on a day, as fortune would:
> (For that, that shalbe, nedes must fall)
> I sat me down, as though I should
> Have ended then my lyfe, and all.
>   And as I sat to wryte my plaint,
> Meaning to shew my great unrest:
> With quaking hand, and hart full faint,
> Amid my plaintes, among the rest,
>   I wrote with ynk, and bitter teares:
> I am not myne, I am not mine:
> Behold my life, away that weares:
> And if I dye the losse is thine. (145–56)

These quatrains match three lines in Petrarch's poem: "*le vive voci m'erano interditte, / ond' io gridai con carta et con incostro: / 'Non son mio, no; s' io moro il danno è vostro'*" (98–100 [words spoken aloud were forbidden me; so I cried out with paper and ink: "I am not my own, no; if I die, yours is the loss"]). The verbal parallels are too specific to be inadvertent. Moreover, the English poet's recourse to the original is not random ambling; he has appropriated two moments in a subplot of the *canzone*, the integration of the love story with the speaker's growing commitment to his poetry. In both poems, misery in love prompts song, and then, after deepening unhappiness, writing; the vocation becomes literally literary. The English poet saw that as the most specific thing he wanted for his poem.

Petrarch's displacement of *viva voce* into *carta et incostro* comes just after the point where manuscript evidence indicates he set the poem aside for a while, as if uncertain what came next. When things resume, the lover has once again managed to collect himself, and even recover some of his confidence: "*Ben mi credea dinanzi agli occhi suoi / d'indegno far così di mercé degno, / et questa spene m'avea fatto ardito*" (101–3) [I thought well thus to make myself in her eyes from unworthy, worthy of mercy, and this hope had made me bold]). But what follows is no alleviation of the speaker's suffering but its repetition in more dire terms; the poem enters the present tense at the end in something close to derangement:

> i' senti' trarmi de la propria imago
> et in un cervo solitario et vago
> di selva in selva ratto mi trasformo,
> et ancor de' miei can fuggo lo stormo. (157–60)

I felt myself drawn from my own image and into a solitary wandering stag from wood to wood quickly I am transformed and still I flee the belling of my hounds.

---

[9] Horace, *Carmina* 4.11.35–6: "*minuentur atrae / carmine curae*" [dark cares are lessened by song].

The English poem continues for a few lines to follow the Italian, but tentatively and shyly:

> Herewith a litle hope I caught:
> That for a whyle my life did stay.
> But in effect, all was for naught.
> Thus lived I styll: tyll on a day ... (157–60)

Suddenly the woman comes around and pledges her love in return. The happy ending is temporary but very real; the innuendo is that she read the poem he had finally had the nerve to write, and that did the trick. The most visible appropriation from "*Nel dolce tempo*" is the hinge to the next chapter of the story, a chapter Petrarch never reaches. Replacing Petrarch's obsessive inwardness with linear narrative progress is the general tenor of what the English poet does in his poem, and the main reason what he writes strikes us as a less compelling, certainly less venturesome poem; but the use he makes of Petrarch in doing so is not imperceptive and not casual.

A half century later another example comes in William Alexander's *Aurora* (1604). Alexander (later Earl of Stirling and, for his ultimately unsuccessful attempt to settle Nova Scotia, Viscount of Canada) is now best remembered for the bridge narrative between the two versions of Sidney's *Arcadia* in the composite 1621 edition. The appearance of his Petrarchan sequence follows the publication of *Darius* (1603), one of what would eventually be four tragedies in the neo-Senecan mode that descends from *Gorboduc*: two of the age's prestige genres not usually attempted by the same writer (a distinction Alexander shares with Daniel and Greville). Alexander may not have thought highly of *Aurora*, which he did not reprint after 1605. When he wrote it, though, his aspirations were sufficient for him to attempt a careful mimicry of the mixture of forms in Petrarch's sequence, with the 105 sonnets punctuated by ten poems identified as "songs," four as "madrigals," three "elegies" in poulter's measure, and two sestinas (each category numbered separately). Of the songs, three follow, more fully than any of the poems mentioned previously, the form of a Petrarchan *canzone*, a complex ad hoc stanza with lines of variable length, repeated a number of times and capped with a shorter stanza serving as a *congedo*. Of these, the third stands out. At 126 lines, it is, like "*Nel dolce tempo*," the longest poem in its sequence, and it begins just about where that *canzone* opens:

> When as my fancies first began to flie,
> Which youth had but enlarg'd of late,
> Enamour'd of mine owne conceit,
> I sported with my thoughts that then were free;
> And never thought to see
> No such mishap at all,
> As might have made them thrall. (1–7)[10]

> Nel dolce tempo de la prima etade,
> che nascer vide et ancor quasi in erba
> la fera voglia che per mio mal crebbe,
> perché cantando il duol si disacerba,

---

[10] I quote *Aurora* from vol. 2 of *The Poetical Works of Sir William Alexander*, ed. L. E. Kastner and H. B. Charlton. The connection of the third song with "*Nel dolce tempo*" is noted by Roche, the only critic to give the poem serious attention (*Petrarch and the English Sonnet Sequences*, p. 278).

> canterò com' io vissi in libertade
> mentre Amor nel mio albergo a sdegno s'ebbe. (1-6)

In the sweet time of my first age, which saw born and still almost unripe the fierce desire which for my hurt grew—because, singing, pain becomes less bitter—I shall sing how then I lived in liberty while Love was scorned in my abode.

The word choice of "thrall" (together with "glide" in ll. 24, 72, 97) suggests that Alexander may have taken some small cues from "Syth syngyng gladdeth oft the harts" (ll. 80, 62, 103, 107), though it is of more moment that he ignores the motive for singing that his English predecessor highlights by placing it first. Alexander also has no place later on for the trope of crying aloud with paper and ink; he excises precisely the subplot of *"Nel dolce tempo"* that Tottel's poet is at pains to reproduce. At the same time, the Scots poet ventures something like the mythic turbulence that the English poet surgically removes, when the third stanza leads into a fantastic voyage that, with different details, evokes the lover's metamorphic adventures in Petrarch's *canzone*:

> Then when I had receiv'd the deadly wound,
> And that the goddesse fled my sight,
> Inveigled with her beauties light:
> First having followed ore the stable ground,
> Unto the deepe profound,
> My course I next did hold,
> In hope the truth t'unfold.
> If *Thetis* by her might,
> Or some sea-nimph had us'd the fatall slight:
> In th'Haven I did a barke behold,
> With sailes of silke, and oares of gold,
> Which being richly deckt, did seeme most sound. (25-36)

An opulent but ominous invitation; he accepts it and heads off for another seven stanzas.

They are extravagantly out of key with the rest of Alexander's sequence, where the Petrarchan conceits have for the most part an inept orderliness. Beneath some conventional expressions of hyperbolic emotion we catch glimpses of a proud and settled confidence in knowing what he is doing and getting where he means to go:

> The thoughts of those I cannot but disprove,
> Who basely lost their thraldome must bemone:
> I scorne to yeeld my selfe to such a one,
> Whose birth and vertue is not worth my love ...
>   At least by this I have allow'd of fame,
>   Much honour if I winne, if lose, no shame.
> (sonnet 27.1-4, 13-14)

The focus on "birth," first in a list of two, has a particularly candid sound. The speaker's confidence is not misplaced. *Aurora* turns out to be the second English-language Petrarchan sequence of the period to end in marriage, a seldom noticed companion to Spenser's *Amoretti*—in this case Alexander's marriage to Janet Erskine in 1601. Alexander's expectation that his troubles will be worth it echoes sonnets in Spenser's sequence in which the lover understands the difficulties and humiliations of courtship as appropriate means to a well-sanctioned end: "thinke not long in taking litle paine, / to knit the knot, that ever shall remaine" (*Amoretti* 6.13–14). But Spenser effectively guides his whole sequence to this end, climaxing it with the grand release of his *Epithalamion*, while *Aurora* seems of at least two minds about its destination.

What it displays in its most ambitious and memorable poem is a narrative line like that in Petrarch's *canzone*: an ostensible continuity of action repeatedly and sometimes violently confused by its own tumult. When the ship on which the lover embarks is wrecked in a storm, he is brought by "her whom I sought at last" (48) to a "chamber made of pearle" (52) where he "proudly sought, / In state with *Jove* to strive" (53–4) until the room bursts into flame. The woman then "on my backe two wings did bind" (63) and he flies aloft until he encounters "a mightie wind" (69) and "glided to the ground almost quite slaine" (72). The same woman, "(as it seem'd) growne kinder then before" (73), makes him a bed of flowers, feeds him with nectar, and sings him to sleep "betwixt two yvorie rounds" (81). When "cur'd of every thing save care" (85), he is led into a labyrinth "made of precious stones" (90) where "A world of men shed weightie grones, / That tortur'd were with th'engines of despaire" (95–6). Wandering there, he "did embrace, / A nymph like th'other in the face, / But whose affections were more mildly bent" (110–12) and who "Plaid *Ariadnes* part, / And led me by the heart / Out of the guilefull place" (114–16). Two especially perplexing lines possibly contain a misprint: "And like th'ungratefull *Theseus* in this case, / I made not my deliverer smart" (117–18). Since the ungrateful Theseus notoriously did make his deliverer smart by deserting her on Naxos, "And like" could be a mistake (in dictation?) for "Unlike." In any case, the outcome is a shaken, tentative calm: "Thus oft affraid my panting hart, / Can yet scarce trust t'have scap'd some bad event" (119–20). The *congedo* concludes with a self-conscious assertion—in effect replacing Petrarch's opening hope for singing to lessen the pain—that the poem is meant to be hard to understand:

> If any muse misterious song,
> At those strange things that thou hast showne,
> And wot not what to deeme;
> Tell that they do me wrong,
> I am my selfe, what ere I seeme,
> And must go mask'd, that I may not be knowne. (121–6)

The poet affirms his own identity through concealment.

The present-tense terror to which the lover in "*Nel dolce tempo*" comes just before the *congedo* completes the transit from narrative to lyric. The different conclusion in Alexander's *canzone* is, by contrast, what gives that poem's emotional excesses a narrative shape, and one which applies, if less interestingly, to the sequence as a whole. The alternating waves of exhilaration and dejection beginning in the third stanza intimate an almost bipolar erotic experience that threatens to be as endlessly cyclic as the reversals in "*Nel dolce tempo*." But the cycles are not like those in Petrarch; lines are crossed that Petrarch never crosses. This woman's explicit agency is stronger than Laura's, and more fully sexual. When the man strives to be like Jove in state, it is after she has brought him to her chamber; it is she who gives him an eagle's wings and feeds him with nectar on a bed of flowers and then lulls him to sleep between her breasts. The cycles in "*Nel dolce tempo*" are endless because the goal of sexual consummation is never reached; here something climactic happens as early as the fourth stanza, yet the story keeps going. When the woman leads the man into her jeweled maze, he compares his now addled will, in a touch of local color, to the ambiguous tidal flow in the Firth of Forth, which "glides as t'were in doubt, / What way she should direct her course" (97–8). He has no idea where to go: "So wandred I about / In th'intricated way" (101–2). The groans around him are sounds from Dante's world; he has come to a place of permanent damnation, where mortals suffer a torment that is a concrete metaphor for their sin.

That is an ending of sorts, but one that confirms the speaker in a state of hopeless agitation. At that point Alexander, showing a mythographic adroitness not generally associated with him, has the conceit generate its own escape route: the labyrinth summons its Ariadne. She shows up after the unnamed "beauteous guide" of the earlier action had "fled quite away" (106); the new she resembles her predecessor facially, but is calmer in her effect on the speaker. Thomas Roche sees a straightforward allegory: "The two nymphs have the same face because human desire has but one face and becomes cupidity or charity according to the object and degree to which reason maintains control."[11] We could also see the second woman as a previously unencountered aspect of the earlier woman; the moment in "*Nel dolce tempo*" which Sidney's Musidorus unwittingly reenacts results from Petrarch's coming upon Laura "*in altro abito*" (75, in another garment) and treating her as if she were someone different. Or she may indeed be another woman; that possibility violates the strict canons of Petrarchism, but does have precedents—in for one Thomas Wyatt's sonnet "If waker care" (R28/MT97)—and also some biographical warrant.[12] However we understand it, the change opens a way out of passion's labyrinth, and one that anticipates at least tentatively the conclusion of the whole sequence. After the third song, located between sonnets 19 and 20, Alexander's poems track some familiar vicissitudes of hope and despair, but just past the century mark announce a new understanding of what has been going on:

> Long time I did thy cruelties detest,
> And blaz'd thy rigor in a thousand lines;
> But now through my complaints thy vertue shines,
> That was but working all things for the best. (103.1–4)

The lover now sees that the woman's intent had been pedagogical, instruction in disciplining his unruly passions:

> Thou of my rash affections held'st the raines,
> And spying dangerous sparkes come from my fires,
> Didst wisely temper my enflam'd desires,
> With some chast favours, mixt with sweet disdaines. (5–8)

In a tenth and concluding song, marriage puts a decisive end to the disorder that love had brought into his life:

---

[11] Roche, p. 279.

[12] See Thomas H. McGrail, *Sir William Alexander*, pp. 26–7. Alexander's sonnet 99 appears prompted by the experience of his beloved's embrace of another, older man—"May I not mourne to see the morning match'd, / With one that's in the evening of his age?" (3–4)—and to signal the end of the speaker's courtship. The episode is never referred to again in the sequence, but an epigram by Alexander's contemporary John Leech confidently identifies Aurora as Elizabeth Shaw, who married John Murray, Earl of Annandale, when he was about forty (some twenty years older than Alexander); Leech, *Epigrammatum Libri Quatuor*, pp. 61–2. Alexander may have gathered under one name both the woman who jilted him and the woman who married him; similar arguments have been advanced about the *Amoretti* (e.g., Lever, *Elizabethan Love Sonnet*, pp. 96–103).

> Great god that tam'st the gods old-witted child,
>   Whose temples brests, whose altars are mens hearts,
> From my hearts fort thy legions are exild,
>   And *Hymens* torch hath burn'd out all thy darts:
> Since I in end have bound my selfe to one,
> That by this meanes I may be bound to none. (13–18)

This is where his Ariadne's thread had been anchored.

An abrupt finish, especially compared to Spenser's. In the *Amoretti*, the woman's consent comes well before the end of the sequence, and is celebrated in several keys, some austere but some joyously sensual. The wedding itself prompts the ceremonious, sustained exuberance of the *Epithalamion*. But the absence of anything like this in *Aurora* does not look like an oversight. In his *Epithalamion* Spenser makes a point of summoning both the "sonnes of Venus" ("play your sports at will") and Hymen to his wedding night (in that order: 364, 405). When Alexander represents his marriage as the victory of Hymen over Cupid, he is making a different statement about marriage. Shakespeare's Prospero makes a version of it in *The Tempest* (4.1.60–138) when he stages a wedding masque from which Venus and Cupid are banished. Medical and moral advice, going back to antiquity and running into the twentieth century, warned against excessive sexual gratification even (perhaps especially) when sanctioned within the bonds of marriage—not without dissent, but Alexander seems to be siding with the common wisdom.[13] It is not just erotic excitement of which he is divesting himself; in the final sonnet of his sequence he divests himself of the pleasures of love poetry:

> Awake my Muse, and leave to dreame of loves,
> Shake off soft fancies chaines, I must be free,
> Ile perch no more, upon the mirtle tree,
> Nor glide through th'aire with beauties sacred doves. (105.1–4)

(Prospero has a similar dismissal to make after his wedding masque.) The speaker hurries on to other projects—"Ile tune my accents to a trumpet now, / And seeke the Laurell in another field" (9–10)—by which he presumably means his Monarchike Tragedies, and married love is simply not a subject that, as a poet, interests him. (For Alexander's own wedding, his friend Walter Quin supplied an unmemorable epithalamium.)[14] There is a consistency to this, and, again, a measure of candor. In the quick shift of tone at the end of *Aurora*, the rage of Petrarchan desire is replaced (for better or worse) with the sober virtues of marriage. Alexander's unique adaptation of "*Nel dolce tempo*" does not dispense with its mythic turmoil, but uses it to serve his own brand of storytelling that leads to a happy ending.

---

[13] See Lawrence Stone, *The Family, Sex and Marriage in England*, pp. 493–501; on the conflict between moderate and excessive passion in love literature, see Joshua Scodel, *Excess and the Mean in Early Modern English Literature*, pp. 145–96.

[14] McGrail, p. 8.

## APPENDIX C

# The *Trionfi*

Petrarch's other major work of vernacular poetry, an allegorical narrative of some 2000 lines in *terza rima*, has faded from view even among scholars, but was in its time widely read and influential, possibly even more so than the *Canzoniere*. It is an ambitious work, a venture outside whatever comfort zone the *Canzoniere* may have represented, though with uncertain success. The choice of meter, one Petrarch never used elsewhere, inevitably invites comparison with Dante (its inventor), a formidable predecessor who had been a guest of Petrarch's father when Petrarch was a boy but whom, he tells Boccaccio in a letter (*Epistolae familiares* 21.15), he long avoided imitating or even reading. Boccaccio's own Dantean *Amorosa visione* may have been the prompt for adapting a conceit from Ovid—Cupid leading a military triumph in the high Roman mode (*Amores* 1.2)—for an agenda comparable to that of Dante's *Commedia*. A lovesick speaker indistinguishable from Petrarch beholds the god of love as "*un vittorioso e sommo duce, / pur com'un di color che 'n Campidoglio / triumfal carro a gran gloria conduce*" (*Triumphus Cupidinis* 1.13–15 [a victorious and supreme leader, like one who drives a triumphal chariot to great glory on the Capitoline Hill]), leading a huge parade of captives, among whom the speaker recognizes a fellow Florentine (otherwise unidentified) who then serves as a guide in identifying the various historical and mythological figures passing by and hearing in some cases their stories. The triumph of Love passes into a succession of what the Latin section titles identify as further triumphs, in which each power is overmastered by the next: Love is conquered by Chastity (*Pudicitia*), in turn conquered by Death, followed by Fame, Time, and ultimately Eternity. The speaker's initial *malaise* is thereby set against a vision of the whole course of human experience as a moral education under God's ultimate guidance.

The inevitable comparison with the *Commedia* does Petrarch no favors. Dante's allegory is fully worked out on the literal level as Dante and Vergil travel through the geography and architecture of hell and purgatory, while Petrarch's succession of triumphs goes in and out of focus. Illustrators, who loom large in the poem's afterlife,[1] visualize a crisp array of the six conquerors signalled in the section titles, but you will have trouble finding them in the text, and the narrative line more than once becomes pointlessly blurred and confusing. The neo-Vergilian guide somehow gets lost track of. The conversations with the dead, moreover, which give Dante's poem its most indelible moments, are in the *Trionfi* surprisingly few and (with one exception, noted later) unmemorable; a grim amount of time is taken up with inert cataloguing of their names, as if the poet's inventiveness had deserted him as he tried to fill out his ambitious plan. Petrarch elsewhere suggests he was frustrated with the poem and considered it unfinished. A dated autograph manuscript of the *Triumphus Eternitatis* may indicate that Petrarch was still working at it three months before his death.

In the fifteenth and sixteenth centuries, though, the poem's popularity was not crimped by what now seem like its defects.[2] On the continent it circulated widely in manuscript and (beginning in 1470) in print, often in combination with the *Canzoniere*, but also on

---

[1] Eisenbichler and Iannucci, in *Petrarch's Triumphs*, devote an entire section to these; Sara Charney, "Artistic Representations of Petrarch's *Triumphus Famae*," gives a sense of the big picture.

[2] For an up-to-date survey, see Alessandra Petrina's Introduction to her *Petrarch's* Triumphi *in the British Isles*, from which the following examples are taken.

its own; like the *Canzoniere*, it attracted the kind of annotation that gave Petrarch's vernacular poetry the look of a classical text on the page. In England and Scotland we can place some edition of it in numerous personal and institutional libraries, including those of Henry VIII's first and last wives (in the former case, a Castilian translation) and Mary Queen of Scots. It was a work people of consequence sought out; there is correspondence in which Edmund Bonner, a significant player in Henry's court, asks Thomas Cromwell for a copy. Roger Ascham in *The Scholemaster* complains of its popularity. The earliest writings of Thomas More's that we have, from the mid-1490s, are some verse captions for a series of painted tapestries in his father's home representing, in sequence, Chyldhod, Manhod, Venus and Cupyde, Age, Deth, Fame, Tyme, and Eternitee. The tapestries have not survived and More's poems show no particular familiarity with Petrarch's text, but the scheme of the project is unmistakably based on that of the *Trionfi*, inflected so that the progress of the soul emerges from the ages of man; even before the younger Henry began to leave his mark on the English court, Petrarch's poem, or at least the idea of it, was a presence in English literate circles.

Two complete translations of the *Trionfi* into English were done in the sixteenth century. Lord Morley's, in unsteady rhymed couplets of variable length, was written during Henry's reign and printed ca. 1554 during Mary's, possibly with political intent.[3] William Fowler's, in poulter's measure, survives in a manuscript dated 1587 and makes a pair with *The Tarantula of Love*, his Petrarchan sonnet sequence. In 1644 another Scot, Anna Hume, published (in Edinburgh) a translation of the first three triumphs into pentameter couplets which show the finesse that that meter was acquiring in English, and in an "Advertisement to the Reader" promised: "If they afford thee either profit or delight, I shall the more willingly bestow some of my few leasure hours on turning the other three."[4] They never surfaced, though what remains, with the triumph of Love ending in the triumph of Death, has a sinister if unintended integrity. Translations of various passages from the poem turn up in different contexts; a manuscript version of the first ninety lines of the *Triumphus Eternitatis* in rhymed quatrains may be by Elizabeth I.[5] The most proficient of these is a complete translation of the *Triumphus Mortis* done sometime before 1600 by Mary Sidney, the only one of these translators to use *terza rima* (which Wyatt had introduced into English, though not for translating Petrarch). This triumph has always been of particular interest; including Morley, Fowler, and Hume, there are six translations from it during this period. In the second of its two *capitoli* everything else going on recedes to allow a *tête-à-tête* between Petrarch and Laura in which, after her almost total silence in the *Canzoniere*, she openly speaks of her own reciprocal love for him. Only concern for both their reputations had caused her to conceal it during her life:

> Mai diviso
> da te non fu 'l mio cor, né già mai fia;
> ma temprai la tua fiamma col mio viso,
> perché a salvar te e me null'altra via
> era, e la nostra giovenetta fama (2.88–92)

---

[3] Kenneth R. Bartlett, "The Occasion of Lord Morley's Translation of the *Trionfi*"; Oliver Wort, "Marian Literary Culture."

[4] *The Triumphs of Love: Chastitie: Death*, p. 100.

[5] In addition to the ones edited by Petrina, see Stuart Gillespie, "Manuscript Translations of Italian Poetry," p. 49.

In Sidney's version:

> Never were
> Our hearts but one, nor never two shall be:
> Onelie thy flame I tempred with my cheere:
> The onelie waye could save both thee and me;
> Our tender fame did this supporte require[6]

Laura is saying of course what Petrarch at this point would want to hear her say, and having her speak is less an escape from lyric self-absorption into narrative than wish fulfillment. Sidney if anything heightens the romance of it. When Laura in Italian affirms, "*Fur quasi iguale in noi amorose fiamme*" (139 [the amorous fires between us were as if equal]), Sidney erases *quasi*: "In equale flames our loving hearts were tryde."[7]

Something fiercer and more disruptive, though, does elsewhere seem to have been injected by Petrarch's poem into English literature. In the third *capitolo* of *Triumphus Cupidinis* he gives a percussive catalogue of his erotic symptoms:

> Or so come da sé 'l cor si disgiunge,
> e come sa far pace, guerra, e tregua,
> e coprir suo dolor quand'altri il punge;
> e so come in un punto si dilegua
> e poi si sparge per le guance il sangue,
> se paura o vergogna avèn che 'l segua;
> so come sta tra' fiori ascoso l'angue... (3.151–7)

And so on for thirteen iterations of *so*. Surrey, in the earliest known translation from the *Trionfi* into English, uses this passage for the last three-quarters of a poem of his own:

> Lo, by these rules I know how sone a hart can turne
> From warr to peace, from trewce to stryf, and so again returne.
> I know how to convert my will in others lust;
> Of litle stuff unto my self to weyve a webb of trust;
> And how to hide my harme with soft dissembled chere,
> When in my face the paynted thoughtes wolde owtwardlye appere.
> I know how that the blood forsakes the faas for dredd,
> And how by shame it staynes agayne the cheke with flaming redd.
> I know under the grene the serpent how he lurckes ...
> (13.15–23)

The incantatory anaphora was not the least of the attractions; "I know" outdoes Petrarch by occurring fourteen times, the result of Surrey's insertion of an emphatic new metaphor into the middle of the list: "The hamer of the restles forge I know eke how yt workes" (24). This is more like Wyatt than like Petrarch ("Such hammers worke within my hed / That sound nought els unto my eris"; 121R/209MT.7–8), and the line radiates its force into the

---

[6] I quote from *The Collected Works of Mary Sidney Herbert Countess of Pembroke*, ed. Margaret P. Hannay, Noel Kinnamon, and Michael G. Brennan. Line numbers are the same as for the Italian.

[7] Kennedy, *Site of Petrarchism*, p. 243. As Kennedy also notes (pp. 244–5), Sidney makes a decision on a textual crux debated by Italian commentators when she has Laura recall for Petrarch "when I thy words' alone did entretaine / Singing for thee" (149–50). Doing so summons up a scene of charged intimacy fit for her brother's sonnet sequence (*Astrophil and Stella* 36, 57).

surroundings, giving the Surrey canon, usually remembered for its smoothness and elegance, its strongest representation of love as an obsessive, throbbing fatality. There is no hint in the poem that the hammers will ever stop.

The nightmarish quality of Surrey's poem is continuous with the most unnerving triumphal procession in English Renaissance literature, the Masque of Cupid in Spenser's House of Busirane (1590). There the god of Love, "riding on a Lion ravenous" (*Faerie Queene* 3.12.22.2), commands a dour parade of allegorical figures manifesting the tyrannous effects of love. They accompany their general's prize trophy, a dazed young woman with "Deathes own ymage figurd in her face" (19.6) and an open wound in her exposed breast, being conducted by the allegorical figures of Despight and Cruelty toward some horrid ritual:

> At that wide orifice her trembling hart
>   Was drawne forth, and in silver basin layd,
>   Quite through transfixed with a deadly dart,
>   And in her blood yet steeming fresh embayd:
>   And those two villeins, which her steps upstayd,
>   When her weake feete could scarcely her sustaine,
>   And fading vitall powers gan to fade,
>   Her forward still with torture did constraine,
> And evermore encreased her consuming paine. (21)

This sado-masochistic spectacle is performed in a cavernous hall to awe an audience of one, the armed and armored female knight who embodies the virtue of Chastity. She successfully resists and eventually rescues the victim, more or less, but it is a close-run thing; the nihilistic power on display lingers like a scene from a David Lynch film.

Two and a half centuries later another English poet steeped in Italian literature will find in the *Trionfi* even darker medicine. At the end of his life Percy Shelley adopts Petrarch's conceit and verse form for a poem in which he envisions the victorious conqueror not as Love but as Life. "The Triumph of Life" (1822) is not a poem of affirmation but one of despair at what the experience of living does to everyone:

> From every firmest limb and fairest face
> The strength and freshness fell like dust, and left
> The action and the shape without the grace
>
> Of life. The marble brow of youth was cleft
> With care; and in those eyes where once hope shone,
> Desire, like a lioness bereft
>
> Of her last cub, glared ere it died; each one
> Of that great crowd sent forth incessantly
> These shadows, numerous as the dead leaves blown
>
> In autumn evening from a poplar tree. (520–9)

The poem builds to the uncomprehending outburst, "Then, what is life? I cried" (544), and trails off, interrupted by its author's possibly intentional death by drowning. The chilling deceptiveness of the title is like that of Yukio Mishima in naming his own last work *The Sea of Fertility*—meaning when he does so not a place of earthly nurture and renewal but the airless, lifeless surface of the Moon.

# Bibliography (Works Cited)

## Primary Sources

Alexander, William (Earl of Stirling). *Poetical Works*. Ed. L. E. Kastner and H. B. Charlton. 2 vols. Manchester: Manchester University Press, 1929.

Andreas Capellanus. *The Art of Courtly Love*. Trans. John Jay Parry. New York: Columbia University Press, 1941.

Aubrey, John. *"Brief Lives," Chiefly of Contemporaries*. Ed. Andrew Clark. 2 vols. Oxford: Clarendon, 1898.

Bacon, Francis. *The Felicity of Queen Elizabeth*. London: Thomas Newcomb for George Latham, 1651.

Bacon, Nathaniel. *The Papers of Nathaniel Bacon of Stiffkey*, vol. 2. Ed. A. Hassell Smith and Gillian M. Baker. Norfolk: Norfolk Record Society, 1983.

Bale, John. *Illustrium Maioris Britanniae Scriptorum ... Summarium*. Wesel: Derick van der Straten for John Overton, 1548.

Balzac, Honoré de. *The Human Comedy: Selected Stories*. Ed. Peter Brooks, trans. Linda Asher et al. New York: NYRB, 2014.

*The Bannatyne Manuscript Writtin in Tyme of Pest 1568*. Ed. W. Tod Ritchie. 3 vols. STS. Edinburgh: Blackwood, 1928–34.

Barnes, Barnabe. *Parthenophil and Parthenophe*. Ed. Victor A. Doyno. Carbondale, IL: Southern Illinois University Press, 1971.

Barnfield, Richard. *Complete Poems*. Ed. George Klawitter. Selinsgrove, PA: Susquehanna University Press, 1990.

Bembo, Pietro. *Opere in volgare*. Ed. Mario Marti. Florence: Sansoni, 1961.

Bembo, Pietro. *Lettere*. Ed. Ernesto Travi. 4 vols. Bologna: Commissione per i Testi di Lingua, 1987–93.

Berryman, John. *Berryman's Sonnets*. Intro. April Bernard. New York: FSG, 2014.

Bodenham, John. *Englands Helicon*. London: James Roberts for John Flasket, 1600.

Bradstreet, Anne. *The Tenth Muse Lately Sprung Up in America*. London: Stephen Bowtell, 1650.

Breton, Nicholas. *The Pilgrimage to Paradise, Joyned with the Countesse of Penbrookes Love*. Oxford: Joseph Barnes for Tobey Cooke, 1592.

Breton, Nicholas. *Wits Trenchmour, in a Conference Had betwixt a Scholler and an Angler*. London: James Roberts for Nicholas Ling, 1597.

Bright, Timothe. *An Abridgement of the Booke of Acts and Monuments of the Church*. London: Joan Orwin for Matthew Law, 1589.

C., E. *Emaricdulfe: Sonnets*. London: John Windet, 1595.

C., J. *Alcilia: Philoparthens Loving Follie*. London: Robert Robinson for William Mattes, 1595.

Campensis, Johannes (Jean de Campen). *Enchidirion Psalmorum*. Lyon, 1533.

Il Cariteo (Benedetto Gareth). *Le rime*. Ed. Erasmo Pèrcopo. Naples: Biblioteca Napolitana di Storia e Letteratura, 1892.

Castiglione, Baldassare. *The Book of the Courtier*. Trans. Charles S. Singleton. Garden City, NY: Doubleday, 1959.

Cavafy, C. P. *Collected Poems*. Ed. George Savidis, trans. Edmund Keeley and Philip Sherrard. Princeton: Princeton University Press, 1975.

Caxton, William. *Caxton's Eneydos 1490*. Ed. W. T. Culley and F. J. Furnivall. EETS. London: Oxford University Press, 1890.

Chamberlain, John. *Letters*. Ed. Norman Egbert McClure. 2 vols. Philadelphia: American Philosophical Society, 1939.

Charles d'Orléans. *Fortunes Stabilnes: Charles of Orleans's English Book of Love*. Ed. Mary-Jo Arn. Binghamton, NY: MRTS, 1994.

Clarendon, Earl of (Edward Hyde). *The History of the Rebellion and Civil Wars in England*, vol. 1. Oxford: At the Theater, 1702.

Constable, Henry. *Poems*. Ed. Joan Grundy. Liverpool: Liverpool University Press, 1960.

*The Court of Venus*. Ed. Russell A. Fraser. Durham, NC: Duke University Press, 1955.

Craig, Alexander. *Amorose Songes, Sonets, and Elegies*. London: William White, 1606.

Daniel, Samuel., trans. *The Worthy Tract of Paulus Jovius*. London: George Robinson for Simon Waterson, 1585.

Daniel, Samuel. *Poems and a Defence of Ryme*. Ed. Arthur Colby Sprague. 1930; rpt. Chicago: University of Chicago Press, 1965.

Davies, John (of Hereford). *Wittes Pilgrimage, (by Poetical Essaies)*. London: Richard Bradock for John Browne, 1605[?].

Davison, Francis. *A Poetical Rhapsody*. Ed. Hyder E. Rollins. 2 vols. Cambridge, MA: Harvard University Press, 1931.

della Porta, Giambattista. *Commedie*. Ed. Vincenzo Spampanato. 2 vols. Bari: Laterza, 1910–11.

*The Devonshire Manuscript: A Women's Book of Courtly Poetry*. Ed. Elizabeth Heale. Toronto: Iter, 2012.

——— *A Social Edition of the Devonshire Manuscript (BL MS Add 17,492)*. Ed. Raymond Siemens, Karin Armstrong, and Constance Crompton. Toronto: Iter, and Tempe, AZ: ACMRS, 2015.

Dickinson, Emily. *The Poems of Emily Dickinson: Variorum Edition*. Ed. R. W. Franklin. 3 vols. Cambridge, MA: Harvard University Press, 1998.

Donne, John. *Poetical Works*. Ed. Herbert Grierson. London: Oxford University Press, 1933.

Drayton, Michael. *Ideas Mirrour*. London: James Roberts for Nicholas Ling, 1594.

Drayton, Michael. *Poemes Lyrick and Pastorall*. London: Richard Bradock for Nicholas Ling and John Flasket, 1606.

Drayton, Michael. *Poems*. London: William Stansby for John Smethwick, 1619.

Erasmus, Desiderius. *De conscribendis epistolis*. Ed. Jean-Claude Margolin. *Opera omnia Desiderii Erasmi Roterodami*, vol. 1.2. Amsterdam: North-Holland, 1971. Pp. 153–79.

Essex, Earl of (Robert Devereux). "The Poems of Edward DeVere, Seventeenth Earl of Oxford and of Robert Devereux, Second Earl of Essex." Ed. Steven M. May. *Studies in Philology* 77.5 (1980): 43–64.

Filosseno (Philoxeno), Marcello. *Sylve*. Venice: Marchio Sesso and Pierodi Ravani, 1516.

Finch, Allan George. *Report of the Manuscripts of Allan George Finch, Esq.*, vol. 1. Historical Manuscripts Commission. London: HMSO, 1913.

Fletcher, Giles, the Elder. *The English Works*. Ed. Lloyd E. Berry. Madison, WI: University of Wisconsin Press, 1964.

*Four Years at the Court of Henry VIII.* Ed. and trans. Rawdon Brown. 2 vols. London: Smith Elder, 1854.
Fowler, William. *Works.* Ed. Henry W. Meikle. 2 vols. STS. Edinburgh: Blackwood, 1914.
Gascoigne, George, trans. *The Noble Arte of Venerie or Hunting.* London: Henry Bynneman for Christopher Barker, 1576.
Gascoigne, George. *A Hundreth Sundrie Flowres.* Ed. C. T. Prouty. Columbia, MO: University of Missouri Press, 1942.
Gascoigne, George. *The Complete Works.* Ed. J. W. Cunliffe. 2 vols. 1907; rpt. New York: Greenwood, 1969.
Gascoigne, George. *A Hundreth Sundrie Flowres.* Ed. G. W. Pigman III. Oxford: Clarendon, 2001.
Gillespie, Stuart, ed. "Manuscript Translations of Italian Poetry, c. 1650–1825: A Miscellany." *Translation and Literature* 28 (2019): 44–67.
Goldwel, Henry. *A Briefe Declaration of the Shews, Devices, Speeches, and Inventions, Done & Performed before the Queenes Majestie, & the French Ambassadours.* London: Robert Waldegrave, 1581.
Gorges, Arthur. *Poems.* Ed. Helen Estabrook Sandison. Oxford: Clarendon, 1953.
Greville, Fulke (Lord Brooke). *Poems and Dramas.* Ed. Geoffrey Bullough. 2 vols. New York: Oxford University Press, 1945.
Greville, Fulke (Lord Brooke). *Selected Poems.* Ed. Thom Gunn. Chicago: University of Chicago Press, 1968.
Griffin, Bartholomew. *Fidessa, More Chaste then Kinde.* London; Joan Orwin for Matthew Lownes, 1596.
H., N. *The Ladies Dictionary: Being a General Entertainment for the Fair-Sex.* London: John Dunton, 1694.
Hall, John. *Certayn Chapters Taken out of the Proverbes of Salomon, wyth Other Chapters of the Holy Scripture.* London: Thomas Raynald, 1550.
Hall, John. *The Court of Virtue.* Ed. Russell A. Fraser. New Brunswick, NJ: Rutgers University Press, 1961.
Harington, John, trans. *Orlando Furioso in English Heroical Verse.* London: Richard Field, 1591.
Harington, John. *Nugae Antiquae.* Ed. Henry Harington. 3 vols. London: James Dodsley, 1779.
Harington, John. *The Arundel Harington Manuscript of Tudor Poetry.* Ed. Ruth Hughey. 2 vols. Columbus, OH: Ohio State University Press, 1960.
Harvey, Gabriel. *Marginalia.* Ed. G. C. Moore Smith. Stratford: Shakespeare Head, 1913.
Herbert, George. *English Poems.* Ed. C. A. Patrides. London: Dent, 1974.
Jonson, Ben. *The Cambridge Edition of the Works of Ben Jonson.* Ed. David Bevington et al. 7 vols. Cambridge: Cambridge University Press, 2012.
Langham, Robert. *A Letter.* Ed. Roger Kuin. Leiden: Brill, 1983.
Lauder, George. *The Popes New-Years Gift, Anno 1622.* St. Andrews: Edward Raban, 1622.
Lauder, George. *The Anatomie of the Romane Clergie: or, A Discoverie of the Abuses Thereof.* London: Richard Field for Robert Milbourne, 1623.
Leech, John. *Epigrammatum Libri Quatuor.* London: Bernard Alsop, 1623.
Leland, John. *Naeniae in Mortem Thomae Viati Equitis Incomparabilis.* London: Reyner Wolfe, 1542.
Leland, John. *Principum, ac Illustrium Aliquot & Eruditorum in Anglia Virorum, Encomia, Trophaea, Genethiliaca, & Epithalamia.* London: Thomas Orwin, 1589.

Lodge, Thomas. *Phillis: Honoured with Pastorall Sonnets, and Amorous Delights*. London: James Roberts for John Busby, 1593.

Lowell, Robert. *The Dolphin*. Ed. Saskia Hamilton. New York: FSG, 2019.

Lynche, Richard. *Diella: Certaine Sonnets*. London: James Roberts for Henry Olney, 1596.

Malipiero, Girolamo. *Il Petrarcha spirituale*. Venice: Francesco Marcolini, 1536.

Metham, John. *Amoryus and Cleopes*. Ed. Stephen F. Page. Kalamazoo, MI: Medieval Institute Publications, 1999.

Michelangelo Buonarotti. *Rime*. Ed. Enzo Girardi, intro. Giovanni Testori. Milan: BUR, 1975.

Moryson, Fynes. *An Itinerary*. London: John Beale, 1617.

Murray, David. *Cælia: Containing Certaine Sonets*. London: George Eld for John Smethwick, 1611.

Nashe, Thomas. *Have with You to Saffron-Walden*. London: John Danter, 1596.

Naunton, Robert. *Fragmenta Regalia*. London, 1641.

Nugent, Richard. *Cynthia*. Ed. Angelina Lynch, intro. Anne Fogarty. Dublin: Four Courts, 2010.

*The Paradise of Dainty Devices (1576–1606)*. Ed. Hyder E. Rollins. Cambridge, MA: Harvard University Press, 1927.

Peele, George. *Polyhymnia: Describing, the Honourable Triumph at Tylt, before Her Majesty, on the 17. of November, Last Past*. London: Richard Jones, 1590.

Pembroke, Earl of (William Herbert). *Poems*. London: Matthew Inman for James Magnes, 1660.

Percy, William. *Sonnets to the Fairest Coelia*. London: Adam Islip for William Ponsonby, 1594.

Petrarch (Francesco Petrarca). *Il Petrarcha con la spositione di Giovanni Andrea Gesualdo*. Venice: Gabriel Giolito, 1553.

Petrarch (Francesco Petrarca). *Opera ... quae extant omnia*. 3 vols. Basel: Heinrich Petri, 1554.

Petrarch (Francesco Petrarca). *The Triumphs of Love: Chastitie: Death*. Trans. Anna Hume. Edinburgh: Evan Tyler, 1644.

Petrarch (Francesco Petrarca). "La 'collatio laureationis' del Petrarca." Ed. Carlo Godi. *Italia medioevale e umanistica* 13 (1970): 1–27.

Petrarch (Francesco Petrarca). *Lord Morley's* Tryumphes of Fraunces Petrarcke: *The First English Translation of the* Trionfi. Ed. D. D. Carnicelli. Cambridge, MA: Harvard University Press, 1971.

Petrarch (Francesco Petrarca). *Petrarch's Lyric Poems*. Ed. and trans. Robert M. Durling. Cambridge, MA: Harvard University Press, 1976.

Petrarch (Francesco Petrarca). *Triumphi*. Ed. Marco Ariani. Milan: Mursia, 1988.

Petrarch (Francesco Petrarca). *Petrarch's* Triumphi *in the British Isles*. Ed. Alessandra Petrina. Cambridge: MHRA, 2020.

Phillips, Edward. *Theatrum Poetarum*. London: Charles Smith, 1675.

*The Phoenix Nest 1593*. Ed. Hyder E. Rollins. Cambridge, MA: Harvard University Press, 1931.

Piccolomini, Aeneas Sylvius. *Storia di due amanti e Rimedio d'amore*. Ed. and trans. Maria Luisa Doglio. Turin: UTET, 1973.

Piccolomini, Aeneas Sylvius. *The Goodli History of the Ladye Lucres of Scene and of Her Lover Eurialus*. Ed. E. J. Morrall. EETS. Oxford: Oxford University Press, 1996.

Poliziano, Angelo. *The Stanze*. Ed. and trans. David Quint. Amherst, MA: University of Massachusetts Press, 1979.
Puttenham, George. *The Arte of English Poesie*. Ed. Gladys Doidge Willcock and Alice Walker. Cambridge: Cambridge University Press, 1936.
*The Queenes Majesties Entertainement at Woodstock*. London: Richard Tottel, 1585.
Ralegh, Walter. *The History of the World*. London: William Stansby for Walter Burre, 1614.
Ralegh, Walter. *Sir Walter Rawleighs Farewell to His Lady*. London: R. H., 1644.
Ralegh, Walter. *Poems*. Ed. Agnes Latham. Cambridge, MA: Harvard University Press, 1951.
Ralegh, Walter. *Letters*. Ed. Agnes Latham and Joyce Youings. Exeter: University of Exeter Press, 1999.
Ralegh, Walter. *The Poems of Sir Walter Ralegh: A Historical Edition*. Ed. Michael Rudick. Tempe, AZ: ACMRS, 1999.
*A Relation, or Rather a True Account, of the Island of England*. Ed. and trans. Charlotte Augusta Sneyd. 1847; rpt. New York: AMS, 1968.
Roberts, Josephine A., ed. "The Imaginary Epistles of Sir Philip Sidney and Lady Penelope Rich." *English Literary Renaissance* 15 (1985): 59–77.
Sanderson, William. *Aulicus Coquinariae: or a Vindication in Answer to a Pamphlet, Entituled the Court and Character of King James*. London: Henry Seile, 1651.
Sandys, George. *Ovid's Metamorphosis Englished, Mythologized, and Represented in Figures*. Ed. Karl K. Hulley and Stanley T. Vandersall. Lincoln, NE: University of Nebraska Press, 1970.
Sannazaro, Jacopo. *Arcadia and Piscatorial Eclogues*. Trans. Ralph Nash. Detroit: Wayne State University Press, 1966.
Serafino dall' Aquila. *Die Strambotti*. Ed. Barbara Bauer-Formiconi. Munich: Fink, 1967.
Shakespeare, William. *Supplement to the Edition of Shakspeare's Plays ... by Samuel Johnson and George Steevens*. 2 vols. London: C. Bathurst et al, 1780.
Shakespeare, William. *The Plays of William Shakspeare*. Ed. Samuel Johnson and George Steevens. 15 vols. London: Thomas Longman et al, 1793.
Shakespeare, William. *Sonnets*. Ed. Robert Cartwright. London: Russell, 1859.
Shakespeare, William. *Sonnets*. Ed. Hyder E. Rollins. 2 vols. New Variorum. Philadelphia: Lippincott, 1944.
Shakespeare, William. *The Riverside Shakespeare*. Ed. G. Blakemore Evans et al. Boston: Houghton Mifflin, 1974.
Shakespeare, William. *Shakespeare's Sonnets*. Ed. Stephen Booth. New Haven, CT: Yale University Press, 1977.
Shakespeare, William. *The Complete Works: Original-Spelling Edition*. Ed. Stanley Wells, Gary Taylor et al. Oxford: Clarendon, 1986.
Shakespeare, William. *The Sonnets and A Lover's Complaint*. Ed. John Kerrigan. Harmondsworth: Penguin, 1986.
Shakespeare, William. *Complete Sonnets and Poems*. Ed. Colin Burrow. Oxford: Oxford University Press, 2002.
Shakespeare, William. *Shakespeare's Sonnets*. Ed. Katherine Duncan-Jones. The Arden Shakespeare. 2nd ed. London: Bloomsbury, 2010.
Shelley, Percy Bysshe. *Poetical Works*. Ed. Thomas Hutchinson and G. M. Matthews. London: Oxford University Press, 1970.
Sidney, Mary (Countess of Pembroke). *Collected Works*. Ed. Margaret P. Hannay, Noel Kinnamon, and Michael G. Brennan. 2 vols. Oxford: Clarendon, 1998.
Sidney, Philip. *The Countesse of Pembrokes Arcadia*. London: William Ponsonby, 1590.

Sidney, Philip. *Syr P. S. His Astrophel and Stella*. London: John Charlewood for Thomas Newman, 1591.
Sidney, Philip. *Poems*. Ed. William A. Ringler, Jr. Oxford: Clarendon, 1962.
Sidney, Philip. *A Defence of Poetry*. Ed. Jan van Dorsten. Oxford: Oxford University Press, 1966.
Sidney, Philip. *Correspondence*. Ed. Roger Kuin. 2 vols. Oxford: Oxford University Press, 2012.
Sidney, Robert. *Poems*. Ed. P. J. Croft. Oxford: Clarendon, 1984.
Smith, G. Gregory, ed. *Elizabethan Critical Essays*. 2 vols. London: Oxford University Press, 1904.
Smith, William. *Poems*. Ed. Lawrence A. Sasek. Baton Rouge, LA: LSU Press, 1970.
Southern (Soowthern), John. *Pandora: The Musyque of the Beautie, of His Mistresse Diana*. London: Thomas Hacket, 1584.
Spenser, Edmund. *The Yale Edition of the Shorter Poems of Edmund Spenser*. Ed. William A. Oram et al. New Haven, CT: Yale University Press, 1989.
Spenser, Edmund. *The Faerie Queene*. Ed. A. C. Hamilton et al. London: Longman, 2001.
Spingarn, J. E., ed. *Critical Essays of the Seventeenth Century*. 3 vols. Bloomington, IN: Indiana University Press, 1957.
*State Papers of the Reign of King Henry VIII*. 11 vols. Record Commission. London, 1830–52.
Surrey, Earl of (Henry Howard). *Poems*. Ed. Emrys Jones. Oxford: Clarendon, 1964.
Sylvester, Richard S., ed. *The Anchor Anthology of Sixteenth-Century Verse*. Garden City, NY: Doubleday, 1974.
*The Tanner Letters: Original Documents and Notices of Irish Affairs in the Sixteenth and Seventeenth Centuries*. Ed. Charles McNeill. Dublin: Stationery Office, 1943.
Tassoni, Alessandro. *Considerazioni sopra le rime del Petrarca*. Modena: Giulian Cassiani, 1609.
Tofte, Robert. *Laura. The Toyes of a Traveller. Or: The Feast of Fancie*. London: Valentine Simmes, 1597.
Topsell, Edward. *The Historie of Foure-Footed Beastes*. London: William Jaggard, 1607.
Tottel, Richard. *Tottel's Miscellany (1557–1587)*. Ed. Hyder E. Rollins. 2 vols. 2nd ed. Cambridge, MA: Harvard University Press, 1966.
Tottel, Richard. *Richard Tottel's Songes and Sonettes: The Elizabethan Version*. Ed. Paul A Marquis. Tempe, AZ: ACMRS, 2007.
Varchi, Benedetto. *The Blazon of Jealousie: A Subject Not Written of by Any Heretofore*. Trans. Robert Tofte. London: Thomas Snodham for John Busby, 1615.
W., T. *The Tears of Fancie. Or, Love Disdained*. London: John Danter for William Barley, 1593.
Watson, Thomas. *The Ἑκατομπαθία or Passionate Centurie of Love*. London: John Wolfe for Gabriel Cawood, 1582.
*The Welles Anthology: MS Rawlinson C. 813*. Ed. Sharon L. Jansen and Kathleen H. Jordan. Binghamton, NY: MRTS, 1991.
Whetstone, George. *The Rocke of Regard*. London: Henry Middleton for Robert Walley, 1576.
Whetstone, George. *A Remembraunce of the Wel Imployed Life, & Godly End, of George Gascoigne Esquire*. London: Edward Aggas, 1577.
Whetstone, George. *Sir Phillip Sidney, His Honorable Life, His Valiant Death, and True Vertues*. London: Thomas Orwin for Thomas Cadman, 1587.
Whythorne, Thomas. *Autobiography*. Ed. James M. Osborn. Oxford: Clarendon, 1961.

Whythorne, Thomas. *Autobiography: Modern-Spelling Edition.* Ed. James M. Osborn. London: Oxford University Press, 1962.
Wroth, Mary. *Poems.* Ed. Josephine A. Roberts. Baton Rouge, LA: LSU Press, 1983.
Wroth, Mary. *The First Part of the Countess of Montgomery's Urania.* Ed. Josephine A. Roberts. Binghamton, NY: MRTS, 1995.
Wroth, Mary. *The Second Part of the Countesse of Montgomery's Urania.* Ed. Josephine A. Roberts, Suzanne Gossett, and Janel Mueller. Tempe, AZ: ACMRS, 1999.
Wroth, Mary. *Pamphilia to Amphilanthus in Manuscript and Print.* Ed. Ilona Bell, with Steven W. May. Toronto: Iter, 2017.
Wyatt, Thomas. *The Collected Poems of Sir Thomas Wyatt.* Ed. Kenneth Muir and Patricia Thomson. Liverpool: Liverpool University Press, 1969.
Wyatt, Thomas. *The Complete Poems.* Ed. R. A. Rebholz. New Haven, CT: Yale University Press, 1981.
Wyatt, Thomas. *Complete Works: Prose.* Ed. Jason Powell. Oxford: Oxford University Press, 2016.
*Zepheria.* London: Joan Orwin for Nicholas Ling and John Busby, 1594.

## Secondary Sources

Alexander, Gavin. "Constant Works: A Framework for Reading Mary Wroth." *Sidney Newsletter and Journal* 14.2 (1996–97): 5–32.
Alexander, Gavin. "Final Intentions or Process? Editing Greville's *Caelica*." *Studies in English Literature* 52 (2012): 13–33.
Alexander, Gavin. *Life after Sidney: The Literary Response to Sir Philip Sidney 1586–1640.* Oxford: Oxford University Press, 2006.
Alexander, Gavin. "Writing and the Hermeneutics of Posthumous Publication: Greville's Afterlives." In *Fulke Greville and the Culture of the English Renaissance*, ed. Russ Leo, Katrin Röder, and Freya Sierhuis. Oxford: Oxford University Press, 2018. Pp. 279–93.
Almasy, Rudolph P. "Stella and the Songs: Questions about the Composition of *Astrophil and Stella*." *South Atlantic Review* 58.4 (1993): 1–17.
Auhagen, Ulrike. "*Ad Stellam et Philastrum amantes (Epigr. 2, 53)*—Janus Dousa, Catull und Martial." In *Ianus Dousa: neulateinischer Dichter und klassischer Philologe*, ed. Eckard Lefèvre and Eckart Schäfer. Tübingen: Gunter Narr, 2009. Pp. 27–38.
Austen, Gillian. *George Gascoigne.* Cambridge: Brewer, 2008.
Bartlett, Kenneth R. "The Occasion of Lord Morley's Translation of the *Triumphi*: The Triumph of Chastity over Politics." Eisenbichler and Iannucci, pp. 325–34.
Bates, Catherine. *Masculinity and the Hunt: Wyatt to Spenser.* Oxford: Oxford University Press, 2013.
Bates, Catherine. *Masculinity, Gender and Identity in the English Renaissance Lyric.* Cambridge: Cambridge University Press, 2007.
Beer, Anna. *My Just Desire: The Life of Bess Ralegh, Wife to Sir Walter.* New York: Ballantine, 2003.
Beer, Anna. *Patriot or Traitor: The Life and Death of Sir Walter Ralegh.* London: Oneworld, 2018.
Beilin, Elaine V. *Redeeming Eve: Women Writers of the English Renaissance.* Princeton: Princeton University Press, 1987.
Bell, Ilona. *Elizabethan Women and the Poetry of Courtship.* Cambridge: Cambridge University Press, 1998.

Bell, Ilona. "Rethinking Shakespeare's Dark Lady." Schoenfeldt, *Companion*, pp. 293–313.
Bell, Ilona. "'A too curious secrecie': Wroth's Pastoral Song and 'Urania.'" *Sidney Journal* 31.1 (2013): 23–50.
Bonanno, Vincenzo. *Serafino l'Aquilano e Sir Thomas Wyatt*. L'Aquila: Marcello Ferri, 1980.
Bond, Garth. "Amphilanthus to Pamphilia: William Herbert, Mary Wroth, and Penshurst Mount." *Sidney Journal* 31.1 (2013): 51–80.
Borris, Kenneth. "'Ile hang a bag and a bottle at thy back': Barnfield's Homoerotic Advocacy and the Construction of Homosexuality." In *The Affectionate Shepherd: Celebrating Richard Barnfield*, ed. Borris and George Klawitter. Selinsgrove, PA: Susquehanna University Press, 2001. Pp. 193–248.
Boswell, Jackson Campbell, and Gordon Braden. *Petrarch's English Laurels 1475–1700: A Compendium of Printed References and Allusions*. Farnham: Ashgate, 2012.
Braden, Gordon. "Hero and Leander in Bed (and the Morning After)." *English Literary Renaissance* 45 (2015): 205–30.
Braden, Gordon. *Petrarchan Love and the Continental Renaissance*. New Haven, CT: Yale University Press, 1999.
Braden, Gordon. "Shakespeare's Petrarchism." Schiffer, pp. 163–83.
Braden, Gordon. "Translating the Rest of Ovid: The Exile Poems." In *Early Modern Cultures of Translation*, ed. Karen Newman and Jane Tylus. Philadelphia: University of Pennsylvania Press, 2015. Pp. 45–55.
Brennan, Michael G. "'A SYDNEY, though un-named': Ben Jonson's Influence in the Manuscript and Print Circulation of Lady Mary Wroth's Writings." *Sidney Journal* 17.1 (1999): 31–52.
Brigden, Susan. *Thomas Wyatt: The Heart's Forest*. London: Faber, 2012.
Brown, Russell M. "Sidney's *Astrophil and Stella*, Fourth Song." *The Explicator* 29.6 (1971), item 48.
Buchan, Alexander M. "Ralegh's *Cynthia*—Facts or Legend." *Modern Language Quarterly* 1 (1940): 461–74.
Campbell, Marion. "Inscribing Imperfection: Sir Walter Ralegh and the Elizabethan Court." *English Literary Renaissance* 20 (1990): 233–53.
Cecioni, Cesare G. *Thomas Watson e la tradizione petrarchista*. Milan: Giuseppe Principato, 1969.
Charney, Sara. "Artistic Representations of Petrarch's *Triumphus Famae*." Eisenbichler and Iannucci, pp. 223–33.
Clanton, Stacy M. "The 'Number' of Sir Walter Ralegh's *Booke of the Ocean to Scinthia*." *Studies in Philology* 82 (1985): 200–11.
Clegg, Cyndia Susan. *Press Censorship in Elizabethan England*. Cambridge: Cambridge University Press, 1997.
Cohen, Walter. *A History of European Literature: The West and the World from Antiquity to the Present*. Oxford: Oxford University Press, 2017.
Coldiron, A. E. B. *Canon, Period, and the Poetry of Charles of Orleans: Found in Translation*. Ann Arbor, MI: University of Michigan Press, 2000.
Coldiron, A. E. B. "Sidney, Watson, and the 'Wrong Ways' to Renaissance Lyric Poetics." *Renaissance Papers 1997*, pp. 49–62.
Coldiron, A. E. B. "Watson's *Hekatompathia* and Renaissance Lyric Translation." *Translation and Literature* 5 (1996): 3–25.
Coogan, Robert. "Petrarch's *De Remediis* and Gascoigne's *Griefe of Joye*." *Salzburg Studies in English Literature: Elizabethan and Renaissance Studies* 71 (1981): 32–46.

Cotter, James Finn. "The 'Baiser' Group in Sidney's *Astrophil and Stella*." *Texas Studies in Literature and Language* 12 (1970): 381–403.
Cressy, David. *Birth, Marriage, and Death: Ritual, Religion, and the Life-Cycle in Tudor and Stuart England*. Oxford: Oxford University Press, 1997.
Crewe, Jonathan. *Trials of Authorship: Anterior Forms and Poetic Reconstruction from Wyatt to Shakespeare*. Berkeley, CA: University of California Press, 1990.
Cropp, Glynnis M. *Le Vocabulaire courtois des troubadours de l'époque classique*. Geneva: Droz, 1975.
Crosman, Robert. "Making Love Out of Nothing at All: The Issue of Story in Shakespeare's Procreation Sonnets." *Shakespeare Quarterly* 41 (1990): 470–88.
Cruttwell, Patrick. *The Shakespearean Moment and Its Place in the Poetry of the 17th Century*. 1954; rpt. New York: Columbia University Press, 1970.
Cummings, Brian. *The Literary Culture of the Reformation: Grammar and Grace*. Oxford: Oxford University Press, 2002.
Dasenbrock, Reed Ray. *Imitating the Italians: Wyatt, Spenser, Synge, Pound, Joyce*. Baltimore: Johns Hopkins University Press, 1991.
Davenson, Henri (H. I. Marrou). *Les Troubadours*. Paris: Seuil, 1961.
Davie, Donald. "A Reading of 'The Ocean's Love to Cynthia.'" In *Elizabethan Poetry*, ed. John Russell Brown and Russell Harris. London: Arnold, 1960. Pp. 71–89.
de Grazia, Margreta. "The Scandal of Shakespeare's Sonnets." Schiffer, pp. 89–112.
Demetriou, Tania. "The Non-Ovidian Elizabethan Epyllion: Thomas Watson, Christopher Marlowe, Richard Barnfield." In *Interweaving Myths in Shakespeare and His Contemporaries*, ed. Janice Valls-Russell, Agnès Lafont, and Charlotte Coffin. Manchester: Manchester University Press, 2017. Pp. 41–64.
Dempsey, Charles. *The Portrayal of Love: Botticelli's* Primavera *and Humanist Culture at the Time of Lorenzo the Magnificent*. Princeton: Princeton University Press, 1992.
Desai, Adhaar Noor. "George Gascoigne's 'Patched Cote': Writing Pedagogy and Poetic Style in the Literature Classroom." *English Literary Renaissance* 52 (2022): 1–33.
Dillon, Janette. "Pageants and Propaganda: Robert Langham's *Letter* and George Gascoigne's *Princely Pleasures at Kenilworth*." Pincombe and Shrank, pp. 623–36.
Dronke, Peter. *Medieval Latin and the Rise of the European Love-Lyric*. 2nd ed. Oxford: Clarendon, 1968.
Dubrow, Heather. "'And Thus Leave Off': Reevaluating Mary Wroth's Folger Manuscript, V.a.104." *Tulsa Studies in Women's Literature* 22 (2003): 273–91.
Dubrow, Heather. *Captive Victors: Shakespeare's Narrative Poems and Sonnets*. Ithaca, NY: Cornell University Press, 1987.
Dubrow, Heather. *Echoes of Desire: English Petrarchism and Its Counterdiscourses*. Ithaca, NY: Cornell University Press, 1995.
Dubrow, Heather. "'Incertainties now crown themselves assur'd': The Politics of Plotting Shakesepare's Sonnets." Schiffer, pp. 113–33.
Duncan-Jones, Katherine. "The Date of Ralegh's '21th: And Last Booke of the Ocean to Scinthia.'" *Review of English Studies* n.s. 21 (1970): 143–58.
Duncan-Jones, Katherine. "Sidney, Stella and Lady Rich." In *Sir Philip Sidney: 1586 and the Creation of a Legend*, ed. Jan van Dorsten, Dominic Baker-Smith, and Arthur F. Kinney. Leiden: Brill, 1986. Pp. 174–81.
Duncan-Jones, Katherine. *Sir Philip Sidney: Courtier Poet*. New Haven, CT: Yale University Press, 1991.
Dunnigan, Sarah. *Eros and Poetry at the Courts of Mary Queen of Scots and James VI*. Basingstoke: Palgrave Macmillan, 2002.

Eccles, Mark. "Samuel Daniel in France and Italy." *Studies in Philology* 34 (1937): 148–67.

Edwards, Edward. *The Life of Sir Walter Ralegh*. 2 vols. London: Macmillan, 1868.

Einstein, Alfred. *The Italian Madrigal*. Trans. Alexander H. Krappe et al. Princeton: Princeton University Press, 1949.

Eisenbichler, Konrad. "Political Posturing in Some 'Triumphs of Love' in Quattrocento Florence." Eisenbichler and Iannucci, pp. 369–81.

Eisenbichler, Konrad, and Amilcare A. Iannucci, eds. *Petrarch's Triumphs: Allegory and Spectacle*. Toronto: Dovehouse, 1990.

Elliott, Elizabeth. "*Eros* and Self-Government: Petrarchism and Protestant Self-Abnegation in William Fowler's *Tarantula of Love*." *Scottish Literary Review* 4.1 (2012): 1–14.

Empson, William. "They That Have Power: Twist of Heroic-Pastoral Ideas into an Ironical Acceptance of Aristocracy." In *Some Versions of Pastoral*. New York: New Directions, 1974. Pp. 87–115.

Estrin, Barbara L. *Laura: Uncovering Gender and Genre in Wyatt, Donne, and Marvell*. Durham, NC: Duke University Press, 1994.

Fallon, Samuel. "Astrophil, Philisides, and the Coterie in Print." *English Literary Renaissance* 45 (2015): 175–204.

Ferry, Anne. *All in War with Time: Love Poetry of Shakespeare, Donne, Jonson, Marvell*. Cambridge, MA: Harvard University Press, 1975.

Ferry, Anne. *The "Inward" Language: Sonnets of Wyatt, Sidney, Shakespeare, Donne*. Chicago: University of Chicago Press, 1983.

Fienberg, Nona. "The Emergence of Stella in *Astrophil and Stella*." *Studies in English Literature* 25 (1985): 5–19.

Fineman, Joel. *Shakespeare's Perjured Eye: The Invention of Poetic Subjectivity in the Sonnets*. Berkeley: University of California Press, 1986.

Fleming, John F. "A Book from Shakespeare's Library Discovered by William Van Lennep." *Shakespeare Quarterly* 15.2 (1964): 25–27.

Fowler, Alastair. *Triumphal Forms: Structural Patterns in Elizabethan Poetry*. Cambridge: Cambridge University Press, 1970.

Fox, Alistair. *Politics and Literature in the Reigns of Henry VII and Henry VIII*. Oxford: Blackwell, 1989.

Frankis, P. J. "The Erotic Dream in Medieval English Lyrics." *Neuphilologische Mitteilungen* 57 (1956): 228–37.

Freedman, Sylvia. *Poor Penelope: Lady Penelope Rich, an Elizabethan Woman*. Bourne End: Kensal, 1995.

Friedman, Donald M. "The Mind in the Poem: Wyatt's 'They Fle From Me.'" *Studies in English Literature* 7 (1967): 1–13.

Friedman, Donald M. "Wyatt and the Ambiguities of Fancy." *Journal of English and Germanic Philology* 67 (1968): 32–48.

Friedman, Laura. "Displaying Stella: Anatomical Blazon and the Negotiation of Male Social Status." *Sidney Journal* 30.1 (2012): 101–15.

Frye, Northrop. "How True a Twain." In *Northrop Frye's Writings on Shakespeare and the Renaissance*, ed. Troni Y. Grande and Gary Sherbert. Toronto: University of Toronto Press, 2010. Pp. 95–113.

Goldring, Elizabeth. "Gascoigne and Kenilworth: The Production, Reception, and Aftererlife of *The Princely Pleasures*." *English Literary Renaissance* 44 (2014): 363–87.

Gray, Erik. "Sonnet Kisses: Sidney to Barrett Browning." *Essays in Criticism* 52 (2002): 126–42.

Greenblatt, Stephen. *Renaissance Self-Fashioning: From More to Shakespeare*. Chicago: University of Chicago Press, 1980.
Greenblatt, Stephen. *Sir Walter Ralegh: The Renaissance Man and His Roles*. New Haven, CT: Yale University Press, 1973.
Greene, Thomas M. *The Light in Troy: Imitation and Discovery in Renaissance Poetry*. New Haven, CT: Yale University Press, 1982.
Hainsworth, Peter. *Petrarch the Poet*. London: Routledge, 1988.
Hall, Kim F. "'These bastard signs of fair': Literary Whiteness in Shakespeare's Sonnets." In *Post-Colonial Shakespeares*, ed. Ania Loomba and Martin Orkin. London: Routledge, 1998. Pp. 64–83.
Hamilton, A. C. "Sidney's *Astrophel and Stella* as a Sonnet Sequence." *ELH* 36 (1969): 59–87.
Hannay, Margaret P. "The 'Ending End' of Lady Wroth's Manuscript of Poems." *Sidney Journal* 31.1 (2013): 1–22.
Hannay, Margaret P. *Mary Sidney, Lady Wroth*. Farnham: Ashgate, 2010.
Harding, D. W. "The Poetry of Wyatt." In *The Age of Chaucer*, ed. Boris Ford. Harmondsworth: Penguin, 1954. Pp. 197–212.
Harris, William O. "Early Elizabethan Sonnets in Sequence." *Studies in Philology* 68 (1971): 451–69.
Harrison, G. B. *Shakespeare at Work, 1592–1603*. London: Routledge, 1933.
Heale, Elizabeth. "Women and the Courtly Love Lyric: The Devonshire MS (BL Additional 17492)." *Modern Language Review* 90 (1995): 296–313.
Hedley, Jane. "Allegoria: Gascoigne's Master Trope." *English Literary Renaissance* 11 (1981): 148–64.
Helgerson, Richard. *The Elizabethan Prodigals*. Berkeley, CA: University of California Press, 1976.
Herford, Charles H. *Studies in the Literary Relations of England and Germany in the Sixteenth Century*. Cambridge: Cambridge University Press, 1886.
Hetherington, Michael. "Gascoigne's Accidents: Contingency, Skill, and the Logic of Writing." *English Literary Renaissance* 46 (2016): 29–59.
Holton, Amanda. "An Obscured Tradition: The Sonnet and Its Fourteen-Line Predecessors." *Review of English Studies* n.s. 62 (2011): 373–92.
Horner, Joyce. "The Large Landscape: A Study of Certain Images in Ralegh." *Essays in Criticism* 5 (1955): 197–213.
Howe, Ann Romayne. "*Astrophel and Stella*: 'Why and How.'" *Studies in Philology* 61 (1964): 150–69.
Hughes, Felicity A. "Gascoigne's Poses." *Studies in English Literature* 37 (1997): 1–19.
Hull, Elizabeth M. "All My Deed But Copying Is: The Erotics of Identity in *Astrophil and Stella*." *Texas Studies in Literature and Language* 38 (1996): 175–90.
Hull, Elizabeth M. "The Remedy of Love." *Hellas* 6.1 (1995): 101–26.
Hulse, Clark. "Stella's Wit: Penelope Rich as Reader of Sidney's Sonnets." In *Rewriting the Renaissance: The Discourses of Sexual Difference in Early Modern Europe*, ed. Margaret W. Ferguson, Maureen Quilligan, and Nancy J. Vickers. Chicago: University of Chicago Press, 1986. Pp. 272–86.
Hunt, Marvin. "Be Dark but Not Too Dark: Shakespeare's Dark Lady as a Sign of Color." Schiffer, pp. 368–89.
Hutson, Lorna. *The Invention of Suspicion: Law and Mimesis in Shakespeare and Renaissance Drama*. Oxford: Oxford University Press, 2007.

Huttar, Charles A. "Wyatt and the Several Editions of *The Court of Venus*." *Studies in Bibliography* 19 (1966): 191–5.

Ioppolo, Grace. "Those Essex Girls: The Lives and Letters of Lettice Knollys, Penelope Rich, Dorothy Perrott Percy, and Frances Walshingham." In *The Ashgate Research Companion to the Sidneys, 1500–1700*, ed. Margaret P. Hannay, Michael Brennan, and Mary Ellen Lamb. Farnham: Ashgate, 2015. Pp. 77–92.

Irish, Bradley J. "Gender and Politics in the Henrician Court: The Douglas-Howard Lyrics in the Devonshire Manuscript (BL Add 17492)." *Renaissance Quarterly* 64 (2011): 79–114.

Ives, Eric. *Anne Boleyn*. Oxford: Blackwell, 1986.

Izard, Thomas C. *George Whetstone: Mid-Elizabethan Gentleman of Letters*. 1942; rpt. New York: AMS, 1966.

Jack, R. D. S. "William Fowler and Italian Literature." *Modern Language Review* 65 (1970): 481–92.

Johnson, Ronald C. *George Gascoigne*. New York: Twayne, 1972.

Jones, Ann Rosalind, and Peter Stallybrass. "The Politics of *Astrophil and Stella*." *Studies in English Literature* 24 (1984): 53–68.

Kalstone, David. *Sidney's Poetry: Contexts and Interpretations*. Cambridge, MA: Harvard University Press, 1965.

Kau, Joseph. "Daniel's *Delia* and the *Imprese* of Bishop Paolo Giovio: Some Iconographical Influences." *Journal of the Warburg and Courtauld Institutes* 33 (1970): 325–38.

Kelliher, W. Hilton. "The Warwick Manuscripts of Fulke Greville." *British Museum Quarterly* 34 (1970): 107–21.

Kennedy, William J. *Petrarchism at Work: Contextual Economies in the Age of Shakespeare*. Ithaca, NY: Cornell University Press, 2016.

Kennedy, William J. *The Site of Petrarchism: Early Modern National Sentiment in Italy, France, and England*. Baltimore: Johns Hopkins University Press, 2003.

Kerrigan, John. *Motives of Woe: Shakespeare and "Female Complaint."* Oxford: Clarendon, 1991.

Kingsley-Smith, Jane. *The Afterlife of Shakespeare's Sonnets*. Cambridge: Cambridge University Press, 2019.

Kinney, Clare R. "'Beleeve this butt a fiction': Female Authorship, Narrative Undoing, and the Limits of Romance in *The Second Part of the Countess of Montgomery's Urania*." *Spenser Studies* 17 (2003): 239–50.

Kinney, Clare R. "Escaping the Void: Isolation, Mutuality, and Community in the Sonnets of Wroth and Shakespeare." Salzman and Wynne-Davies, pp. 25–36.

Kinney, Clare R. "Mary Wroth's Guilty 'secrett art': The Poetics of Jealousy in *Pamphilia to Amphilanthus*." In *Write or Be Written: Early Modern Women Poets and Cultural Constraints*, ed. Barbara Smith and Ursula Appelt. Aldershot: Ashgate, 2001. Pp. 69–85.

Kinney, Clare R. "Turn and Counterturn: Reappraising Mary Wroth's Poetic Labyrinths." Larson and Miller, pp. 85–102.

Klein, Lisa M. *The Exemplary Sidney and the Elizabethan Sonneteer*. Newark: University of Delaware Press, 1998.

Koeppel, Emil. "Studien zur Geschichte des englischen Petrarchismus im sechzehnten Jahrhundert." *Romanische Forschungen* 5 (1890): 65–97.

Koller, Kathrine. "Spenser and Ralegh." *ELH* 1 (1934): 37–60.

Kuin, Roger. *Chamber Music: Elizabethan Sonnet-Sequences and the Pleasure of Criticism*. Toronto: University of Toronto Press, 1998.

Kuin, Roger. "More I Still Undoe: Louise Labé, Mary Wroth, and the Petrarchan Discourse." *Comparative Literature Studies* 36 (1999): 146–61.
Laam, Kevin. "'Lyke Chaucers Boye': Poetry and Penitence in Gascoigne's *Griefe of Joye*." *Early Modern Literary Studies* 14.1 (2008).
Lamb, Mary Ellen. "'Can you suspect a change in me?': Poems by Mary Wroth and William Herbert, Third Earl of Pembroke." Larson and Miller, pp. 53–68.
Lamb, Mary Ellen. *Gender and Authorship in the Sidney Circle*. Madison: University of Wisconsin Press, 1990.
Lamb, Mary Ellen. "'Love is not love': Shakespeare's Sonnet 116, Pembroke, and the Inns of Court." *Shakespeare Quarterly* 70 (2019): 101–28.
Lanham, Richard. "*Astrophil and Stella*: Pure and Impure Persuasion." *English Literary Renaissance* 2 (1972): 100–15.
Larson, Katherine R., and Naomi J. Miller, with Andrew Strycharski, eds. *Re-reading Mary Wroth*. New York: Palgrave Macmillan, 2015.
Leishman, J. B. *Themes and Variations in Shakespeare's Sonnets*. 2nd ed. London: Hutchinson, 1963.
Levao, Ronald. *Renaissance Minds and Their Fictions: Cusanus, Sidney, Shakespeare*. Berkeley: University of California Press, 1985.
Lever, J. W. *The Elizabethan Love Sonnet*. 2nd ed. London: Methuen, 1974.
Lewalski, Barbara Kiefer. *Writing Women in Jacobean England*. Cambridge, MA: Harvard University Press, 1993.
Lewis, C. S. *English Literature in the Sixteenth Century, Excluding Drama*. Oxford: Clarendon, 1954.
Loewenstein, Joseph. "Sidney's Truant Pen." *Modern Language Quarterly* 46 (1985): 128–42.
Lyons, Mathew. *The Favourite: Ralegh and His Queen*. London: Constable, 2012.
Marotti, Arthur F. *Manuscript, Print, and the English Renaissance Lyric*. Ithaca, NY: Cornell University Press, 1995.
Marotti, Arthur F. "Shakespeare's Sonnets and the Manuscript Circulation of Texts in Early Modern England." Schoenfeldt, *Companion*, pp. 185–203.
Mason, H. A. *Humanism and Poetry in the Early Tudor Period: An Essay*. London: Routledge, 1959.
Mason, H. A. *Sir Thomas Wyatt: A Literary Portrait*. Bristol: Bristol Classical Press, 1986.
Mason, H. A. "Wyatt and the Psalms." *Times Literary Supplement* 52 (27 Feb. and 6 Mar., 1953): 144, 160.
May, Steven W. "The Countess of Oxford's Sonnets: A Caveat." *English Language Notes* 29.3 (1992): 9–19.
May, Steven W. *The Elizabethan Courtier Poets: The Poems and Their Contexts*. Columbia: University of Missouri Press, 1991.
May, Steven W. *Sir Walter Ralegh*. Boston: Hall, 1989.
Maynard, Winifred. "The Lyrics of Wyatt: Poems or Songs?" *Review of English Studies* n.s. 16 (1965): 1–13, 245–57.
McCanles, Michael. "Love and Power in the Poetry of Sir Thomas Wyatt." *Modern Language Quarterly* 29 (1968): 145–60.
McCarthy, Penny. "Autumn 1604: Documentation and Literary Coincidence." Salzman and Wynne-Davies, pp. 37–46.
McCoy, Richard C. "Gascoigne's '*Poemata castrata*': The Wages of Courtly Success." *Criticism* 27 (1985): 29–55.

McCoy, Richard C. *Sir Philip Sidney: Rebellion in Arcadia*. New Brunswick, NJ: Rutgers University Press, 1979.

McGrail, Thomas H. *Sir William Alexander, First Earl of Stirling*. Edinburgh: Oliver and Boyd, 1940.

Miller, Edward Haviland. "Samuel Daniel's Revisions in *Delia*." *Journal of English and Germanic Philology* 53 (1954): 58–68.

Montrose, Louis Adrian. "Of Gentlemen and Shepherds: The Politics of Elizabethan Pastoral Form." *ELH* 50 (1983): 415–59.

Montrose, Louis Adrian. "'Shaping Fantasies': Figurations of Gender and Power in Elizabethan Culture." *Representations* 2 (1983): 61–94.

Moody, Ellen. "Six Elegiac Poems, Possibly by Anne Cecil de Vere, Countess of Oxford." *English Literary Renaissance* 19 (1989): 152–70.

Mumford, Ivy L. "Petrarchism and Italian Music at the Court of Henry VIII." *Italian Studies* 26 (1971): 49–67.

Murphy, Peter. *The Long Public Life of a Short Private Poem: Reading and Remembering Thomas Wyatt*. Stanford, CA: Stanford University Press, 2019.

Murphy, William M. "Thomas Watson's *Hekatompathia* [1582] and the Elizabethan Sonnet Sequence." *Journal of English and Germanic Philology* 56 (1957): 418–28.

Nathan, Leonard E. "Tradition and Newfangleness in Wyatt's 'They Fle from Me.'" *ELH* 32 (1965): 1–16.

Neely, Carol Thomas. "The Structure of English Renaissance Sonnet Sequences." *ELH* 45 (1978): 359–89.

Newman, Joel. "An Italian Source for Wyatt's *Madame, withouten many wordes*." *Renaissance News* 10 (1957): 13–15.

Oakeshott, Walter. *The Queen and the Poet*. London: Faber, 1960.

O'Connor, John J. *Amadis de Gaule and Its Influence on Elizabethan Literature*. New Brunswick, NJ: Rutgers University Press, 1970.

Orgel, Stephen. *Impersonations: The Performance of Gender in Shakespeare's England*. Cambridge: Cambridge University Press, 1996.

Paden, William D., Jr. "*Utrum Copularentur*: Of *Cors*." *L'Ésprit créateur* 19.4 (1979): 70–83.

Pequigney, Joseph. *Such Is My Love: A Study of Shakespeare's Sonnets*. Chicago: University of Chicago Press, 1985.

Pèrcopo, Erasmo. "Dragonetto Bonifcaio, Marchese d'Oria, rimatore napolitano del sec. xvi." *Giornale storico della letteratura italiana* 10 (1887): 197–233.

Pincombe, Mike, and Cathy Shrank, eds. *The Oxford Handbook of Tudor Literature*. Oxford: Oxford University Press, 2009.

Poirier, Michel. *Sir Philip Sidney, le chevalier poète élisabéthain*. Lille: Bibliothèque Universitaire de Lille, 1948.

Prendergast, Maria Teresa Micaela. *Renaissance Fantasies: The Gendering of Aesthetics in Early Modern Fiction*. Kent, OH: Kent State University Press, 1999.

Prouty, C. T. *George Gascoigne: Elizabethan Courtier Soldier, and Poet*. New York: Columbia University Press, 1942.

Pugh, Syrithe. "Ovidian Reflections in Gascoigne's *Steel Glass*." Pincombe and Shrank, pp. 571–86.

Quilligan, Maureen. "Sidney and His Queen." In *The Historical Renaissance: New Essays on Tudor and Stuart Literature and Culture*, ed. Heather Dubrow and Richard Strier. Chicago: University of Chicago Press, 1988. Pp. 171–96.

Rebholz, R. A. *The Life of Fulke Greville First Lord Brooke*. Oxford: Clarendon, 1971.

Rees, Joan. *Fulke Greville, Lord Brooke, 1554–1628: A Critical Biography*. London: Routledge, 1971.
Rees, Joan. *Samuel Daniel*. Liverpool: Liverpool University Press, 1964.
Rickman (Luthman), Johanna. *Love, Lust, and License in Early Modern England: Illicit Sex and the Nobility*. Aldershot: Ashgate, 2008.
Robertson, Jean. "Sir Philip Sidney and Lady Penelope Rich." *Review of English Studies* n.s. 15 (1964): 296–7.
Roche, Thomas P., Jr. *Petrarch and the English Sonnet Sequences*. New York: AMS, 1989.
Rohr Philmus, M. R. "Gascoigne's Fable of the Artist as a Young Man." *Journal of English and Germanic Philology* 73 (1974): 13–31.
Rudenstine, Neil L. *Ideas of Order: A Close Reading of Shakespeare's Sonnets*. New York: FSG, 2014.
Rudick, Michael. "The 'Ralegh Group' in *The Phoenix Nest*." *Studies in Bibliography* 24 (1971): 131–7.
Salamon, Linda Bradley. "A Face in 'The Glasse': Gascoigne's 'Glasse of Governement' Re-Examined." *Studies in Philology* 71 (1974): 47–71.
Salzman, Paul, and Marion Wynne-Davies, eds. *Mary Wroth and Shakespeare*. New York: Routledge, 2015
Sanchez, Melissa. "'In My Selfe the Smart I Try': Female Promiscuity in *Astrophil and Stella*." *ELH* 80 (2013): 1–27.
Sandison, Helen Estabrook. "Arthur Gorges, Spenser's Alcyon and Ralegh's Friend." *PMLA* 43 (1928): 645–74.
Sargent, Ralph M. *The Life and Lyrics of Sir Edward Dyer*. 1935; rpt. Oxford: Clarendon, 1968.
Scarry, Elaine. *Naming Thy Name: Cross Talk in Shakespeare's Sonnets*. New York: FSG, 2016.
Schiffer, James, ed. *Shakespeare's Sonnets: Critical Essays*. New York: Garland, 1999.
Schoenfeldt, Michael. "The Matter of Inwardness: Shakespeare's Sonnets." Schiffer, pp. 305–24.
Schoenfeldt, Michael, ed. *A Companion to Shakespeare's Sonnets*. Oxford: Blackwell, 2007.
Scodel, Joshua. *Excess and the Mean in Early Modern English Literature*. Chicago: University of Chicago Press, 2002.
Scott, Janet G. *Les Sonnets élisabéthains: les sources et l'apport personnel*. Paris: Honoré Champion, 1929.
Sedgwick, Eve Kosofsky. *Between Men: English Literature and Male Homosocial Desire*. New York: Columbia University Press, 1985.
See, Sam. "Richard Barnfield and the Limits of Homoerotic Literary History." *GLQ: A Journal of Lesbian and Gay Studies* 13 (2007): 63–91.
Sessions, W. A. *Henry Howard, the Poet Earl of Surrey: A Life*. Oxford: Oxford University Press, 1999.
Shore, David R. "Whythorne's *Autobiography* and the Genesis of Gascoigne's *Master F. J.*" *Journal of Medieval and Renaissance Studies* 12 (1982): 159–78.
Shulman, Nicola. *Graven with Diamonds: The Many Lives of Thomas Wyatt*. Hanover, NH: Steerforth, 2013.
Simon, Margaret. "Refraining Songs: The Dynamics of Form in Sidney's *Astrophil and Stella*." *Studies in Philology* 109 (2012): 86–102.
Skura, Meredith Anne. *Tudor Autobiography: Listening for Inwardness*. Chicago: University of Chicago Press, 2010.

Smith, Bruce R. *Homosexual Desire in Shakespeare's England: A Cultural Poetics.* Chicago: University of Chicago Press, 1991.
Smith, Hallett. *Elizabethan Poetry: A Study in Conventions, Meaning, and Expression.* Cambridge, MA: Harvard University Press, 1952.
Sokolov, Danila. "Love under Law: Rewriting Petrarch's Canzone 360 in Early Modern England." *Philological Quarterly* 96 (2017): 426–35.
Solomon, Deborah C. "Representation of Lyric Intimacy in Manuscript and Print Versions of Wyatt's 'They Flee from Me.'" *Modern Philology* 111 (2014): 668–82.
Southall, Raymond. *The Courtly Maker: An Essay on the Poetry of Wyatt and His Contemporaries.* New York: Barnes and Noble, 1964.
Spiller, Michael R. G. *The Development of the Sonnet: An Introduction.* London: Routledge, 1992.
Spriet, Pierre. *Samuel Daniel.* Paris: Didier, 1968.
Stamatakis, Chris. *Sir Thomas Wyatt and the Rhetoric of Rewriting: 'Turning the Word.'* Oxford: Oxford University Press, 2012.
Steggle, Matthew. "Greville's Buxton Poem: A Text and Commentary." *Sidney Journal* 20.1 (2002): 55–68.
Stein, Arnold. "Wyatt's 'They Flee from Me.'" *Sewanee Review* 67 (1959): 28–44.
Stevens, John. *Music and Poetry in the Early Tudor Court.* London: Methuen, 1961.
Stewart, Alan. "Gelding Gascoigne." In *Prose Fiction and Early Modern Sexualities in England, 1520–1640*, ed. Constance Relihan and Goran V. Stanivukovic. New York: Palgrave Macmillan, 2003. Pp. 147–69.
Stillman, Robert E. "'Words cannot knytt': Language and Desire in Ralegh's *The Ocean to Cynthia.*" *Studies in English Literature* 27 (1987): 35–51.
Stirling, Brents. *The Shakespeare Sonnet Order: Poems and Groups.* Berkeley: University of California Press, 1968.
Stone, Lawrence. *The Family, Sex and Marriage in England 1500–1800.* New York: Harper and Row, 1977.
Strier, Richard. *The Unrepentant Renaissance: From Petrarch to Shakespeare to Milton.* Chicago: University of Chicago Press, 2011.
Strycharski, Andrew. "Literacy, Education, and Affect in *Astrophel and Stella.*" *Studies in English Literature* 48 (2008): 45–63.
Svensson, Lars-Håkan. *Silent Art: Rhetorical and Thematic Patterns in Samuel Daniel's Delia.* Lund: Gleerup, 1980.
Talvacchia, Bette. *Taking Positions: On the Erotic in Renaissance Culture.* Princeton: Princeton University Press, 1999.
Targoff, Ramie. *Eros and the Afterlife in Renaissance England.* Chicago: University of Chicago Press, 2014.
Taylor, Gary. "Some Manuscripts of Shakespeare's Sonnets." *Bulletin of the John Rylands Library* 68 (1985–6): 210–46.
Tennenhouse, Leonard. *Power on Display: The Politics of Shakespeare's Genres.* London: Routledge, 1986.
Thompson, John. *The Founding of English Metre.* New York: Columbia University Press, 1961.
Thomson, Patricia. *Sir Thomas Wyatt and His Background.* Stanford, CA: Stanford University Press, 1964.
Thomson, Patricia. "Sonnet 15 of Samuel Daniel's Delia: A Petrarchan Imitation." In *Übersetzung und Nachahmung im europäischen Petrarkismus*, ed. Luzius Keller. Stuttgart: Metzler, 1974. Pp. 210–17.

Trevelyan, Raleigh. *Sir Walter Raleigh*. New York: Holt, 2002.
Varlow, Sally. *Lady Penelope: Passion and Intrigue at the Heart of the Elizabethan Court.* London: André Deutsch, 2014.
Vendler, Helen. *The Art of Shakespeare's Sonnets*. Cambridge, MA: Harvard University Press, 1997.
Verweij, Sebastiaan. "The Manuscripts of William Fowler: A Revaluation of *The Tarantula of Love*." *Scottish Studies Review* 8.2 (2007): 9–23.
Wakeman, Rob. "Shakespeare, Gascoigne, and the Hunter's Uneasy Conscience." *Exemplaria* 29 (2017): 136–56.
Walker, Kim. *Women Writers of the English Renaissance*. New York: Twayne, 1996.
Wall, Wendy. *The Imprint of Gender: Authorship and Publication in the English Renaissance*. Ithaca, NY: Cornell University Press, 1993.
Waller, Gary. "The Rewriting of Petrarch: Sidney and the Languages of Sixteenth-Century Poetry." Waller and Moore, pp. 69–83.
Waller, Gary. *The Sidney Family Romance: Mary Wroth, William Herbert, and the Early Modern Construction of Gender*. Detroit: Wayne State University Press, 1993.
Waller, Gary, and Michael D. Moore, eds. *Sir Philip Sidney and the Interpretation of Renaissance Culture: The Poet in His Time and Ours*. London: Croom Helm, 1984.
Warkentin, Germaine. "The Meeting of the Muses: Sidney and the Mid-Tudor Poets." Waller and Moore, pp. 17–33.
Waswo, Richard. *The Fatal Mirror: Themes and Techniques in the Poetry of Fulke Greville*. Charlottesville: University Press of Virginia, 1972.
Weinberg, Bernard. "The *Sposizione* of Petrarch in the Early Cinquecento." *Romance Philology* 13 (1959): 374–86.
Weiner, Andrew D. "'In a grove most rich of shade': A Figurative Reading of the Eighth Song of *Astrophil and Stella*." *Texas Studies in Literature and Language* 18 (1976): 341–61.
Whigham, R. G., and O. F. Emerson. "Sonnet Structure in Sidney's 'Astrophel and Stella.'" *Studies in Philology* 18 (1921): 347–52.
Whittington, Leah. *Renaissance Suppliants: Poetry, Antiquity, Reconciliation*. Oxford: Oxford University Press, 2016.
Williamson, George. "The Convention of *The Extasie*." *Seventeenth Century Contexts*. Rev. ed. Chicago: University of Chicago Press, 1969. Pp. 63–77.
Winters, Yvor. *Forms of Discovery: Critical and Historical Essays on the Forms of the Short Poem in English*. Chicago: Swallow, 1967.
Wong, Alex. *The Poetry of Kissing in Early Modern Europe: From the Catullan Revival to Secundus, Shakespeare and the English Cavaliers*. Cambridge: Brewer, 2017.
Wong, Alex. "Sir Philip Sidney and the Humanist Poetry of Kissing." *Sidney Journal* 31.2 (2013): 1–30.
Wood, Dennis. *Benjamin Constant*. London: Routledge, 1993.
Wort, Oliver. "Marian Literary Culture: Petrarch and the Rapprochement of Cultures." *English Literary Renaissance* 51 (2021): 153–89.
Woudhuysen, H. R. *Sir Philip Sidney and the Circulation of Manuscripts 1558–1640*. Oxford: Clarendon, 1996.
Wynne-Davies, Marion. "'So Much Worth': Autobiographical Narratives in the Work of Lady Mary Wroth." In *Betraying Our Selves: Forms of Self-Representation in Early Modern English Texts*, ed. Henk Dragstra, Sheila Ottway, and Helen Wilcox. London: Macmillan, 2000. Pp. 76–93.
Yoch, James J. "Brian Twyne's Commentary on *Astrophel and Stella*." *Allegorica* 2.2 (1977): 114–16.

Young, Richard B. "English Petrarke: A Study of Sidney's *Astrophel and Stella*." In *Three Studies in the Renaissance: Sidney, Jonson, Milton*. New Haven, CT: Yale University Press, 1958. Pp. 39–88.

Zarnowiecki, Matthew. *Fair Copies: Reproducing the English Lyric from Wyatt to Shakespeare*. Toronto: University of Toronto Press, 2014.

# Index

"Absence" (anonymous poem): 130
*Alcilia* (by J. C.): 92, 148
Alençon, François, Duc d': 122, 192
Alexander, Gavin: 123, 128, 132, 170
Alexander, William, Earl of Stirling: 148, 154, 157, 164–8
Alleyn, Edward: 208
Almasy, Rudolph P.: 90
Alquemade, Petronella de: 70
Andreas Capellanus: 102
Aretino, Pietro: 154
Ariosto, Lodovico: 41, 51, 93, 167, 197, 201
Aristotle: 76
Arundel manuscript: 26, 82, 124
Ascham, Roger: 270
Aubrey, John: 113, 184
Auhagen, Ulrike: 111
Austen, Gillian: 44–5, 47, 51

Bacon, Francis: 180
Bacon, Nicholas: 68
Baïf, Jean-Antoine de: 152
Bale, John: 42–3
Balzac, Honoré de: 77
Bannatyne manuscript: 34
Barnes, Barnabe: 148, 152–5, 261
Barnfield, Richard: 129, 148, 157–8, 217
Bartlett, Kenneth R.: 270
Bates, Catherine: 70, 73, 79, 195, 202
Bayly, Lewis: 131
Beach Boys: 226
Beadle, Samuel A.: 242
Beer, Anna: 184, 196–7
Beilin, Elaine V.: 160
Bell, Ilona: 57, 159, 163–4, 169, 175, 211
Bembo, Pietro: 30, 32, 93
Benson, John: 211
Bernard of Clairvaux: 42
Berryman, John: 206
Best, Charles: 199
Bèze, Théodore de: 39, 46
Blage, George: 16
Blage manuscript: 27
Blount, Charles, Earl of Devonshire: 255–6, 259
Boccaccio, Giovanni: 29, 32, 42, 269

Bodenham, John (*Englands Helicon*): 158, 185, 258
Boethius, Anicius Manlius Severinus: 193
Boleyn, Anne: 16, 20, 22, 82
Boleyn, George, Viscount Rochford: 82
Bolton, Edmund: 85
Bonifacio, Draagonetto: 15–17
Bonanno, Vincenzo: 14
Bond, Garth: 163
Bonner, Edmund: 16, 270
*Book of Common Prayer*: 187, 236
Booth, Stephen: 236, 242
Borris, Kenneth: 158
Botticelli, Sandro: 179
Boyes, Edward: 58–9
Bradstreet, Anne: 87
breasts (female): 7, 33, 78, 105, 125, 155–7, 168, 173, 175, 240–1, 266, 272
Brennan, Michael: 161
Breton, Nicholas: 84, 161, 183
Brian, Francis: 84
Brigden, Susan: 17, 20
Brown, Russell M.: 253–4, 257
Buchan, Alexander M.: 196
Buckingham: *see* Villiers
Bullough, Geoffrey: 123–4, 127
Burleigh: *see* Cecil, William
Burrow, Colin: 221, 245, 248
Bynneman, Henry: 82

Campbell, Marion: 197
Campen, Jean de (Ioannis Campensis): 7
Campion, Thomas: 141, 152
Carew, George: 197
Carew, Thomas: 142
Cariteo, Il (Benedetto Gareth): 29
*carpe diem*: 142–5, 185, 212–13, 224–5, 233
Cartwright, Robert: 226
Castiglione, Baldassare: 149, 160–1
Catullus, Valerius: 111, 113, 142–3, 185
Cavafy, C. P.: 34–5
Cavendish, Christian, Duchess of Newcastle: 168–9
Caxton, William: 33
Cecil, Robert, Earl of Salisbury: 194, 196–7, 205
Cecil, William, Lord Burghley: 44, 90, 194

Cecil de Vere, Anne, Countess of Oxford: 90
Cecioni, Cesare G.: 91, 93
Cervigni, Dino: 4
Chamberlain, John: 162–3
Charles, Duc d'Orléans: 30, 33–4, 151, 208
Charney, Sara: 269
Chaucer, Geoffrey: 18, 40, 42–3, 50–1, 82, 89, 92, 260, 262
Churchyard, Thomas: 82, 84
Cicero, Marcus Tullius: 93
Clanton, Stacy: 195
Clarendon, Edward Hyde, Earl of: 168
Clement V (Pope): 231
Cohen, Walter: 88
Coldiron, A. E. B.: 91, 151
Constable, Henry: 147–8, 182, 186, 191, 209–10, 217, 235, 238
constancy: 11–12, 21–6, 31–7, 62, 127–8, 165–7, 172–7, 221–2, 225, 236–8
Constant, Benjamin: 29
Coogan, Robert: 51
Cotter, James Finn: 111
*Courte of Venus, The*: 38–9, 41
Craig, Alexander: 148–9
Crewe, Jonathan: 24, 79–80
Cromwell, Thomas: 270
Cropp, Glynnis: 178
Crosman, Robert: 212
Cruttwell, Patrick: 207, 210, 245, 248
Cummings, Brian: 131–2

Dandolo, Francesco: 231
Daniel, Samuel: 84, 135–48, 172, 227, 264
 *Complaint of Rosamond, The*: 136
 *Defence of Ryme, A*: 137, 141–2
 *Delia* (first edition, 1592) *5*: 138; *6*: 145–6; *12*: 137, 139; *14*: 137; *15*: 141; *16*: 137; *17*: 137; *19*: 137; *20*: 137; *26*: 138; *30*: 137, 140, 145; *31*: 140; *32*: 144; *33*: 137, 144; *34*: 137, 145; *35*: 144–5; *40*: 136; *44*: 138; *45*: 146–7; *46*: 146; *48*: 146; *49*: 147; *50*: 147
 "Like as the spotlesse *Ermelin*": 139–40
 *Musophilus*: 141, 150
 "O whether (poore forsaken)": 138
 "Ode": 136
 "Oft do I muse, whether my *Delias* eyes": 140
 "A Pastorall": 136, 142–3
 "The slie Inchanter": 137
 "Still in the trace of my tormented thought": 139
Dante Alighieri: 41–3, 54, 167–8, 202, 267, 269
Darrell, Elizabeth: 5, 20
Dasenbrock, Reed Ray: 10
Davenson, Henri (H. I. Marrou): 253

Davie, Donald: 200
Davies, John: 148
Davies, John, of Hereford: 149, 151–3, 157
Davison, Francis (*A Poetical Rapsody*): 199, 122, 130
de Grazia, Margreta: 211, 240
della Porta, Giambattista: 125
Demetriou, Tania: 106
Dempsey, Charles: 179
Denny, Edward, Lord: 162–3
Desai, Adhaar Noor: 47
Desportes, Philippe: 140–1, 181
Devereux, Penelope: *see* Rich
Devereux, Robert: *see* Essex
Devonshire manuscript: 7, 14, 26–7, 36, 38
Dickinson, Emily: 81
Dillon, Janette: 44
dimples: 157
Diogenes Laertius: 138
Donne, John: 117, 130–1, 134, 174, 196, 219
Douglas, Margaret: 27
Dousa, Janus (Jan van de Does), father and son: 111
Doyno, Victor A.: 152
Drake, Francis: 59
Drayton, Michael: 84–6, 91, 93, 148, 150, 187
dreams: 29–37, 146–7, 155–6, 194, 225–8, 258
Dronke, Peter: 135, 161
Drummond, William: 135, 161
DuBellay, Joachim: 181
Dubrow, Heather: 170, 211–12, 216, 231, 254, 256–7
Dürer, Albrecht: 201
Duncan-Jones, Katherine: 78, 86, 96, 181, 195–7, 208, 223, 229, 236, 242, 259
Dunnigan, Sarah: 149
Durling, Robert M.: 4
Dyer, Edward: 84, 122, 125, 181
Dymoke, George: 135

Eccles, Mark: 140
Egerton manuscript: 3, 19–20, 23, 26, 38, 40
Eisenbichler, Konrad: 179
Eliot, George: 208
Elizabeth I (Queen of England): 43–5, 50–1, 73, 80, 86, 90, 122, 147, 179–205, 209, 230, 254–6, 270
Elliott, Elizabeth: 149
*Emaricdulfe* (by E. C.): 148, 157
Empson, William: 221
Erasmus, Desiderius: 53, 75, 114
Essex, Robert Devereux, Earl of: 92, 182–4, 191, 154
Estrin, Barbara: 24, 36

eyes (of the beloved): 4, 17, 33, 63, 94, 99, 105–6, 112, 117, 120–1, 128, 138, 140, 156, 159, 169, 174, 182, 185, 201, 212, 215–16, 228, 240–1, 246–7, 249, 255, 259, 263

Fallon, Samuel: 113
Ferry, Anne: 7, 232, 239
Ficino, Marsiglio: 220
Fienberg, Nona: 254
Filosseno, Marcello: 32
Finch, Moyle: 197
Fineman, Joel: 248
Fitton, Mary: 168
Flacius Illyricus, Mathias: 42
Fleming, John F.: 39
Fletcher, Giles (the elder): 92–3, 148, 155–6
Fogarty, Anne: 149
*Four Foster Children of Desire, The*: 122, 258
Fowler, Alastair: 151
Fowler, William: 135, 148–9, 155, 270
Fox, Alistair: 22–3
Foxe, John: 42
Frankis, P. J.: 30, 34
Freedman, Sylvia: 256, 259
Friedman, Donald M.: 25, 37
Friedman, Laura: 98
Frye, Northrop: 233–4

Gascoigne, Elizabeth Bacon Breton: 44, 58–9
Gascoigne, George: 43–88, 93–5, 161, 253, 260
  "A cloud of care hath covered all my coste": 52
  *Adventures of Master F. J., The*: 54–61, 65, 67, 76, 82, 90, 253
  "And if I did what then?": 60
  "Beholde (good Quene) A poett with a Speare": 45
  *Certayne Notes of Instruction*: 84–6, 150
  *Complaynt of Phylomene, The*: 47, 84
  "Dame Cinthia hir selfe": 52
  *Dan Bartholmew of Bathe*: 52, 61–8, 71, 83, 90
  *Delicate Diet, A*: 48
  *Droome of Doomes Day, The*: 48, 84
  *Dulce Bellum Inexpertis*: 75
  "From depth of doole": 52
  *Fruite of Fetters, The*: 62, 67–72, 81, 83, 90
  "Gascoignes councell to *Douglass Dine*": 61
  "Gascoignes good morrow": 61
  "Gascoignes good nyghte": 61
  "Gascoignes praise of his Mystres": 53
  "Gascoignes wodmanship": 72–81, 84
  *Glasse of Governement, The*: 47–8, 50
  *Grief of Joye, The*: 48–51, 70
  *Hundreth Sundrie Flowres, A*: 45–7, 51, 55, 57, 59, 61, 72

  "I could not though I would": 61
  "In haste post haste": 52–3, 74, 150
  "In prime of lustie yeares": 58
  *L'escü d'amour*: 51
  *Noble Arte of Venerie or Hunting, The*: 79, 86
  "Of thee deare Dame, three lessons would I learne": 52
  *Posies, The*: 46–7, 54, 57, 67, 72, 82, 84
  *Spoyle of Antwerpe, The*: 44
  *Steele Glas, The*: 47, 84, 184
  "The thriftles thred which pampred beauty spinnes": 62–3
  "This *Apuleius* was in Affricke borne": 52
Gesualdo, Giovanni Andrea: 51, 94
Gillespie, Stuart: 270
Giovio, Paolo: 139
Golding, Arthur: 87
Goldring, Elizabeth: 44
Goldwel, Henry: 258
Googe, Barnabe: 46
*Gorboduc* (Thomas Sackville and Thomas Norton): 45, 264
Gorges, Arthur: 181–2, 197, 201
Gower, John: 82
Greenblatt, Stephen: 8, 22, 24, 35, 37, 189–90, 195, 201
Greene, Thomas: 260
Greville, Fulke, Lord Brooke: 99, 123–35, 140–1, 164, 252, 264
  "A tale I once did heare a true man tell": 124
  *Cælica 10*: 128; *11*: 122–3; *18*: 125; *21*: 127; *25*: 124; *29*: 135; *30*: 124; *36*: 127; *38*: 126–7; *40*: 125–6; *41*: 127; *42*: 128–9, 261; *45*: 129–30, 226; *56*: 124–5, 130–1, 155; *58*: 124; *66*: 129; *71*: 127–8; *73*: 124; *75*: 124; *76*: 127; *78*: 99; *83*: 128; *84*: 124; *85*: 133; *86*: 132; *89*: 132–3; *95*: 132; *98*: 133–4; *101*: 133; *102*: 129; *103*: 133; *109*: 134
  *Treatie of Humane Learning, A*: 129
Grey, Thomas, Lord: 72–5, 78, 85, 202
Grierson, Herbert: 130
Griffin, Bartholomew: 148, 152–3
Guarini, Giambattista: 140
Gunn, Thomas: 124
Gwynne, Matthew: 135

Hainsworth, Peter: 156
Hall, John: 38–9
Hall, Kim F.: 240
Hamilton, A. C.: 89
Hannay, Margaret P.: 164–5, 169–70, 172
Harding, D. W.: 22
Hardwick, Elizabeth: 206
Harington, John: 82, 93, 118, 180–1

294  INDEX

Harris, William O.: 52
Harrison, G. B.: 240
Harvey, Gabriel: 85, 231
Hawes, Stephen: 34
Heale, Elizabeth: 27
Hedley, Jane: 77
Helgerson, Richard: 47, 55
Heneage, Elizabeth: 197
Henri IV (King of France): 147
Henry VIII (King of England): 3, 8, 22, 27, 41, 43, 57, 270
Henry, Prince of Wales: 187
Herbert, George: 133, 252
Herbert, William: *see* Pembroke
Herford, Charles H.: 47
Herrick, Robert: 143–4
Hetherington, Michael: 65, 80
Holton, Amanda: 2
homosexuality: 157–8, 216–19
Hopkins, Gerard Manley: 81
Horace (Horatius Flaccus): 224, 263
Horner, Joyce: 195
Hoskyns, John: 130
Howe, Ann Romayne: 89, 107, 257
Hughes, Felicity A.: 70
Hull, Elizabeth: 28, 254, 256
Hulse, Clark: 254, 257–8
Hume, Anna: 270
Hunt, Marvin: 240
Hutson, Lorna: 65
Huttar, Charles A.: 38

Innocent III (Pope): 48
Ioppolo, Grace: 256
Izard, Thomas C.: 84

Jack, R. D. S.: 149
James VI and I (King of Scotland and England): 147–9, 189, 197, 205, 209, 256
jealousy: 1, 8–9, 58–60, 83, 102, 169, 173–7, 220, 228–32, 239
Jewel, John: 42
Johnson, Ronald C.: 81
Jones, Ann Rosalind: 254
Jonson, Ben: 161–2, 164, 223, 261

Kalstone, David: 89, 95–6
Katherine of Aragon: 5, 22, 41, 270
Kau, Joseph: 139
Kelliher, W. Hilton: 123, 125
Kenilworth entertainment: 44, 84, 86
Kennedy, William J.: 94, 271
Kerrigan, John: 136, 221
Kingsley-Smith, Jane: 208–10, 212, 240, 242
Kinney, Clare: 159, 165, 167, 170, 173–5, 177

kisses: 96, 107–13, 130, 142–3, 149, 152, 155–8, 178, 218, 242
Klein, Lisa: 87
Koeppel, Emil: 261
Koller, Kathrine: 195
Kuin, Roger: 90, 135, 159, 174
Kyd, Thomas: 134

Laam, Kevin: 51
*Ladies Dictionary, The* (by N. H.): 41
Lamb, Mary Ellen: 162, 166
Langham, Robert: 44
Lanham, Richard: 96–7
Latham, Agnes: 184, 195
Lauder, George: 42
laurel: 5–7, 9, 45–50, 145–6, 149–50, 224, 260, 268
Lawes, Henry: 236
Leech, John: 267
Leicester, Robert Dudley, Earl of: 100, 182, 191
Leishman, J. B.: 224–5, 232
Leland, John: 42–3
Levao, Ronald: 254
Lever, J. W.: 95, 99, 267
Lewalski, Barbara: 160, 167, 175
Lewis, C. S.: 5, 8, 24, 90–1, 195, 261–2
Lock, Anne Vaughan: 52
Lodge, Thomas: 148, 156–7, 171, 261
Loewenstein, Joseph: 95
Lowell, Robert: 206
Lynch, David: 272
Lynche, Richard: 92, 148, 153
Lyons, Mathew: 202

Machiavelli, Niccolò: 192
Malipiero, Girolamo: 39
Malone, Edmund: 208, 210–11, 223, 226, 229
Mantuan (Baptista Spagnuoli): 42
Marino, Giambattista: 251
Marlowe, Christopher: 106, 134, 155–6, 185
Marotti, Arthur: 208
Marsiglio of Padua: 42
Marston, John: 152
Marvell, Andrew: 143, 185
Mary (Queen of Scotland): 149, 270
Mason, H. A.: 8–9, 33
May, Steven W.: 90, 96, 122, 125, 159, 181–2, 184, 191–2, 202, 205
Maynard, Winifred: 8
McCoy, Richard: 47, 253–4
McGrail, Thomas H.: 267–8
McMurtry, Larry: 213
Medici, Lorenzo de': 143, 178–9
Meres, Francis: 84, 208
Metham, John: 2

Michelangelo Buonarroti: 219–20
Miller, Edward Haviland: 136–7
Milton, John: 149–50, 226
Mishima, Yukio: 272
Montrose, Louis Adrian: 180, 195
More, Thomas: 189–90, 270
Morley, Henry Parker, Lord: 41, 270
Mornay, Philippe de: 87
Moryson, Fynes: 255
Mumford, Ivy: 3
Murphy, Peter: 36, 40
Murphy, William: 92
Murray, David: 148

Nashe, Thomas: 135, 152–3, 162
Naunton, Robert: 124
"Naye, phewe nay pishe?" (anonymous poem): 154
Neely, Carol: 151
Nott, George: 261
Noves, Laurette de: 92
Nugent, Richard: 149

Oakeshott, Walter: 190–1
Orgel, Stephen: 217
Ovid (Ovidius Naso): 2, 51, 55, 85, 111, 113, 149, 153, 155–6, 196, 212, 251, 260, 269
Oxford, Edward de Vere, Earl of: 90, 133, 181

Paden William D., Jr.: 253
Page, Samuel: 84
*Paradyse of Daynty Devises, The*: 84, 261
Parker, Robert: 139
Parr, Katherine: 270
Pasqualigo, Piero: 3
*Passionate Pilgrim, The*: 185, 208–9
Peele, George: 255
Pembroke, Mary, Countess of: *see* Sidney, Mary
Pembroke, William Herbert, Earl of: 163–5, 168, 209, 258
Pequigney, Joseph: 212, 217–19, 231, 238–9
Percy, William: 37, 148
Persius Flaccus: 93
Petrarch (Francesco Petrarca)
  *Canzoniere 1*: 7, 40; *3*: 40; *11*: 40; *12*: 144, 186; *23*: 9–10, 40, 52, 58, 109–11, 128, 138, 150, 152, 168, 260–8; *35*: 140, 147; *37*: 5, 7, 156, 260; *45–6*: 212; *105*: 52; *116*: 227; *121*: 3–4, 10, 40; *123*: 103; *124*: 4; *126*: 156; *129*: 1–2, 52, 206–7, 227, 260; *134*: 18; *136–8*: 42; *140*: 23, 110, 140; *164*: 92; *189*: 52; *190*: 4–5, 30; *199*: 4–5, 11; *201*: 11–12; *206*: 10; *207*: 171; *224*: 18, 141; *238*: 156, 178; *248*: 94–5; *264*: 234, 260; *310*: 89; *323*: 260; *341*:

155; *360*: 5–6, 10, 260; *364*: 93, 250; *365*: 91, 250; *366*: 183, 250–1
  *Collatio laureationis*: 45
  *De remediis*: 22, 41, 51
  *Epistolae familiares*: 92, 269
  *Liber sine nomine*: 41–2
  *Trionfi*: 41, 118–19, 149, 161, 269–72
Petrina, Alessandra: 269
Petronius, Gaius: 223
Phillips, Edward: 132
*Phoenix Nest, The*: 93, 190–1, 261
Piccolomini, Aeneas Sylvius (Pope Pius II): 115
Piero, Zuan: 3
Pigman, G. W., III: 51–2, 74, 80, 82
Pindar: 98
Plato: 215, 220
Platonic love: 54, 95, 174, 159–60, 222
Plutarch: 22
Poirier, Michel: 116
Poliziano, Angelo: 143, 179
Prendergast, Maria Teresa Micaela: 101
Prouty, C. T.: 47, 49, 58
Psalms: 6–7, 161, 182
Pugh, Syrithe: 47
Pulci, Luigi: 179
Puttenham, George: 19, 41, 52, 85, 91, 184, 191, 193, 229

Quilligan, Maureen: 180
Quin, Walter: 268

Ralegh, Elizabeth (Bess) Throckmorton: 196–8, 205
Ralegh, Walter: 84, 93, 184–205, 258
  "Fortune hath taken thee away": 191–4
  "Give me my Scallop shell of quiet": 187–9
  *History of the World, The*: 187
  "If all the world and love were young": 185
  "If Synthia be a Queene": 194
  "Many desire, but few or none deserve": 258
  "My boddy in the walls captived": 194
  "My dayes delights, my springetyme joies fordunn": 195, 203–5, 252
  "Nature that washt her hands": 185–7
  "Now Serena, bee not coy": 185
  "Now we have present made": 195
  "Sufficeth it to yow my joyes interred": 195, 198–203
  "What is our Life": 189
  "Yeoven suche ys tyme": 187
Rebholz, Ronald A.: 13, 31–2, 124, 131, 134
Récamier, Juliette: 29
Rees, Joan: 125, 139

Rich, Penelope Devereux, Lady: 92, 97–8, 118, 122, 148, 158, 164, 180, 182–3, 254–6, 259
Rich, Robert, Lord: 92, 102, 255
Rickman, Johanna: 255–6
Rilke, Rainer Maria: 232
Ringler, William A., Jr.: 92, 99, 114, 116, 135, 253
Roberts, Josephine A.: 254
Robertson, Jean: 259
Roche, Thomas, Jr.: 119, 121, 131, 136, 149–51, 231, 264, 267
Rohr Philmus, M. R.: 60
Rollins, Hyder E.: 209, 211, 261
Romei, Annibale: 260
Ronsard, Pierre de: 19, 30, 91, 143, 186, 260–1
Rudenstine, Neil: 217
Rudick, Michael: 184, 189–90, 193

Sagudino, Nicolo: 3
Saint-Gelais, Mellin de: 17
Salamon, Linda Bradley: 47
Sanchez, Melissa: 96, 106, 119, 256
Sanderson, William: 256
Sandison, Helen Estabrook: 197
Sandys, George: 153
Sanford, Hugh: 137
Sannazaro, Jacopo: 23
Sargent, Ralph M.: 181
Savonorola, Girolamo: 42
Scarry, Elaine: 209–10, 217, 235, 238
Scève, Maurice: 140
Schiffer, James: 215
Schoenfeldt, Michael: 221–2
Schonhoven, Petronella van: 70
Scipio Africanus: 93
Scodel, Joshua: 268
Scott, Janet: 84, 93
Secundus, Janus (Jan Everaerts): 111, 143–4
Sedgwick, Eve Kosofsky: 233, 239, 244, 254
See, Sam: 158
*semper eadem*: 179, 192
Seneca, Lucius Annaeus: 115
Serafino dall'Aquila: 13–14
Sessions, W. A.: 40
Shakespeare, William: 84, 104, 151, 154, 163, 180, 207–51
  *Cymbeline*: 208
  *Hamlet*: 223–4, 240
  *Henry V*: 208
  *Macbeth*: 189
  *Merry Wives of Windsor, The*: 39
  *Midsummer Night's Dream, A*: 28, 226
  *Much Ado about Nothing*: 60, 92
  *Romeo and Juliet*: 53, 152

Sonnets: *1*: 212; *2*: 212; *3*: 213; *10*: 213–14; *12*: 214; *13*: 214–15; *15*: 215; *16*: 215; *17*: 215; *18*: 216; *19*: 217; *20*: 216–18, 228, 238; *21*: 241; *25*: 234; *26*: 230; *30*: 213, 225; *33*: 218, 228–9; *34*: 229; *35*: 229–30, 232; *41*: 243; *42*: 239; *43*: 225–7; *57*: 230–1, 234; *59*: 208; *71*: 234; *73*: 232–3; *85*: 235; *87*: 227–8, 239; *89*: 218; *93*: 222, 234–5; *94*: 220–2; *99*: 235; *102*: 235–6; *104*: 209; *113*: 226–7; *114*: 227; *116*: 236, 238; *118*: 237; *119*: 237; *120*: 237; *123*: 225, 238; *126*: 238; *127*: 240–3; *128*: 208, 242; *129*: 223, 242–3, 251; *130*: 62–3, 240–2; *131*: 242–3; *133*: 243; *134*: 243–4; *135*: 241; *137*: 218; *138*: 244–5; *139*: 246; *140*: 246–7; *144*: 208, 210, 240; *145*: 209; *146*: 251; *147*: 232, 247–8; *148*: 248; *149*: 249; *150*: 249; *152*: 211, 248–9; *153*: 209; *154*: 209; *155*: 208
  *Richard III*: 114, 189
  *Tempest, The*: 268
  *Timon of Athens*: 242
  *Troilus and Cressida*: 69
  *Venus and Adonis*: 157, 217
Shelley, Percy Bysshe: 272
Shelton, Mary: 20, 27
Shore, David: 57
Shulman, Nicola: 19–20, 27, 36
Sidney, Elizabeth: 161
Sidney, Mary, Countess of Pembroke: 122, 135, 137, 162–3, 259, 270–1
Sidney, Philip: 84, 86–124, 126, 134–5, 137, 140, 147–8, 149, 160–1, 164–5, 167, 180, 182–3, 208
  *Arcadia*: 87, 96, 109–11, 113, 116, 122, 135, 149, 165, 258–60, 264, 267
  *Astrophil and Stella*. Sonnets: *1*: 89; *2*: 97–8; *3*: 98; *5*: 99; *8*: 122–3; *9*: 93, 98; *13*: 97–8; *14*: 99, 148; *15*: 78, 93, 156–7; *17*: 129; *20*: 99; *21*: 99, 148; *24*: 92, 97, 118; *30*: 99–100, 167; *31*: 100–1; *34*: 122; *35*: 101; *36*: 101, 103, 105, 113, 271; *37*: 92, 101–2, 118; *39*: 135; *41*: 102–3; *44*: 48, 104; *45*: 257; *47*: 104–5; *52*: 105; *57*: 105, 271; *62*: 105; *63*: 151, 253, 257; *66*: 106, 257; *69*: 106–7; *71*: 94, 107, 151, 176; *72*: 107; *73*: 109; *74*: 93; *76*: 112; *78*: 102; *81*: 112; *82*: 113; *85*: 113; *86*: 115, 253; *87*: 120; *89*: 121; *101*: 148; *103*: 120, 197; *108*: 121. Songs: *2*: 107–8, 155; *3*: 113; *4*: 107, 113–15, 253–4, 257–8; *5*: 115–16; *8*: 116–20, 124, 185, 257–8; *9*: 120, 203; *11*: 120
  *Certain Sonnets*: 128
  *Defence of Poesie*: 77, 86, 88, 96, 154
Sidney, Robert, Lord: 148, 161, 165, 256
Simon, Margaret: 117, 119, 257

Skura, Meredith Anne: 73
Smith, Bruce R.: 231
Smith, Hallett: 104
Smith, Richard: 82
Smith, William: 92
Sokolov, Danila: 13
Solomon, Deborah: 36
sonnet form: 2, 40–1, 87–90, 137, 147–8, 165
sonnet sequence: 90–2, 123–4, 150–1
Soowthern (Southern), John: 90–1
Sophocles: 92
Southall, Raymond: 22
Spearing, A. C.: 34
Spenser, Edmund: 84–5, 87, 89, 135, 140, 144–5, 148, 150, 154, 157, 183–5, 195, 199, 203, 246, 260, 265–8, 272
Spiller, R. G. Michael: 90, 95, 150
Spriet, Pierre: 140
Stallybrass, Peter: 254
Stamatakis, Chris: 17, 38
Stampa, Gaspara: 19, 168, 170–1, 232
Steevens, George: 207–8, 210, 217
Steggle, Matthew: 124
Stein, Arnold: 35
Stevens, John: 8
Stewart, Alan: 56
Stewart, Patrick: 207–8
Stillman, Robert: 201
Stirling, Brents: 211
Stone, Lawrence: 268
Strier, Richard: 242
Strycharski, Andrew: 95
Surrey, Henry Howard, Earl of: 2, 39–41, 52, 82, 84, 89, 137, 140, 271–2
Svensson, Lars-Håkan: 138, 146, 150
Sylvester, Richard S.: 26
"Sythe singyng gladdeth oft the hartes" (anonymous poem): 261–5

Targoff, Ramie: 261–2
Tasso, Torquato: 140, 142–4
Tassoni, Alessandro: 101
Taylor, Gary: 208
*Tears of Fancie* (by T. W.): 84, 148, 151
Tennenhouse, Leonard: 180
Thomson, Patricia: 14, 141
Tofte, Robert: 102, 148, 154, 159–60, 260
Topsell, Edward: 153
Tottel, Richard (*Songes and Sonettes*): 14, 36–7, 39–41, 52–3, 261, 265
troubadours: 8, 22, 28, 54, 178, 194, 253
Turbervile, George: 46, 95
Twyne, Brian: 99
Twyne, Thomas: 41

Varchi, Benedetto: 102, 260
Varlow, Sally: 255, 259
Vendler, Helen: 208, 210, 214, 225, 229, 231–3, 235, 238, 248
Vergil (Vergilius Maro): 33, 62, 92, 143, 269
Verweij, Sebastiaan: 149
Villiers, George, Duke of Buckingham: 162

Walker, Kim: 176
Waller, Gary: 165, 254
Walsingham, Frances: 256
Walsingham, Francis: 44, 134–5, 140
Warkentin, Germaine: 95
Waswo, Richard: 123
Watson, Thomas: 91–3, 129, 148
Weiner, Andrew: 119
Welles manuscript: 4, 17–18, 29–30, 33–4
Whetstone, George: 59, 82–4, 87, 122
Whitgift, John: 256
Whittington, Leah: 231
Whythorne, Thomas: 57
Wilde, Oscar: 211
Williamson, George: 117
Winters, Yvor: 27, 72, 78, 131, 231
Withypoll, Bartholomew: 61
Wolsey, Thomas: 22
Wong, Alex: 111–13
Woodstock entertainment: 45, 181
Wort, Oliver: 270
Woudhuysen, H. R.: 122, 135, 140
Wroth, Mary Sidney: 149, 159–77, 240, 258
  "Hirmophradite in sense in Art a monster": 162
  "Lindamira's Complaint": 176–7
  *Pamphilia to Amphilanthus*. Manuscript: 4: 170–1; *55*: 170–1; *63*: 168; *65*: 173; *77*: 169; *96*: 159; *110*: 171; *113*: 159, 168; *116*: 165; *117*: 171. Print: *1*: 168; *2*: 159; *3*: 159, 173; *4*: 170; *5*: 159–60; *10*: 165; *14*: 168; *20*: 175; *23*: 168; *24*: 160; *26*: 167; *30*: 159; *35*: 170; *43*: 168; *45*: 205; *47*: 159; *54*: 170; *55*: 170–1; *56*: 169; *59*: 170; *64*: 175; *71*: 169; *74*: 172; *76*: 172; *77*: 172–3; *78*: 160, 173; *79*: 173; *81*: 159, 173; *82*: 174; *84*: 174; *85*: 175, 243; *86*: 175; *89*: 176; *90*: 176; *91*: 159; *97*: 175; *103*: 171–2
  "Sweete solitarines joy to those hartes": 164
  *Urania*: 160, 164–6, 169, 171–3, 176–7
Wroth, Robert: 161, 163–6
Wyatt, Thomas: 2–41, 43, 51, 57, 82, 84, 95, 116, 270
  "A face that shuld content me": 5
  "Altho thow se": 6–7
  "Behold, love": 3–4, 10, 40
  "Blame not my lute": 9

Wyatt, Thomas: (*Continued*)
   "Dryven by Desire I Dyd this Dede": 24
   "Dryven by dissyr to set affection": 38
   "Eche man me telleth": 21–2
   "Ffarewell, Love, and all thy lawes": 128
   "From thowght to thowght from hill to hill": 260
   "I fynde no peace": 18
   "If fansy would favour": 25–6
   "If waker care": 19–21, 37, 240, 267
   "It was my choyse": 27
   "Lament my losse": 7
   "Love and fortune and my mynde": 4
   "Lyke as the Swanne": 114
   "Madame, withouten many wordes": 15–16, 21–3
   "My galy charged wth forgetfulnes": 52
   "My lute, awake": 7, 39, 82
   "My pen, take payn a lytyll space": 7
   "Myne olde dere En'mye": 5–6, 260
   "Myne owne John Poyntz": 75
   "O goodely hand": 4–5, 12–13
   "Perdy I sayd hytt nott": 10, 14
   "Sins you will nedes that I shall sing": 271
   "So feble is the threde": 5, 7, 20, 260
   "Spight hath no powre": 16
   "Suffised not (madame)": 7
   "Suffryng in sorrowe": 27
   "Syethe yt ys so": 27
   "Tanglid I was yn loves snare": 14
   "The flaming Sighes that boile within my brest": 52–3
   "The longe love": 23, 140
   "There was never ffile": 7
   "They fle from me": 33–7, 53, 58, 126–7, 194, 252, 258
   "To cause accord": 18
   "Unstable dreme": 31–2
   "What nedeth these thretning wordes": 14
   "What rage is this": 18
   "What vaileth trouth": 23
   "Who so list to hounte": 4–5, 30–1
   "Yf amours faith": 18, 141
   "You that in love finde lucke": 31
Wycliffe, John: 42
Wynne-Davies, Marion: 164

Xenocrates: 138

Yeats, William Butler: 250
Young, Richard B.: 96–7, 121

Zarnowiecki, Matthew: 46, 55
*Zepheria*: 148–50, 156–7
Zouche, Anne: 20